ITALIAN FARMHOUSE COOKBOOK

by SUSAN HERRMANN LOOMIS

Illustrations by Anne Smith

WORKMAN PUBLISHING · NEW YORK

The recipe for Fried Potato Balls originally appeared in *Metropolitan Home;* Trentino Christmas Cake and Trentino Christmas Cake II originally appeared in *Bon Appétit.*

Cover and book design by Lisa Hollander and Lori S. Malkin
Cover art by Jane Rey

Library of Congress Cataloging-in-Publication Data
Loomis, Susan Herrmann.
Italian farmhouse cookbook/by Susan Herrmann Loomis.
p. cm.
ISBN 0-7611-1791-1 (hc) — ISBN 0-7611-0527-1 (pb)
1. Cookery, Italian. I. Title.

TX723 .L595 2000
641.5945 —dc21   99-053776

Workman books are available at special discounts when purchased in bulk for premiums and sales promotions as well as for fund-raising or educational use. Special editions or book excerpts can be created to specification. For details, contact the Special Sales Director at the address below.

Workman Publishing Company, Inc.
708 Broadway
New York, NY 10003-9555
www.workman.com

First printing February 2000
10 9 8 7 6 5 4 3 2 1

To Michael, Joe,
and now Fiona

Acknowledgments

This book went together with the help of so many fine people: friends, people who became friends, and people who simply helped along the way because they are endowed with that wonderful characteristic called generosity. Among these I must particularly mention three dear friends who gave, gave, and gave some more. Thank you Karen Kaplan, Susan Lord, Beverly Crofoot.

Danilo Barroncini, with Susan Lord, agreed to lend his considerable wine knowledge, honed after years of journalistic work pursuing the finest Italy has to offer, by suggesting wines to go with the dishes in this book. I am honored to have his assistance. Danilo and Susan read the manuscript as well, and their valuble suggestions have helped make it what it is.

Barbara and Herb Haber were readers for part of the manuscript, and their help was invaluble.

Other friends and colleagues helped immeasur-

ably and I am so grateful. They include Lidia Bastianich, Rolando Beremendi, Elliott Coleman and Barbara Damrosch, Nancy Harmon Jenkins, Judy Kao, Steven Rothfield, and Patricia Wells.

Thank you to Bill Garry and Barbara Fairchild at *Bon Appétit* magazine, to Nancy Newhouse at *The New York Times* and to Lisa Higgins and Donna Warner at *Metropolitan Home* for their support.

Dozens of people helped me in Italy, and I mean helped in the true sense of the word, with cheerfulness, openness, and generosity. Among them are the warm and wonderful—and talented—Caputo and Casa family of Nerano, Maria Grazia Daolio, Fabio Picchi, Benedetta Vitali, Andreina and Andrea Bucci, Sylvia Melosi Hernandez, Giovanni Ceretelli and Luna Lattarulo, Francesco Masiero, Buzzi Pucinelli, Barbara de Rham, Angela Marconi, Sara Jenkins, Lisa Bonacossi and family, the marvelous Lancellotti family, the warmer-than-warm Nano and Laura Morandi, the Passatempi family, the unforgettable Ricci family, especially Antonella, Kristy Davis, Doctor Andrea Ceccine, charming Signore Soine who is giving the world a lot with his Vino della Pace, Josko Sirk, Bruno Vesnaver, Giovanni Vesnaver, the Nonino family, Piero Selvaggio, the very special Corrado Assenza, and Giusto Occhipinti. A particular thanks goes to Donatella Colombini, for her interest and support of my work. Each of these people, with with all of the others you will meet in this book, were unstintingly generous and gracious with me, a northener to the bones, who through their efforts now has a valuble veneer of southernness!

When it comes to testing the recipes in the United States with American ingredients, I don't know where I would be without the invaluable Marion Pruitt and Barbara Leopold. Thank you both for fine work and fine friendship. And thank you to Cal Burgett, whose expert opinions inform the sweet side of this book.

I would like to thank everyone at Workman Publishing who works tirelessly, patiently, and with a sense of giving their best including Peter Workman, Suzanne Rafer, the unflappably patient Lisa Hollander and Lori S. Malkin, Barbara Ottenhoff for her careful copyediting, Kylie Foxx for her able assistance, and Andrea Glickson and Jim Eber for their ideas. Thank you also to Arthur Klebanoff.

At home I must thank friends who wished me well, sampled the recipes, and generally supported my wild enthusiasm for my Italian discoveries. Thank you Edith and Bernard Leroy, Marie Lawrence Gaudrat, Honorine and Mark Tepfer, the Bourillon family all, Iuliano and Nadège, Collette Soustre, and Patrick Merlin. Thank you to the équipe at Chez Clet and to Monique and Jean-Claude Martin, who continually humor my demands for fine and foreign produce.

I must thank my sister, Kate Lilly, for passing along names and tips which proved so helpful, and the rest of my family, particularly my parents, Joseph and Doris Herrmann, who remain constantly supportive and entertaining.

Finally, finally, I thank my three favorite traveling companions in this life. Two of them kept the home fires burning and accompanied me when it was possible. They remain my darling Michael, and our darling Joseph. The third person, darling Fiona, arrived one fine early spring day and fills our life with sun.

Contents

PRIMI PIATTI

First Courses 99

At the farm table, dishes are presented like a vast patchwork, seemingly without rules and without end. However, in Italy, pastas always come first, and so they lead off this chapter as well. The second part of the chapter includes a tempting selection of other classic first courses—Garlicky Cheese Polenta, Spinach and Ricotta Dumplings, Artichoke Frittata—that can easily be turned into entrees.

artichokes

SECONDI PIATTI

Second Courses 187

In the past, farmers reserved meat and fish for celebratory occasions, and in fact still treat them with infinite care. Lamb is a favorite, as is pork, and chicken as well as guinea hen and rabbit are fixtures. Plates of succulent Herb-Marinated Leg of Lamb, or richly spirited Guinea Hen with Vin Santo, take their rightful place as the nourishing *secondi*.

L'ORTO *The Vegetable Garden* **243**

The farmhouse table would be incomplete without the many offerings from the garden. Whether from an open-air market, a truck garden, a country field, or someone's small kitchen garden, fresh vegetables and herbs are the epicenter of Italian farmhouse cooking.

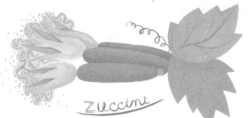

DAL FORNO *From the Bread Oven* **289**

There is nothing more welcoming than the warm scent of freshly baked bread, or the golden heat that emanates from the hearth. For the Italian baker, the fruits of this labor of love are crisp-crusted loaves, fragrant pizza and *focacce* (flat breads), and biscotti, all of which you will find in the pages of this chapter.

DOLCE, DOLCE *Sweet, Sweet* **335**

Desserts are one of the great pleasures of the Italian farm table. Finish a meal with fresh fruit heaped in a bowl and served alongside

a richly flavored *torta di nocciole* (hazelnut cake), or with pastries like *crostate*, crisp-crusted tarts bursting with everything from ripe apricots to lemon marmalade. These simple and delicious desserts beg to be made often, and with abandon.

LA DISPENSA

The Pantry 387

The well-stocked pantry, with its lively array of pepper- and herb-infused oils, jars of fresh tomato sauce, and jam made with ripe figs and grapes straight off the vine, hints at the many possibilities of the Italian farmhouse kitchen.

RICETTI DI BASE

The Basics 421

The basics are the simple little recipes that every Italian farmhouse cook knows inherently. They are the rustic tomato sauce, the home-made pastas, the perfect dough for tender pizza—all the from-scratch foods and seasonings that are elemental to the success of any dish.

An Introduction to Italian Farmhouse Cooking

When I was in my early twenties, I went to Paris to study the fundamentals of cooking and apprenticed at the famed La Varenne Ecole de Cuisine. My passion for France and the sophisticated and ordered French way of life flourished, but Italy beckoned as well, and whenever I could, I jumped on a train headed for either Florence or Rome. Once there, I investigated every *pasticceria* (pastry shop), *rosticceria* (shop offering roasted meats), *fornaio* (bakery), that I passed. Everything seemed so much more earthy, less orderly yet so much more intriguing and contemporary, that I was seduced and sometimes wondered why I'd chosen to live in France. Of course, once back in Paris I remembered.

Since those days I've wanted to write about Italy in order to know it better. When I had the chance to do this book I jumped at it, and I cannot say how happy I am to have been able to travel through such a glorious country, and meet such fine people, learning about their traditions and foods along the way.

I confess that when I began the research my eagerness and enthusiasm was matched by trepidation at entering a country where my facility with the language was just passing, and where techniques and standards were as yet unknown to me. I needn't have worried, however, for I found that the language came easily, that people I met were willing to help, welcoming my sometimes stammering ques-

tions and speaking slowly enough for me to understand. Regarding culinary technique, I soon learned that the Italian cuisine, like the Italian way of life, is one of spontaneity and informality rather than rule.

What I also knew, and what supported and spurred me along, was farming and its winding ways. I'd already written two extensive books about farming, one in the United States, the second in France. For each of those I'd spent months traveling to farms and interviewing farmers, getting to know them and their families, trying to help make the connection between these hard-working people and the food we all put on our tables. I have found that though methods and crops may differ, farmers have the same verve, drive, and fierce attachment to the land whether they live in America or France or Italy.

I relished traveling through Italy and its farmland, which is surprisingly vast given the size of the country and its population of 60 million. Italy's wheat fields, orchards, and vegetable fields stretch on and on. Because of its large tracts of land and surprisingly sophisticated approach to farming—many rural horizons are endowed with mile after mile of greenhouses—much of Italy reminded me of California. In fact, I found that many Italian farmers turn to California's farmers for inspiration, technology, and guidance.

But so much of Italy reminded me of Italy. That is, my vision of Italy, which is an admittedly romantic one. For every large farm there is a small one where cows and sheep keep company with a pig and a handful of guinea hens, where rabbits sit in hutches and the family garden supplies fresh vegetables, herbs, and fruit. The soul of Italy is the vegetable gardens on every tillable centimeter of soil, whether next to an urban front door or behind a sprawling farmhouse or squeezed between the railroad tracks and a hill. And whether the produce from these gardens is intended for the market or for personal use, it is varied and rich as it bursts out here and there with sheer joy, it seems.

One aspect of the Italian rural landscape I found particularly alluring is the deliciously faded colors and fanciful architecture of even the simplest farmhouse. So often I arrived at a farm and found myself charmed by the faded pink walls and light green windows, or ocher washed walls accented with blue. But Italy can be aesthetically challenging too, particularly in the south where cinder block monstrosities rear their heads next to lush vegetation, homes, or monuments, their cheap ugliness begun and never completed because of some clever political machination. The contrast can be harsh, the surrounding loveliness intensified by the unfinished construction.

Though Italian farmers resemble their colleagues in other countries, many things set them apart as well. Foremost is the depth of poverty they and their forebears experienced well into the twentieth century. Over time, Italian farm life has evolved through a number of painful incarnations, including one of near slavery, which changed gradually to tenant farming, or *mezzadria*. The *mezzadria* system, where tenant farmers were required to give half of what they cultivated to the landowner, who provided them with housing, existed well into the 1960s. Then, the government turned land ownership upside down. Either the landowners were required to sell small plots to their *mezzadri*, who bought the land with money given them by the government, or straight transfers were arranged between the landowner and the tenant farmer. The idea was to free the *mezzadri* from what was too often a yoke of poverty and lack of self-determination.

In reality the program was awkward, for often in areas where peasants were most in need, no money was appropriated to help them, or land they were allotted was too poor to farm. In areas where the *mezzadri* did obtain land, the plots were usually too small to provide a viable living, so they were worse off. They had too little land and no safety net. Many former *mezzadri* sold their land, often back to the original owner, and moved to towns and cities to work, with the result that the countryside gradually emptied.

The countryside had experienced a previous emptying during the Second World War. Then, men left to fight and women were called into the war effort. When farmers returned home, they often found the women relocated to the city. The men followed and the combined exoduses resulted in a gradual diminishing of farmers on the land. In the 1940s there were more than eight million Italian farmers. There are now fewer than two million.

Despite the drastic change in numbers of people on the land, there is a vibrancy to Italian agriculture. The government is doing its best to create programs that will allow farmers to expand their holdings, and lure young people to the land. And the history of Italian agriculture has made the Italian farmer hungry for success. Italian farmers are as good as or better than American farmers at identifying mar-

kets and doing what is necessary to supply them. They are not nostalgic for old times—who would be when old times were so meager—nor do their egos require that they continue to farm the way their ancestors did; inside, every Italian farmer is an entrepreneur, ready to turn land into profit. The generally small size of farms allows the Italian farmer to be flexible in responding to new market demands.

There are huge industrial farms in Italy producing wheat, soybeans, and corn (in part to better compete in the European Union). There is also a vast network of small, productive market gardens that produce everything from lettuces to fat purple garlic, to peppers of every size and shape. In between are good-sized family farms, many of which have joined with neighbors to create thriving, well-organized farm cooperatives.

Much alternative farming thrives in Italy as well, from organic to biodynamic. Its development has been spurred on by huge markets to the north, in Germany and Austria, by a growing market in Italy, and with the help of foresighted government programs.

Seven organic certification organizations exist already in Italy, and their representatives survey, inspect, and help farmers with marketing strategies. Each organization is aligned to a political party and they tend to work against rather than with each other, but the collective result of their work is a strong organic farm movement. At least one Italian supermarket chain has cast its support for alternative farming by devoting shelf space to organic produce.

From what I saw, in Italy the transition to farming without synthetic chemicals is somewhat easier than it has been in other countries. Italy's rural communities remained "underdeveloped" until very recently, and they had fewer synthetic chemicals at their disposal, and less money to purchase them. The same isola-

tion meant limited access to hybrid seeds so that pure fruit and vegetable strains are more common in Italy. Both factors contribute to the astonishingly rich and purer flavor of Italian tomatoes, peppers, garlic, corn, wheat, onions, zucchini, cabbage, and greens.

A curious thing about Italy is its lack of farmers' markets. Most large cities have them, but rural outposts don't. What passes for a farmers' market in small towns from Piedmont to the wilds of Sicily are small trucks bursting with produce which pass through towns, loudspeakers blaring to announce their arrival. Sometimes errant trucks laden with a single item, say, artichokes or broccoli or fennel, will rattle into town, and be emptied within a matter of minutes, no one bothering to ask where the produce comes from because, I was told, they don't really want to know, in case it was highjacked from a field or transporter.

Among several reasons I was offered for the lack of markets was that traditionally most rural Italians cultivated their own food, and poor roads made it difficult for farmers to travel even if they did have something to sell.

The Roots of Italian Farm Food

mezzaluna

The recipes in this book come direct from the Italian farm and farm country, and they represent the sensuous core of Italian cuisine. For all Italian food, whether it be served at a starred restaurant, a simple *osteria* (an Italian version of a pub), or in a *cucina di casa* (home kitchen), has a strong, direct link to what is still prepared each day on the Italian farm. You will find many familiar recipes within these pages, each marked by the individual personality of the cook who gave it to me.

Italian farm food is easy to love. It is delightfully unpretentious, artfully combined, and appropriately economical. The major single influence on all Italian farmhouse cooking has been poverty, and it has the same influence on the food as it has had on the rural character. Italian farmhouse dishes, from silken chestnut pasta to restoring soups,

are a study in simplicity yet intensity of flavor. The food is joyous, unexpected, fresh. I have never experienced such vibrant tomatoes, greens of every description, olive oils, herbs, peppers, cardoons, fennel, radicchio, mushrooms, and artichokes as those I had on the Italian farm. Italian farmhouse cooking can be complex, but the complexity comes from the way ingredients and flavors are melded together, not from technique.

Until the mid-nineteenth century, Italy was a nation of independent regions, each with its distinct personality and its own cuisine. The regional cuisines have evolved throughout the country's stormy history, influenced by whatever culture swept through, yet each has retained its own characteristics. Even the creation of the Kingdom of Italy in 1861 did little to blur distinctions, so that one still finds a different cuisine in each region. The spicy dishes of the Abruzzo, for instance, are not replicated in Piedmont, and there is no way that Lombardi's rich and bubbling *polenta taragna*, with its earthy buckwheat and rich melted cheese, would be served in Sicily.

Generally speaking, Italy can be divided by its butter and cream half—the North—and its olive oil half—the South. It is also divided by corn and wheat. In the North, corn rules, while in the South, wheat is king. Another dividing line is by color—the sauces in the North tend to be white (without tomatoes) while those in the South are red (with tomatoes), though one finds some of both everywhere. Staying with general observations, bread improves and flavors become more gutsy and spicy as one moves south. Basilicata, Abruzzo, and Calabria win prizes for the most peppery cuisine, while Tuscany and Puglia honor olive oil the most. The cuisine of Sicily surprises with its delightful contrast between earthy rusticity and high sophistication. The cuisine of the Veneto has an international allure, influenced as it is by its heart, the great port city of Venice, and whispers of influence from as far away as Asia.

In many regions, starches and vegetables are the basics for the cuisine, but in some, such as Tuscany and Piedmont, meat plays a starring role. Beef, however, is always a luxury. Lamb is common the further south you go (and what lamb!), while pork is typical in the North. Guinea hen, with its dark and sensuous flesh, is more popular than chicken on the Italian farm, and rabbit is a mainstay.

Though Italy has a vast coastline, there is very little seafood on the Italian farm table. Most of Italy's coastline was swampy and impossible to cultivate until the middle of the twentieth century, when various land reclamation projects were

A Note About Agriturismi

I visited many an *agriturismo,* or farm that opens its rooms and often its table to paying guests. I had wonderful experiences on some, but in many instances I was disappointed. My expectations were based on what I experienced in France, where a farm stay is simple, authentic, and a real opportunity to meet farmers and learn about their lives. This is seldom so in Italy where all too often an *agriturismo* is simply a business run by people—some farmers, some not—who were able to get large government grants to remodel crumbling farmhouses, build swimming pools, construct restaurants, and create resorts where farms once stood. I chalk this up to that fine art of Italian survival. Who wouldn't take advantage of such a program and make the most of it? These commercial *agriturismi* are often lovely; they just don't offer a real Italian farm experience.

Fortunately I did find authentic situations where I was able to step into rural Italy in a warm, rich, and authentic way. For reliable farm-stay addresses, contact *http://www. initaly.com* for information. You may also want to refer to a fine book, *Karen Brown's Italian Country Bed & Breakfasts,* by Nicole Franchini.

instituted. Thus, farmers didn't live near the sea, they lived in the hills and mountains, and though they fished some from rivers and lakes, fishing had little impact on the cuisine. Roads were simply too rustic, transportation all but impossible to allow for the distribution of fresh seafood.

Surprisingly, Italian farmers aren't big on salads, either. Though there are delectable exceptions, like the *Insalata d'Acetaia* with its drizzle of *aceto balsamico tradizionale,* or balsamic vinegar, they tend to prefer their leafy greens cooked and lightly seasoned.

About the Recipes

As I stood by Italian farmhouse cooks in their big, square, low-lit kitchens with a grill or fireplace on one side, a big pot for deep-frying on another, it became clear to me that the Italian farm cook adheres to one main rule as

Olive oil, preferably extra-virgin, is the ideal oil for deep frying because it adds its incomparable flavor to foods, plus it has a high burning point.

she (or he—it is not uncommon to find a man at the stove, preparing dishes with great pride) creates fine, simple food. That rule is *quanto basta*, "when there is enough." Often that, along with a big smile, was as much of an answer as I could get when I asked how much of an ingredient to add.

I came to learn that, perhaps more than in any cuisine I've experienced, Italian farmhouse cooking is a question of *accortezza*, or knowing. It is an inherent knowing that leads one to that special place in the woods at the right time of year to pick nettles or wild fennel, *giri,* or wild asparagus. It is the knowing that can

turn three simple but exquisite ingredients into something wonderful, a dish that caresses rather than overpowers.

As you travel through this book you will encounter exciting recipes and wonderful people, and through them you will develop that necessary "knowing."

Buon appetito, e buon viaggio!

—Susan Herrmann Loomis

Please visit me at my Web site:
www.susanloomis.com

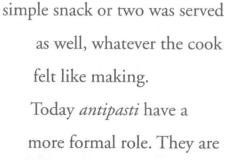

ANTIPASTI E MERENDE

APPETIZERS AND SNACKS

*A*ntipasti, those large inviting platters of sausages, pickled vegetables, stuffed anchovies, and other tasty, savory bites served before a meal, have roots on the Italian farm. As for snacks and afternoon *merende*, they, too, can trace their beginnings to rural Italy. These piquant morsels that accompany a glass of wine and fill the void between meals, like *gnocchi* (light pillows of fried dough) and thick slices of freshly toasted bread topped with a variety of tempting mixtures, called *crostini*, have abated a farmer's hunger for centuries.

The local village *osteria*—the Italian version of a pub with several chairs and tables for card playing and not much else—served wine to farm and factory workers in their pause from labor. Because it was unthinkable to drink without nibbling, a simple snack or two was served as well, whatever the cook felt like making.

Today *antipasti* have a more formal role. They are

Sage

served to prepare the palate for the meal that follows, usually accompanied by a chilled glass of Prosecco in the north or spritzy, often homemade, red wine in the south. The snack and *merenda* are still strong farm customs and have stayed much as they were—a short break for sustenance, company, and conversation.

I've enjoyed many snacks and *merende* on Italian farms, and one of the most memorable occurred in Emilia-Romagna in a tiny family-owned cheese factory. The crew of four had been hard at work since before sunup. Several hours later, when the milk was resting after having been skimmed of its cream and lightly heated, the work stopped and everyone trooped into the adjacent family kitchen. There, a bottle of wine, sausages, and slabs of bread awaited, and the crew members tucked in until each was satisfied, the local economy had been discussed, and everyone was refreshed. It took all of fifteen minutes. Another favorite *merenda* I shared was in Tuscany. The

Snack and Merenda

The word "snack" has been appropriated by the Italians, and they use it to describe a little bite taken in the morning between meals. *Merenda* is a similar little bite, only one that is eaten in the afternoon.

farmer's twelve-year-old son came in after school, casually cut a slab of bread, rubbed a half tomato on it, and nibbled it as he walked outside to sit on a bench in the sun. All of the adults present followed suit; it was simply delicious.

Antipasti memories are legion too, though one of my favorites remains the selection I ate on a farm in the mountains of Basilicata when, at the end of the day, I sat with the farm family around a table and ate aromatic home-cured olives, home-pickled vegetables, homemade sausage, a sumptuous egg and pepper dish, and *crostini* topped with herbed beans, all washed down with liters of homemade wine.

Each dish in this chapter has its roots in such experiences, and in the simple *antipasti,* snack, and *merende* of rural Italy, the small dishes and snacks that are enjoyed either at table in the farmhouse or, when weather and work oblige, in the field under the shade of an almond tree. They are vivid and satisfying, both to the palate and to the eye. Serve these dishes singly or together, before a meal or for an alfresco picnic, in the flavorful tradition of the Italian farm.

Olives with Garlic, Hot Peppers, and Fresh Mint

OLIVE CON AGLIO, PEPERONCINO, E MENTA

2 CUPS OLIVES

This is an antipasto from Grazia Ienonolo, who moved from her cattle farm in the Sicilian countryside, not far from Ragusa, to the nearby country town of Frigintini, where she opened a small trattoria with her husband, Giovanni, her son, Emanuele, and her daughter, Maria Fidone. She didn't like living way out in the country and convinced her husband to lease their farmland and try to make a go of it in town. Their experiment has been a huge success, and their unpretentious restaurant, called simply Trattoria and the only one in town, is rarely empty.

They do a tremendous business with local people, which might seem odd since the Ienonolos—who all work together in the large, square kitchen, each tending to his or her specific task—make the wonderful rustic food of the local farms. Their success, however, is based on fine products, skillful preparation, and a generosity uncommon in any restaurant, anywhere.

Among other things, the Ienonolos grow and cure their own olives, then season them lightly with hot pepper for a back-of-the-throat tang and with mint, which underlies the rich olive flavor with its aromatic essence. They put a bowl of these olives on the table to nibble before the meal. I follow their lead, using fine Ligurian or Nyons olives as a base. I allow them to macerate in the seasoning for at least twenty-four hours, then serve them with a simple glass of white or red wine.

Signora Ienonolo said she freezes her olives, but I've never had enough left over to try and see if it works!

Mint

2 tablespoons extra-virgin
   olive oil
½ teaspoon red wine vinegar
1 clove garlic, green germ removed,
   minced

⅛ teaspoon crushed red pepper flakes
⅓ cup fresh mint leaves
2 cups (about 11 ounces) black
   olives cured in brine, preferably
   from Liguria or Nyons

1. Whisk together the oil, vinegar, garlic, and red pepper flakes in a medium bowl.

2. Mince the mint and add it to the oil mixture, then add the olives and toss to coat thoroughly. You may either serve the olives immediately or cover and let them sit overnight. Stir them up again before serving so they are coated lightly with the oil. Refrigerated, the olives will keep well for at least 2 weeks. Be sure to bring them to room temperature before serving.

Lemon-Spiced Olives

OLIVE CON LIMONE

2 CUPS OLIVES

Sergio Maggion lives and gardens on Lido di Venezia, an island in the Venetian lagoon about forty-five minutes by boat from Venice (see essay, page 7). There he grows and cures enough olives to supply his family and his small *pasticceria* for the year. His recipe is simple: He harvests the olives when they're black and ripe, runs water over them for several days to help remove the bitterness, then puts them in salt to cure. Once they are cured, he adds herbs and spices according to his whim, and seals and keeps the aromatic olives on hand in his outdoor kitchen to nibble with a glass of his homemade white wine, a bottle of which is always hanging by a rope in his well.

2 cups (about 11 ounces) black olives cured in brine, preferably from Liguria or Nyons
About 1 teaspoon minced lemon zest (see Note)

¼ teaspoon crushed red pepper flakes
2 imported dried bay leaves, crumbled
2 cups extra-virgin olive oil (see Note)

1. Combine the olives in a 4-cup jar with the lemon zest, pepper flakes, and bay leaves. Close and shake the jar so the ingredients are combined. Open the jar and pour the oil over all so that the olives are completely covered. Close the jar and store in the refrigerator; the olives should be ready to eat within 1 week and will keep well for several weeks. Be sure to bring them to room temperature before serving.

NOTES: The amount of lemon zest called for gives the right hint of lemony flavor; too much will mask the actual flavor of the olives themselves. If your olives are particularly strongly flavored, however, you may want to add a bit more lemon zest.

In this recipe, the olives are mixed with a generous amount of oil, which lends them moistness as well as flavor. Once you've eaten the olives, use the oil in salad dressing, to dress pasta, or to sauté vegetables.

Bay leaves

A VERY HAPPY FARMER—OR IS HE A BAKER?—ON LIDO

I think Sergio Maggion has more fun in his vast *orto,* or farm garden, than any farmer I've met. Of course, he's not technically a farmer; he's a baker and owner of Laboratorio di Pasticceria e Torte Maggion, the best-known *pasticceria* on the island of Lido di Venezia, in the Venice lagoon. But he spends every free moment in his gardens on Lido, cultivating hundreds of varieties of herbs, vegetables, and fruits. These he uses in sweet and savory tarts and traditional pastries for the *pasticceria.* I'd heard about him from farming friends, and I knew from their description that I had to meet him.

Over the phone Sergio Maggion told me where to get the boat to the island and promised to meet me at the dock. After a dazzling forty-five-minute ride past Venice and its treasures, the boat docked at Lido, a surprisingly fashionable little town. I spotted Sergio Maggion immediately among the attractively dressed crowd awaiting the boat, for he had on farmer's clothes—comfortable pants and a T-shirt— his skin was dark from the sun, and his car had dirt on the tires. "My kind of guy," I thought.

He explained as we drove to his pastry shop that he'd been a baker for twenty-four years. "I work with my wife, Leonilde, and my son, Matteo," he said. "I've got one of the oldest *pasticceria* in town." Sergio is well known on Lido, where he is considered the father of *pasticcerie.* At least three young bakers have left his training and opened their own successful shops on the island.

But Sergio has always had a feeling for the soil. I got the distinct impression, in fact, that his bakery is a well-loved hobby, while his land and his *orto* are his passion. As he explained it, he bought his first parcel of land as soon as he could, then proceeded to import 480 truckloads of soil from nearby Padua to build it up. "There

wasn't near enough soil in this area for cultivating, nor the right kind," he said. "That
soil from Padua was incredibly rich, and
when I started digging through it I found
old things, pieces of ancient vases, treasures
of all kinds."

Over the years, he bought more land
and now has two separate parcels, which total about 7,500 square feet. On one, which
is just steps from the sea and where he plans
to retire, he built a small, well-equipped
house and surrounded it with grass and a
tidy garden. The other is a riot of productivity and experimentation. One wouldn't expect such agricultural dynamism in this chic
community, for the land is hidden away behind busy commercial streets and residential
areas, but Lido has a small, secret society of
gardeners, mostly male, who coax untold
riches from the soil.

Sergio explained the origins of Lido,
how it was developed long ago to protect
Venice from invasions, how it became a
haven for the ill, the religious, and finally for
the general populace as they fled attackers
from inland. They found the land arable
enough to cultivate, realized they could produce all they needed, and never left.

"The soil here is perfect for vegetables
like asparagus, artichokes, eggplant, but it's
scarce. Trees have trouble, for instance. They
have to be propped up because they can't
put down roots, but we can live with that,"
he said.

Wind is another drawback to cultivation, but as we walked into his lush garden,
I saw he had overcome all obstacles. Surrounded by a thick hedge, it overflowed
with tomatoes, green beans, shell beans,
eggplant, peppers, cucumbers, zucchini.
There were huge lavender bushes to attract
bees, which provide him with enough
honey for his family for the whole year, a
plot of artichokes, an olive tree or two, and
special melons grown from Sicilian seeds.
"I pick and hang them outside, and they
keep until Christmas, when they are so
good," he said.

zucchini

I looked around at the garden and felt
transported. Just a minute ago we were driving through a crowded, affluent neighborhood. Here, we were in nature, surrounded
by lush greenery. Sergio's garden is one of
several that sit side by side. From what I
could see of the others, his was the most
energetic, with its solar shower in one corner, a well in another, and its little shack for
chickens. Sergio, visibly relaxed, almost
danced over to his pride and joy—a fully
equipped kitchen, enclosed on three sides
and open to the elements on the fourth.

Pots and pans hung everywhere. "When
the wind blows, the noise is tremendous,"
he said, laughing. He parted a curtain that

hid shelves laden with jars of pickled egg-plant, spiced dandelion buds, bottles of *rosolio* or rose petal liqueur, honey, cured olives. He opened them all so I could taste. The olives were deliciously aromatic, the pickled eggplant spicy and rich tasting, the dandelions puckery tart. The *rosolio* was delicate and sweetly perfumed, the honey mild and alluring.

Suddenly he ran from the kitchen into an open patch of grass and started calling, "Booshi, booshi!" From behind a clump of greens waddled a family of ducks, their heads held high. "They go out into the garden and eat all the slugs," he said. "I don't use any chemicals here."

He turned back to the kitchen and un-corked three bottles for me to sniff. One smelled intensely of sage, another knocked me over with garlic, and the third seared my nose with its peppery heat. These were his flavored oils that he uses on grilled fish, which he nets straight from the sea.

Sergio walked over to his well and pulled up a rope that had a bottle hanging from it to keep it cool. "Let's have a drink," he said. "This is last year's wine."

We took the bottle next door to share with his neighbor, another passionate gardener who is a truck driver in real life. "We spend a lot of time out here together," Sergio said, sitting down at a long table sheltered by a grape ar-bor. He poured while his friend, a shy man who putters endlessly in his tidy, perfectly arranged garden, brought out from his little house platters of sliced prosciutto, pancetta, salami, and a mountain of wonderfully crisp cracker bread. We nibbled and sipped in this quiet spot, and the two joked with each other about how this was their universe, their society. "Oh, my wife is welcome whenever she wants to come," Sergio ac-knowledged. "But she usually just shows up for dinner!"

Sergio is viewed by his community as a warm, generous eccentric, and he proved this by trying to give me half his supply of pickled vegetables as I got ready to leave. I insisted he keep them and left instead with a bottle of his wine, a handful of recipes, and the happy memory of a day spent with this joyous man.

Caramelized Onions

Cooked slowly in balsamic vinegar and water, these onions become meltingly sweet and sour. In Italy they are served warm or cold, either as a side dish or as part of an antipasto tray. I think they are best served at room temperature, along with a selection of other pickled vegetables or along with roasted meats, poultry, or fish. Refrigerated, they keep well for several days.

*1 pound small onions or pearl
    onions, peeled*

½ cup balsamic vinegar

1. Cut a shallow cross into the root end of each onion. Place them in a medium-size heavy saucepan and add the vinegar and 1 cup of water. Shake the pan to blend the liquids, then bring to a boil over high heat. Reduce the heat so the liquid is simmering merrily and cook, shaking the pan and turning the onions occasionally so they cook evenly. You may need to adjust the heat to keep the liquid from evaporating too quickly or too slowly. After about 15 minutes you should have about ¼ cup thick liquid remaining. Shake the pan so the onions roll around and are covered with the liquid as it reduces. Continue cooking until the onions are tender throughout but not mushy and the liquid is caramelized and almost entirely evaporated. The entire cooking process from the time the liquid boils will take about 25 minutes.

2. Remove the onions from the heat and let cool to room temperature before eating.

Vegetable Carpaccio

CARPACCIO
VEGETALE

6 SERVINGS

Segreti

To shave Parmesan cheese, use a vegetable peeler and simply "peel" the curls from the hunk of cheese, holding it right over the salad.

Robbio is a farming town in Lombardy, near Alessandria, not too far from the Piedmont border. In the heart of rice-growing country, Robbio is surrounded by paddies, which produce Italy's famed Baldo, Arborio, and Carnaroli rice. Da Mino, a small restaurant located in the center of town, specializes in typical rural dishes of the area, and I was particularly taken by Chef Enrica Abatte's unusual fresh vegetable *carpaccio*. Made with produce from the garden of Pietro Lorizzo, her husband and the restaurant's owner, the macerated paper-thin vegetables came to the table lightly chilled, tender, and full of texture and flavor.

When I have the time, I prepare the carpaccio as they do at Da Mino, but when I don't want to wait, I simply toss all the vegetables and seasonings together and serve it immediately. The styles are different; both are delicious. Try this with a light, luscious, and dry red, such as Bonarda dell'Oltrepò Pavese.

4 medium zucchini, trimmed and
    cut into paper-thin rounds
2 teaspoons best-quality red wine
    vinegar
2 small red bell peppers, stemmed,
    seeds and pith removed, cut into
    paper-thin strips
Fine sea salt

Freshly ground black pepper
    (optional)
2 cups arugula, rinsed, patted dry,
    and torn into bite-size pieces
2 ounces Parmigiano-Reggiano,
    shaved into paper-thin curls
    (see Segreti)
2 tablespoons extra-virgin olive oil

1. Cover the bottom of a 12-inch round nonreactive dish with a layer of the zucchini, using half the rounds, slightly over-lapping them in concentric circles. Using a pastry brush, brush half the vinegar as evenly as possible over the zucchini. Scatter

half the bell pepper slices over the zucchini, then season lightly with salt and, if desired, black pepper. Arrange half the arugula leaves on top with half the Parmesan cheese curls. Drizzle with half the olive oil and season lightly again with salt and, if de-sired, pepper. Repeat the layers using the remaining ingredients.

2. Cover the dish tightly with aluminum foil and refrigerate for 18 to 24 hours. Remove from the refrigerator about 15 minutes before serving.

Roberta Camboule's Roasted Eggplant

**MELANZANE
ARROSTO DI
ROBERTA
CAMBOULE**

4 SERVINGS

I'd heard that Zia Maria, on the island of Sardinia, was the real deal—not just an *agriturismo* and working farm, but a warm, authentic spot, a window into rural Sardinian life. It seemed like the perfect destination for my first visit to Sardinia. But, when I arrived, the stucco farmhouse and its surroundings were dusty from lack of rain. The place seemed deserted, and I wondered if my choice had been well made.

By dinnertime however, Zia Maria was filled with a lively crowd, a curious blend of highway workers who boarded there, local people, and tourists. My table in the dining room was literally covered with plates heaped with all manner of delicious-looking combinations. There was a boar stew that gave off a heady, vinegar-spiked aroma, peppers in oil, zesty tripe salad, a vegetable *frittata,* a tiny pot of hardened sheep cheese, a portion of peppery goat stew, a basket of the Sardinian crisp bread *carta da musica,* and a dish of beautiful celadon green, lightly translucent eggplant. Where to begin?

I sampled them all in a delightful voyage of discovery, but it was the eggplant, my favorite dish, that I finished. The next day, Roberta Camboule, daughter of the owners and occasional chef, showed me how to make the eggplant I'd found so delicious. The first step in her recipe is to run outside and pick eggplants from the field, a luxury most people, including myself, don't have. I was concerned that I'd never be able to recreate the eggplant dish in all the richness of flavor, but I needn't have worried. Roberta would be quite happy, I believe, to eat it at my house, for it is a true facsimile of what she so cheerfully served me that evening.

This calls for a robust red, such as Nebbiolo di Sardegna.

Segreti

Choose very, very firm eggplants (you may use small Japanese eggplants as well as standard) with tight skins, to be sure that they are fresh and won't be bitter. Before roasting them, prick them many times with a trussing needle or skewer so they won't explode in the oven.

4 small roundish eggplants (each about 5 ounces)
2 teaspoons plus 2 tablespoons extra-virgin olive oil

Fine sea salt
2 cloves garlic, cut in half, green germ removed
1 cup fresh flat-leaf parsley leaves

1. Preheat the oven to 450°F.

2. Prick the eggplants all over with a trussing needle or skewer, then rub them all over with oil, using about 2 teaspoons, and place them on a baking sheet. Bake in the oven, turning once, until the skins turn dark and crackle slightly, and the eggplant is soft through but not mushy, about 35 minutes.

3. Remove the eggplants from the oven and transfer them to a rack. When they are cool enough to handle, trim off the stems and carefully peel off the skins, being careful not to take too much flesh with the skin and to leave the eggplant intact.

4. Place the skinned eggplants in a colander and let drain for 1 hour so they give up some of their liquid (see Note).

5. To serve, cut the eggplants carefully in half lengthwise. Arrange them, cut side up, on a serving plate or platter and sprinkle with sea salt to taste. Mince the garlic and parsley together and sprinkle over the eggplant, then drizzle with the remaining 2 tablespoons oil and serve immediately.

NOTE: Don't skip this step. Not every eggplant will give up liquid, but those that have it to give up will be much more flavorful without it.

Fattoria dei Barbi's Seasoned Chicken Liver Spread on Toasts

CROSTINI DI FEGATINI ALLA FATTORIA DEI BARBI

10 TO 20 SERVINGS

*C*rostini, which literally means "toasts," is a term applied to one of the most common antipasti in various parts of Italy, particularly in Tuscany and Umbria. Perhaps the best known is called *fettunta,* a thick slice of Tuscan bread toasted over the fire, rubbed with garlic, drizzled with fresh olive oil, and sprinkled with salt and sometimes pepper.

This *crostino* is very common in Tuscany and it typically includes the spleen of the chicken as well. My favorite was served at a comfortable stone trattoria on the grounds of the Fattoria dei Barbi, a huge farm and *agriturismo* outside Montalcino, known internationally for its wines and locally for its sheep's milk cheese, hams, and sausages. There, Franca Ciaci and her kitchen partners, Luciana Lorenzini and Vania Papi, chop, stir, and taste their way through its preparation, then toast the bread, drizzle it with olive oil, and top it with the warm mixture. These *crostini* are equally delicious served at room temperature as they are warm.

8 oil-packed anchovy fillets, drained

¼ cup milk

¼ cup extra-virgin olive oil, plus additional for serving

1 small onion, coarsely chopped

3 cloves garlic, green germ removed, coarsely chopped

12 ounces chicken livers, trimmed of any green parts and minced or finely ground in a meat grinder

⅓ cup dry white wine, such as Pinot Grigio

½ cup fresh flat-leaf parsley leaves

⅓ cup capers, rinsed, and patted dry

10 slices (each ½ inch thick) Tuscan Bread (page 311), cut in half

20 fresh sage leaves for garnish (optional)

1. Place the anchovy fillets in a shallow bowl and pour the milk over them. Let soak for 20 minutes, then drain, rinse quickly under cold running water, and pat dry gently with paper towels.

2. Heat the oil in a large saucepan over medium heat. Add the onion and garlic and sauté until softened, about 2 minutes. Add the anchovies and stir to break them apart, then add the livers and cook, stirring occasionally, until they have changed color but are not quite cooked through, about 2½ minutes. Pour in the wine, cover, and cook gently until the wine has evaporated, about 7 minutes, reducing the heat as necessary.

3. Preheat the broiler.

4. Mince the parsley leaves.

5. Add the parsley and capers to the liver mixture. Stir, then re-cover and cook until the mixture is heated through, about 2 minutes. If the mixture seems very wet, let it cook, uncovered, a few seconds longer, until it is just pleasantly moist; do not overcook. Remove from the heat and transfer the mixture to a heatproof bowl while you toast the bread.

6. Arrange the bread slices in a single layer on a baking sheet and toast about 3 inches from the heat source until crisp and golden, about 1 minute per side.

7. Transfer the toasted bread to a serving platter. Drizzle each piece lightly with oil and spread with some of the still-warm liver mixture, dividing evenly. Garnish with the sage leaves if desired, and serve immediately.

Aperitivi

There were no pre-lunch drinks as there would have been in Britain. Such aperitivi were unknown in rural Italy. No hanging about either. As soon as the quorum of participants at the feast had been made up someone uttered the magic words, "Avanti, andiamo a tavola!" and we went to the table.

A Small Place in Italy, Eric Newby

Crostini with Herbed Beans

CROSTINI CON
FAGIOLI ALLE
ERBE

10 TO 20
SERVINGS

This antipasto idea comes from Pomurlo Vecchio, a luxurious *agriturismo* and working farm tucked into the Umbrian hills not far from Orvieto. There, owner Lazzarro Minghelli and his daughter, Daniela, raise cattle, goats, and horses, and the grounds are landscaped with vegetables. Geese hiss and chickens cackle from their pen, which is also home to rabbits.

Eola Bianchi is chief cook at the trattoria on the grounds of Pomurlo Vecchio, and though she may cook for as many as sixty in an evening in the large and contemporary kitchen, she does so like an Italian mama, making her own fresh pastas and sauces and stepping into the dining room now and then to cheerfully explain the dishes.

Tender, aromatic beans on toasted bread are a perfect example of Umbrian cuisine, which is rustic and rests solidly on dried beans and other legumes. Today this dish is an antipasto, but there was a time when a dish like this was the main meal for an Italian farm family.

Before eating these *crostini*, enhance their flavor by drizzling them with some fine-quality extra-virgin olive oil to enhance this hearty appetizer.

Try this with a simple Rosso Piceno to put you in the Umbrian state of mind.

2 pounds fresh borlotti, Jacob's cattle, or cranberry beans, shelled or 3 cups (19 ounces) dried beans, such as borlotti or cranberry

6 sprigs fresh thyme

1 long sprig fresh rosemary

2 imported dried bay leaves

4 tablespoons extra-virgin olive oil,

   plus additional for serving

Fine sea salt

10 slices (each ½ inch thick) Tuscan Bread (page 311), cut in half

1 clove garlic, cut in half, green germ removed

1. If you are using fresh beans, go right to step 2. If you are using dried beans, place them in a large saucepan and cover generously with water. Bring to a boil, cover, and remove from the heat. Let the beans soak for 1 hour, then drain.

2. Place the fresh or dried beans in a large saucepan. Add water to cover by 2 inches and the thyme, rosemary, and bay leaves. Bring to a boil over medium-high heat, then reduce the heat so the beans are just simmering. Cover and cook until the beans are tender and very soft but not mushy, 20 to 30 minutes for fresh beans, about 1 hour for dried (see Note).

3. Drain the beans, reserving the cooking liquid, and transfer to a large bowl. Add 2 tablespoons of the oil and toss to coat, then season generously with salt. The beans should be pleasantly moist and tender enough so you can mash them lightly on the toast when you add them. If they need more moisture, add a little of the reserved cooking liquid. Set aside while you toast the bread.

4. Preheat the broiler.

5. Arrange the bread slices in a single layer on a baking sheet and toast about 3 inches from the heat source until crisp and golden, about 1 minute per side.

6. Rub each piece of toast on one side with a cut garlic clove, then brush generously with oil, using the remaining 2 tablespoons. Arrange the pieces, seasoned side up, on a serving platter and cover each with a generous amount of warm beans. Serve accompanied by a cruet of extra-virgin olive oil and additional sea salt for sprinkling.

NOTE: The cooking time for dried beans will be longer or shorter depending on their age; the older they are, the longer they will take. Start testing the beans after 45 minutes.

Gorgonzola and Goat Cheese Crostini

I tasted these delicately delicious *crostini* at La Caprina, a small *agriturismo* farm near Lake Como. Tiny and tucked off the side of the road, La Caprina has a local reputation for serving fine, simple farm food, and that is exactly what I found there.

When I arrived, the long dining table was covered with antipasti. There were home-pickled eggplant and thinly sliced air-cured and spiced meats—including goat—of all shapes and colors. There were also these *crostini*, topped with a light blend of the farm's fresh cheese, a touch of Gorgonzola, and a bit of cream, and while everything was delicious, the crostini stood out.

Try these plain, sprinkled with fresh minced chives, or dusted with coarsely ground black pepper. And accompany them with a lightly chilled light and edgy red, such as Sassella della Valtellina.

The cheese blend keeps in the refrigerator for several days, ready when the need or desire for a quick *crostini* arises.

6 ounces fresh, soft goat cheese
2 ounces Gorgonzola cheese
⅓ cup heavy (whipping) cream,
*   preferably not ultrapasteurized*
Plenty of thinly sliced crusty bread,
*   toasted*

1 small bunch fresh chives, for
*   garnish (optional)*
Coarsely ground black pepper, for
*   garnish (optional)*

1. Using a wooden spoon, blend the cheeses with the cream in a small bowl to obtain a smooth, relatively homogeneous mixture.

2. Thickly spread the mixture on toasts and arrange attractively on a platter.

3. Mince the chives if using.

4. Serve the toasts plain or sprinkled with chives and pepper.

Olympic Wine

In the fifth century B.C., Sophocles praised Italy as the land preferred by Bacchus, and the country was often referred to as Enotria, land of wine and vineyards. Italy has had some rough spots in its wine production, but within the last twenty years it has once again become a land that Sophocles might praise.

Out of the hundreds of notable wines produced in Italy, one of them, Cirò, has a particularly illustrious history. Cirò is produced in Calabria, the rough and rocky region that forms the toe of Italy's boot. In ancient times it was awarded as a prize to victorious Olympic athletes, for it was thought to be sustaining, nourishing, and a source of physical power and prowess.

Today Cirò, which is made primarily with Gaglioppo grapes, is gaining an international reputation as Calabrian vintners update their production methods to produce an increasingly better-quality wine. Red Cirò is very rich, full, and surprisingly flavorful. The white is simple but refreshing. And when you drink a glass be aware, for you may notice your muscles taking on new vigor.

Bagna Cauda

6 TO 8 SERVINGS

Maria Manera, a farmer and fantastic cook, lives in the town of San Rocco Senod'Elvia, right outside Alba in Piedmont. She made her family's favorite dish, *bagna cauda*—which means "hot bath"—for the last night of my visit with them. I'd arrived several days before, invited to help with the grape harvest, but because it was unseasonably warm, Maria and her husband, Luciano, like all the other growers in the area, were leaving the grapes on the vines as

Segreti

When cardoons are in season, Maria always serves them with *bagna cauda,* remembering that the old varieties were much more bitter and flavorful than the new hybridized varieties she grows now. She serves the cardoons either raw or cooked, depending on her whim. When Maria prepares them for cooking, she doesn't wash them but rubs them clean with a tea towel, then with lemon, because washing a cardoon with water causes it to discolor.

long as possible, so their sugar content would continue to rise. The Maneras are paid according to the sugar content of their grapes, so they were happy to let them hang as long as possible.

It was a tense time, and Luciano went out several times a day to check the grapes and confer with neighboring farmers. But it was also quieter than usual on this industrious farm, and the Maneras and I had a chance to spend time together.

Though neither Maria nor Luciano, nor their children, Barbara and Daniele, said anything that last evening as we dipped vegetables into this garlic-redolent *bagna cauda,* I realized it was a rare treat to eat this midweek in September, for *bagna cauda* is usually reserved for holidays or big family gatherings. Maria's version—a rich, creamy, almost souplike garlic sauce with a distinct anchovy flavor—was divine, truly worthy of a celebration, and I, too, make it now when I want to celebrate a special occasion.

Serve a light red alongside, such as Nebbiolo delle Langhe.

4 heads garlic, cloves separated and peeled, cut in half, green germ removed

1⅓ cups whole milk

1 pound small waxy potatoes, peeled

1 small head cauliflower (1 pound), cut into florets

12 oil-packed anchovy fillets, not rinsed

¼ cup heavy (whipping) cream

2 tablespoons unsalted butter

1½ cups extra-virgin olive oil

1 pound fresh fennel, trimmed and cut into ½-inch-thick strips

3 stalks cardoon, trimmed, strings removed, rubbed with a tea towel, then with ½ lemon, and cut into 4-inch lengths

1 or 2 red bell peppers, stemmed, seeds and pith removed, cut into ¼-inch-thick strips

1. Combine the garlic and milk in a medium-size heavy saucepan and bring to a simmer over medium heat. Cook, partially covered, until the garlic is soft but not mushy, 20 to 30

Segreti

If you have guests who object to the salt in anchovies, simply soak them in milk for 10 minutes and discard the milk. The anchovies will be gentled and much less salty.

minutes. Any milk that has not been absorbed will have thickened substantially.

2. While the garlic is cooking, bring water to a boil in the bottom of a steamer over medium-high heat. Add the potatoes to the steamer and cook until almost tender, about 12 minutes. Add the cauliflower to the steamer and steam until both vegetables are tender, about 5 minutes longer. Transfer the vegetables to a platter to cool to lukewarm.

Bagna Cauda

Bagna cauda, which translates as "hot bath," is a dish reserved for *feste,* or celebrations, in the northern region of Piedmont. No real *festa* would be worthy of its name without a pot of this fragrant garlic- and anchovy-rich sauce and the vegetables that accompany it, but that said, it changes from farm to farm, village to village, and no two *bagna caude* are the same.

Recipes in Italy have never traveled far, for until recently poor roads over forbidding landscape kept most people—and ideas and cooking methods—close to home. So while *bagna cauda* is always made with the same basic ingredients, its individual character depends upon the inspiration and habits of the cook who makes it.

3. Meanwhile, remove the pan containing the garlic from the heat. Crush the garlic with a fork until smooth and creamy. Place the pan over very low heat and add the anchovies, cream, and butter. Stir, crushing the anchovies into the mixture, until you have a thick cream. While the mixture bubbles over the heat, whisk in the oil until thoroughly incorporated. Remove from the heat (see Note).

4. Arrange the fennel, cardoons, and red pepper strips on the platter with the now-lukewarm potatoes and cauliflower. Serve accompanied by the hot *bagna cauda* for dipping.

NOTE: The *bagna cauda* must be served very hot. If you have a chafing dish or fondue pot, serve the *bagna cauda* in it, keeping the flame lit underneath and stirring it with the vegetables as you eat.

Peppers in Hot Garlic and Anchovy Sauce

**PEPERONI IN
BAGNA CAUDA**

**8 TO 10
SERVINGS**

Segreti

Red or yellow peppers are best here, as the flesh of most green peppers is soft, the "walls" of the vegetable too thin to withstand grilling and still keep their shape. Besides, according to Elvira, red and yellow are more traditional in the Italian *orto.*

Elvira Padovan is housekeeper of the Principato di Lucedio near Torino, in Piedmont, a rice estate owned by the Contessa Rosetta Clara Cavalli d'Olivola (see essay, page 172). Signora Padovan lives year-round on the estate with her son, Pierangelo, who works the rice fields with four other hired hands. A large-boned woman with reddish blond hair and a lovely open face, she is also gardener of a small *orto,* or vegetable garden, general handyperson, and cook.

She and I sat under a huge old apple tree in the massive graveled courtyard of the Principio—an otherworldly kind of place that is somewhat rundown yet has a lovely, ancient allure—and talked recipes. Peeling apples all the while, she told me about her favorite dishes, the things she makes regularly. This recipe, which Elvira prepares in summer when her garden is in full pepper production, is a standout for its garlic and pungent anchovy flavor softened by the sweetness of the peppers. She grows red and yellow peppers and uses them singly or together when she makes this.

Serve a delightfully rich Nebbiolo d'Alba along with this simple dish.

*2 pounds red or yellow bell peppers,
   roasted (see box, page 23)*
2 tablespoons unsalted butter
2 tablespoons extra-virgin olive oil
*2 cloves garlic, cut in half, green
   germ removed*
8 oil-packed anchovy fillets, drained
*1 tablespoon best-quality red wine
   vinegar*

Pinch of hot paprika, or to taste
1 cup heavy (whipping) cream
Small bunch basil, for garnish

1. After removing the seeds and any white pith from the roasted peppers, cut them into ½-inch-wide strips and lay them on paper towels to drain.

2. Melt the butter with the oil in a small heavy saucepan over low heat. Add the garlic and cook, stirring occasionally, just until translucent, 3 to 4 minutes. Remove and discard the garlic, then stir in the anchovies, vinegar, and cayenne pepper. Whisk in the cream until the mixture is emulsified and bring to a simmer. Simmer, stirring, until the sauce is thickened enough to lightly coat the back of a metal spoon, 5 to 10 minutes. Remove from the heat.

3. Place the pepper strips in a shallow serving dish. Pour the sauce over the peppers and serve immediately, garnished with the basil if desired.

Roasting Peppers

While some people in Italy still roast bell peppers over a wood fire, the most common way these days, there as elsewhere, is over the flame from a gas burner. To do it this way, turn on your burner or burners, depending on how many peppers you are going to roast, to medium-high and place one pepper on each. When the area of skin exposed to the flame is charred and blackened, turn the peppers with tongs, and continue to roast, turning, until the peppers are charred all over; the skins will be crackled and flaking. Watch carefully to prevent the peppers from burning. Remove the peppers from the burners and wrap in a kitchen towel or a sheet of aluminum foil or place them in a plain brown paper bag for 15 minutes or so. The steam from the peppers' own heat will loosen the skins. When cool enough to handle, rub the skin off the peppers, scraping off stubborn bits with the blade of a small sharp knife. Remove the seeds and pith from the peppers (preferably over the sink, since there will be a fair amount of liquid), then pat dry with paper towels and proceed with your recipe.

If you don't have a gas stove, preheat the broiler. Place the peppers on a baking sheet and broil, turning as necessary, until charred and blackened all over. Remove from the broiler and wrap and peel as described above.

Tomatoes with Herb Sauce

**POMODORI CON
SALSA VERDE**

6 SERVINGS

Here's another recipe from Maria Manera (see essay, page 27). She makes the herb sauce—a regional specialty—with her mezzaluna, a curved, very sharp knife with wood handles on either end. Maria prefers this old-fashioned kitchen implement over her food processor because, as she told me, the processor mashes the ingredients and muddies the flavor. Inspired by Maria, I got my own mezzaluna.

Maria serves this tonic herbal sauce spooned over fully ripe but firm halved tomatoes straight from her garden. I usually serve it that way too, though I do love it over roasted red bell peppers as well. Accompanied by plenty of bread for sopping up the sauce and a light but aromatic red, such as Dolcetto delle Langhe, this is sure to become a summer staple.

6 small ripe tomatoes, cored and cut crosswise in half
½ teaspoon fine sea salt, plus additional to taste
1 teaspoon red wine vinegar
4 oil-packed anchovy fillets, drained
4 cups (loosely packed) fresh flat-leaf parsley leaves

1 small clove garlic, cut in half, green germ removed
1 piece (½ to 1 inch) fresh chili pepper, such as serrano or jalapeño (optional)
5 tablespoons extra-virgin olive oil
Pinch of cayenne or other hot ground pepper (optional)

1. Sprinkle the cut sides of the tomatoes with ½ teaspoon salt and let sit for 15 minutes.

2. Combine the vinegar and ⅓ cup water in a small bowl. Add the anchovies and let them soak for 5 minutes. Drain and pat dry.

3. Turn each tomato half upside down over the sink and shake out any liquid, then arrange the halves, cut side up, on a serving platter.

4. Mince the anchovies, parsley, garlic, and chili pepper

Parsley

(if using) together, using a mezzaluna or a sharp, heavy knife. Transfer the mixture to a bowl, then stir in the oil and season with salt to taste and cayenne if using. Spoon an equal amount of the sauce over the top of each tomato. Serve immediately or let sit at room temperature for 30 minutes before serving.

Stuffed Sage Leaves

FOGLIE DI SALVIA FARCITE

MAKES 45 STUFFED LEAVES; 4 OR 5 APPETIZER SERVINGS

In Tuscany, the sage grows leaves as big as baby shoes, and they often are deep-fried and served as an appetizer. I can't find them quite so big where I live, but it doesn't matter for this recipe. Regular sage leaves, which are about 3 inches long, work just fine. Stuffed with anchovies, garlic, and capers, then dipped in a *pastella*, or light batter, and fried, they make a flavorful antipasto.

I got this recipe from Lisa Bonacossi, owner with her husband, Ugo Contini Bonacossi, of the Tenuta di Capezzana, a winery outside Florence, in the Carmignano hills near Pistoia. The winery produces a handful of luscious wines, including Villa di Capezzana Carmignano and Villa di Capezzana Carmignano Riserva, all made from a blend of the traditional Tuscan grape Sangiovese and a very atypical grape for Tuscany, Cabernet Sauvignon. What sets Capezzana apart from other Tuscan wineries is that it was the first recorded to have planted Cabernet Sauvignon grapes several hundred years ago.

Serve the sage leaves with a chilled Villa di Capezzana Carmignano in combination with other antipasti, such as Lemon-Spiced Olives, Prosciutto and Cheese Snails, or any of the Crostini (see Index).

15 oil-packed anchovy fillets,
    drained
¼ cup white wine or milk
45 good-size (2½ to 3 inches long)
    fresh sage leaves
45 capers (heaping ¼ cup), rinsed,
    drained, and patted dry

2 large cloves garlic, minced
⅓ cup all-purpose flour
½ cup carbonated mineral water or
    seltzer
3 cups olive oil or a blend of mild
    vegetable and olive oils

1. Place the anchovies in a small bowl, cover with the wine or milk, and soak for 15 minutes. Drain, rinse, pat dry, and cut them lengthwise into thirds.

2. To fill the sage leaves, lay them out on a work surface and lay a piece of anchovy fillet in the center of each. Top it with a caper, then sprinkle on some minced garlic (judge by eye, so that you have enough garlic for each sage leaf). Roll up the sage leaf lengthwise, from the stem end up to the tip, keeping all in the center (which isn't as difficult as it sounds), and pierce with a toothpick to hold it together, putting the toothpick through the caper. Continue with the remaining sage leaves, capers, and garlic.

3. Place the flour in a medium-size bowl and whisk in the carbonated water until blended and smooth. You will have a very liquid batter that will fizz up, then die down as you mix. Line 2 baking sheets with several layers of clean plain brown paper or paper towels.

4. Heat the oil in a deep, heavy saucepan over medium-high heat until it shimmers on the surface but isn't smoking. To test, drop some of the batter in the oil. It should rise to the top and turn pale golden within 30 seconds.

5. Dip a stuffed sage leaf in the batter to thoroughly coat. Then hold it just above the oil and push it off the toothpick with a fork, right into the oil. The batter will hold it together if it has been rolled securely. Remove it from the oil when it is crisp and golden, after about 1 minute. Let any excess oil drip from it, then transfer it to the prepared baking sheets to drain, then transfer to a serving platter and serve.

THE MANERAS OF PIEDMONT

I spent all of a hot summer morning with Luciano Manera, walking through his Moscato, Dolcetto, and Barbera vineyards and gazing across the hills at the incredible countryside near Alba, in Piedmont. The Manera family lives in a modern house just a footpath over the hill from the old family farmhouse, a large, spare stone building.

Luciano took me down into the *cantina*, or wine cellar, of the old farmhouse, which holds wine tanks from the thirties, their doors each painted a shade of blue, rose, or turquoise green that have all faded into a delicious array of muted colors. Luciano has both Dolcetto and Barbera wines aging in the tanks, and he filled a couple of bottles to take back to his house. As we left, he pointed out his homemade sausages, which hang from the ceiling to cure in the dry air of the cellar.

Luciano is a proud man. He and his wife, Maria, work hard in their vineyards and are doing very well now.

"It's thanks to the Moscato," Luciano said as we hiked back over the hill to his house. "We happen to have the best patch of land for Moscato in all of Alba, and the market for that grape has exploded. We always sell every grape we grow." The Cinzano company buys the Moscato to make the very sweet apéritif wine that bears the company name and is sold worldwide.

So proud is Luciano of his section of Piedmont that he offered me a tour. We drove up and down hills and over country roads, finally stopping at a knoll that dominated the area. "You see, there isn't anything like this in the world," he said, as we looked at the steep hillsides covered with manicured vineyards, interrupted now and then by deep-green groves of hazelnut trees.

"Those trees produce the best hazelnuts in Italy," Luciano said. "I raised them too, but it made more sense for me to plant grapes. Besides, I don't have a 'feeling' for hazelnuts. I don't enjoy caring for the trees, while I do love tending the vines."

When we returned to the Maneras' house, I met the delightful Maria, a passionate cook. "Maria used to cook for the local *osteria* when times weren't quite as good for us as they are now," Luciano said. "She is the best cook in town."

Maria countered his "Times weren't as good" with an "I really miss it too!" for she loved cooking for the public who somehow found their way to the tiny pub in their town of San Rocco Senod'Elvia. She keeps her hand in by taking over for the chef there when he needs it and when she can get a break from working in the vineyard, helping in the vegetable garden, or preparing meals for Luciano, their daughter, Barbara, and son, Daniele.

Anchovies Are Worth a Fortune

When it comes to anchovies, don't skimp on the price. Even at their most expensive, a container of anchovies rarely rivals the price of a good bottle of wine, and the contents go much, much further. I recommend top-quality anchovies either packed in sea salt (from Spain, France, Italy, Morocco) or wonderful silken fillets packed in oil (from the same countries). If you can find whole salted anchovies from Sicily, try those, remembering to gently pull the fillets from the bone before cooking them.

Generally a very low price on anchovies means a mushy, salty, fishy mash inside. Good-quality anchovies should be firm, not so salty they make you pucker, have integrity of texture, and not smell so fishy that you have to hold your nose. A good, intense anchovy aroma and flavor are normal—and desirable. Funky fishiness isn't.

A good anchovy will only add to a dish where anchovies are called for, and unless it is specified in the recipe, neither rinsing nor soaking is necessary.

That said, if you still think the anchovies you're using are too salty, and possibly too anchovy-ish in flavor, try using the following Italian farmhouse tricks for gentling them:

Soak them for 5 minutes in ⅓ cup water mixed with 1 teaspoon red wine vinegar or soak them for 10 minutes in milk.

After soaking, pat them dry and proceed with the recipe.

Frittata with Mint

FRITTATA CON MENTA

6 SNACK SERVINGS; 2 TO 4 MAIN-COURSE SERVINGS

This recipe comes from Giuseppe Vena, who, with his brother, Mauro, and his father, Salvatore, are still sharecroppers in the lush, fertile Madonie mountains in north-central Sicily (see essay, page 30). When I visited them at the end of March, their garden was a maze of the last of winter produce. The few remaining cabbages and leeks were giving way to spring crops—the favas were low and bushy, some lettuce was sprouting, the fennel was a bright green. A huge mint plant flourished, and when I asked Giuseppe what he did with it, he described a mint frittata, emphasizing, as he carefully described its making, that one must use neither too much nor too little mint, but just enough to give a fresh flavor.

I like to make this in advance and serve it at room temperature. It is a perfect little snack or appetizer, but can also be served as a main course with a salad.

Serve this frittata with a white wine of some strength, such as Etna Bianco Superiore.

6 large eggs
¼ teaspoon fine sea salt
⅓ cup (loosely packed) peppermint
  leaves, rinsed and patted dry

¼ cup finely grated Parmigiano-
  Reggiano
Hot paprika or cayenne pepper
1 tablespoon olive oil

1. Preheat the broiler.

2. Whisk together the eggs and salt in a large bowl just until they are broken up. Mince the mint and whisk it immediately into the eggs along with the cheese. Season lightly with hot paprika.

3. Heat the oil in a 9½-inch ovenproof skillet over medium-high heat until it is hot but not smoking. Add the eggs, which will puff up, and cook without stirring until they are set on the bottom, which will take 2 to 3 minutes. You will detect a somewhat toasty smell, and the eggs will be set except for about ¼ inch on the top.

4. Remove the pan from the heat and place it under the broiler, about 5 inches from the heat source. Cook until the top is just set and no egg is left uncooked, which should take 1 to 2 minutes; be careful not to overcook.

5. Remove from the heat and flip the frittata onto a warmed serving platter. Serve immediately or let it cool to room temperature.

THE VENA BROTHERS
OF GANGI

The Vena brothers, Giuseppe and Mauro, live with their father, Salvatore, deep in the Madonie mountains of north-central Sicily. They are among the last farmers in this lush, fertile agricultural area, for in the past thirty years the countryside has nearly emptied of farm families, many of whom have moved into nearby towns.

Traditionally, farming in the Madonie was done by *mezzadri,* or sharecroppers, who gave half of what they raised to the landowner in exchange for housing. When the sharecropping system was abolished in the 1960s, the state freed the *mezzadri* and gave them small plots of land and the choice of whether or not to farm it. Many

elected to sell the land and move to town. Often they were hired back to work it, and many still do, commuting daily from town. During the day the fields buzz with tractors and the conversation of farmworkers. In the evening all is quiet.

Through some wrinkle in the system, the Venas have continued to live under the sharecropper system, and they feel extremely lucky to be doing so. They cultivate the land, which is owned by a man from Palermo, raising all their own food as well as feed for their six cows and ten sheep, whose milk and meat they sell. They continue to give half of everything they raise and earn to the landowner, in return for the farmhouse and a small pension. "We've got the best life," Giuseppe said. "No one bothers us, we're lucky enough to have a landlord who is happy that we're taking care of his land, and we're left alone to live a great, simple life."

The Venas built a small house on the land the state gave them, which is just down the road. Since they've never needed to live in it, it serves as a storage shed, surrounded by a garden filled with flowers and herbs.

What has happened in the Madonie mountains is a perfect example of postwar

agriculture in Sicily, where more land is under cultivation than ever before, but few farmers live on it. Simple, old stone farmhouses like the Venas' are vacation homes for city folk from Palermo, and weekends and holidays finds them filled. Only vestiges of an agricultural society remain.

I was visiting the Venas because I wanted to see how they survived in their old way of life. I found that *thrive* was a better word to describe what they were doing. Although the day was gray, they were all sitting comfortably in a one-room lean-to—really a large kitchen with a table in it—at the side of their large, comfortable farmhouse. A fire burned in the woodstove, a wonderful creamy smell from freshly made cheese filled the air, and the room—stuccoed bright pink—was cozy and warm. A relative from town was visiting, and the cards were about to be dealt.

"We have the life, don't we?" Giuseppe said, laughing and sipping a glass of wine. They'd been up since dawn working and were taking an extended morning break. "We try not to brag about it," he added. "We don't want to act too happy. It might cause another agricultural revolution if we did!"

The lean-to acts as their daytime sitting room, and from its windows they can survey their fields and simultaneously keep an eye on dishes simmering atop the stove.

Giuseppe and Mauro keep a sizable kitchen garden—filled with mint, which they use in a frittata (page 28), and late-season vegetables—just outside the farmhouse. They also do the cooking, and judging from the aromas issuing from that morning's hearty chicken and potato stew, they do a terrific job.

They took me on a tour of their farm, introduced me to their animals, then offered me coffee. As I prepared to leave, the sun came out, and I stood with them in the farmyard and looked down and over the fields and mountains, a stunning blue-tinged vista. It was obvious why the Venas felt lucky. They've kept their life simple and uncomplicated and have enough company to keep them from getting lonely and a nearby town to visit whenever they feel the need. They help out their few neighbors when necessary, and otherwise go about the business of farming and living. They know they've got it good.

Roasted Peppers with Tuna

PEPERONI AL TONNO

8 TO 10 SERVINGS

This dish was sitting on the table in the Maneras' (see box, page 27) family dining room, the prelude to one of the finer meals I've ever eaten, and the first of many I've since taken in their company. I make these *peperoni* often in summer, when red bell peppers are plentiful. It's very easy and fast, and perfect for a large group. You can easily cut the recipe in half to suit a smaller group.

Serve this, as Luciano did, with a dry but fruity red, such as Dolcetto.

6 medium red bell peppers, roasted (see box, page 23)
2 cans (6 ounces each) tuna packed in olive oil, drained
6 tablespoons capers, preferably preserved in salt (see box, page 66)

½ cup extra-virgin olive oil
¼ cup fresh flat-leaf parsley leaves, for garnish

capers

1. After removing the seeds and any white pith from the roasted peppers, cut them lengthwise into quarters. Arrange, insides up, on a serving platter and set aside.

2. Combine the tuna and capers in a food processor and process until finely chopped. With the machine running, add the oil in a steady stream through the feed tube and continue processing until the mixture has turned an ivory color and is quite smooth, 8 to 10 minutes.

3. Fill the pepper quarters with the tuna purée, using about 1 generous tablespoon per pepper.

4. Mince the parsley leaves if using and garnish the filled peppers. Serve immediately.

Batter-Fried Vegetables

Next time you find yourself in the process of making party plans, include these tender vegetables wrapped in a delicately crisp batter, then fried in olive oil. I make *frittura vegetale* often for family and friends, and we stand and eat them as they emerge from the oil, savoring each mouthful, looking forward to the next.

The variety of vegetables and herbs I suggest using is typically Italian, but you may use other favorites, such as broccoli, cauliflower, or green beans, mixing them according to your tastes. Try to serve these just out of the oil, for they won't get any better if they are left to sit.

A lightly chilled Pomino Bianco makes a perfect complement to the lightly fried vegetables.

3 pounds mixed vegetables, such as
   zucchini, bell peppers, potatoes, and
   eggplant, rinsed and patted dry
1 cup (or more) fresh sage leaves and
   small, tender sprigs
⅔ cup all-purpose flour
1 cup carbonated mineral water or
   seltzer

5 cups mild olive oil
   (see Note)
3 to 4 cloves garlic, cut
   lengthwise into thin
   slices
Fine sea salt, for sprinkling

1. Trim and peel or core and seed the vegetables if necessary. Cut them all into very thin lengthwise slices. Separate all but the little sprig of sage leaves at the end of the stem, leaving that intact.

2. Place the flour in a large bowl and whisk in the carbonated water until blended and smooth. You will have a very liquid batter that will fizz up, then die down as you mix. Line a baking sheet with several layers of clean plain brown paper or paper towels.

3. Heat the oil in a large

heavy saucepan or deep fryer until hot but not smoking, 370°F on a deep-fry thermometer.

4. When the oil is ready, dip into the batter as many vegetables and herbs, including the garlic, as will fit into the pan without crowding. Hold them with your fingers or with tongs and let any excess drip off. Place them in the oil so they float in an even layer on the surface without crowding each other. Cook until they are golden, which will vary from about 35 seconds for bell peppers, sage, and garlic, to slightly over 1 minute for the zucchini and potatoes. The timing depends on several things, including the temperature of the oil, the temperature of the vegetables,

and the thickness of the slices.

5. Remove the vegetables and herbs from the oil, let drain briefly on the prepared baking sheet, then transfer to a warmed serving platter. Sprinkle with salt and serve immediately.

NOTE: In the south of Italy, frying in pure olive oil is still a common practice. In the north, pork fat was the frying medium of choice but has been replaced by a variety of oils. Many farm cooks I spoke with in both northern and southern Italy suggested a blend of oils, as I've indicated, which they feel results in a lighter, better dish. I agree with them, but sometimes I like to indulge my passion for olive oil, and I use it pure, for frying. Do as your own palate indicates.

Fried Potato Balls

POLPETTE DI PATATE

MAKES ABOUT 25

On one of my trips to Tuscany, I was introduced to basil grower Vittorio Miniati (see essay, page 36). While visiting him, I marveled at the lushness of the basil he had growing in his greenhouses and asked him if he had any special basil recipes. The naiveté of that question became clear when the answer I got was a rousing round of

laughter. "We put basil into everything we eat," Catia, his daughter, said. "We laugh because to us it's the best part of our cooking."

They agreed, however, that these savory little potato balls were a family favorite, something they make often and never fail to enjoy. Crisp on the outside and scented with basil within, they should be served hot from the oil with a glass of light Montecarlo Rosso alongside.

1 pound russet potatoes
Fine sea salt
¾ cup (2 ounces) fresh bread
    crumbs
1 clove garlic, green germ removed,
    minced

1½ cups (gently packed) fresh
    basil leaves
½ cup (gently packed) fresh flat-leaf
    parsley leaves
3 to 4 cups mild olive oil

1. Place the potatoes in a large saucepan, cover with water, and add 1 tablespoon sea salt. Bring to a boil over high heat, then reduce the heat so the water is boiling gently, and cook, partially covered, until the potatoes are tender, 20 to 30 minutes.

2. Drain the potatoes. When they are cool enough to handle, peel them and put them through a ricer or food mill into a large bowl. Gently stir in the bread crumbs.

3. Mince the garlic with the herbs and add to the potato mixture. Season to taste with salt.

4. Form small balls, using 1 heaping tablespoon of the mixture for each one, and place them on a plate.

5. Pour the oil into a deep, heavy saucepan and heat until a deep-fry thermometer registers 375°F.

6. Line a plate with several layers of clean plain brown paper or paper towels. Fry the *polpette*, 4 to 6 at a time, being careful not to crowd the pan, until they are golden on the outside and very hot through, about 2 minutes. Transfer to the prepared plate and let sit just long enough to drain slightly, then transfer to a serving platter and serve.

AN AGRONOMIST, A GENIUS, AND A LUCKY FARMER

It was not quite ten o'clock on an early summer morning in Tuscany, and the sun was already crushing. I had just parked my car in a spot of shade near the Poggibonsi exit on the highway between Perugia and Florence to wait for Giovanni Ceretelli, an agronomist, heirloom vegetable specialist, and organic farming consultant. I heard someone call my name and spied a handsome, rangy, blond-haired man unfold himself from a tiny car. He waved and I went to meet him. As I got in his car, I turned to meet his wife, Luna. "My assistant," he said with a wink. Together they would take me to meet some of the farmers Giovanni works with. I already knew from talking with Giovanni on the phone that he spent most of his waking hours tussling with farming issues. What I didn't know was that Luna shares his passions and that together they farm (organically, of course) a small plot of land surrounding the ancient farmhouse they call home, and where they also keep chickens in a hutch Luna built by hand.

Giovanni's personal and professional mission is to increase the amount of organic farming in Tuscany, and in these efforts he wears many hats. Aside from consulting and advising, he will, when asked, actually step in to run a farm, particularly one that is making the transition from conventional farming, based on synthetic chemicals, to organic. As a certifier for one of Italy's three organic certification organizations, he inspects farms to be sure organic farming practices are being followed. As an heirloom vegetable sleuth, he helps ensure the future of Tuscany's flavorful vegetables.

He conducts most of his business from his car, which he drives with a phone clamped to one ear. When he leaves the house early in the morning, Luna knows that, unless they're working together that day, she won't see him again until late evening. His consulting clients range from an artisanal basil production to one of the largest dairies in Tuscany. While turning Tuscany organic is uphill work, Giovanni feels progress is being made.

We stopped by a winery where Giovanni consults and where he and Luna were scheduled to give a wine tasting. As we waited for the group to arrive, Giovanni talked about his heirloom vegetable project. His investigations take him throughout Tuscany, poking around in gardens on the lookout for noncommercial varieties of tomatoes, zucchini, onions, and peppers. He has a high success rate because he often runs across older people who cultivate plants grown from seeds they've saved year after year. He photographs and catalogs the vegetables and, working with the University of Florence agricultural school and the State Department of Agriculture and Forests, has published much of his work. He grows as many varieties as possible in his own garden.

Sitting on a stone bench under an olive tree, we looked through some of his slides—of smallish Nespoli artichokes, deep red *rossa* onions, the distinctive scalloped Florentine tomato, *nero* shell beans and spotted brown butter beans, huge and dusty-skinned *moscatello* watermelons, ruffle-leafed basil, and dozens of other varieties. Some of these I'd already seen at markets I'd visited, which is just about the only place most people find them.

The wine tasting was brief and revivifying, then we were on our way, twisting and turning through countryside that was mostly covered with vines, punctuated by orchards of silvery olive trees.

As we drove along Giovanni prepped me for the next visit. As a retirement project, a former factory worker named Vittorio Miniati had developed a revolutionary way to raise basil that was making him wealthy and employing his whole family. He'd sought out Giovanni some months before, and today's trip was scheduled because he wanted advice on organic cultivation. Giovanni

also thought I'd be interested in seeing the farming operation.

We drove down a gravel road and pulled up under a shade tree in a small farmyard. A man rushed out of the house, hurriedly chewing his last mouthful of lunch, and Giovanni hailed him. "*Ciao, Vittorio!*" Vittorio Miniati greeted us enthusiastically, and we headed off for a clutch of greenhouses a short distance away. Passing a large, lush vegetable garden on the way, I craned my neck to look at the Tuscan triumvirate of fava beans, tomatoes, and zucchini growing there.

Though the weather had been dry for almost a week, the ground squelched slightly under our feet as we approached the long greenhouses. "The ground here is damp because we're near the river," Miniati explained. "To absorb the dampness in the greenhouses, I put down straw, covered it with a fine layer of soil, and planted basil seeds in it. They all came up."

Layering straw and organic soil that has been commercially heated to a temperature hot enough to destroy any noxious seeds is the accidental secret to Miniati's success. He didn't know how well it would work when he first did it, but realized it made sense as soon as he saw the results. Weeds are the bane of the organic farmer, who doesn't use herbicides to kill them. By stacking straw on the soil, then covering it with more soil followed by a nondecomposing fabric, intended to keep weeds down and in which he makes holes for the basil plants, Miniati circumvents expensive and time-consuming weeding almost entirely.

We stepped inside the greenhouse, where it was so hot and humid it was almost impossible to breathe. What made it bearable was the rich basil aroma. The floor was a green carpet of vibrant basil plants, and Miniati stepped among them, picking sprigs and handing them to us, talking, gesticulating as Giovanni thoughtfully rubbed his chin, shook his head.

Giovanni turned to explain. "Every six months Vittorio adds new straw to his raised beds as the old decomposes to make soil. That, combined with the fabric and the even temperatures provided by the greenhouses, has proved a total success," he said. "The only problem is yellow leaves on the plants, which probably means the soil has become too rich." With Giovanni's help, Miniati will find a solution.

Miniati harvests basil year-round. Once a week in summer, he snips the top branches from half the plants, pulling the rest of them out so he can replant. The snipped tops are bundled in bouquets to sell. Those he pulls out are sold with the roots still on, which gives them a longer shelf life. The plants that are trimmed will continue to produce all summer. In winter he harvests every eight days, pulling up the entire plant because leaf production is less lush.

When Giovanni first saw what Miniati was doing, he was both flabbergasted and enchanted. "Such a simple system, and it works so well," he said. "This guy is a genius."

His eldest daughter, Catia, watched her father closely as he worked, helping him harvest pounds of produce, wondering with him what to do with it all. One morning without saying a word to her family, she got up early, packed all the extra produce from the day before in some crates, and went with a friend to the Florence wholesale market.

She returned home with empty crates and full pockets. The following day she did the same, and a small business was born.

"I was twenty-one at the time," Catia, now twenty-nine, said. "I was the youngest and smallest producer at the market, and the only woman except for some farmer's mother. People bought everything I had!"

When her father retired, he gardened full time and started his basil project. The basil—a key ingredient in most Italian cuisines, Tuscan no exception—soon became their most important crop. Catia began bringing bunches of basil to the market, their roots swathed in newspapers, their leaves in a big plastic bag. Once again she returned home with empty crates. As Miniati developed his cultivation method, he built up to producing tons of the peppery, licorice-flavored green leaves a year. Catia still sells through the wholesale market, and the family also sells to supermarkets and to the local school system, where basil goes into school lunches.

Dough Pillows

GNOCCHI FRITTI

ABOUT 20 FRITTERS

These lovely, light little pockets of crisp dough, traditionally served on the farms and in the rural *osterie,* or pubs, around Modena and Reggio-Emilia, in Emilia-Romagna, are not to be confused with the well-known boiled dumplings called simply gnocchi. Laura Morani, a Modenese shopkeeper, has taken the idea right to the heart of town. She makes *gnocchi fritti* at the small trattoria she and her husband, Nano, own at the back of Giusti's, their shop in Modena that specializes in regional specialties.

Laura invited me into the kitchen so I could see how she made them. I watched her roll out the dough, then cut it into rectangles and deftly fry it in fat so hot it was nearly smoking. Each and every *gnocchi* came out light, golden, and perfect; not one refused to puff up.

On the farm these *gnocchi* played a significant part in a meal, a foil for sausage, ham, or cheese. Now they have become a palate teaser, emerging from the hot fat light as a feather. (Every now and then you may get a non-cooperator that stays flat in the fat—just discard it and continue.)

1 teaspoon active dry yeast

3 tablespoons lukewarm water

3¾ cups (1 pound) all-purpose flour

4 tablespoons unsalted butter, melted

Fine sea salt (see Note)

¾ cup carbonated mineral water or seltzer

3 to 4 cups mild olive oil

1. Dissolve the yeast in the warm water in a large bowl. Add ½ cup flour and stir, then stir in the melted butter until combined. Add a pinch of salt and the mineral water, then add the remaining flour, 1 cup at a time, to make a soft, smooth dough. Turn the dough out onto a lightly floured work surface and knead just until satiny, about 5 minutes. Cover with an overturned bowl and let

rest for 1 hour.

2. Heat oil to a depth of 1 inch in a large heavy skillet until it shimmers on the surface but is not smoking. It should be very, very hot; a deep-fry thermometer should register at least 375°F.

3. Roll out one-quarter of the dough at a time to a thickness of $1/16$ inch. Cut the dough into rectangles approximately 4½ x 2½ inches and add 2 at a time to the hot oil. Fry, turning

once, until the fritters fill with air and turn pale golden on each side, less than 1 minute per side.

4. Using a slotted spoon, transfer the fritters to a plate covered with a double thickness of paper towels to drain while you roll out, cut, and fry the remaining fritters. Lightly salt them and serve as soon as possible.

NOTE: Sea salt is a must for sprinkling the *gnocchi.*

Ligurian Artichoke Torte

**TORTA
PASQUALINA
LIGURE
6 S E R V I N G S**

This recipe, made with fresh artichokes, ricotta cheese, parsley, and basil, is traditional to the countryside of Liguria and as common to the farmhouse kitchen as are the fresh eggs that go into it. The oldest, and claimed to be the truest, version calls for either Swiss chard or artichokes, many more eggs than are called for here, marjoram, and bread crumbs and is traditionally made at Eastertime. It has spawned a variety of recipes, like this one, generally referred to as *torta pasqualina.* This version is lighter and more contemporary, though still very traditional.

I've adapted it by adding some basil, which is both characteristic of Liguria and a wonderful flavor enhancer, and rather than make my own strudel dough, I use packaged phyllo dough, as suggested by my Ligurian friend and culinary specialist Paola Repetto.

Serve this with a wine from Liguria, such as Cinque Terre Bianco, lightly chilled.

1 lemon, cut in half
5 large artichokes (each about
1 pound) or 5 pounds small
artichokes
2 tablespoons extra-virgin olive oil
1 medium onion, thinly sliced
2 cloves garlic, minced
1 cup ricotta
2 large eggs
1 cup (about 1¾ ounces) grated
Parmigiano-Reggiano

1 cup (loosely packed) fresh
basil leaves
1 cup (loosely packed) fresh
flat-leaf parsley leaves
Fine sea salt
5 sheets phyllo dough, thawed
if frozen
Extra-virgin olive oil, for brushing
the dough
(2 tablespoons)

1. Squeeze the juice of the lemon into a large bowl of water. If using large artichokes, trim them down to the hearts (see box, page 42); cut them into thin slices, and place them in the acidulated water for about 15 minutes. If using small artichokes, trim all the leaves down to the inner tender yellow ones, cut them into thin slices, and place in the water for 15 minutes. Drain the artichokes and pat dry with paper towels.

2. Preheat the oven to 400°F.

3. Heat the oil in a large skillet over medium heat. Add the onion and garlic and cook until the onion begins to turn translucent, about 5 minutes. Add the artichokes, cover, and cook, stirring occasionally, until they are tender but not mushy, about 20 minutes.

4. Place the ricotta in a food processor and process until it is smooth and somewhat light. Add the eggs and Parmigiano and process until thoroughly blended, then transfer to a medium-size bowl. Mince the basil and parsley and whisk them into the cheese mixture, then season generously with salt.

5. Working with one sheet of phyllo dough at a time and

Preparing Artichoke Hearts

First pull off all the large outer leaves of the artichoke with your fingers. Using a large heavy knife, slice off the top of the remaining cone of leaves. Using a paring knife, trim the stem and all the dark green parts remaining on the outside of the light green heart. Scrape out the hairy choke with a teaspoon. Rub the artichoke heart with half of a lemon to keep it from darkening or drop it into a bowl of cold water mixed with lemon juice.

with oil. Repeat with 4 more sheets, brushing each with oil and leaving the edges of the phyllo hanging over the sides of the pan. Spread the artichoke mixture over the pastry, then top with the cheese mixture. Fold the ends of the phyllo dough, one layer at a time, back over the top of the filling, brushing each layer lightly with oil. Place the pan on a baking sheet and bake in the center of the oven until the torte is golden on top, about 30 minutes.

6. Remove the torte from the oven, remove sides of the pan, and slip the torte onto a serving platter. Cut into wedges, like a pie, and serve immediately.

keeping the remainder covered with a damp kitchen cloth, line a 9-inch springform pan with the first phyllo sheet and brush it

Cured Pork with Sage and Vinegar on Pizza

PIZZA CON BARBOZZA, SALVIA, E ACETO

6 TO 8 *MERENDE* SERVINGS

At Agriturismo Malvarina, a working farm outside Assisi, owner Maria Maurillo makes this wonderfully savory mixture to top her equally delicious, puffy pizza dough. Serve a flavorful and hearty red, such as Montepulciano d'Abruzzo, alongside.

Segreti

When adding vinegar to the pan, use a long-handled utensil and stand back so the vapor from the vinegar doesn't sear your eyes.

1 tablespoon extra-virgin olive oil
6 ounces pancetta or prosciutto, sliced thin but not paper thin, and cut crosswise into 2-inch strips

2 cups (gently packed) fresh sage leaves
¾ cup best-quality red wine vinegar
1 recipe Maria's Pizza Dough (page 432), baked

1. Heat the oil in a large nonreactive skillet or saucepan over medium-high heat. Add the pancetta and stir so the pancetta is coated with oil, then sauté until it begins to turn golden on both sides. Reduce the heat to medium, cover, and cook, checking occasionally so the pancetta doesn't burn, until it is deep golden and beginning to get quite crisp, about 3 minutes.

2. Increase the heat to medium-high and add the sage leaves, mixing them in among the pancetta. Stir them so they are coated with oil. Reduce the heat just slightly, cover, and cook, shaking the pan occasionally, until the leaves are curled and dark at the edges, about 3 minutes.

3. Pour the vinegar carefully into the pan, standing back to avoid the vapor, and shake the pan so the ingredients combine. Remove from the heat and let sit for at least 5 minutes before serv-

ing so that the flavors have a chance to mellow and blend.

4. Cut the baked pizza crust into 3- to 4-inch squares. Place one or two squares on each serving plate, and divide the sauce evenly among them, pouring it right on the pizza. Alternatively, serve the pizza and the sauce separately.

THE BUFFALO AND THEIR CHEESE

It was hot and the traffic was so snarled I faltered. But the taste memory of smooth, freshly made mozzarella and my desire to learn more about how and where it was made kept me going, and I finally emerged from the din of Neapolitan traffic.

I was on my way to Battipaglia, a noisy town that is the heart of buffalo-milk mozzarella production. It is surrounded by flat, fertile land—the Piana del Sele, or Sele River flats—which bursts with cherry, apricot, and plum trees, vegetables, herbs, wheat, and forage for animals.

Just outside Battipaglia is La Morella, a large farm that was once the domain of a wealthy landowner. As such, it resembles an enclosed village with its own chapel, bread oven, granary, and red brick–topped tower, which once served as a lookout for marauding armies. I drove into the large courtyard, and Cucino Generoso, one of the farm's owners, emerged from his office with a warm greeting, ready to tell me all he could about water buffalo and mozzarella cheese.

He immediately led me across the courtyard to show me the thoroughly modern milking installation in one of the old farm buildings. Morning and evening the farm's thirty-odd head of water buffalo troop through to be milked. The day's milk is blended and refrigerated and each morning delivered to a dairy in Battipaglia.

We emerged from the milking room and walked the outside periphery of the walled farm while Generoso told me his story. Though he wasn't raised on a farm, he was brought up near La Morella and always had a fascination for agriculture, with a particular interest in and affection for water buffalo. "When I was a child, the buffalo were left to wander in the marsh during the day, and the herders called them back at night by singing couplets," he said. "They were very poetic, and each one described the characteristics of a specific animal and was recognizable to it as its name. I remember those haunting songs floating over the air at night, and perhaps that is why I love water buffalo so much."

Generoso pursued a career in business until several years ago, when he finally combined his agricultural interest with his training by purchasing La Morella with a group of friends. Now he oversees the farming and plans to gradually increase the herd of buffalo, as well as the production of fruits and vegetables.

We rounded the final corner of the wall and headed for a back field to see the buffalo. Generoso became increasingly animated as we approached them. "These animals are like friends," he said. "They're gentle, sensitive, and intelligent, and I always have the feeling they're happy to see me." Indeed, as we approached, the buffalo lined up in two orderly lines and calmly watched us.

With their placid faces, stocky bodies, and curved, upturned horns, the water buffalo resemble their Asian relatives who work rice paddies. Because they have no sweat glands they must have water nearby when it's hot, and according to Generoso, they'll do just about anything to get into it. He recounted the time the buffalo broke through their fence and jumped into an irrigation canal on the other side.

"It was hot earlier than usual that year, and we hadn't dug them a pond yet, so their natural instinct was to head for the canal," he said. "I've never seen anything funnier, but they wouldn't come out when we called, so we had to pull them out with a tractor. Now our fences are stronger, and we make sure to dig them a pond early in the season, before it gets too hot!"

That night I stayed in one of the clean, spacious apartments on the farm, and the following morning met Generoso so we could go to the cooperative dairy where the milk from his buffalo is turned into cheese. By 10 A.M. we were standing among the white-clad crew busy stirring, forming, and braiding cheeses.

Though small, the dairy is fully automated, and machines whir, clank, and spin as water and whey splash everywhere.

He explained over the din how milk is heated before being turned into cheese.

"It's not technically pasteurized," he hastened to say. "But it does amount to about the same thing." He acknowledged that heating damages the delicate "flower" of the milk's flavor, but he feels it is a necessary step. "We're small but we make a lot of cheese, and we have to be assured of a market," he said. "We market in northern Europe, and northern Europeans won't buy it if the milk hasn't been heated."

The hot milk has rennet and a bit of salt added, then it is left for about twenty minutes to form a curd, which looks like a big, white Jell-O. We watched as it was cut into tiny pieces, then drained in a copper sieve called a *stregatura,* where the curds compress into a near-solid mass. The mass was transferred to a table, cut in four large chunks, and left to drain again.

The young *caciaro,* or head cheesemaker supervising the process, was extremely absorbed in his task.

At his signal, two other young workers slipped the curd into a vat of boiling water and stirred until it was transformed into an elastic, homogeneous mass, the beginnings of mozzarella cheese. This particular batch was destined to become tiny balls, formerly shaped by hand but now done by machine. Into the machine went the warm mass, and out plopped little balls into a waiting pan of water, where they would cool before being put into a brine of whey, water, and salt, and shipped to stores in the area. The cheeses are considered prime for twenty-four hours, though they keep well in the brine for several days. Generoso fished out two balls of cheese and gave one to me, while he bit into the other. It hadn't yet absorbed any saltiness from the brine, and it had the fresh, rich flavor of the milk—which is higher in fat than cow's milk—balanced by a slight acidity.

In a far corner of the dairy, a gray-haired man was bent over a table, working with another ball of fresh cheese made that morning. He pinched off pieces and rolled them into fat ropes, which he deftly

braided. When all were finished, he handed me a particularly fat braid, offering it with an artisan's shy pride.

A small percentage of each batch of mozzarella is smoked, and we walked outside to a corner of the parking lot where a metal drum sat up-ended over a straw fire. This was the dairy's far-from-sophisticated smoker. Two sticks were balanced across the opening, and several cheeses hung from them, enveloped in smoke. They stay there just long enough to develop a golden veneer and slight smoky flavor, about ten minutes. "Smoking cheeses was originally a way to preserve them," Generoso said. "Most people have refrigeration now, but they still like the smoky taste on the cheese."

We walked back into the dairy and were met at the door by the *caciaro,* who held out samples of still-warm ricotta—a cheese made from the solids left in the whey. Before I knew it, I'd finished the entire creamy, custardy bowlful. It was ethereal, so delicious that it changed my opinion of ricotta forever.

Generoso is visibly proud of his new and thriving farm, the dairy that he is now part of, the cheese that comes from it. "I'm still a businessman," he said. "But now I'm at the farm helping it come to life. And I finally have the water buffalo I always wanted."

For information about Antica Masseria La Morella, call (011.39) 828.51008 or 336.853516. Or write Cucino Generoso, Via Cilentana, 18 Battipaglia (SA).

INSALATE

SALADS

Salads on the Italian farm are not legion, and their rarity makes them that much more appealing. From curls of zucchini, carrot, and Parmesan cheese dressed in freshly pressed extra-virgin olive oil, to abundant tomatoes obscured by minced basil and parsley, each is a sonnet to the season, the region, the particular farm that inspired it.

Having said that, there is always something unexpected about an Italian farm salad. Even what appears to be a simple toss of greens, turns out to be a spicy, gutsy blend whose wild flavors are brought together with a touch of extra-virgin olive oil and a sprinkle of salt. Panzanella, typical to the Tuscan farm table, combines bread, sun-ripened tomatoes, and the surprisingly crisp purple onions of the region. In Sicily in February, when the citrus fruit hangs ripe and heavy on the trees, the most common salad is a savory one of oranges liberally seasoned with parsley. In Emilia-Romagna, arugula provides a smoky bed for ripe pears and tart raspberries

mezzaluna

dressed in balsamic vinegar.

One of my favorite salads is another gem from Tuscany, made with lightly aged sheep's milk cheese, fresh fava beans, a drizzle of golden olive oil, and a sprinkling of herbs. It couldn't be simpler, yet it offers a satisfying contrast of lush flavors and textures—just like all the salads in this chapter.

Radicchio with Anchovy Sauce

**RADICCHIO IN
SALSA
D'ACCIUGHE**

**4 TO 6
SERVINGS**

Treviso, in the Veneto region, is world renowned for its radicchio, which is long and narrow with milky white ribs and deep burgundy-red, white-veined leaves (as opposed to the more readily available, round-headed radicchio). It has a meaty texture and wonderful bitterness and has traditionally been available only from November to mid-January, though new cultivation techniques involving greenhouses have now lengthened the season into February.

Purists, those who love their *radicchio di Treviso* in its season, believe that it should be indulged in then and never thought of again until the following year. Domenico Camerotto, chef and owner of the country trattoria Da Domenico, outside Treviso, is such a purist. He haunts his own garden and local farms for the first radicchio,

Segreti

This salad is wonderful as it is, though you may also like to try it with Parmigiano-Reggiano shaved over it.

which he serves in dozens of ways, including dressed like this. When the season is in full swing, he offers an all-radicchio menu, which brings diners as passionate as he is into the restaurant. For that meal, most of the radicchio is cooked—teamed with polenta or used as a bed for roast poultry, for instance—with other dishes such as this salad providing a raw, crunchy foil.

I love to make this when I find any variety of radicchio, for its bitter leaves are perfectly complemented by the salty-acidic dressing. Serve it as part of an antipasto offering or to begin a meal all on its own, accompanied by a lightly chilled dry sparkling wine, such as Prosecco di Conigliano-Valdobbiadene.

4 anchovy fillets (see Note)
2 teaspoons best-quality red wine vinegar
⅓ cup extra-virgin olive oil

2 medium heads radicchio (each about 8 ounces), trimmed
Fine sea salt and freshly ground black pepper (optional)

1. Crush the anchovies with a mortar and pestle. Add the vinegar, continuing to work the anchovies, then slowly whisk in the oil until the mixture is combined. Transfer the mixture to a large salad bowl.

2. Cut the radicchio crosswise into ¼-inch-thick slices, then cut the slices crosswise into ¼-inch pieces. Add to the dressing in the bowl and toss well until it is thoroughly coated. Taste for seasoning, adding salt and pepper if desired, and serve immediately.

NOTE: If the anchovies are packed in oil, pat any excess oil from them. If they are packed in salt, rinse them quickly under running water and pat dry.

Cherry Tomato and Arugula Salad

**INSALATA DI
POMODORINI E
RUCOLA**

4 SERVINGS

Abruzzo is on Italy's east-central coast, directly across the country from Rome; on a clear day, if you stand in a high spot in the mountains that cover most of the region, you can see the *autostrada* that was originally laid down by ancient Romans and has connected Rome to the port city of Pescara for centuries.

Abruzzo landscape is rugged, with mountains that run right to the sea. The cuisine is hearty, liberally spiced with hot peppers and heavy on mountain lamb, which is almost always served with this simple salad. With the diminutive tomato halves nestled in their bed of tender arugula, the salad is both lovely to look at and uncommonly refreshing. A bit of salt and the barest drizzle of extra-virgin olive oil and lemon juice are the only seasonings needed.

Try this as part of an antipasto selection or alongside Herb Marinated Leg of Lamb (page 206).

24 ripe cherry tomatoes, stemmed
Fine sea salt
8 cups (loosely packed)
    arugula leaves, rinsed and
    patted dry

2 tablespoons extra-virgin
    olive oil
1 teaspoon fresh lemon
    juice

1. Cut the cherry tomatoes in half, sprinkle their cut sides lightly with salt, and let them sit for 10 minutes.

2. Arrange the arugula on 4 serving plates, dividing evenly. Working over the sink, shake off any excess liquid from the tomatoes, then arrange 12 halves, cut side up, on each serving of arugula. Drizzle first with the oil, then with the lemon juice. Season the arugula with salt and serve immediately.

Antonella DiRosolini's Lush Tomato Salad

Antonella DiRosolini and her husband, Giuseppe Cicero, a consultant for the state who works to develop organic agriculture in Sicily, have a small farm not far from Modica, in southeastern Sicily. Among the glories it produces are bushels of juicy tomatoes, which Antonella puts on pizza dough, eats whole like apples, and uses in this delicious salad.

I make this often too, when fresh tomatoes are abundant. At the DiRosolini-Cicero household, it was served as a first course, along with several different versions of the tight-grained Sicilian *pane di casa,* the typical bakery bread with an alluring cinnamon taste (see essay, page 319). Giuseppe said that, for him, no meal is complete without bread. I have always held dear the same philosophy, and urge you to adopt it too!

I have added the option of freshly ground black pepper, though Antonella wouldn't use it on her salad. Pepper is generally considered superfluous when basil is present, but for those who are pepper fanatics, go ahead and add a sprinkling!

Try a lightly chilled somewhat full-bodied white wine, such as Etna Bianco, as accompaniment.

*1½ pounds not-too-ripe cherry
tomatoes, stemmed and cut in half*

*3 pounds large not-too-ripe tomatoes,
cored and coarsely chopped*

*1 small onion (4 ounces), sliced
paper thin*

*½ cup top-quality capers,
preferably preserved in salt (see
box, page 66)*

*½ cup (gently packed) fresh
flat-leaf parsley leaves*

*3 cups (gently packed) fresh
basil leaves*

½ cup extra-virgin olive oil

Fine sea salt

*Freshly ground black pepper
(optional)*

1. Combine the tomatoes, onion, and capers in a large salad bowl.

2. Mince the parsley and tear the basil leaves into small pieces (see Note).

3. Sprinkle the herbs over the tomatoes and capers, then drizzle with the oil and toss gently so that all the ingredients are thoroughly combined. Season with salt and, if desired, pepper. Toss again and serve.

NOTE: If using basil with tiny leaves, this step won't be necessary.

Tomato, Red Onion, and Basil Salad

**INSALATA DI
POMODORI,
CIPOLLE ROSSE,
E BASILICO**

**4 TO 6
SERVINGS**

Angelo Lancellotti described this simple, and simply luscious, salad to me while we stood in his incredibly verdant vegetable garden near the family restaurant in Soliera, outside Modena. It is a very simple dish, but you will enjoy the salad for its looks as well as its sublime flavor. Angelo uses purple basil as garnish, though I find green basil is delicious too.

Serve this salad with an edgy red, such as Sangiovese di Romagna, alongside.

*1 pound not-quite-ripe
tomatoes, cored and cut
into ¼-inch-thick slices
15 purple or green basil leaves*

*1 small red onion, sliced paper thin
2 tablespoons extra-virgin olive oil
Fine sea salt*

Arrange the tomato slices on a large platter, interspersing them irregularly with the whole basil leaves. Strew the onion on top and drizzle the oil over all. Season with salt and serve.

The Real Panzanella

**LA VERA
PANZANELLA**

**8 TO 10
SERVINGS**

Panzanella, or bread salad, may be one of the better-known dishes of the Tuscan farm. It is one born of the farm wife's frugality, her distaste for getting rid of anything that could nourish, including days-old bread.

I received two good *panzanella* lessons while in Tuscany. One was from Ghiselda Bini, a farmer outside Radda, in Chianti, and the other was from Carlo Cioni, owner of the restaurant Da Delfina in Artimino, near Pistoia (see box, page 54). With these two experts as guides, I fashioned this simple recipe and found it as delightful as those tasted in Tuscany. Heady with basil and rich with tomatoes and oil, it is a true farm dish, born of little and elevated to something wonderful.

Try it with a lightly chilled crisp white wine, such as Bianco Vergine della Valdichiana.

Did You Know?

For most people, images of Tuscan cuisine conjure up platters laden with fat slices of flavorful tomatoes garnished with a drizzle of incomparable Tuscan olive oil and sprigs of fresh basil, set on a table alfresco against a backdrop of verdant hills planted in grapevines. This may be true now, but the tomato, common to the south of Italy, was practically unknown in Tuscany until the end of the Second World War. Before then, the Tuscan diet relied on traditional crops like chickpeas, lentils, chard, olives, *cavolo nero* (black cabbage) arugula, leeks, lemons, and chicory. Improved transportation and a roving population—with many people from the south moving north in search of work—changed all that, and the tomato was introduced to Tuscany.

*8 slices (each ½ inch thick) 1- to 2-
    day-old Tuscan Bread (page 311)*
*¾ cup (gently packed) fresh basil
    leaves*
*1 medium red onion, cut lengthwise
    in half, then into crosswise paper-
    thin slices*
*2 pounds ripe tomatoes, cored and
    coarsely chopped*
¼ cup best-quality red wine vinegar
1 tablespoon extra-virgin olive oil
*Fine sea salt and freshly ground
    black pepper*

1. Place the bread in a large bowl, cover with cold water, and soak until the bread has absorbed the water and is heavy with it, 8 to 10 minutes. To drain the bread, pick it up by small handfuls and place it in the palm of one hand. Cover it with the palm of your other hand so your hands are cupped, and squeeze very gently, slowly, and firmly, so that you squeeze out the water without mashing the bread, allowing the bread to retain its integrity. The bread should be just slightly moist, not wet. Some of

Panzanella Tips from the Experts

Ghiselda Bini, who farms in Chianti, is recognized by her neighbors as one of the area's best cooks. Signora Bini makes *panzanella* for her family year-round, and she told me, "Traditionally the dish had just four ingredients—bread, basil, tomatoes, onion."

According to her husband, Bruno, it is one of his favorite breakfasts, after a good morning's work in the fields. He gets up and has coffee and yogurt (he called this the "modern farmer's early-morning breakfast," as opposed to the sausages and wine his father ate), then goes to work and comes back around nine o'clock for *panzanella*.

Signora Bini insisted that the best ingredients must be used, and the bread mustn't be too wet. "That," she said, "is a matter of opinion, but to me, too much water in a *panzanella* isn't any good."

Restaurateur Carlo Cioni, who was taught the secrets of good farm cooking by his mother, concurs. He cautioned me that *panzanella* was deceptive. "It seems simple, but great care must be taken to make it slowly, to not rush," he said. Here, too, well-squeezed bread is the secret, and his mother is often the one who painstakingly squeezes it for the restaurant's version. Cioni showed me how she does it, taking a small handful of day-old bread that had been soaking in water and, neither twisting nor mashing it, removing the water by gently pressing it between his slightly cupped palms. "It mustn't be so wet it can't absorb the flavors of the other ingredients," he said. "And while it loses the shape of a slice of bread, it must keep a grainy, rather than mashed, texture. The secret is time—take your time."

the bread may disintegrate into very wet crumbs in the water at the bottom of the bowl; discard these as well as the water.

2. Place the bread in a large bowl. Coarsely chop the basil and add it with the onion and tomatoes to the bread. Toss gently until all the ingredients are thoroughly combined. Drizzle with the vinegar and oil and

toss gently again. Season with salt and pepper and toss a final time. As you toss, the bread will break up into small pieces and, depending on its state of freshness, may even come to resemble couscous.

3. Refrigerate the *panzanella* for at least 1 hour or up to 4 before serving. Do not keep it longer than a day.

The Vinegar Maker's Salad

INSALATA DELLA ACETAIA

4 TO 6 SERVINGS

This salad comes from the Leonardi family (see essay, page 57), who make rich and luscious *aceto balsamico tradizionale*, the true balsamic vinegar, right outside the lovely little city of Modena. I spent an unforgettable day with them, touring their *acetaia*, or vinegar works, then enjoying a meal in their large, cool dining room. It didn't matter that outside the sun was blazing. Inside we were awash in wonderful food, vivid wine, and dishes like this zesty salad, made with home-produced ingredients.

This salad might be considered the Italian farm version of a chef salad, for it has all the necessary ingredients—but here the ham is flavorful pancetta or prosciutto, the cheese is nutty Parmigiano-Reggiano, and the dressing is made with the delicately sweet and aromatic balsamic vinegar. Make and serve this by itself, as a single antipasto, or along with other antipasti. You'll be surprisingly satisfied.

Serve a warming, refined, not too heavy red, such as Sangiovese di Romagna, alongside.

1 large head tender lettuce, such as oak leaf or Bibb, or a mixture, rinsed, patted dry, and very thinly sliced

3 tablespoons good-quality balsamic vinegar

2 tablespoons plus 1 teaspoon extra-virgin olive oil

2 large ripe tomatoes, cored and cut into 8 wedges

4 large eggs, hard-cooked and cut into thin rounds

4 ounces Parmigiano-Reggiano, in one piece

6 ounces very thinly sliced pancetta or prosciutto, cut into very thin strips

1. Place the lettuce in a large bowl. Drizzle 2 tablespoons each vinegar and oil over the lettuce and toss thoroughly. Transfer the lettuce from the bowl to the center of a serving platter, leaving any juices in the bowl. Add the tomatoes to the bowl with 1 teaspoon of the remaining vinegar, toss, and arrange the tomatoes on the outside of the platter, reserving any juices in the bowl.

2. Arrange the egg slices, overlapping, around the outside of the lettuce, alongside the tomatoes. Using a vegetable peeler, shave very thin slices of the cheese over the center of the lettuce so they fall in a delicate mound.

3. Add the pancetta or prosciutto to the bowl and toss with 1 teaspoon of the remaining vinegar. Arrange it around the cheese curls atop the salad, and drizzle any juices in the bowl over the tomatoes. Finally, drizzle the entire salad, focusing on the cheese, with the remaining 1 teaspoon each vinegar and oil. Serve immediately.

THE REAL BALSAMIC VINEGAR

Light streams through small windows into the upstairs room of a good-size barn just outside Modena, in Emilia-Romagna. It casts pale light on the unpolished wood floors and puts farmer Leonardi in shadow as he inserts a long glass tube into a small barrel. He puts his finger over the top of the tube, trapping dark brown vinegar from the barrel inside, and pulls it out. He lifts his finger and releases the vinegar into a glass, swirling it around as he inhales its aroma.

He carefully hands me the glass, containing its sample of thirty-year-old balsamic vinegar, as proud as if it were his first-born child. I notice that the vinegar, which smells sweet, is thick like syrup. He suggests I put a drop on the flat space between the base of my thumb and forefinger, a good place from which to taste. I do, and the drop sits right up without even trying to drizzle away.

I taste it and am immediately carried through years of patient waiting, tasting, blending. This is true balsamic vinegar, *aceto balsamico tradizionale,* made with juice from the Trebbiano Lambrusco grape. The grape variety is important, of course, but it is Signore Leonardi who holds the key to the quality of this vinegar, in lessons he learned from his father and grandfather about temperature, acidity, sugar, and simple patience.

The history of *aceto balsamico* began with the Romans, who cooked *mosto* (the juice of crushed grapes) to produce a sweet-tart liquid they called *sapa.* A highly valued substance, it was used both as condiment and as cure. Today's *sapa* is *aceto balsamico,* which is most valued at table.

Like many farm families in and around Modena, the Leonardis have always made vinegar. "Ninety percent of farmers here made vinegar," Leonardi said, "but only about five percent made balsamic."

That's easy enough to understand. Making traditional *aceto balsamico* resembles winemaking without the aid of technology. It requires a finely honed palate, plenty of space, and lots of time. A decision made one year here in Leonardi's *acetaia,* or vinegar works, will have repercussions on the quality of his vinegar for years to come.

The Leonardi family has a diversified farm and many agricultural occupations. They raise cattle and the grain to feed them, cultivate fruit, and have a commercial jam business. But they are most dedicated to the vinegar, which has developed from production for the family's use, begun at least two generations ago, to a commercial one that now produces between 25,000 and 30,000 three-ounce bottles a year.

The Leonardis transformed the beautiful old barn into an *acetaia* with a tasting room, a production room with state-of-the-art double-walled stainless-steel tanks, and several floors dedicated to nothing but providing space for hundreds of small barrels while the vinegar "works."

When I visited on a hot early summer day, the *acetaia* was still. Grapes destined for *aceto balsamico* are harvested in fall, as late as possible so they can develop a maximum amount of sugar. The grapes are crushed and the *mosto* runs into large barrels, where it rests briefly. This is the first critical stage of the process, for the *mosto* must not ferment.

The *mosto* is transferred into one of the steel vats, where it will cook under careful supervision for thirty hours to concentrate the sugar between 30 and 70 percent, depending on the grapes that year. Between the walls of the vat, which is custom-built for this purpose, runs oil that protects the *mosto* from direct contact with the heat. The temperature of the *mosto* must never exceed 122° F so that the natural yeasts survive, for it is those yeasts that will eventually transform the *mosto* into vinegar.

Once cooked, the *mosto* cools to a deep red, thick liquid. It is transferred to other vats to rest for a month or two so that impurities and solids can fall to the bottom, and then it is ready to go into barrels. Before accepting the cooked *mosto*, a new barrel is first filled with wine and left to "age" for two months. The wine is then discarded. The *acetaia* isn't heated, and the extremes of temperature common in this area are beneficial to the

bacteria, encouraging it to work. Without them the vinegar wouldn't be as silken, as rich in flavor.

Leonardi explained that the vinegar requires different woods at different stages for flavor. Though most balsamic vinegar producers use the same woods, the amount of time they leave the vinegar in contact with them is a personal choice, and according to Leonardi, it is part of what makes the difference between a good and an excellent vinegar.

The Leonardis start the *mosto* in oak for aroma, then move it into cherry for sweetness. From cherry it goes into *robinia* (locust), which is considered neutral, then into chestnut for color. Over time the vinegar undergoes a complex and vibrant microbiological action as it develops acidity and sweetness, simultaneously mellowing, thickening, becoming more rich.

Leonardi keeps some vinegar in barrels made of juniper wood, which adds a distinctive pungency. He uses the juniper vinegar as a seasoning, blending it in by the tiniest amount, to balance the flavor of the *aceto balsamico*. Other producers use barrels made with a stave or two of juniper to achieve the desired flavor.

The basic vinegar-making process is simple. It consists of decanting one-third of the contents of one barrel to another containing an older vinegar, year after year, until the desired flavor is achieved.

Decanting and bottling are done in winter, when the bacteria are dormant.

By five years the vinegar is dark and lively, its consistency that of normal vinegar. At ten years it has thickened significantly and developed a heavier sweetness. At twelve years the vinegar is slightly more intense. At twenty years it begins to take on the texture of a syrup. By thirty years it is as thick as maple syrup, and at a hundred years, the oldest I have tasted, its texture and color resemble molasses, without the ropiness. At that venerable age, it must be judiciously licked from a tiny spoon or from a drop placed on your hand.

Production of true *aceto balsamico* has always been limited because of the time, care, and expense that go into it, and its use was strictly regional until recently. As word got out about the qualities of this fine substance, it was inevitable that industry would try to copy it, and now imitations are made throughout the world.

Encouraged by regional producers hoping to protect their vinegar, the Italian government created a DOC, or area of origin, in 1987 that limited the production of traditional, or *tradizionale,* vinegar to the Modena and Reggio areas. In 1993, using the term *balsamico* and the names of the regions was also limited.

Two consortiums of vinegar producers— one for the Modena area and one for the Reggio area—now supervise both labeling and bottling of all *aceto balsamico tradizionale.* They operate somewhat differently, and there is some confusion in the marketplace about their relative merits. I am most familiar with the Modena consortium (which publishes its rules and readily responds to questions).

To merit the label *aceto balsamico tradizionale di Modena, acetaie* are subject to inspections, and the vinegar must undergo a rigorous tasting by a panel of experts, who grade it on a 400-point scale. If it scores more than 250, it merits the label *tradizionale,* which almost guarantees its sale. To win a prize, it must score much higher. If it doesn't achieve 250, it is generally returned to the barrel for further aging.

To further distinguish true *aceto balsamico tradizionale di Modena,* it is all bottled in a central location in the same chunky 3-ounce bottle designed by Italian artist Giorgetto Giuggiaro. Each producer puts his own label on the bottle and determines his own price.

For now Leonardi remains independent from the consortia. He has chosen his own bottle, which resembles a small flask of perfume, and sells vinegars that range in age from five to more than thirty years. He exports some of his vinegar, particularly that which has aged for five years (and is not allowed by law to be called *aceto balsamico tradizionale,* because it is deemed too young, so it is called simply *aceto balsamico*). He wants traditionally made balsamic vinegar to be available to the widest possible number of people, and he reasons the best way to do that is make sure its quality is high and its age relatively young so it is affordable, though old enough so it has a rich mantle of flavor.

Angelo's Pear, Raspberry, and Mixed Green Salad with Balsamic Vinegar

INSALATA DI
PERE, LAMPONI,
ERBE
AROMATICHE,
E ACETO
BALSAMICO DI
ANGELO

4 TO 6
SERVINGS

Segreti

When you can't get fresh raspberries and have to use frozen ones, don't thaw them before crushing them in the balsamic vinegar and oil.

This is a first-course specialty at the Lancellotti Hotel in Soliera, not far from the town of Modena, in Emilia-Romagna. Chef-owner Angelo Lancellotti (see essay, page 86) created it one fine day in early autumn, when the seasons for pears and raspberries overlap. The salad was such a hit with diners that Angelo makes it year-round—using frozen raspberries when he can't get them fresh. Should he run out of local pears, he resorts to imports. Though out-of-season ingredients aren't his style, for this salad he makes an exception. "Diners want it and I get wonderful ingredients," he says. "If I don't find the ingredients I like, I don't serve the salad, but that is rare."

This salad is like a celebration on a plate, bright in color and tartly delicious in flavor. It must be served immediately after being assembled, for the pears begin to oxidize once they are cut.

The signature lightly fizzy red wine of Emilia-Romagna, Lambrusco, goes particularly well with this salad. If you don't like fizz in your wine, try a light, fruity red, such as Monterosso Val d'Arda or a fruity Chianti.

4 teaspoons balsamic vinegar

⅓ cup extra-virgin olive oil

2 cups fresh or frozen raspberries

4 smallish not-overripe pears (each about 5 ounces)

8 cups (about 6 ounces) arugula or blend of greens, such as butter or oak leaf lettuce with some arugula, rinsed and patted dry (see Note)

Fine sea salt and freshly ground black pepper

Nasturtium and borage flowers, for garnish (optional)

1. Whisk together the vinegar and oil in a large salad bowl, then add the raspberries and crush into the mixture with the back of a wooden spoon. Do not strain the raspberries.

2. Peel and core the pears, cut crosswise into very thin slices, and add to the dressing, then scissor-cut the greens into the bowl. Toss gently until the ingredients are thoroughly coated. Season lightly with salt and pepper, then transfer to serving plates and garnish, if possible, as Angelo does, with nasturtium and borage flowers. Serve immediately.

NOTE: As for greens, Angelo uses tender, garden-fresh *misticanza,* a wonderful blend of different lettuces that is heavy on arugula. I often use arugula exclusively, my favorite way to eat this salad. Some arugula, with its smoky flavor, is essential. Other lettuces must be tender rather than crisp, so avoid romaine, iceberg, and similar lettuces.

Aceto Balsamico Tradizionale

The recipes in this book that call for balsamic vinegar were originally made with *aceto balsamico tradizionale,* the rich, thick, aged vinegar of Emilia-Romagna. Unfortunately, true balsamic vinegar is often so expensive by the time it is exported to the United States that even the small amounts called for make a dish prohibitively expensive. Thus, in my recipes I call for best-quality balsamic vinegar, and leave each cook to his or her own devices and pocketbook.

A little hint: To improve commercially made balsamic vinegar and approximate that made in Emilia-Romagna, empty a small (250ml) bottle of balsamic vinegar into a nonreactive saucepan, whisk in 2 tablespoons unpacked dark brown sugar, and bring to a boil over medium heat. Cook until the mixture is about the consistency of maple syrup. Remove it from the heat and let cool. Use this in recipes that call for balsamic vinegar. The vinegar will keep for several months in a darkened bottle stored in a cool spot.

Sicilian Orange Salad

**INSALATA
DI ARANCE DI
SICILIA**

4 SERVINGS

"Life is for
people who
merit it. If you
don't like it, you
don't get it."

—SICILIAN PEASANT
SAYING

This recipe is from Giuseppina Morello, whose son, Gaetano, has recently begun an olive plantation on eight acres of family land near Grammichele, in south-central Sicily (see essay, page 106). Within a couple of years Gaetano will have plenty of organic oil to supply the entire family and, he hopes, an international clientele. For now, the family uses a deep, fruity oil from a relative's production to dress dishes like this salad, which is a hallmark of Sicilian cuisine. Every family has their own combination and way of presenting *insalata di arance,* and this variation—simple, fresh, and lively—is the one I prefer.

Try to make the salad with blood oranges, which have an alluring acidity. Otherwise use the best, juiciest oranges you can find. Do not be concerned that too much parsley is called for. It is an essential part of the salad.

Serve with a lightly chilled somewhat full-bodied white, such as Etna Bianco.

*2 pounds blood oranges or
other juicy, lightly tart
oranges
2 tablespoons extra-virgin olive oil
Fine sea salt*

*¼ teaspoon hot paprika or
crushed red pepper flakes, or
to taste
1 generous cup (gently packed) fresh
flat-leaf parsley leaves*

1. Remove the skin and the white pith from the oranges, then cut each crosswise into ⅛-inch-thick rounds. Arrange the rounds, slightly overlapping, on a large serving platter.

2. Drizzle the oranges with the oil, then season with salt and the paprika or red pepper flakes.

3. Mince the parsley and sprinkle it over the oranges. Serve immediately.

Chickpea Salad

INSALATA DI
CECI

6 SERVINGS

had chickpea salad in Liguria and chickpea salad in Tuscany, and though they were similar, there was enough of a difference to consider each a regional dish. I chose to combine the recipes, incorporating the Ligurian recipe, with its garlic and onions, with the Tuscan, which relies heavily on the fine olive oil produced there. The combination is sublime, so much so that a friend of mine who tried it said, "I could have eaten it all for breakfast, while it was still warm. Next time I'll make a double batch!"

Serve the chickpeas as a first course or as part of a selection of antipasti. Or, in summer, turn it into a meal with some good Tuscan bread and fresh fruit for dessert.

Try a lightly chilled dry yet flavorful white wine, such as Vermentino, alongside.

1 pound dried chickpeas
⅓ cup extra-virgin olive oil
1 small onion, sliced paper thin
2 cloves garlic, green germ removed,
  minced

Fine sea salt and freshly ground
  black pepper
½ cup fresh basil leaves,
  for garnish

1. Place the chickpeas in a large heavy saucepan and cover with 2 inches of water. Bring to a boil over high heat, then remove from the heat and let sit for 1 hour. Drain, return the chickpeas to the pan, and cover with at least 3 inches of cold water. Bring to a boil over high heat, then reduce the heat to medium and cook, partially covered, until the chickpeas are tender but not mushy, 50 minutes to 1½ hours (see Note).

2. While the chickpeas are cooking, combine the oil, onion, garlic, and salt and pepper to taste in a large bowl.

3. When the chickpeas are tender, drain and add them to the oil mixture in the bowl. Toss until they are well coated with the oil, then taste for seasoning, adding salt and pepper as necessary. Gar- nish with basil leaves and serve hot or at room temperature.

NOTE: The length of time it takes to cook the chickpeas will depend on their age; start check- ing after 50 minutes.

Fava Bean Salad with Cheese and Fresh Herbs

INSALATA DI FAVE, PECORINO, E ERBE AROMATICHE FRESCHE

4 SERVINGS

Fava beans have a prized spot in every kitchen garden and farm in Tuscany. Come May and June, prime *fava* season, one cannot have a farm (or restaurant for that matter) meal in Tuscany with- out them in it somewhere. This ubiquitous salad, which I enjoyed dozens of times while in Tuscany, is one of the best ways of serving them. Seasonings, I found, varied; sometimes it was simply salt, sometimes fresh oregano, once a touch of fresh thyme. Salt is imper- ative, and I use thyme or oregano and sometimes combine both to give the salad a gentle herbal kick.

Try this pretty salad with a light and crisp white, such as Val d'Arbia, or with a light, fruity Chianti.

*2½ pounds fresh fava beans in their
    pods, shelled but not skinned*
*4 ounces young sheep's milk cheese,
    cut into small cubes*
*3 tablespoons extra-virgin olive oil,
    preferably from Tuscany*

Fine sea salt
*1 tablespoon fresh thyme leaves
    (optional)*
*1 tablespoon fresh oregano leaves
    (optional)*

1. Bring a large pot of water to a boil over high heat. Add the fava beans, return the water to a boil, and drain the fava beans. To remove their skins, make a slit in one side and squeeze gently so the bean pops out. Continue until all of the fava beans are skinned.

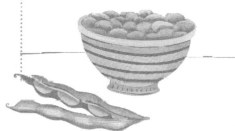

2. In a medium-size shallow serving bowl, combine the fava beans, cheese, and oil and toss gently until the favas and cheese are well coated with oil. The amount of oil is intentionally generous.

3. Sprinkle the salad with salt to taste, then sprinkle the herbs over the top if desired. Carefully toss all the ingredients so they are well mixed and serve.

Caper and Potato Salad

INSALATA DI
PATATE E
CAPPERI

4 TO 6
SERVINGS

This salad from the island of Salina, off the west coast of Sicily, is the creation of Maria Francesca Bongiorno, whose husband cultivates several acres of the famed Salina capers.

Capers on Salina are cured to a delicate tenderness in sea salt for several months, and before using them Maria Francesca rinses and soaks them. They give this salad a delicious floral dimension, which nicely complements the tender potatoes and crisp onions. The inspired addition of mint, very common in Sicilian cuisine, is another key to its light, fresh flavor.

Serve a lightly chilled pleasantly fruity white, such as Regaleali Bianco, alongside.

Segreti

The best, most flavorful, and toothsome capers are medium size, about the size of a plump raisin, rather than the tiny, barely formed buds we're used to thinking of as best.

⅓ cup extra-virgin olive oil
1 small onion, sliced paper thin
2 pounds waxy potatoes, peeled and
    quartered
3 tablespoons capers, preferably
    preserved in salt (see box below)

⅓ cup fresh mint leaves
Fine sea salt
Freshly ground black pepper
    (optional)
⅛ teaspoon hot paprika, or
    to taste

1. Combine the olive oil and onion in a large serving bowl and toss to thoroughly coat the onion with the oil. Set aside.

2. Bring a large saucepan of salted water to a boil over high heat and add the potatoes. Cook, covered, until they are tender throughout but not mushy, 15 to 20 minutes. Drain and immediately add the potatoes to the oil and onion. Toss gently but thoroughly and let cool to room temperature.

3. When the potatoes are cool, stir in the capers.

4. Just before serving, mince the mint leaves, add them to the potato salad, and toss gently until all the ingredients are thoroughly combined. Season with salt, pepper, and paprika to taste. Serve.

Salt-Cured Capers

Salt-cured capers are increasingly easy to find in the United States, thanks in part to Manicaretti Italian Foods (5332 College Avenue, Suite 200 Oakland, California, 94618; phone, 800-799-9830; www.manicaretti.it), which exports them from Italy. If you simply can't find them, use capers in vinegar (see page 316). Rinse salted capers of excess salt under cold running water, then soak them in hot water for about an hour. Drain and pat dry before using. Soak them for more or less time, depending on how salty you like them.

THE CAPERS OF SALINA

In late September and early October the island of Salina, part of the Eolian archipelago off the west coast of Sicily, smells like capers. The aroma isn't overpowering, but it is persistent, round, intensely green, and alluring.

Salina produces about 100,000 pounds annually of *Capparis spinosa,* considered to be among Italy's best capers. Their quality is due to a combination of dry atmospheric conditions, volcanic soil, careful cultivation techniques honed over many thousands of years, and variety. The tightly closed green buds are harvested painstakingly, by hand, from the end of April through July. Women do the work, for their touch is gentle as they pick the buds off the lithe branches from among the plant's shiny round leaves and deposit them by the handful in their aprons. They begin before dawn to avoid the heat and to get the capers when they are at their most fragrant, working until noon.

On Salina nearly every household has enough plants to produce the family supply, and at least one company, the Società Onofrio in Pollara, produces enough to export. Feverish production accounts for the island's wonderful aroma and the appearance of capers in everything from salads to pasta sauces.

It was a cool, sunny fall morning in Santa Marina, one of Salina's larger communities. A mutual friend had introduced me to Santino Rossello, Santa Marina's full-time policeman and part-time caper promoter. Santino had offered to take me to the other side of the island to visit the caper farm of Giuseppe De Lorenzo, president of Società Onofrio.

The journey went quickly. We sped along, all car windows open despite the unseasonably cool air. And as the car climbed up the winding road that looks out across the sea to the island of Lipari, I had only to raise my head and look up the hill above me to see the Medusa-like caper plants that covered it. Santino navigated the death-defying road with ease, propelling the car around bends with a speed that threatened to send us hurtling into the sea below. I was relieved when we finally turned down a little road that led us to the coastal community of Pollara.

The car shuddered to a stop outside a cheerful house with a terrace nearly obscured by bunches of cherry tomatoes hanging in the sun.

"Those tomatoes will keep until March," Santino said as he showed me into the dark kitchen. There we met

Giuseppe De Lorenzo, the president of the company, and his wife, Maria Francesca Bongiorno. We sat down to a glass of local, house-produced Malvasia, a very sweet white wine, and talked capers.

According to De Lorenzo, there was once a vital commercial caper production on Salina that declined because of the increased interest in producing Malvasia on the same land. Santino shook his head. "The Malvasia isn't good, because the vines don't like the salt air here," he said. "The caper plants tolerate it—one might even say they thrive on it."

Since 1985, De Lorenzo has produced capers commercially, helping revive the reputation of Salina's capers, familiarly called *nocellara* or *tondino*, or small round. He has six acres under cultivation and is developing others. He also buys capers from other growers.

We stepped outside to look at the field nearest the house. The capers were long gone, the flowers too, but the seed pods—called *cucunci*—had just been harvested and were spread out to dry in the shade. Once salted, they make a tasty snack with a flavor similar to capers.

We bent down to examine one of the plants, whose branches departed from a central stem and fell to the ground in a wide, graceful arch. Santino showed me where the buds grew on little stems, and explained that they are all different sizes and they mature at different times, so that on one stem at one time there are both the stunning

pinkish white, passionlike flowers referred to on the island as the "orchid of Eolie," tiny buds, and buds as big as a fat chickpea. Each plant can produce up to ten pounds of capers if the soil is worked regularly and the buds are harvested often.

The plants require relatively little care, according to Santino. In January the land around them is cultivated, and the branches that produced fruit the previous year are removed and cuttings are taken if needed. In March the plants are fertilized, and in April they begin to produce new branches.

"The women pick every bud on the plant, then return in eight to ten days to renew the harvest," Santino said. As he explained it, that is the ideal time interval, giving the buds the chance to develop to their ideal maturity.

Past the end of July, the buds are inferior and are left to blossom. Then, in the fall, the blossoms develop into the seedpods that, if left on the plant, will eventually turn red and burst, sending seeds across the field (unless they are harvested to turn into *cucunci*). Because the plants don't grow well from seed, there is little interest in letting the seedpods grow.

Once the capers are harvested, they rest in the shade for the afternoon. In the cool of the evening, they undergo a quick selection according to size, then are layered with coarse gray sea salt in big barrels for ten days, giving up liquid as they cure. "We turn them every single day," Santino said, a job he fits in around his duties as policeman. "If we didn't, they would heat up and turn yellow and soft."

After ten days the capers are drained and transferred to large barrels, where they are left to cure until the fall.

The salted capers, which are firm and a slightly deeper green than when they were harvested, are rolled across calibrated screens to size them, then packaged according to size with 25 percent of their weight in sea salt, so that they almost appear buried in it in the bags they are sold in. Santino says they will keep well for five years but admits they would probably be fine forever.

At Società Onofrio the simple processing is done in a tidy tiled laboratory out behind the De Lorenzo house, overlooking the Tyrrhenian Sea. Though warm outside, it is naturally cool indoors, and the barrels of salted capers emit the familiar, intense caper aroma. Santino darted fingers into each barrel, pulling out buds so we could taste them. Though they were too salty to really enjoy (they must be soaked and rinsed before they are eaten), their lovely aromatic flavor nonetheless came through.

Capers are calibrated on Salina from numbers 6 to 14, and according to island caper connoisseurs, the medium-size (number 10s) are the best. The size of a raisin or chickpea, they offer a wonderful floral flavor and toothsome texture and couldn't be further removed from the tiny capers in vinegar Americans are used to buying. In fact, packing a caper in vinegar is considered heresy on Salina. "Oh no," Santino said, "they're not any good in vinegar."

Though salted capers are the bulk of the Società Onofrio business, they also get into a bit of caper fantasy. Their caper sauce, a purée of mostly capers flavored with spices and a bit of oil, is delicious on freshly toasted bread. They break their own rule by preserving some capers with hot peppers in oil and a touch of vinegar—allowable in this instance, according to Santino—and are always experimenting with other recipes.

We walked out onto the porch of the laboratory and looked out over the caper fields to the sea beyond. We could see the island ferry approaching and some small fishing boats nose into the port at Pollara. Surrounded by the heady aroma of capers, Santino talked of his dream. "I'm ready to do something else besides be the local policeman," he said. "Oh, it's a good job, but after you've done it as long as I have, you know all the stories."

"Agriculture is my love," he continued. "And capers are the future." And with that we walked back to his car and made the return trip to Santa Marina, windows wide open, containers packed full of capers stacked in the back seat.

Amalfi Seafood Salad

**INSALATA DI
FRUTTI DI MARE**

6 SERVINGS

The cuisine of Campania, the southeastern region that includes Naples, the Amalfi peninsula, and the Lattari mountains, is a rugged and romantic mélange of land and sea. It incorporates fish and shellfish, uses prodigious amounts of olive oil, and makes the most of its world-renowned lemons. While farmers in most parts of Italy traditionally didn't eat much seafood because they couldn't get it fresh, the fertile Amalfi peninsula was—and still is—different. There, in that part of Campania, farmland runs practically right down to the sea.

This salad is a breath of fresh Amalfi air. The inspiration for it comes from Grazia Caso, who, along with her son, Alfonso Caputo, cooks at their family restaurant, the Taverna del Capitano, in the small fishing port of Marina del Cantone, on the southern side of the Amalfi peninsula. Grazia walks down the steps from her kitchen and across the pebbly beach to choose her shellfish each day from a fisherman who fishes just for her; the vegetables she uses are grown on her own land. Lemons rain from the sky, it seems, for lemon trees are planted everywhere on the peninsula, and they produce their fruit year-round.

Serve a lightly chilled full-flavored white wine, such as Fiano di Avellino, and plenty of fresh and crusty bread alongside.

Cleaning Squid

To clean squid, gently pull the head with the tentacles from the body, or mantle. Most of the viscera will come out with the head. Cut off the tentacles right in front of the eyes. Gently squeeze the hard "beak" from the center of the tentacles and discard it, along with the viscera. Remove the hard, transparent "pen" from the mantle. Rinse the mantle well, removing any viscera that may have remained inside.

Segreti

There is no salt in the recipe, and none is needed, for the shellfish provides its own ample supply!

FOR THE SHELLFISH

5 pounds small clams, such as
   littleneck or Manila
1½ pounds mussels
1 generous pound squid, cleaned
   (see box, page 70)
1 pound shrimp, in the shell
½ cup fresh flat-leaf parsley
   leaves
6 tablespoons extra-virgin
   olive oil
6 tablespoons fresh lemon juice,
   plus additional if needed

1 clove garlic, green germ removed,
   minced
Freshly ground black pepper

FOR THE SALAD

¼ cup extra-virgin olive oil
1 tablespoon fresh lemon juice
13 cups mixed salad greens, such as
   radicchio, escarole, and/or curly
   endive, rinsed, patted dry, and
   cut or torn into bite-size pieces
1 lemon, cut into 6 wedges
   (optional)

1. Scrub the clams well under cold running water, using a stiff brush, then purge of sand and grit by placing them in a large bucket or bowl of salted water (⅓ cup salt mixed with 1 gallon water). Mix in 1 tablespoon cornmeal and let stand for 1 to 3 hours, in the refrigerator if longer than an hour. Drain and refrigerate until ready to cook.

2. Right before cooking, scrub the mussels well under cold running water. Pull off and discard the tufts of coarse fiber (the beards) that protrude from the shells, then place the mussels in a colander and rinse thoroughly. Drain and transfer to a large pot.

3. Add the purged clams to the mussels in the pot and set over high heat. It's not necessary to add any liquid. Cover and cook just until the shellfish open, 3 to 7 minutes, uncovering the pot frequently to check. Using tongs, remove each mussel or clam as it opens and place in a large bowl, then re-cover and continue to cook until all have

opened (discard any that remain closed).

4. When all the shellfish have been removed from the pot, strain the cooking juices through a sieve lined with a double layer of dampened cheesecloth into a medium-size saucepan. Set over medium heat and bring to a simmer.

5. Cut the squid bodies in quarters lengthwise, then crosswise into ¼-inch-wide strips. Quarter the tentacles, then cut them into pieces similar in size to the body pieces. Add the squid to the simmering liquid in the saucepan and cook, uncovered, until opaque and just tender, 2½ to 3 minutes. Check the squid as it cooks to make sure it is not getting tough; it will cook very quickly and must be tender-crisp. Using a slotted-spoon, transfer the squid to a large shallow bowl.

6. Add the shrimp to the simmering liquid in the saucepan and cook, uncovered, until pale pink and just curled, 2 to 3 minutes. Drain and set aside.

7. Remove and discard the shells from the mussels and clams; add the shellfish to the

squid. When the shrimp is cool enough to handle, shell, devein if necessary, and add to the shell-fish mixture.

8. Rinse the parsley.

9. Combine the 6 tablespoons each oil and lemon juice, the parsley, garlic, and pepper to taste in a small bowl and whisk to mix. Pour over the shellfish mixture in the bowl and toss gently until thoroughly coated with the sauce. Cover and refrigerate for 2 to 3 hours, tossing occasionally.

10. When ready to serve, prepare the salad. Combine the ¼ cup oil and 1 tablespoon lemon juice in a large bowl and whisk to blend. Add the salad greens and toss until the leaves are thoroughly coated, then divide the greens among 6 serving plates. Taste the shellfish mixture for seasoning, adding more lemon juice, salt, and pepper as necessary. Spoon the shellfish over the salad greens, dividing it up evenly, and serve immediately, with lemon wedges if desired.

NOTE: The mix of shellfish will depend on seasonal availability. Try octopus, oysters, lobster, or whatever is best and most fresh.

MINESTRE E ZUPPE

SOUPS

Traditionally, soup on the Italian farm table needed to sustain, but it needed to be good too, because it was often the only dish there was. Even if made from just an ingredient or two—this usually meant garlic, fragrant olive oil, a ham bone or chunk of cured pork fat, and wild herbs—the result was a revivifying, tasty blend, the kind of dish that energized hard-working souls.

Today those same soups born of the ever-provident farm wife's skill are still a vital part of the country's rural cuisine. Times have changed, but soups remain the same.

In Italy soups go by various names. There are *zuppa, minestra,* and *minestrone,* and though there are definitions for each soup, people use them differently. As I traveled and shared meals with farmers, I found that each person applied his or her own name to a soup, and what one person called *minestra* was *zuppa* to someone else.

In the end, names don't really matter. What matters is the inspired way that Italian farm cooks take a few simple greens and herbs and create an ethereal *zuppa di verdura,* for example, or the way they turn a cupful of wheat berries, some lentils, and a few strips of pancetta enlivened with deep green chard leaves into a delicately delicious meal.

In the Italian farm repertoire there are soups made with bread, with beans, with greens, with herbs. There are thick soups and thin, hot soups and cold. There are soups that take moments to prepare, and those that simmer for several hours. The flavors are uncomplicated, and because the Italian farm tradition calls for a base of water rather than stock, they are thrifty as well.

An Italian farm soup is an inspiration, a bit of spontaneity in a bowl. Relish these, make them often, and eat them with gusto, in the spirit of Italian farm cooking.

Country Vegetable Soup

Segreti

When "sweating," or gently cooking, vegetables until they are translucent, add them to the skillet along with the oil. This way, the ingredients heat up gently and you avoid burning them around the edges.

It is almost impossible to codify *minestra*, for it is to Italy what *potage* is to France—a basic, delicious vegetable soup that is composed of what is fresh and in season. This straightforward recipe, given to me by Ghiselda Bini, a cook and farmer in Tuscany, is simply prepared with just a handful of ingredients. She gets hers—except for the prosciutto—fresh from the ground.

You can recreate this revivifying and delicious *minestra* easily and in very little time. Serve it piping hot or at room temperature—it is delicious either way. And if you prefer your vegetables less cooked, simply reduce the cooking time. Make sure the richly flavored garnish, a tasty blend of diced vegetables and prosciutto, is served warm, for it is unappealing when cold. If serving the *minestra* the day after you make it, store it in the refrigerator and heat it at least slightly, as it loses some of its flavor when chilled.

Serve this with Chianti Classico.

FOR THE SOUP
2 medium carrots, cut lengthwise into quarters, then crosswise into small chunks
8 ounces green beans, trimmed and cut into 1-inch lengths
1 large bunch Swiss chard (about 2 pounds), leaves separated from stems, stems coarsely chopped, leaves thinly slivered
2 small zucchini, trimmed and cut lengthwise into quarters, then crosswise into small chunks

Fine sea salt
Freshly ground black pepper

FOR THE GARNISH
1 tablespoon extra-virgin olive oil
1 small onion, diced
1 clove garlic, green germ removed minced
2 small ribs celery, strings removed, diced
3 ounces ¼-inch-thick slices prosciutto, rind removed, cut into tiny dice

1. Place the carrots, beans, chard stems and zucchini in a large soup pot and add water to cover by about 2 inches. Bring to a boil, reduce the heat to low, and simmer, uncovered, until all the vegetables are tender, about 40 minutes. Add the chard leaves and the salt; cook until the leaves are wilted and tender, about 35 minutes. Season with salt and pepper and remove from the heat.

2. While the vegetables are cooking, prepare the garnish. Place the oil, onion, garlic, celery, and prosciutto in a medium-size skillet and cook over medium heat, stirring frequently, until the vegetables are tender and completely translucent, about 20 minutes. Be vigilant, adjusting the heat so the vegetables don't brown. Remove from the heat and set aside.

3. Serve the soup and the garnish hot or at room temperature. Either way, stir the garnish in the *minestra* just before serving.

zucchini

Hot Zucchini Soup with Fresh Herbs

MINESTRA DI ZUCCHINI IN BIANCO

6 TO 8 SERVINGS

In the verdant region of Campania, which includes Naples and the Amalfi peninsula, every square inch of soil that isn't consecrated to industry or tourism is cultivated. The farmland produces nearly all year, and farm cooks turn the local bounty into dishes that are simple, yet intensely exciting to the palate. An ode to zucchini and herbs, this soup is a perfect example of Campania's vibrant cuisine.

Segreti

Do not use huge, overgrown zucchini in this recipe. The tenderness and delicate flavor found in small zucchini are paramount to its success.

I always welcome creative uses for zucchini, so I was delighted to find the recipe among a collection from Grazia Caso, a wonderful chef and owner of Taverna del Capitano in Nerano, on the Amalfi peninsula. Though much of what Grazia cooks at the restaurant is a fancy version of the region's hearty cuisine, this soup is as traditional as the lemon trees that grow there with their enormous, fragrant fruit. *In bianco,* or cooked in the white style, describes mixtures without tomato; they are usually dressed simply with oil or oil and herbs. Try serving a lightly chilled white wine alongside, such as Biancolella.

½ cup olive oil
2 cloves garlic, green germ removed
*   if desired, coarsely chopped*
4 pounds fresh garden zucchini,
*   trimmed and cut into ½-inch*
*   cubes*
1 small dried hot pepper, such as
*   bird's-eye pepper, crushed (see*
*   Note)*

1 cup (gently packed) flat-leaf
*   parsley leaves*
2½ cups (gently packed) fresh
*   basil leaves*
Fine sea salt

1. Place the oil and garlic in a medium-size saucepan over medium-high heat. Stir and add the zucchini immediately. Cook, stirring constantly, until the zucchini and garlic begin to turn golden, 5 to 6 minutes. Add the hot pepper and reduce the heat to medium.

2. Coarsely chop the parsley and 2 cups of the basil and add to the zucchini mixture. Stir, season to taste with salt, and cover with 3 inches boiling water. Cook, partially covered, until the zucchini is tender, about 20 minutes. Adjust the seasoning. Tear the remaining ½ cup basil into small pieces and serve the soup garnished with the basil.

NOTE: As for the amount of hot pepper to use in this recipe, your own taste must dictate. In Campania this soup isn't searing, but there is a definite slow tingle on the back of the palate after a bowl, the resultant heat of one

small, but very hot, dried pepper added at the start.

Spring Greens Soup

ZUPPA DI VERDURA

6 TO 8 SERVINGS

Springtime was just arriving in Campania, and I was sitting in a country restaurant not too far from Naples with my family and a group of friends. Throughout a simple and delicious meal of roasted meats and cheese, a mixed green salad, and exquisite *prosciutto crudo,* we discussed one particular recipe, *zuppa di verdura.* Our inspiration was the market we'd just visited near Avellino. There wild greens of every description were offered, mostly by women shrouded in peasant clothes who had undoubtedly spent their very early morning hours gathering them. Tidily displayed on upturned crates, the wild greens—and some herbs—lay awaiting purchase. They were intended, according to my friends, for this soup, which is a ritual of early spring when the greens are at their best.

Similar to *acqua cotta,* or cooked water, a well-known dish from Sutri, north of Rome, *zuppa di verdura* is a blend of seasonal wild greens cooked and served over toast. It is easy to make, but it takes a certain amount of know-how, for the flavors of the greens must blend well, and one must not overpower the others. If you have wild nettles, lamb's quarters, and/or borage, use them as part of the mix suggested below.

Try a light but flavorful white wine, such as Greco di Tufo, alongside.

FOR THE SOUP
2 tablespoons extra-virgin olive oil
1 large onion, diced
1 medium carrot, diced
2 ribs celery, strings removed,
  diced
4 cups (gently packed) turnip or
  dandelion greens, trimmed and
  well rinsed
4 cups arugula leaves, trimmed and
  well rinsed
2 pounds spinach leaves and stems,
  very well rinsed

4 cups (gently packed) chervil leaves,
  or 3 young chervil plants,
  trimmed and coarsely chopped
About 7 cups water
1 tablespoon fine sea salt

FOR THE TOASTS
6 slices (¼ inch thick) Tuscan or
  other country bread, cut
  in half crosswise
1 large clove garlic, peeled
3 tablespoons extra-virgin
  extra-virgin olive oil

1. Place the oil, onion, carrot, and celery in a large heavy soup pot over medium-high heat and sauté just until the onion turns golden, about 10 minutes. Add the turnip greens and arugula; stir and cook until they soften and wilt a bit, about 3 minutes. Stir in the spinach, cover, and cook, stirring occasionally, until the spinach has wilted and turns bright green, about 6 minutes.

2. Add the chervil, stir, then add enough of the water to cover the vegetables. Stir in the salt, cover, and cook until the vegetables are tender, about 25 minutes. Continue cooking, partially covered, until the vegetables are completely tender, about 20 minutes more. Adjust the seasoning.

3. Toast the bread and gently rub it with the garlic. Place each slice in a warmed shallow soup bowl and drizzle each with 1½ teaspoons oil. Ladle the soup over the toast and serve immediately.

THE LANCELLOTTIS:
A Farm Family off the Farm

The Florence to Bologna *autostrada* is mostly one long, winding tunnel through the heart of the Apennine mountains. I first drove it on a hot summer day, heading north to a small farming town outside Modena called Soliera. I was scheduled to visit Ristorante Lancellotti, which is widely known for the quality of its cuisine. I was going for additional reasons, however, for the Lancellottis, who own and run the restaurant, were once farmers. The last vestige of their farming is a huge organic garden that supplies the restaurant with much of its produce. It is cited by many gardeners and cooks throughout northern Italy as the most beautiful and productive garden of its kind in the country. Angelo, one of the three Lancellotti brothers, is the gardener as well as the restaurant's chef, and *brilliance* is a word often associated with his name. Another brother, Francesco, makes balsamic vinegar whose quality has merited the label *aceto balsamico tradizionale di Modena,* a local and highly esteemed pedigree for vinegar. The third brother, Emilio, is the Maitre d'Hotel and accountant, as well as a staunch supporter of local, traditional gastronomic specialities, and his current project is saving a much-revered sausage called *culatello* from extinction.

I arrived in Soliera, which seemed itself to have developed organically out of the cornfields and vineyards that surround it, on a Sunday afternoon. The streets were empty, the air hot, the sun vivid. I found the restaurant and hotel and was immediately greeted by Emilio, a handsome man with striking black hair.

"Welcome, welcome," he said, simultaneously shaking my hand and taking my bags. He announced my arrival to a group sitting in the cool dining room, and they immediately left their table in a body to come meet me. One man held out his knobby, gnarled hand. "Angelo Lancellotti, eldest brother," he said, then pulled a short woman to his side and indicated a young man. "Szdena, my wife here; there Francesco, my brother." I met their parents, Ida and Camillo, and a niece and nephew. Emilio whisked me upstairs to my room, returning three minutes later with a bowl of cherries in ice water and a bottle of water, a remedy for the heat. He suggested I come downstairs in half an hour.

We began in the dining room, where he gave me the lively family history, through the family's dairy farming years, which lasted until 1967. "My parents cried when they sold the cows," he said. "My father still wishes he were a farmer, but he's realistic. Farming was just too difficult." The family kept a small farm Ida owned, their toehold in the farming community.

The Lancellottis bought an *osteria,* a small bar where farmworkers came for a glass of fizzy Lambrusco and a plate of fried dough or organ meats, sliced sausages and bread, or other simple delicacy prepared by Ida. The family worked together and the *osteria* prospered. By 1973 the *osteria* was no longer big enough to support the entire family, so they opened the restaurant and were immediately successful. Ida, Camillo, and Angelo cooked, preparing both the farm specialties they knew and the light, fresh, herb-laced dishes that have become Angelo's signature. After training at a hotel school, Emilio took over the dining room, and Francesco became the wine steward.

All the Lancellotti brothers are nostalgic for their life on the farm. They have a collective goal to move the restaurant down the road to the farmhouse on Ida's farm, where Angelo has his garden.

Angelo told me to meet him there the next day, and Francesco was to be my escort. "Do you want to go in the car or on a bicycle?" Francesco asked. I chose the bicycle, and we joined the many other cyclists on the flat road between the restaurant and the outskirts of Soliera, which cut through silent fields of corn,

wheat, and grapevines. Waves of heat shimmered up from the ground, stopping at about chest level, where humidity held them.

We turned off the road, went through a gate, and entered a fragrant oasis where the temperature was several degrees cooler. There was birdsong. There were flowers. And there was Angelo, bent over a shovel, his dog Pipo by his side. He straightened, gave a little salute, and proceeded to walk—or more accurately run—me through the garden, which he cultivates organically, irrigates with cool well water, and watches over like a mother hen. We began at the thick, lush hedge that separates the garden from the road. "This helps with the temperature," Angelo said. "It shades the greenhouse where I grow lettuces, provides a home for birds and insects that are both good and bad, and muffles the noise." He explained that before the war the land all around them had been divided by hedges, there to provide habitat for animals, birds, and insects and to help regulate the temperature. Now the landscape stretches forever without a break except for the huge, stocky farmhouses that former dictator Benito Mussolini encouraged people to build.

Inside the greenhouse was a new planting of wild arugula. "The one with the real flavor," he said, handing me a jagged leaf that

burned my tongue with its pleasant smokiness. He combines it with pears, raspberries,
and *aceto balsamico tradizionale di Modena* in
a sublime salad (see page 60).

Outside, we walked to a patch of lacy
flowers in several intense shades of blue.
"They're for butterflies and bees," Angelo
said. "And this," he said, pointing to a pile of
sticks and twigs leaning up against a tree, "is
for hedgehogs." I must have looked surprised,
for he turned to face me full on, brought his
hands together, and leaned forward, instruct-
ing. "You can't believe the quantity of insects
they eat," he said intensely. "Why, they're
absolutely necessary here."

Francesco, at my side, was as enraptured
as I. "I don't come in here much," he explained. "Angelo doesn't like company!"

We walked on. "This area here," Angelo
said, pointing to a low patch of grass, "is for
harmful insects. I don't encourage them to
come—they're already here and they're necessary to create a balance." He pointed up to
a small wooden birdhouse on the side of a
tree. "The birds need insects, and they don't
like just the so-called good ones! I've got
thirty of those placed around the *orto,* and
the size of the hole determines the kind of
bird that will come. I've encouraged birds
that eat the most insects and that eat the lar-
vae that attack our grapes," he said, pointing
to the vineyard a short distance away where
Francesco gets the Trebbiano and Lambrusco
de Santo Croce grapes to make his *aceto balsamico tradizionale di Modena.*

I nearly stumbled over what looked like

a haphazard pile of tiles against a stump.
"Careful, that's for lizards." Angelo said.
"They like to hide under the warm tiles.
They're insect eaters too." He turned and
pointed to the old house on the property
where his parents used to live and which
the brothers are hoping to transform into a
new restaurant. "See the roof tiles?" he asked.
"They're home to the *pipistrelli* [bats]. Vora-
cious insect eaters. There would be more bats
if more old houses were left standing."

I recognized lovage next to Chinese garlic
and alongside that a patch of lettuce. "They
help each other grow," he said. And they all
end up in his legendary salads. Onions grew
next to calendula and tarragon. There were
several towering hollow-stemmed angelica
plants, their flowers like big umbrellas, which
he plants for shade. That the angelica winds
up in one of his most popular pasta sauces
is almost incidental.

We passed the thyme. "I like to sprinkle
that on roasts," he said. And the borage? "It
tastes a bit like fish. I use it in salads." The
tall and hearty bronze fennel, which he
plants far away from its green cousin to prevent it from reverting to green itself, he tosses
into rice just before serving.

We headed for the shade of a huge walnut tree, whose foot was surrounded with
dusty green absinth. "It repels insects that
like walnuts," Angelo said. He values walnuts
not only for pastries but also for a sweet wine
made from the still-green nuts.

"Organized chaos!" laughed Angelo as he
waved goodbye. "That's what I've got here."

Potato and Lovage Soup

**ZUPPA DI
LEVISTICO E
PATATE**

**6 TO 8
SERVINGS**

Angelo Lancellotti, chef at the Lancellotti restaurant in Soliera, makes this delicate soup using potatoes and lovage from his remarkable garden (see essay, page 80), and he told me I would not just love it but adore it. He was correct. The intense celery-like flavor of the lovage is gentled by the potatoes and semolina, and the result is an elegant and satisfying soup.

No one who has sampled it at my home believes it's so easy to put together—nor did I when Angelo first made it for me—but it is a quick dish and one that never fails to please. Make it in spring when the lovage is young and tender and new potatoes are abundant. You'll love it.

Try this with a slightly fizzy red wine, such as Lambrusco Salamino di Santa Croce.

*1½ pounds russet potatoes, peeled
and cut into quarters
Scant 1 tablespoon coarse sea salt
1 tablespoon extra-virgin olive oil
1 small onion, thinly sliced
1 tablespoon sweet paprika
1 large egg*

*½ cup semolina
Pinch of hot paprika or cayenne
pepper, or to taste
About 20 lovage leaves (to give
2 tablespoons thinly slivered;
see Note)*

1. Place the potatoes and 8 cups of water in a large heavy saucepan. Add the salt, cover, and bring to a boil over medium-high heat. Reduce the heat and cook until the potatoes are very soft and beginning to fall apart, about 25 minutes.

2. Place the oil and onion in a small heavy skillet over medium-high heat and cook until the onion is deep golden, 10 to 12 minutes. Stir in the sweet paprika and cook for about 1 min-

ute, then remove from the heat.

3. When the potatoes are finished cooking, whisk the egg and semolina together in a small bowl to make a paste. Whisk 1 cup of the potato cooking water into the paste, then whisk the mixture back into the potatoes, breaking the potatoes up at the same time. Stir the onion mixture into the potatoes and add the hot paprika.

4. Stack the lovage leaves and thinly sliver crosswise. Stir the lovage into the soup and cook for 1 minute. Adjust the seasoning and allow the soup to sit for several minutes before serving so it isn't blistering hot.

NOTE: Lovage is called many things, including "poor man's celery" and "common celery." It is becoming increasingly easy to obtain, but if you can't find it, use the the pale green leaves from celery—their flavor is sharper than lovage and has less depth, but they will substitute nicely in this soup.

Pasta and Potato Soup

This chunky, flavorful soup is so common to the Sicilian farm that I got dozens of recipes for it, no two identical. I've included two in this collection (see also Chicken with Pasta and Potatoes, page 219)—this is the simpler one. The soup is very robust and flavorful, with the garlic prevalent but gentled by slow cooking, and the parsley adding a wonderful, colorful freshness. You'll find yourself making and serving it often, just as the Sicilian farm cook does.

Try this with Cerasuolo di Vittoria, a robust red from Sicily.

2 tablespoons extra-virgin olive oil

4 cloves garlic, crushed, green germ removed

12 ounces waxy potatoes, such as Yellow Finn, peeled and cut into quarters

2 medium carrots, cut into ¼-inch-thick rounds

Fine sea salt

1½ cups (gently packed) flat-leaf parsley leaves (about 1 medium bunch)

12 ounces small dried pasta, such as orecchiette

1. Place the oil and garlic in a large heavy saucepan over medium heat and cook until the garlic is golden, about 3 minutes. Remove the garlic from the pan and add the potatoes and carrots. Sauté the vegetables until they are golden on all sides, 4 to 5 minutes. Season them generously with salt.

2. Mince the parsley and add it to the vegetables. Add water to cover by about 2 inches, cover, and bring to a boil. Reduce the heat to keep the liquid at a low boil and cook until the vegetables are tender but not mushy, 10 to 15 minutes. Make sure the vegetables stay covered with 2 inches of water.

3. Return the cooking liquid to a vigorous boil over medium-high heat. Again, make sure the vegetables are covered with 2 inches of water, which you will need to cook the pasta. Add the pasta, stir, cover, and cook just until it is al dente (tender but still firm to the bite), 7 to 10 minutes. Remove from the heat, adjust the seasoning, and serve immediately.

Potato and Artichoke Soup from Campania

**ZUPPA DI PATATE
E CARCIOFI
DELLA
CAMPANIA**

**6 TO 8
SERVINGS**

I found the recipe for this soup in an old collection of traditional farm recipes lent to me by a friend who lives in Campania. The area, which includes the Amalfi Peninsula, Naples, Pompei, and Herculaneum, is a gorgeous stretch of rustic landscape punctuated by sophisticated cities and small towns. This soup is a culinary reminder of Campania. Its texture is rustic, yet its light herbal flavor, balanced by the nuttiness of artichokes and the sweet acidity of tomatoes, is sophisticated.

Try a light, lively white wine, such as Fiano di Avellino, alongside.

1 lemon, halved
4 large artichokes
3 pounds waxy potatoes, peeled and
*   cut into ½-inch dice*
3 medium onions, cut crosswise
*   into thin slices*

12 ounces ripe tomatoes (about
*   5 small), peeled, cored, and*
*   quartered*
Fine sea salt and freshly ground
*   black pepper*
¼ to ¾ teaspoon dried oregano
*   (see Note)*
2 tablespoons extra-virgin olive oil

1. Squeeze the juice of the lemon into a bowl of cold water. Trim the artichokes to their hearts (see box, page 42). Place them in the acidulated water for 30 minutes.

2. Drain and cut the artichokes into ½-inch dice.

3. Combine the artichokes, potatoes, onions, and tomatoes in a large heavy saucepan. Season with salt and pepper and about ¼ teaspoon of the oregano. Add water to cover by about ½ inch, add the oil, and bring to a boil over medium-high heat. Cover and cook until all of the vegetables are tender, about 40 minutes. Taste for seasoning and add additional oregano, salt, and pepper as desired. With the soup uncovered, continue cooking for

10 to 15 minutes more. The soup should be quite thick.

4. Remove from the heat, adjust the seasoning, and serve immediately.

NOTE: Dried oregano is superior in flavor to fresh oregano for nearly everything. The amount of dried oregano you use will depend greatly on its freshness, so taste as you go, being careful not to add too much. Too much oregano can destroy an otherwise wonderful soup.

Seasonal Soup

This soup is a universal Italian farm cook's ode to spring—when artichokes are wonderful, favas are at their best, and the first peas of the year make their appearance. All combine in this earthy spring mélange.

I've adapted the recipe from the traditional farm version, which calls for the peas to be cooked until they are olive green. I prefer them cooked through but still bright green so they offer flavor, sweetness, and a bit of texture to the soup.

Try a lovely red wine, such as Aglianico, with this.

1 lemon, cut in half
4 large artichokes (1 pound each), or 4 pounds small artichokes (see Note)
6 small onions (less than 1 ounce each, 5 ounces total)
1 tablespoon extra-virgin olive oil
5 ounces pancetta, sliced into very thin (⅛-inch) strips

2 pounds fresh fava beans in the pod, shelled but not skinned (generous 2 cups; see box, page 91)
Fine sea salt and freshly ground black pepper
2 pounds fresh peas in their pods, shelled (1¾ cups)
1 cup (gently packed) flat-leaf parsley leaves

1. Squeeze the lemon into a bowl of cold water. Trim the large artichokes to their hearts or the small artichokes to their inner tender cone of leaves (see box, page 42).

2. Peel the onions. Leave 4 of the onions whole and cut the other 2 in half.

3. Place the oil, halved onions, and pancetta in a large heavy saucepan over medium heat and sauté until the onions are golden, 3 to 5 minutes. Add the favas, the whole onions, and ¼ cup water and season lightly with salt and pepper. Stir, cover, and cook until the favas are tender, about 10 minutes.

4. If using large artichoke hearts, cut them crosswise into ¼-inch-thick strips. If using baby artichokes, slice them lengthwise about ¼ inch thick. Add the artichokes to the fava mixture, stir, and add enough water to just cover the vegetables. Cover and cook until the artichokes are tender, about 20 minutes. Check occasionally to be sure there is enough water and the vegetables aren't sticking. Add the peas, stir, and cook to your liking. If you like them just cooked and tender, they will take about 10 minutes, but you may let them cook as long as 20 minutes with no real ill effect.

5. Just before serving, mince the parsley and stir it into the soup. Remove from the heat, adjust the seasonings, and serve.

NOTE: In Italy this is made with tiny *violetto* artichokes, what we call "baby" artichokes, or the secondary growth of a regular artichoke plant. I make them with the smaller purple Italian artichokes when I can find them, but otherwise use large artichokes, which generally weigh in at 1 to 1½ pounds each.

Bibi's Fava, Fennel, and Pasta Cream

MACCO DI BIBI

4 TO 6 SERVINGS

I met Bibi Loffredo at the home of mutual friends who live in Palermo, Sicily. We had been invited for lunch and I had asked everyone to tell me about their favorite farm recipes. When the conversation turned to *macco,* the group really became animated— they all had something to say about this well-loved dish, and they all spoke at once. Bibi's voice rang above the others, however, describing how this dish is made of the humblest of ingredients yet is so delicious that it is eaten all the time, on the farm and in the city, by people of every economic class. "No other dish, I think, represents Sicilian farm cooking as well as *macco,*" she said.

Seasoned lightly with onion and the wild fennel that grows in the Sicilian hills, it is earthy and delicately anise flavored. I make it in the winter with dried favas, though it can be made in the spring as well, with fresh green favas. When made with dried favas, it is monochromatic, so reserve some fennel fronds for sprinkling on top. Not too much, for the fennel flavor must be subtle, not overwhelming.

Try a Cerasuolo di Vittoria with *macco* for the full Sicilian effect.

*1 pound dried fava beans, or
   3 pounds fresh fava beans in
   their pods*
1 large onion, minced
3 tablespoons extra-virgin olive oil
*1 cup (gently packed) fresh fennel
   fronds (about ⅓ bunch), plus
   additional for garnish*

*8 ounces dried spaghetti, broken
   into thirds*
Fine sea salt
*Freshly ground black pepper
   (optional)*
*Extra-virgin olive oil,
   for serving*

1. Place the dried favas in a large saucepan, cover generously with water, and bring to a boil. (If using fresh favas, see box, page 91). Remove from the heat, cover, and let sit for 1 hour. Peel each fava by slitting the outer skin and popping out the bean inside. Remove the little "tongue" on the curved inner part of the bean as well (it generally comes off with the skin).

2. Rinse the saucepan and return the favas to it. Add water to cover them by about 3 inches, cover the pan, and bring to a boil. Reduce the heat so the water is simmering, adjust the lid so the beans are partially covered, and cook, stirring occasionally, until the favas are tender, about 30 minutes. Check occasionally to see that there is plenty of water covering the favas, which absorb a surprising amount; they should remain soupy, and as they cook and you stir, they will break down and become the consistency of heavy cream. When they are cooked through, stir them vigorously until they are creamy. Using a whisk or a wand mixer will also incorporate some air and make the

macca lighter. If the cooked favas are thicker than heavy cream, add enough boiling water to thin them.

3. Place the onion and ¼ cup water in a medium-size skillet and heat over medium heat. When the water has evaporated, add 2 tablespoons of the oil, stir, and cook until the onion is translucent, about 7 minutes. Mince the fennel fronds and add them to the onion. Stir and continue cooking for another 2 minutes. Remove from the heat and stir into the fava purée. You may make the *macco* several hours ahead of time, but I suggest at least 1 hour so the flavors have a chance to mellow.

4. Bring a large pot of salted water to a boil. Add the pasta, stir, and cook until it is al dente (tender but still firm to the bite), about 7 minutes. Drain, reserving some of the cooking water. Transfer the pasta to a large bowl and toss with the remaining 1 tablespoon olive oil.

5. To serve the *macco,* reheat the fava purée very gently over low heat, whisking it as it heats and adding spoonfuls of the

pasta cooking water if necessary to make it creamy. Stir in the pasta and continue heating until the pasta is hot, 3 to 4 minutes. Season generously with salt and, if you like, with pepper and let sit for at least 10 minutes before serving.

6. In Sicily *macco* is eaten either piping hot or at room temperature. To serve, ladle the soup into wide shallow soup bowls and garnish with fennel fronds. Pass a cruet of olive oil alongside.

NOTE: In many parts of the United States, fennel grows wild, its full, deep green fronds sending out a sweet scent. If you find it, use it (after verifying that it hasn't been sprayed). If you can't find it, use the feathery fronds from commercially grown fennel bulbs.

Peeling and Cooking Fava Beans

Inside the bulbous fava's husk rests the bean, and inside the bean rests the true treasure of the fava, the tender, bright green bean. In Italy when the beans are small and young, they are often eaten with their outer peel on, for they haven't yet developed a bitterness. However, when they get larger, about the size of a lima bean, the outer peel is usually removed. I recommend removing the outer peel for all the dishes in this book that call for fresh fava beans, unless otherwise specified.

To remove the peel from the fava bean, bring a medium-size pot of water to a boil, covered, over high heat. Add the fava beans, return the water to a boil, and drain. When the beans are cool enough to handle, slit the skin of each and gently squeeze out the bright green fava bean within. Proceed with any recipe that calls for fresh fava beans or continue to cook them.

Cover the favas with 2 inches of water and bring to a boil. Reduce the heat so the water is simmering, adjust the lid so the beans are partially covered, and cook, stirring occasionally, until the beans are tender, about 15 minutes. Using a wand mixer, purée the favas. If the fava purée is thicker than heavy cream, add a bit of water to thin it.

Wheat and Lentil Soup from Catania

I met Carmelo Chiaramonte after eating a fascinating meal he prepared at the chic Cantine del Cugno Mezzano in Catania, a city on Sicily's east coast not far from Modica. Much of the reason his food is so good, he explained, is a result of his weekend "shopping" trips. "I go to my parents' farm every weekend, get what I can there, then visit all the neighbors to buy rabbits, chickens, vegetables. Good ingredients are one key," he said.

The other key? "A mama who cooks like mine," he added.

When I joined him at his parents' farm a couple of days later his mother was in the kitchen and generously offered me tastes of the handful of dishes she was preparing for lunch, including the most delicious stewed chickpeas I'd ever eaten. It was Carmelo, however, who made me this light yet substantial soup, which he grew up eating at home.

The substantial nature of this soup calls for a rich, red wine, like Signorio Barone la Lumia.

1 cup wheat berries
1 cup lentils
1½ ounces pancetta, diced
2 tablespoons extra-virgin olive oil
1 medium onion, diced
1 rib celery, strings removed, diced

2 medium carrots, diced
5 ounces Swiss chard leaves, stems
    trimmed, rinsed, and coarsely
    chopped (see Note)
Sea salt and freshly ground pepper

1. Place the wheat berries in a large saucepan, cover them amply with water, and bring to a boil over medium-high heat. Remove from the heat and let sit, covered, for 1 hour. Drain and cover generously with fresh water. Bring to a boil and cook, partially covered, until the wheat berries are tender but still somewhat chewy, about 30 minutes. Drain, discarding the cooking liquid.

2. Place the lentils in a medium-size heavy saucepan, cover with 6 cups water, and bring to a boil over medium-high heat. Reduce the heat so the lentils are boiling very gently, almost simmering, and cook, partially covered, until they just begin to get tender, 15 to 20 minutes. (The amount of time you cook the lentils depends a great deal on the variety you use.) Add the pancetta and continue cooking until the lentils are tender but still slightly firm, 10 to 15 minutes more. Drain the lentils and pancetta, reserving the cooking liquid.

3. Heat the oil in a medium-size skillet over medium heat. Add the onion, celery, and carrots and cook, stirring occasionally, until the vegetables are tender but not browned, about 10 minutes. Add the chard, stir, and cook, stirring occasionally, until it is wilted and dark green, about 8 minutes. Season to taste with salt and pepper and remove from the heat.

4. When all the ingredients are cooked, combine them in a large saucepan with the lentil cooking liquid. Cover and bring to a boil, then reduce the heat immediately and simmer just long enough so the soup is hot, about 5 minutes. Adjust the seasoning and serve.

NOTE: Carmelo's mother uses slightly bitter wild chard in this soup, and so does Carmelo. I use Swiss chard, which is delicious, but if you can find the wild variety, try it.

Bean Soup with Swiss Chard

ZUPPA DI FAGIOLI E BIETOLE

6 TO 8 SERVINGS

This robust soup comes from a lovely, robust land, the Amalfi peninsula in the region of Campania. A typical farm soup, it is rich in flavor and sustaining, a meal in a pot for hungry workers. It is just one of many recipes given to me by Grazia Caso, who was born and raised in the area and is now chef and owner with her husband, Salvatore, of Taverna del Capitano, a lovely restaurant in the picturesque fishing port of Marina del Cantone, near Nerano on the south side of the peninsula.

Grazia and Salvatore own farmland tucked up in the mountains about an hour and a half from their seaside home and restaurant. Its fertile soil gives them all the vegetables and herbs they serve, as well as lemons so sweet you can just about eat them as you would an orange. When the farmer who works the land includes chard in his vegetable delivery, this soup is likely to be on the menu.

Swiss chard is available from late summer through the winter months. I, however, prefer it after it has gone through its first freeze and sugars begin to course through it. The sweet depth of chard combined with the summery tomato sauce makes for a welcoming, hearty dish.

Try a hearty Piedirosso alongside.

3 tablespoons extra-virgin olive oil

1 pound yellow onions (about
    4 medium), diced

2 long ribs celery, with leaves if
    possible, strings removed, diced

1 small carrot, diced

2 cloves garlic, green germ
    removed, diced

1½ pounds Swiss chard, stems
    trimmed, rinsed, and coarsely
    chopped

1 pound dried cannellini beans,
    cooked (see box, facing page)

¼ cup Nunzio's Tomato Sauce
    (page 424)

2 small dried bird's-eye peppers,
    crushed, or ¼ to ½ teaspoon
    crushed red pepper flakes

Fine sea salt

1 medium red onion, sliced
    paper thin

1. Heat the oil in a heavy soup pot over medium heat and add the diced onions, celery, carrot, and garlic. Cook, stirring, until the onions are golden and translucent and the celery is tender, about 20 minutes.

2. Add the chard, stir, cover,

Cooking Dried Beans

Pick over the beans, removing any pebbles or other debris. Place the beans in a heavy saucepan and add water to cover by 2 inches. Bring to a boil, remove from the heat, and let sit, covered, for 1 hour. Drain, return the beans to the saucepan, and add fresh water to cover by 3 inches. Bring to a boil over medium-high heat, reduce the heat so the beans are simmering, and cook, partially covered, until they are al dente, tender but still slightly firm, about 45 minutes. (The cooking time can vary substantially, depending on the freshness of the beans.) Drain the beans so they don't get overly soft, reserving the cooking liquid.

and cook until it has softened, about 15 minutes.

3. Add the beans with their cooking liquid and enough water to just cover the vegetables. Add the tomato sauce and peppers and stir. Season lightly with salt, cover, and bring to a boil, raising the heat if necessary. Reduce the heat so the liquid is boiling gently and cook, partially covered, until the vegetables are tender and soft but the beans aren't mushy, about 45 minutes. Adjust the seasoning and serve with the red onion slices alongside for diners to add to the steaming soup as they prefer.

Ligurian Chickpea Soup

ZUPPA DI CECI LIGURE

6 TO 8 SERVINGS

Bean soups of all kinds have always been staples on the Italian farm, for beans are abundant, nourishing, and inexpensive. This soup is traditional to Liguria and typical of that region's cuisine, for it is aromatic and rich with the flavors of chard, onions, and fresh tomato sauce. Liguria has always been a region of fishermen, and in the past they were at sea much of the year, subsisting on fresh-caught fish and dried foods. When they returned home, they wanted their meals to include fresh vegetables, and the cuisine developed around their desire. Fortunately for the fishermen, there were always enough people left at home to cultivate the land and prepare the bounty, turning it into delicious dishes like this fresh soup.

This soup was traditionally served on feast days honoring the dead. Perhaps it was to reassure their spirits that those behind were eating well, if simply.

Try a light red wine, such as Rossese di Dolceacqua, with this for a taste of the Mediterranean viewed from the hills of Liguria.

8 ounces dried chickpeas
1 large onion, diced
1 good-size bunch Swiss chard
    (generous 1 pound), stems
    trimmed, rinsed, and diced

2 cups Light and Lively Tomato
    Sauce (page 423)
Fine sea salt and freshly ground
    black pepper
Extra-virgin olive oil, for serving

1. Place the chickpeas in a large heavy saucepan. Add water to cover by about 2 inches. Bring to a boil over high heat, remove from the heat, and let sit for 1 hour. Drain, return the chickpeas to the pan, and cover with at least 3 inches of cold water. Bring to a boil over high heat, reduce the heat to medium-high, and cook, partially covered, until the chickpeas are almost but not quite tender, about 35 minutes (see Note). Drain and return the chickpeas to the pan.

2. Add the onion, chard, and tomato sauce to the chickpeas, season lightly with salt and pepper, and bring to a boil. Reduce the heat and cook, at a lively simmer, partially covered, until the vegetables are tender, about 25 minutes. Check occasionally to be sure that the mixture isn't drying out; if it is, add just enough boiling water to moisten it, but not more than a cup or so. Adjust the seasoning and serve with the olive oil alongside.

NOTES: The cooking time for chickpeas will vary depending on their freshness. Freshly dried chickpeas cook more quickly than those that are older.

Hearty Umbrian Soup

**ZUPPA DI
CICERCHIE**

**6 TO 8
SERVINGS**

Maria Maurillo, owner with her son, Claudio, of Agriturismo Malva-rina, dishes up this smoky, chunky soup made with a unique Umbrian specialty, *cicerchie*. An old-fashioned legume, or pulse, little known outside Umbria, *cicerchie* resemble a chickpea with flat sides. Once widely cultivated, they went out of fashion because they were hard to cultivate, the plants were fickle, and the production was small.

Cicerchie no longer sustains the farmers in this rugged region, and although they are still cultivated they have become something of a rarity. Maria has a constant supply for her farm restaurant that she gets from friends and neighbors who still bother to grow them. Like many gastronomically obscure and old-fashioned ingredients, *cicerchie* are starting to be used by chefs in elegant restaurants in Italy, so no doubt their cultivation will revive. For now, however, most remain in the hands of those who grow them.

Maria's soup beguiles guests because of its delicate smokiness, which is the flavor of *cicerchie*. I buy *cicerchie* whenever I go to Italy, but if I don't have them, I make this soup with chickpeas. By adding smoked pork, I can recreate the subtle flavor of *cicerchie*.

To match the special flavor of this soup, try an equally special Chianti Classico or Rufino alongside.

*1 pound dried chickpeas or
   cicerchie (scant 3 cups)*
1 medium onion, coarsely chopped
2 small carrots, coarsely chopped
*2 medium ribs celery, strings
   removed, coarsely chopped*
*16 cherry tomatoes, or 3 medium-
   size ripe tomatoes, cut in half*

*2 ounces smoked ham or bacon in
   one piece, if using chickpeas*
*½ cup extra-virgin olive oil, plus
   additional for garnish*
*20 slices (each ¼ inch thick) fresh
   baguette, cut crosswise in half*
1 clove garlic, peeled
Fine sea salt

1. Place the chickpeas or *cicerchie* in a heavy soup pot and add water to cover by 2 inches. Bring to a boil over high heat and drain. Cover the beans with fresh water by about 3 inches, add the vegetables and the smoked ham, if using chickpeas, and bring to a boil over medium-high heat. Reduce the heat so the liquid is simmering and cook, covered, until the chickpeas are tender and falling apart, about 2 hours. Check to be sure the chickpeas are not drying out as they cook and add water if necessary.

2. While the soup is cooking, heat ½ cup of the oil in a large heavy skillet over medium heat until it is hot but not smoking. Add the bread slices and cook until the pieces are golden on all sides, which should take less than a minute for both sides. Do this in two batches to avoid crowding the pan. Transfer the croutons to paper towels to drain. When they are cool enough to handle, rub each lightly with the garlic clove.

3. Remove the smoked ham from the beans and discard. Using a food processor or wand mixer, purée the beans and vegetables and season to taste with salt.

4. To serve, ladle the soup into 6 to 8 warmed shallow soup bowls. Drizzle each bowl with a teaspoon of olive oil and pass the croutons separately.

PRIMI PIATI

FIRST COURSES

In Italy, where a red traffic light is considered a "suggestion," categorizing dishes becomes something of an artifice. At the farm table, as at any table in an Italian home, dishes are presented without end. Pretty soon what one thought was a *primo,* or first course, turns out to be an extension of the antipasto course, and the *secondo,* or second course, is off even further into the future. Just when you think the meal is winding down, another savory dish emerges.

That wasn't always so on the Italian farm, where, traditionally, farmers ate one-dish meals. There was neither an abundance of food nor a lot of time to prepare it, so to make meals satisfying, the Italian farm cook had to be inventive. The main components of the meal—meat or another source of protein, vegetables (most commonly wild greens), and grains—were combined in one dish with plenty of herbs, oil, nuts, and vinegar to make flavors sing.

Today mealtime on the farm is more elaborate,

Though bread is primordial to the Italian farm table, it is never served alongside pasta. It is reserved for the antipasti and the secondo piatto.

although there seems to be no intrinsic organization to it. However, it doesn't hurt to impose one. Thus, the panoply of dishes within this chapter are considered first courses, although most could probably be served as a main course as well. The chapter opens with pastas, which in Italy are always first courses; the second part of the chapter includes more varied and flexible dishes. Stuffed and fried zucchini blossoms, frittato, risotto, a Ligurian artichoke tart—all definitely substantial enough to qualify as first courses—could also, if reduced in quantity (one stuffed blossom, a skinny wedge of frittata or tart per person), be part of an antipasti offering.

The label or organization really doesn't matter. What matters is flavor, and here you will not be disappointed.

Giusto's Pasta with Mint Sauce

PASTA ALLA GIUSTO

4 SERVINGS

Giusto Occhipinti is a practicing architect and winemaker, part owner of the COS winery in Sicily (see essay, page 124). He lives in the village of Mazzarrone outside Caltagirone, in a small stone house his grandfather gave him. When he inherited it, the house was nothing more than a crumbling ruin. He quickly fixed it up, adding a swimming pool and outdoor grill and kitchen. It is surrounded on three sides by vineyards, but it sits right behind an unsightly factory. He shrugs. "I wanted to keep the land my grandfather worked and the house he gave me, so I decided I would ignore the factory," he says. When he is home, he looks out the back of the house on a beautiful view of vineyards.

During my visit we sat around Giusto's kitchen table, feasting on fresh vegetables and pasta, unbelievable Sicilian bread, and COS wine. We talked food, love, traditions, and Giusto, who is very sentimental, spoke of his grandmother. "She always told me that if I said bad things about people I would be as bad as they were, and if I said good things about people I could hope to be as good as they are."

Giusto says he's not a good cook except for a couple of dishes, and this, with its uniquely Sicilian blend of herbs and raisins, is one.

He claims that the recipe is "an original" and the easiest thing in the world. It is, and one of the best.

Serve a Cerasuolo di Vittoria alongside.

Mint

1 cup (gently packed) fresh mint leaves, plus additional for garnish
⅓ cup extra-virgin olive oil
2 cloves garlic, minced
⅓ cup raisins (optional)
Fine sea salt
Hot paprika or cayenne pepper (optional)

1 pound good-quality short dried pasta, such as fusilli, orecchiette, or penne
1 pound eggplant, unpeeled, cut into 1-inch cubes
¾ cup grated Pecorino Romano or Parmigiano-Reggiano, for serving

1. Bring a large pot of salted water to a boil over high heat.

2. Meanwhile, mince the 1 cup mint, transfer it to a large bowl, and cover with the oil. Stir in the garlic and the raisins if using, then season generously with salt. Stir in hot paprika to taste if using.

3. Add the pasta and eggplant to the boiling water at the same time, stir the pasta, and push the eggplant under the surface of the water often as it cooks. Cook until the pasta is al dente (tender but still firm to the bite) and the eggplant is tender, about 8 minutes for both.

4. Drain the pasta and eggplant in a colander, reserving ½ cup of the cooking water. Add the pasta, eggplant, and cooking water to the mint sauce and toss thoroughly to coat. Taste for seasoning, adding salt as necessary. Serve garnished with mint leaves and accompanied by the grated cheese.

Pasta-Cooking Rules, Gleaned from the Italian Farm Cook

• To cook pasta, use either a big pasta cooker with a fitted colander insert (the pasta cooks in the insert, which makes for easy draining) or a large soup pot.

• And cook it in an abundant quantity of water, which means more than you ever imagined. Six quarts water is about right for 1 pound pasta.

• Add a good quantity of salt to the water, for without salt the pasta will taste bland. Count on using 2 level tablespoons of coarse sea salt to 6 quarts water. (If using table salt, use half the amount.)

• Make sure the water is boiling vigorously before adding the pasta, which you should do slowly so it moves around in the water rather than forming a large clump at the bottom. Stir the pasta once it is all added to the water so it cooks evenly.

• Time the pasta carefully—whether fresh or dried, it will take much less time than you think. Fresh pasta is cooked almost as soon as it is in the water—1½ minutes maximum. Dried pasta, depending on the shape and the brand, takes 7 to 8 minutes for al dente, tender but still firm to the bite, which is the only way to eat good-quality dried pasta. If you are adding pasta to a sauce and heating it together, undercook the pasta by about 1 minute. It will continue to cook in the sauce, absorbing flavor as it does so.

• Drain the pasta by removing the colander insert or by pouring the pasta into a stand-alone colander set in the sink. Or remove it quickly with a hand-held strainer or tongs. That way, you can save the pasta water, which is an invaluable ingredient in many pasta sauces.

Pasta with Sardines

PASTA ALLA CARRETTIERE

6 SERVINGS

Pasta alla carrettiere (literally "cart driver's pasta") is one of Sicily's most typical pasta dishes. Made with fresh sardines when they are in season from early spring through summer, it is a delightful blend of Sicilian flavors—pine nuts, raisins, anchovies, fennel fronds,

Segreti

The *mollica* called for here is a subtle secret of Sicilian cuisine. It is nothing more than the carefully toasted crumbs of *pane di casa,* the simplest of Sicilian bread, which has an alluring hint of cinnamon flavor. I make *mollica* with plain white bread and still get a lovely seasoning (page 427).

and garlic—which perfectly balance the intense flavor of the sardines.

Fresh Mediterranean sardines are robust, firm little fish whose lovely, fatty, dark yet subtle meat is delicious grilled, sautéed as they are here, or stuffed and baked. They bear no relation to sardines in a can, which are usually not sardines at all but herring.

When sardines are in season, I can never get enough, so I was delighted to come across this delicious way of fixing them. It was part of a meal prepared by Signora Giuseppina Morello, the mother of Giuseppe and Gaetano Morello, who are reviving the family olive grove in Sicily. "We Sicilians love sardines," she said. "We eat them all the time. They're poor people's food, but that's what most people in Sicily have always been—poor people."

Although she said this matter-of-factly, she admitted that at first she'd thought this dish too humble to serve to me. Fortunately, Gaetano convinced her this was exactly the kind of spirited, robust dish I was looking for, and he was correct. Serve it with a Bianco d'Alcamo, lightly chilled.

5 tablespoons extra virgin olive oil

2 cloves garlic, minced

1 large onion, minced

8 oil-packed anchovy fillets

⅓ cup pine nuts

⅓ cup raisins

4 medium-size ripe tomatoes, peeled, seeded, and diced

3 cups fresh fennel fronds

Fine sea salt

Hot paprika or cayenne pepper

1½ pounds fresh sardines, cleaned but heads and tails left on (see Notes)

½ cup almonds, toasted (see box, page 348) and cooled

1 pound good-quality dried pasta, such as spaghetti

¼ cup Toasted Bread Crumbs (see page 427)

1. Heat 2 tablespoons of the oil with the garlic and onion in a large heavy skillet over medium-high heat. Cook, stirring frequently, just until the onion and garlic begin to brown, about 3 minutes. Stir in the anchovies. Add the pine nuts and raisins and stir until the mixture is heated through and the pine nuts just begin to

"Gli spaghetti amano la compagnia." According to this Italian dictum, spaghetti loves company, so don't leave your pasta while cooking, for timing is all.

brown, 2 to 3 minutes more. Stir in the tomatoes and cook, stirring frequently, until the tomatoes are tender and have given up much of their liquid, 10 to 12 minutes.

2. Mince the fennel fronds and stir them into the sauce. Reduce the heat to low and cook, uncovered, until all the flavors have had a chance to blend, another 10 to 12 minutes. Season to taste with salt and hot paprika. Remove from the heat and keep warm.

3. Bring a large pot of salted water to a boil over high heat.

4. Meanwhile, rinse the sardines thoroughly and pat dry with paper towels. Heat the remaining 3 tablespoons oil in a large skillet over medium-high heat. Arrange the sardines in the skillet in one layer and cook until they are golden and cooked through, 2 to 3 minutes per side (see Notes). Remove the fish from the heat.

5. Grind the almonds in a food processor until they are coarsely chopped. Add the *mollica* and process several times until the crumbs and almonds are blended and of about the same consistency, though the almonds

will be in slightly larger pieces than the crumbs. Transfer to a serving dish and set aside.

6. Add the pasta to the boiling water, stir, and cook until it is al dente (tender but still firm to the bite), about 7 minutes. Drain well, then transfer to a warmed serving bowl. Add the tomato sauce and toss gently but thoroughly to coat. Taste for seasoning, adding salt as necessary, then toss again. Arrange the sardines on a warmed serving platter and serve along with the pasta. Serve the almond mixture alongside for sprinkling atop the pasta.

NOTES: If you can't find fresh sardines, use boneless mackerel fillets. Prepare them as suggested for the sardines, checking to be sure they don't overcook.

You will need to adjust the cooking time depending on the type and size of the fish you are using. To check for doneness, pierce the fish along the backbone, near the head, with the blade of a sharp knife. Pull back the knife and look at the meat. If it is opaque, it is cooked; if it is still translucent, cook it for a few seconds more.

TWO SICILIAN BROTHERS

Brothers Gaetano and Giuseppe Morello inherited the family farm outside the town of Grammichele, about forty-five miles west of Catania, in Sicily. Their great-grandparents were *mezzadri,* or sharecroppers, who cultivated the land at the turn of the century. According to Giuseppe, the landowner, a wealthy woman who owned a lot of property, didn't care much about the sixteen acres of reclaimed farmland the Morellos worked, leaving them alone to cultivate olives and wheat and raise animals. They worked the land well and diligently, and each year they paid rent with a pair of goats, some chickens, eggs, and part of their wheat and olive harvest. They raised all the food they needed for themselves and their five sons. Anything that was left, they sold.

By 1914 the family had a nest egg, which they used to buy the land they'd worked for so long. Their neighbors thought they were fools to buy it, for the land wasn't considered fertile, but each year the Morellos did well anyway. The family wasn't wealthy, but they worked hard and kept the farm productive.

Gaetano and Giuseppe's father grew up on the farm. He saw how hard his grandparents and parents worked, so when it came time for him to work, he moved to town for an easier life. The closest he ever got to farming after that was cultivating a garden outside town.

Gaetano and Giuseppe, like many young Sicilian men, trained as stonemasons, but by the time they were ready to work, there were too many stonemasons and not enough walls to build. So Giuseppe moved to France because he could get good-paying work there, and Gaetano stayed home.

Giuseppe, in his mid-forties, still lives in France, which is where I met him, but he dreams of returning to Sicily and settling on the farm his father abandoned, for he is convinced he can make a good living from it, as is Gaetano, who shares his dream. Together they are doing everything they can to get there. They already have two hundred olive trees that have been on their land since their great-grandparents' time, and they want to plant more. For many years the trees were neglected, but Giuseppe now returns regularly from France to care for them and help Gaetano keep up the land. With a small crew the brothers harvest the olives and take them to a local mill for pressing. What oil the Morello family doesn't use is sold locally.

When I was in Sicily, I visited the Morellos' land with Gaetano. From Grammichele we drove for a half hour through beautifully rolling and increasingly remote land until Gae-

tano turned off onto a hostile dirt road that led up into the hills. It ended at their property—lovely, calm, and hidden.

Gaetano, visibly excited, walked me through the small crumbling farmhouse that he and Giuseppe hope to renovate. Outside it stand remnants of his ancestors' life—a bay tree and wild oregano shrubs, whose leaves seasoned his grandmother's sauces, and a gate where Giuseppe planted geraniums like those his grandmother had, which lend a cared-for look to the homestead.

Gaetano pointed proudly to a perfectly cultivated field of reddish soil punctuated by a few huge and ancient olive trees. "I've got those fields ready for the two-year-old olive trees I hope to buy," he said. "I've applied for a grant and am waiting to hear about it."

The grant is part of Sicily's efforts to invigorate its agriculture. Sicily is one of few regions in Italy where more land is cultivated now than twenty or thirty years ago, thanks to the Cassa per il Mezzogiorno, the state fund for the south, which allocates money to develop agriculture. Theoretically, the fund is intended to help people like Gaetano and Giuseppe, but that isn't always the case—after I returned home from Sicily, I learned that the money Gaetano was waiting for wasn't awarded.

However, the brothers did apply and receive money from the European Union (EU) because they are cultivating their olive trees organically and the EU has a fund to support organic agriculture. Their dream is to sell organic olive oil throughout Europe. Giuseppe, as the marketing arm of the duo, has re-

searched the organic market and found it almost bottomless, particularly for olive oil.

"We're lucky already," he said. "Our area, the Maruzzella, is known for the quality of its olives and oil, and we sell all we produce now. The fact that our oil is organic is a plus."

Both Gaetano and Giuseppe feel strongly that farming is their hope, since jobs are few in Sicilian towns. Besides that, farm life is what they want. As Gaetano put it, it seems more secure than the life of an occasionally employed stonemason. He admits that he and his brother are in an ironic situation. "Here we are, working so hard to get back to where my grandparents were," he said. "My parents don't understand why we want to work the land. They don't realize that leaving the land as they did doesn't make sense in today's economy. In Sicily, farming is the future."

Giuseppe is even more convinced. Since he lives in France, he's working on finding markets there. He is extremely chauvinistic about Sicily and feels that its products, from olive oil to sun dried tomato paste to wild oregano, are the best in Italy. He is sure that once he finds and develops the markets, the orders will roll in not just for his oil but for a variety of Sicilian products. He often drops off samples to small shops in the area too. "France is the toughest because its consumers are even more chauvinistic about their products than I am about mine," he says with a glint of humor. "If I can get in here, I can get in anywhere."

A Few Common Pasta Questions Answered

• *Fresh or dried pasta, which is best?* The answer is, it depends. Fresh pasta is tender, almost smooth, yet has a bit of texture, and it is wonderful with certain sauces. It is hard to generalize just what kind of sauce is best with fresh pasta, but in this book you will find everything from a rustic yet sophisticated bean ragù to a light and sprightly lemon and pine nut sauce. On the other hand, the vigorous eggplant and mint sauce or the Peduzzis' cherry tomato and pepper sauce are better over dried pasta, which stands up to and complements the sauce.

• *For dried pasta, which brands are best?* The best dried pastas are the most expensive from Italy. I prefer Latini and Rustichella d'Abruzzo, both "boutique" pastas carefully made and presented in lovely packaging. They are made with fine, hard wheat that is dampened before being processed to remove the bran, then ground and sifted many times over before being combined with water and run in small quantities through bronze dyes for shaping. The pasta emerges with a rough, porous surface that easily captures the sauce and provides a satisfying, toothsome texture. The pasta then moves slowly through huge specially built ovens that dry it. If your budget doesn't allow for such artisanal perfection, De-Cecco pasta is perfectly acceptable, as is Barilla.

• *How much pasta is enough?* If you are serving pasta as a main course, 1 pound will easily feed four hungry people. As a first course, it will serve eight.

• *How much sauce is enough?* In Italy the pasta is the thing. Sauce is vital, of course, but pasta is considered delicious in its own right, not simply a vehicle for other flavors, so sauce quantities are less rather than more, enough to season but not overshadow.

• *What if the pasta sauce is dry?* Add pasta cooking water, judiciously of course, to moisten it.

• *What about sauces for flavored pastas?* Do as cooks traditionally do in Abruzzo, where they flavor fresh pasta with pepper, spinach, or tomatoes and then dress it with a simple but spicy sauce.

Giannola Nonino's Summer Zucchini Pasta

Segreti

• Reserving ¼ cup of the pasta cooking water is absolutely essential to this dish, so don't forget it!

• Tearing the basil leaves and adding them to the oil allows their perfume to infuse the oil with flavor.

The pale green of the zucchini, the darker green stripes of basil, and the glisten of wonderful oil make this quick pasta an essential part of anyone's summer repertoire. It was suggested to me by Giannola Nonino, whose family makes soft, delicate grappa in Friuli (see essay, page 246). Try it—it's easy to put together and delicious.

Serve the pasta with a gentle, light Soave Classico for a real treat.

⅓ cup extra-virgin olive oil
1 cup (gently packed) fresh
    basil leaves
1 pound good-quality dried penne
    or fusilli pasta

1 pound small zucchini, trimmed
    and cut into very thin rounds
6 tablespoons grated Parmigiano-
    Reggiano

1. Bring a large pot of salted water to a boil over high heat.

2. Pour the oil into a large bowl. Tear the basil leaves into fairly small pieces (about ¼ inch), add them to the oil, and stir to be sure they are completely immersed.

3. Add the pasta to the boiling water, stir, and cook until it has softened but is still quite firm in the center, 7 to 8 minutes; then add the zucchini and stir. Continue cooking until the pasta is al dente (tender but still firm to the bite), another 2 min-

utes. Drain the pasta and zucchini, reserving ¼ cup of the cooking water.

4. Add the pasta and zucchini to the oil and basil and toss thoroughly, then sprinkle with the cheese and toss. Season to taste with salt, toss, then pour the reserved cooking water over the pasta and toss again. Serve immediately.

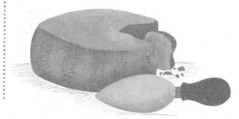

Pasta with Broccoli

In Sicily in winter, broccoli is omnipresent. Tumbling from the backs of trucks that have just come in from the fields, piled high and haphazardly in market stalls, stacked on the sidewalk in front of tiny groceries, it begs to be taken home and transformed into delicious dishes.

Italian broccoli isn't the broccoli Americans know. It looks like vivid green cauliflower, each head weighing upwards of 2 pounds. And its flavor is infinitely more delicate than that of American broccoli. This recipe is the most common preparation for broccoli in Sicily—in both farm and urban kitchens. The blend of raisins, pine nuts, and anchovies—the Sicilian triumvirate—comes from the Arab influence, which dates back centuries.

I first tasted pasta with broccoli in Palermo, where it was prepared by my friend Gabriella Cusimano. I was won over by the subtle Sicilian layers of flavor. Gabriella made this dish several hours in advance and told me it was as typical to serve it at room temperature as it was to serve it piping hot.

Serve a corpulent Sicilian Corvo Rosso along with this exceptional dish.

2 pounds broccoli, stems trimmed, peeled, and cut into ½-inch chunks, and florets separated; or 1 good-size head cauliflower (about 3 pounds), trimmed and cut into florets
Scant ¼ teaspoon saffron (optional)
¼ cup extra-virgin olive oil
5 cloves garlic, cut in half, green germ removed

6 anchovy fillets, rinsed, patted dry, and coarsely chopped
½ cup pine nuts
½ cup currants
¾ cup Nunzio's Tomato Sauce (page 424)
1 pound good-quality dried short pasta, such as fusilli or penne
Fine sea salt

Segreti

• This is at its most delicious when made with very fresh, very green broccoli, though cauliflower makes a worthy substitute.

• To get the most flavor from saffron, soak it first in hot water, then add it with the soaking water to a dish. Don't use Mexican saffron, which has a brighter color but next to no flavor.

1. Bring 3 cups of water to a boil in a large pot over high heat. Place the broccoli in a steamer and set it over the boiling water. Cover, reduce the heat to medium, and steam until it is tender but still resists the point of a knife, about 10 minutes. Remove it from the heat.

2. If using the saffron place it in a cup, add 1 tablespoon of boiling water, and let sit for 5 minutes.

3. Heat the oil with the garlic in a large heavy skillet over medium heat. Cook, stirring, until the garlic turns golden, about 3½ minutes. Add the anchovies and cook, stirring and crushing them with the spatula, until they form a sort of paste. Add the pine nuts, stir, and cook until they become pale golden, about 3 minutes. Add the currants, tomato sauce, ¼ cup water, and the saffron.

4. Reduce the heat to low, add the broccoli, and stir to coat the florets with the sauce. Cover and cook until the broccoli is tender and heated through, about 7 minutes. Remove from the heat and keep covered.

5. While the broccoli is cooking, bring a large pot of salted water to a boil over high heat. Add the pasta, stir, and cook until it is al dente (tender but still firm to the bite), about 7 minutes. Drain, reserving some of the cooking liquid. Transfer the pasta to a warmed serving bowl, add the broccoli mixture, and toss to thoroughly combine the ingredients. If the dish seems dry, add just enough of the cooking water to moisten it to your liking, then season with salt. Serve immediately.

Stromboli's Pasta (or Pasta of the Sun)

This is a traditional pasta dish on the island of Salina, part of the Eolian archipelago off the western coast of Sicily. Salina sits between the islands of Lipari and Stromboli—home of a volatile volcano that puts on a light show, spewing a spume of sparks from its crater every night of the year. It follows that the people of Salina would have a dish that evokes their fiery neighbor, and this is it.

On Salina fresh cherry tomatoes are an important ingredient in the cuisine year-round. In summer they are picked from the plants that grow in every *orto,* or vegetable garden, on the island. As the season wanes, the cherry tomatoes are gathered and hung in bunches from terraces, tree branches, any spot where there is shade.

The traditional cheese of choice for this dish is baked ricotta, which is mild and slightly sweet. You can make your own by baking in a 200°F oven 1 pound of ricotta in a baking dish covered with aluminum foil until it is golden and firm, 3 to 4 hours. Otherwise, simply do as suggested here and use an ample amount of freshly grated ricotta salata or Parmigiano-Reggiano.

The cheese symbolizes the ash on Stromboli's volcano, the hot peppers its fiery heat. This is a lovely, bright, fun dish to be enjoyed with lovely, bright company and a bottle of Colomba Platino.

1 pound good-quality dried
spaghetti
2 tablespoons extra-virgin olive oil
2 cloves garlic, green germ removed,
diced
5 cups ripe, firm cherry tomatoes,
stemmed and cut in half

Hot paprika or cayenne pepper
Fine sea salt
2½ cups (gently packed) fresh basil
leaves
3 cups (about 6 ounces) freshly
grated ricotta salata or
Parmigiano-Reggiano

1. Bring a large pot of salted water to a boil over high heat. Add the spaghetti, stir, and cook until it is al dente (tender but still firm to the bite), about 7 minutes.

2. While the pasta is cooking, heat the oil and garlic in a large heavy skillet over medium heat. When the garlic begins to sizzle, stir it and let it cook until it begins to turn translucent but doesn't brown, 1 to 2 minutes.

Add the tomatoes, stir, and cook just until they begin to lose their shape and are hot, 2 to 3 minutes. Season with hot paprika and salt to taste and remove from the heat.

3. Coarsely chop the basil and stir it into the tomatoes. Drain the pasta and transfer it to a warmed platter. Mound the tomatoes on top, then mound with the cheese so that the effect is somewhat dramatic—like a volcano. Serve immediately!

NOTE: Just before you eat the pasta, which should look like a volcano when it is served, mix the sauce with the pasta so it is well distributed.

Peppers with Pasta Peduzzi

**PASTA CON
PEPERONI ALLA
PEDUZZI**

4 SERVINGS

Lunch with the Peduzzi family of Pianella, a town outside the city of Pescara in Abruzzo, is a lively affair. Signora Nicolina Sergiacomo, the matriarch—and as powerful as all Abruzzo women are reputed to be—sits at the head of the table surrounded by her children, Gianluigi and Stefania Peduzzi, their spouses, and her grandchildren. All the Peduzzis live in the same building, which also houses the offices of Rustichella d'Abruzzo, the family's pasta company.

Each day the family assembles for meals with Nicolina Sergia-como presiding. I sat at her side and took notes as she carefully explained each dish to me. Of course, she double-checked to make sure that I got it all right. How she could tell with my mixture of English, French, and Italian notes I'll never know, but she seemed satisfied.

This dish, she explained, is typical to Abruzzo, where even the poorest family always had a vegetable garden. Their tradition was to cook the vegetables simply and stir them into pasta, then slather them with hot peppers. I watched as the Peduzzis all added hot peppers to the dish with abandon. They in turn watched as I judiciously tasted the pasta—it was fiery but flavorful—and laughed when I added just a little of the peppers. "How can you ever be an Italian if you use so little?" Giancarlo, Stefania's husband, said. "Come on, you need more!"

Simple and delicious, the pasta must be served with the hot peppers for the full Abruzzese effect. But do add them with discretion.

Serve a lively, simple white wine, such as Trebbiano d'Abruzzo, to complement the peppery flavor.

10 ounces good-quality short dried
    pasta, such as penne,
    farfalle, or fusilli
2 tablespoons extra-virgin olive oil
2 cloves garlic, green germ
    removed, cut lengthwise in
    thin slices

1½ pounds cherry tomatoes,
    stemmed and cut into
    quarters
Fine sea salt
1 cup fresh flat-leaf parsley leaves
1 recipe Hot Peppers Abruzzese
    (page 391)

1. Bring a large pot of salted water to a boil over high heat. Add the pasta, stir, and cook until it is al dente (tender but still firm to the bite), about 7 minutes. Drain and keep warm.

2. While the pasta is cooking, place the oil and garlic in a

medium-size heavy skillet over medium-high heat. Cook until the garlic turns golden, about 2 minutes. Add the tomatoes, stir, and cook until they soften but don't entirely lose their shape, 4 to 5 minutes. Season to taste with salt and remove from the heat. Toss the tomato sauce with the pasta.

3. Mince the parsley, add it to the pasta, and toss until all is thoroughly combined. Adjust the seasoning and serve with the Abruzzese peppers alongside.

Pasta with Turnip Greens

ORECCHIETTE ALLE CIME DI RAPE

4 SERVINGS

This recipe is traditional to Pugliese cuisine, which is, by definition, a rural cuisine. Made with young *cime di rape*, or turnip greens, that have just come into flower, it is rich and green tasting, with a wonderful undercurrent of anchovy balanced by the delightful bite of hot peppers.

I have Dora Ricci, chef and owner of Al Fornello da Ricci, her family's restaurant in Ceglie Messapico, outside Ostuni, to thank for the recipe. In the restaurant kitchen she shares with her daughter, Antonella, she showed me not only how to prepare the greens but also how to make the small, ear-shaped orecchiette.

She and Antonella were particularly busy the night I visited them in the kitchen, and she turned the pasta making over to me. I was almost crushed by the responsibility as I tried to replicate the little pastas that flipped so easily from her fingers. No plates of orecchiette were sent back that night, so I guess my efforts were accepted!

Serve a wonderful full-bodied, lush, and slightly tannic red, such as Salice Salentino, along with this simple, flavorful dish.

Segreti

To get an additional layer of flavor from this recipe, cook the pasta in the same water in which you cook the turnip greens.

*1 pound turnip greens, in flower if
    possible, well rinsed*
4 anchovy fillets
5 tablespoons extra-virgin olive oil
*1 clove garlic, green germ removed
    thinly sliced crosswise*
1 imported dried bay leaf
*1 inch-long piece fresh hot pepper,
    such as serrano, with some seeds,
    or hot paprika to taste*
1 pound best-quality dried orecchiette
Fine sea salt

1. Bring a large pot of salted water to a boil over high heat. Add the greens, return to a boil, and cook until they are tender but not mushy, about 7 minutes. Using a slotted skimmer or tongs, remove the greens from the water and let them drain naturally so they aren't completely dry. Cover the pot of water to keep it warm. When the greens have drained, coarsely chop them.

2. Rinse the anchovies well under cool running water and pat them dry.

3. Heat the oil in a large heavy skillet over medium heat until hot but not smoking. Stir in the garlic, then add the bay leaf, hot pepper or paprika, and anchovies; cook, stirring to break up the anchovies, until the garlic begins to turn golden, 2 to 3 minutes. Add the greens to the mixture, stir, and cook until the greens have absorbed the oil and the flavors have had a chance to blend, about 12 minutes.

4. Return the pot of water to a boil. Add the pasta, stir, and cook until it is al dente (tender but still firm to the bite), 7 to 9 minutes. Drain the pasta, reserving some of the cooking water, and transfer it immediately to the greens in the skillet. Stir to combine, and if the pasta seems dry, add enough pasta cooking water to moisten it. Season to taste with salt, remove the bay leaf, and serve immediately.

NOTE: A hint of hot peppers is necessary in this recipe, but the amount you use depends on your own taste. Dora Ricci uses an inch-long piece of a pleasantly hot pepper. I follow her lead and suggest an inch-long piece of a fresh pepper such as serrano, with some seeds removed so it doesn't burn but lends a gentle, insistent heat.

Pasta and Potatoes

PASTA E PATATE

6 SERVINGS

Segreti

Whenever Sicilian cooks brown diced onions to start a sauce or other dish, they add about 2 tablespoons of water and braise the onions for the first few moments of cooking until the water evaporates. This removes any harshness from the onions, rendering them sweeter, softer, more delicious, and more digestible, as well as preventing them from burning.

asta e patate can be found throughout Italy. It's a traditional peasant dish guaranteed, with its mix of two starches, to fill empty stomachs, and typical to the Italian tradition, it happens to taste just delicious too.

I got this particular recipe from Mauro and Giuseppe Vena, two brothers who live and farm in the Madonie mountains, near the small town of Gangi (see essay, page 30). When I asked who cooked for this household of three men, which includes their father, Salvatore, Mauro dissolved in laughter as he replied, "Whichever of us gets up first." They claimed not to cook much, not to be good cooks, not to care, yet when they started talking about their food, I realized this wasn't true at all. Not only do they care about what they eat, but they also are skilled at flavoring and making something more out of a humble dish. This, then, is the Vena brothers' *Pasta e patate*.

Serve a chilled Regaleali Bianco with this, for true Sicilian flavor and flair.

2 tablespoons extra-virgin olive oil
1 medium onion, diced
1 pound waxy potatoes, such as
    Yellow Finn, peeled
1 cup Nunzio's Tomato Sauce
    (page 424)

Fine sea salt
1 pound good-quality dried pasta,
    such as short fusilli or spaghetti
    broken into short lengths, or penne
Hot Pepper Oil (page 389) and/or
    extra-virgin olive oil

1. Heat the olive oil and onion and just enough water to moisten the onion (about ¼ cup) in a large heavy saucepan over medium-high heat. Cook just until the water has evaporated, 4 to 5 minutes.

2. Cut the potatoes in uneven chunks ranging from ½ inch to 2 inches. Add the pota-

toes to the onions, stir, and add 4 to 5 cups water or enough to cover by about 2 inches. Bring to a boil over high heat, then reduce the heat and cook until the potatoes are tender but not mushy, 15 to 20 minutes. Add the tomato sauce, stir until the water returns to a boil, season with salt if necessary, and add the pasta. Stir, cover, and cook until the pasta is al dente (tender but still firm to the bite), about 7 minutes. The pasta should absorb almost all the water. If the mixture seems dry,

add just enough water to moisten the dish. Adjust the seasoning with salt.

3. Ladle the stew into 6 warmed soup bowls and pass the pepper oil and/or olive oil for drizzling on top.

Battuto

A *battuto* is a peculiarly Italian technique for cooking onions that retains their sweetness and lessens their bite. I have found it to be one of the more valuable *segreti*, or tricks, I learned in my travels through the culinary byways of Italy. If you follow this method, you'll never burn the onions that form the basis for so many dishes. When simmered gently in water, protected from the heat, the onions soften and are tender and ready to become the basis of a sauce, stew, or soup when the water has evaporated.

To make a *battuto*, place the required amount of olive oil and onions in a cold pan and add just enough water to moisten the onions—they should be completely moist but not swimming. Turn the heat under them to between medium and medium-high and let them cook until the water has evaporated, 3 to 4 minutes. At this point the onions should be sweet, translucent, and not quite tender—the same stage they would be if they'd been sautéed for 2 minutes in hot oil, only here there isn't a hint of browning.

Pasta with Fava Beans, Potatoes, and Basil

**PASTA CORTA
CON FAVE,
PATATE, E
BASILICO**

**6 TO 8
SERVINGS**

Typical to Liguria, this dish comes in different guises. While potatoes remain a constant, in spring and summer it includes fresh tiny fava beans; in summer and fall green beans are the vegetable of choice. It is wonderfully light and uses the best that Liguria offers: delectably sweet Ligurian basil, extra-virgin olive oil, and fresh vegetables grown close to the sea.

This dish is often made with *trofio*, a funny, homemade pasta. Barbara Piaggio, at Trattoria Ligagin, a country restaurant high in the hills above Santa Margherita Ligure, told me, "You must have crooked fingers to make this pasta, and that's why you don't find it very much!" You may use cavatappi, farfalle, or even fusilli for this dish—each captures the sauce equally well.

Try a lovely light, fruity, lightly chilled white wine, such as Cinque Terre, with this.

FOR THE VEGETABLES AND PASTA
3 pounds fresh small fava beans
*   in their pods, shelled and*
*   skinned (see Note), or*
*   12 ounces green beans,*
*   trimmed and cut crosswise*
*   in half*
12 ounces new potatoes, peeled and
*   cut crosswise into ¼-inch-thick*
*   slices*
1 pound good-quality dried
*   pasta, such as cavatappi,*
*   farfalle, or fusilli*

FOR THE BASIL PESTO
1 clove garlic, cut in half, green
*   germ removed*
⅓ cup (generous ½ ounce) grated
*   Parmigiano-Reggiano*
1 tablespoon pine nuts
7 cups (loosely packed) fresh
*   basil leaves*
¼ cup extra-virgin olive oil
Fine sea salt

TO FINISH THE PASTA
1 tablespoon unsalted butter

1. Bring a large pot of salted water to a boil over high heat. Add the fava or green beans, return to a boil, and boil until they have softened but still have texture, about 3 minutes for favas, 5 to 7 minutes for green beans. If using favas, remove them at this point with a slotted spoon; the green beans require further cooking. Add the potatoes and cook until they are tender, about 5 minutes. Be sure not to overcook the potatoes so they won't fall apart. Using a slotted spoon, remove the vegetables from the pan and loosely cover them so they retain their heat.

2. Return the pot of cooking water to a boil, add the pasta, stir, and cook until it is al dente (tender but still firm to the bite), about 7 minutes.

3. While the pasta is cooking, prepare the pesto. Place the garlic, cheese, and pine nuts in a large mortar or food processor and grind with a pestle or process until they are minced. Add the basil and grind or process until it is minced. Add the oil in a fine stream, mixing or processing all the while so that it combines well with the other ingredients. Sea-

son to taste with salt and transfer to a large shallow serving bowl.

4. When the pasta is cooked, drain it, reserving ½ cup of the cooking water. Add the pasta to the pesto along with the vegetables and toss. Add the butter and toss, then add enough of the cooking water so the pasta is pleasantly moist, not watery. Adjust the seasoning and serve.

NOTE: If your fava beans are very fresh, you may not need to peel them. Sample one and see. If the peel is bitter, the favas will be better off without it (see box, page 91).

Tuscan Basil Belief

Basil should always be torn, not cut with metal, which will destroy its flavor and aroma.

Pasta with Favas and Basil

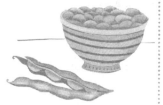

After a long day of research I was back in the small, comfortable apartment I'd rented on the Il Colle farm near Trequanda, a village in the heart of Tuscany. In the back seat of the car were the spoils of the day: a generous bag of fresh favas and bunches of aromatic basil, gifts from the farmers I'd been to visit. I already had a bottle of olive oil from Il Colle and a bag of good hard-wheat pasta, so my dinner menu was set. I made and ate this pasta sitting on the small terrace outside my door that overlooked the village.

The rolling landscape was sculpted in hues of every imaginable green—dusty from the olive trees, kelly from the wheat, forest from the trees, emerald from the wild grasses. I thought as I ate, if you grow up in this part of Tuscany where can you go to see anything more beautiful?

I sipped the 1994 Il Colle Chianti produced on the farm and found it surprisingly gutsy and good. Everyone I'd talked to sniffed at 1994, considering it a poor wine year but the more I learned, the more I realized that the Chianti region is full of microclimates. What is a bad year in one vineyard can be excellent in another. Thus categorizing any year as bad for all Chianti is shortsighted. Chiantis must be judged individually, as should most wines.

When you find a Chianti you like, make this dish to serve along with it. You are sure to be satisfied.

1 tablespoon plus ⅓ cup extra-
   virgin olive oil
2 pounds fresh fava beans in their
   pods, shelled and skinned
   (about 2 cups; see Note)
Fine sea salt

1½ cups (gently packed) fresh
   basil leaves
1 pound good-quality dried
   short pasta, such as penne or
   fusilli

1. Heat the 1 tablespoon olive oil and the favas in a medium-size skillet over medium heat. Add ¼ cup water, stir, and season lightly with salt. Cook, shaking the pan so the favas cook evenly, until they are tender but still bright green, about 20 minutes. Remove from the heat.

2. Meanwhile, bring a very large pot of salted water to a boil over high heat.

3. Tear the basil leaves into large bite-size pieces if they are very large. Combine the basil with the remaining extra-virgin olive oil in a large bowl and stir to moisten the leaves with the oil.

4. Add the pasta to the boiling water, stir, and cook just until it is al dente (tender but still firm to the bite), about 7 minutes. Drain, reserving about ½ cup of the cooking water. Add the pasta to the basil and toss to completely coat the pasta with the oil. Add the fava beans and toss until they are evenly distributed throughout the pasta, adding a bit of the pasta cooking water if the pasta seems dry. Adjust the seasoning and serve.

NOTE: If your fava beans are very fresh, you may be able to leave on the inner peel. Sample one and see. If the peel is bitter, the favas will be better off without it (see box, page 91).

Spaghetti with Bread Crumbs

SPAGHETTI CON MOLLICA

6 TO 8 SERVINGS

This is one of the most basic of Sicilian pastas and, in my opinion, one of the best. The primary ingredient, apart from pasta, is *mollica*, carefully toasted crumbs made from Sicilian *pane di casa*, or everyday bread. Their use is born of inventive frugality: the Sicilian farm cook wouldn't think to throw away leftover bread; instead, she grinds it, then turns it into a distinctive ingredient of its own. Sprinkled over pasta, greens, or vegetables, it adds gives a toasty flavor and crisp texture.

The first time I had this dish was late on a cool spring night at

Anna Sapuppo's farm, Alcala. Her cook, Nunzio San Filippo, had left his tomato sauce and the *mollica* ready, and all Anna did was toss them with the pasta. Sitting at a table lit with a single candle in the little cottage that faced Anna's citrus grove, I was captivated. With the majesty of Mount Etna right behind it, who wouldn't be?

After first tasting this dish at Anna's, I was to have many more variations on the theme, but hers has remained my favorite. This is the recipe she gave me—it works every time—and it has become a favorite at our house. Like many Italian pastas, this is not a "saucy" one but a delicate balance of sauce and pasta.

Try this with a wonderful Cerasuolo di Vittoria from the small COS winery, near Vittoria, or another gutsy, aromatic red wine.

¼ cup extra-virgin olive oil

2 cloves garlic, green germ removed, minced

4 anchovy fillets, coarsely chopped

¼ cup Nunzio's Tomato Sauce (page 424)

½ cup (gently packed) fresh flat-leaf parsley leaves

1 pound good-quality dried spaghetti

¼ cup Toasted Bread Crumbs (page 427)

Hot Pepper Oil, for seasoning (page 389; optional)

1. Bring a large pot of salted water to a boil over high heat.

2. Meanwhile, heat the oil and garlic in a large skillet over medium-high heat. Add the anchovies and stir until they are broken up. Stir in the tomato sauce, bring to a simmer, and remove from the heat.

3. Mince the parsley, stir it into the sauce, and transfer to a large serving bowl.

4. Add the pasta to the boiling water, stir, and cook until it is al dente (tender but still firm to the bite), about 7 minutes. Drain the pasta, add it to the sauce along with the bread crumbs, and toss it all together so the sauce is well mixed with the pasta. Serve immediately with the hot oil alongside.

COS

Giusto Occhipinti, part owner of the very successful COS winery in southeast Sicily, not far from the town of Caltagirone, well known for its ceramics, produces some of the best *cerasuolo* (a gutsy, berry-rich Sicilian red wine made with traditional Nero d'Avola, Nerello Mascarese, and Frappato di Vittoria grapes), claims his interest in wine began as a lark.

"You know those long, hot, high-school summers that stretched on forever with nothing at all to do?" he asked me one evening as we sat in his kitchen over a meal that he had prepared. He explained that when he was a boy, summer holidays stretched from May to October. To alleviate the unending boredom, he and two friends, Pinuccia Strano and Titta Cilia, decided to help crush grapes.

"The father of one of my friends owned a winery, and he put us to work," Giusto said. Following tradition, they strapped wide blocks of wood to their feet, descended the steps carved into the side of the old cool stone vat, and literally stomped the grapes. It's easy to see how Giusto would have been in his element. Gifted with a ready sense of humor, capable of seeing the funny side of just about every situation, he was surely the one who kept the others laughing as they stomped.

The three friends loved the work and continued doing it for many summers. One year they decided to make their own wine, so they bought local grapes and rented the winery for the time it took to crush and blend them. Their wine developed with a rich, deep flavor and was a surprising success. Each year they made a bit more until eventually, in 1980, they bought the winery and renamed it COS (a combination of the first letters of their last names). To their delight, their wine began garnering the attention of the local industry, then it began to win national prizes.

Giusto, who is also a practicing architect, shrugged. He pretends that the winery is simply a hobby, but when he talks about it, it is with excitement. Clearly he invests a lot of love and pride in the winery. He showed me the collection of empty wine bottles he keeps on the mantle in his kitchen, many of their labels signed by those who enjoyed them. "You see those bottles," he said. "Each tells a story—a good, interesting, rich story— just like the bottle we've drunk tonight will tell. That's wine."

Giusto does much of the marketing for the winery, traveling around Sicily and beyond when he can take the time. He's a natural. Though he speaks only Italian and Sicilian, he manages to communicate with everyone. "All you need is a good bottle of wine and some delicious food," he said with a burst of laughter.

Sicily has always produced a substantial river of full-bodied grape juice, much of which was, until ten to fifteen years ago, bought up by French wineries to shore up the body of their wines. The little wine actually made in Sicily was considered uninteresting and low in quality. Sicilian wine makers had to battle two substantial enemies—lack of water and intense heat. The first was always threatening their grapes, the second their wine making. That has all changed, thanks in part to wineries like COS, which was among the first in Sicily to add refrigeration to the process, keeping the grape juice cool and allowing them more time to make their wine. COS is just one of an emerging group of Sicilian

vinters whose wines are being recognized worldwide.

Giusto is very happy with the progress they've made. "We've grown slowly and carefully, asking the advice of the right people along the way," Giusto told me. "We have no debts. All the money we make from the winery we put right back into it." The only problem they do have is that they simply cannot keep up with the demand.

Several years ago Titta Cilia sold her share to Giusto and Pinuccia, who is also a practicing architect, and the two continue to run it successfully. "We are lucky being architects," Giusto acknowledged. "We don't depend on the winery, so we can make the kind of wine we want to make. It's the same for architecture really. Because we have the winery, I, for instance, can afford to do only the jobs I want to do. It all works together very well."

I left Sicily a couple of days after visiting with Giusto, with a half-dozen bottles of COS Cerasuolo di Vittoria. After letting it settle for a couple of weeks at home, I uncorked a bottle. One whiff of its aroma and I was back in that sun-drenched land, eating pasta in Giusto's kitchen with friends, sipping wine, and listening to tales of Sicily's past and future. COS wines are appropriate for this very special island, for they, too, are unforgettable.

Tiny Little Meat Ravioli

AGNOLOTTI

4 TO 6 SERVINGS

These mini ravioli, with their aromatic pork and beef filling, are as much a part of Piedmont as the rolling hills covered with vineyards, the winding roads, the white truffles of fall. They are served in farmhouses and restaurants throughout the region, and each recipe is slightly different from the next, dependent on the tastes of the cook who makes them. Maria Manera, a wine-grape grower near Alba, shaves white truffles over her *agnolotti* if Luciano, her husband and a passionate mushroom hunter, has happened to find one.

This recipe is a distillation of Maria's *agnolotti* and those I sampled at the wonderful country trattoria I Bologna in the small town of Rocchetta Tanara, near Asti, where they also serve them with white truffle when it's in season. Don't feel you must have a truffle to make these, however, for they are sublime without it.

Try these with a delicious sprightly red, like Barbera d'Alba.

FOR THE AGNOLOTTI
7 ounces finely ground beef round
   (generous ¾ cup)
3½ ounces finely ground pork,
   a mixture of lean and fatty
   (scant ½ cup)
1 ounce (about 6 leaves) fresh
   spinach, trimmed, well
   rinsed, and minced
Fine sea salt

1 medium egg
1 cup (about 2 ounces) grated
   Parmigiano-Reggiano
Semolina, for dusting the
   baking sheet
1 recipe Fresh Pasta Dough
   (page 434)

FOR THE SAGE BUTTER
8 tablespoons (1 stick) unsalted
   butter
14 medium fresh sage leaves

1 fresh white truffle (optional)

pasta wheel

Sage

1. Place the beef and pork in a large skillet over medium heat and cook, breaking up the clumps with a wooden spoon, until almost all of it is no longer pink, about 5 minutes. Add the spinach and cook, stirring occasionally, until the meat is cooked through and the spinach is completely wilted, another 5 minutes. Season with salt and let cool to room temperature. Pass the meat mixture through the finest disk of a meat grinder or pulse several times in a food processor until it is very finely ground but not a purée. Transfer the meat mixture to a small mixing bowl, add the egg, and mix well. Add the cheese and mix well, then adjust the seasoning. Set aside while you prepare the pasta.

2. Generously dust 2 baking sheets with an even layer of semolina. Follow the pasta dough directions, steps 1 through 3. Reserve 4 pieces for the agnolotti. Roll the remaining 4 pieces into strips, then dry them and store for future use (see Note).

3. Keeping the dough you're not working with under a lightly dampened tea towel, roll a reserved dough piece through each setting of the rollers once, without folding it, until you have a long strip that is about 6 inches wide. Repeat with the remaining dough pieces. Cut the strip of dough lengthwise in half with a ravioli wheel. Lay one of these 3-inch-wide strips in front of you and cover the other with a lightly dampened tea towel. Place scant teaspoonsful of the filling on the lower half of the strip of dough in front of you, leaving about ¼ inch between each spoonful of stuffing. You should have about 16 mounds of filling on the strip. Fold the top half of the dough over the filling so that the edges meet, and press between the mounds of stuffing so that the pasta dough sticks together and you remove as much air as possible from between the layers. Then press the edges together firmly. Using the ravioli cutter, cut between the agnolotti, trimming off any excess pasta dough. Take each agnolotto and squeeze it gently at each end so the center of it

sits up a bit. Transfer the agnolotti as they are made to a prepared baking sheet. Repeat with the remaining pasta pieces until all the filling is used. You should have about 128 agnolotti.

4. Prepare the sage butter. Melt the butter in a small saucepan over low heat. Stack the sage leaves and cut them crosswise into very fine strips. Add them to the butter, swirl it, and keep warm over very low heat. Don't cook the sage leaves or they will become crisp and bitter.

5. Bring a large pot of salted water to a boil over high heat. Add some of the agnolotti to the pan without crowding them. When they begin to rise to the surface, taste one and keep checking them every 30 seconds or so; remove them from the water with a slotted spoon as soon as they are cooked through, 2 to 3 minutes. Repeat with the remaining agnolotti.

6. Divide the agnolotti among warmed shallow soup bowls and spoon the sage butter over the top. Shave equal amounts of the white truffle, if using, over each serving.

Pasta with Zucchini Flower Sauce

PASTA CON FIORI DI ZUCCA

4 TO 6 SERVINGS

I was at the market in Medicina, a sweet little town in Emilia-Romagna. After stopping at a café for coffee and a *bombolon,* a sort of jelly doughnut, I walked to the town square where a handful of trucks was parked with small tables in front piled with vegetables, fruits, clothing. Francesca Passatempi, a young farmer whose family I had met through mutual friends, had her produce neatly stacked on a makeshift table, and she was in the midst of carefully packing wide-open zucchini blossoms into paper sacks for a customer. The customer, Luisa Piadina, paid and walked away with me close on her heels, for I was curious what she had planned for the flowers. Since they were open, I doubted she would stuff them (the stuffing wouldn't stay inside) and, indeed, that wasn't her intention. Instead, she was going to use them to prepare this pasta sauce.

I was delighted to find such a simple and unusual use for zucchini flowers. They are abundant in summer gardens, and dishes for them are scarce. I jotted down the recipe and made it as soon as I returned to my home and my garden, which was filled with zucchini blossoms. The sauce was as delicious, easy, elegant, and fresh as it sounded. Surprisingly, for such delicate blossoms, the flowers have an intense, lovely, pure flavor, and they lend that as well as their rich golden color to this dish.

With this, try a light Sauvignon Bianco, lightly chilled.

12 ounces good-quality dried fusilli
or penne pasta
9 fresh mint leaves
1 tablespoon extra-virgin olive oil
2 small onions, sliced paper thin

30 zucchini flowers, pistils removed,
rinsed quickly, gently patted dry,
and cut lengthwise into strips
Fine sea salt

1. Bring a large pot of salted water to a boil over high heat. Add the pasta, stir, and cook just until it is al dente (tender but still firm to the bite), about 7 minutes.

2. About 5 minutes before the pasta is cooked, stack the mint leaves and cut crosswise into fine slivers. Heat the oil and onions in a large skillet over medium heat and cook just until the onions begin to turn translucent, about 1½ minutes. Add the zucchini flowers and mint. Stir, season lightly with salt, cover, and cook until the flowers have softened, about 3 minutes. Check the flowers and shake the pan occasionally to be sure they

are cooking evenly. They should be very soft but not at all mushy. Remove from the heat.

3. Drain the pasta, reserving ½ cup of the cooking water.

Place the pasta in a serving bowl, add the zucchini flower mixture along with the cooking water, and toss gently but thoroughly. Adjust the seasoning.

Architect's Sauce

**PASTA ALLA
GIUSTO**

**4 TO 6
SERVINGS**

Giusto Occhipinti is part owner of the exciting COS winery in Sicily (see essay, page 124) and a practicing architect. He travels Sicily a great deal and is particularly drawn to Trapani, on the island's west coast. There one sees in the architecture, culture, and cuisine the results of Arab domination in Sicily many centuries ago.

This sauce is Giusto's ode to Trapani and like Trapani, it reflects rich tradition, mystery, and warmth. He makes it often because it suits his gastronomic sense of adventure with its textures and flavors that pop on the palate. As Giusto says, the sauce must be made and waiting for the hot pasta, whose heat will warm up the herbs and cause their flavors to flow. Mix the pasta into the sauce quickly and thoroughly, and don't linger—eat it immediately, with or without cheese. Don't think there is too much sauce—it is exactly the amount required for one pound of pasta. Giusto says even if you're a garlic lover hold off adding more garlic, for it will imbalance the harmony of flavors. I totally agree with him, but that said, you must do as you like. Also, the sauce is intended for high-quality short dried pasta, such as corkscrew fusilli, farfalle, which are shaped like butterflies (or bow ties), conchiglie, which are shaped like seashells, or lumache, which are shaped like snails.

Serve it with a deep and rich red wine, such as a Cerasuolo di Vittoria (from COS winery, of course!).

⅓ cup almonds, skins removed

3 tablespoons pine nuts

¼ cup walnut halves, skins
removed (see Note)

1 clove garlic, green germ removed,
minced

3 tablespoons capers, rinsed and
patted dry

3 cups (gently packed) fresh
basil leaves

2 tablespoons (gently packed) fresh
mint leaves

¾ cup (gently packed) fresh
arugula leaves

7 tablespoons extra-virgin
olive oil

1 pound ripe tomatoes, cored

Fine sea salt

1 pound good-quality dried short
pasta, such as fusilli, farfalle,
conchiglie, or lumache

4 ounces ricotta salata or ¾ cup
grated Parmigiano-Reggiano
(1½ ounces)

mezzaluna

1. Coarsely chop together the nuts and minced garlic, using a mezzaluna or chef's knife. Place the capers on top of the nut mixture and coarsely chop. Place the basil, mint, and arugula on top of the nuts and capers and continue chopping until the greens are minced very fine. The nuts don't need to be evenly minced; in fact, they should be in uneven pieces. Place the mixture in a large serving bowl and stir in the oil.

2. Finely chop the tomatoes and add them with any juices to the bowl. Stir and season to taste with salt.

3. Bring a large pot of salted water to a boil. Add the pasta to the boiling water, stir, and cook until it is al dente (tender but still firm to the bite), 7 to 10 minutes. Drain the pasta, reserving some of the cooking water, and add the pasta to the sauce. Toss it well, adding up to 3 tablespoons of the cooking water as you toss so the ingredients blend well. Adjust the seasoning and serve with the cheese alongside.

NOTE: Removing the skins from walnuts may seem like a futile exercise, but the results are worth it, for walnut skins contain an appreciable amount of tannin, which can be bitter. Without the skins on them you get the wonderful, buttery walnut flavor in all its completeness. To skin walnuts, bring a small pan of water to a boil over medium-high heat. Plunge the walnuts into the water, return it to a boil, and boil for about 40 seconds. Drain the walnuts and remove the skins, using a sharp-bladed knife to help you loosen them.

Angelo's Fabulous Pasta with Herbs

LA PASTA FAVOLOSA DI ANGELO CON ERBE

6 SERVINGS

I first tasted this dish with the Lancellotti family in Soliera, outside Modena (see essay, page 80). Their restaurant, Ristorante Lancellotti, was closed to celebrate the birthday of Ida Lancellotti, the family matriarch. When Angelo, the eldest sons, brought it to the table, its buttery, herbal aroma preceded it. With the first mouthful I was won over by its simply fresh and subtle taste.

This dish is meaningful to the Lancellotis because it was one of the first Angelo created for the restaurant, which signaled its departure from the traditional cuisine his parents had always prepared. Diners accustomed to pasta dressed with ragùs, beans, or other traditional sauces at first thought it odd, but it has since become a signature favorite. I could have made a meal of it and almost did, for Camillo served me seconds while my head was turned. Oh well, I thought as I picked up my fork again, there are definitely worse things in life than this.

Serve a slightly spritzy Lambrusco di Sorbara alongside.

6 tablespoons (¾ stick) unsalted
   butter
1 cup (loosely packed) fresh oregano
   or marjoram leaves
1 large bunch chives (for 1 cup

   minced)
1 recipe Fresh Pasta Dough (page
   434), cut into tagliatelle
Fine sea salt

1. Bring a large pot of salted water to a boil over high heat.

2. Meanwhile, melt the butter in a small saucepan over low heat, then remove from the heat. Mince the herbs and add them to the butter, mixing well.

3. Add the tagliatelle to the boiling water, stir, and cook until al dente (tender but still firm to the bite), which will take about 1 to 1½ minutes.

4. Drain the tagliatelle and transfer to a warmed serving bowl. Pour the butter and herbs over the tagliatelle, season lightly with salt, and toss until the pasta is thoroughly coated with the herbs and butter. Serve immediately.

Lemon and Pine Nut Tagliatelle

TAGLIATELLE CON LIMONE E PINOLI

6 TO 8 SERVINGS

Segreti

Be sure to let the pine nuts macerate in the oil so they can lend their sweet flavor.

Lisa Bonacossi, her husband, Ugo Contini Bonacossi, and most of their seven children run the Capezzana winery near Pistoia, in Tuscany. Though Lisa Bonacossi is from a noble family, she is the kind of person who can't stay out of the kitchen (any more than she can stay away from the winery), and she often prepares simple country dishes herself.

"This is one of my favorite pastas," Lisa Bonacossi said, citing its simplicity. "It is made with the lemons, pine nuts, and oil that everyone has at hand." The flavors are simple and brilliant. The sauce is best served with fresh tagliatelle. I serve it with lemon wedges too for those who like to squeeze a bit of fresh juice over the pasta.

Serve this with a well-chilled Pinot Grigio for a nice, bright combination.

1 cup (gently packed) fresh flat-leaf
    parsley leaves
½ cup extra-virgin olive oil
Zest of 2 lemons, cut into fine
    (julienne) strips
½ cup pine nuts, lightly toasted
    (see box, page 348)

Fine sea salt
1 recipe Fresh Pasta Dough
    (page 434), cut into tagliatelle
Freshly ground black pepper
1 lemon, cut into 6 wedges
    (optional)

1. Mince the parsley and place it in a large shallow bowl. Add the oil, lemon zest, and pine nuts and mix until well combined. Season with salt, cover, and let sit for at least 2 hours at room temperature.

2. Bring a large pot of salted water to a boil over high heat. Add the tagliatelle, stir, and cook until it is al dente (tender but still firm to the bite), 1 to 1½ minutes. Drain, reserving ½ cup of the cooking water.

3. Add the hot pasta along with the cooking water immediately to the prepared sauce and toss until the sauce is thoroughly distributed. Season with salt and pepper and toss again.

4. To serve, use two spoons and carefully scoop up the pasta, making sure to get pine nuts with each serving (see Note). Serve with the lemon wedges if desired for squeezing atop the pasta.

NOTE: The pine nuts tend to fall to the bottom of the bowl no

Pasta, Beautiful Pasta

In the old days in Emilia-Romagna (some say even now), if a woman didn't know how to make pasta, she would never find a husband. So girls began to learn how to make pasta well before they were ten years old and some as early as six. Ida Marverti Lancellotti, owner, cook, and "mama" at the Lancellotti Restaurant in Soliera, in Emilia-Romagna (see essay, page 80), remembers when she learned. "I was so small I had to stand on a box so I could reach the table to roll out the pasta." She also remembers loving to work beside her mother and grandmother, and the lesson not only took but blossomed. She, indeed, found a wonderful husband, Camillo Lancellotti, and has made a good living for herself and her family by putting her pasta-making skills to work in the family restaurant.

matter how well you toss the pasta. Once the pasta is served, simply return to the bowl and evenly distribute the remaining pine nuts over each serving.

Mama Lancellotti's Simple Ragù

RAGU SEIMPLICE
DI MAMMA
LANCELLOTTI

4
GENEROUS
SERVINGS

Segreti

• Mince (which means cut into tiny, tiny pieces) all the ingredients, and they will yield triple the flavor.

• For the *soffritto*, or vegetable mixture, you are striving for an equal amount of onion, carrot, and celery for flavor and color contrast.

What is a ragù? A ragù is a pasta sauce that is usually made with meat. Within that general definition are variations; for example, there is *ragù alla bolognese* and *ragù alla napoletana*. The first is a standard recipe that is actually registered with the Bologna Chamber of Commerce; it is a blend of meat, lemon zest, prosciutto, vegetables, including tomatoes, and a touch of cream. *Ragù alla napoletana* is more robust, with more meat, more tomatoes, more onions, and more cooking time.

That said, every farm cook has her own ragù, and this is one of two included here that come directly from Ida Lancellotti, the doyenne of Emilian cuisine who cooks at her family restaurant, Ristorante Lancellotti, in Soliera, near Modena. Both are extremely spare and simple, yet packed with flavor.

Try this with a good, toothy Albana di Romagna.

1 tablespoon extra-virgin olive oil
1 small onion, minced
1 medium rib celery, strings removed, minced
1 small carrot, minced
7 ounces prosciutto, cut into tiny dice
½ cup dry white wine, such as Frascati

4 large ripe tomatoes (about 1½ pounds), peeled and coarsely chopped, or the equivalent amount of good-quality canned tomatoes, coarsely chopped
Fine sea salt
1 recipe Fresh Pasta Dough (page 434), cut into tagliatelle

Segreti

Always save 1 cup of the pasta cooking water to add to a sauce or to the pasta once it is sauced in case it is needed to achieve the right moisture balance.

1. Heat the oil in a medium-size saucepan over medium-high heat. Add the vegetables and prosciutto, stir, and reduce the heat to medium-low. Cook, covered, until the vegetables are softened, about 10 minutes; stir occasionally to be sure they aren't sticking to the bottom of the pan.

2. Add the wine, stir, and continue cooking, covered, until the vegetables have absorbed the wine, about 15 minutes. Add ½ cup water, stir, and continue cooking until the vegetables have absorbed much of the water and are very tender, another 20 to 25 minutes.

3. Add the tomatoes, stir, and continue cooking until the sauce has become quite liquid, about 35 minutes. Uncover and cook, stirring occasionally, until the sauce has thickened, about 20 minutes. Season to taste with salt.

4. Bring a large pot of salted water to a boil over high heat. Add the pasta, stir, and cook until it is al dente (tender but still firm to the bite), about 1½ minutes. Drain.

5. Transfer the pasta to a serving platter and top with the sauce. Serve immediately.

Mama Lancellotti's Tagliatelle with Bean Ragù

**RAGU DI FAGIOLI
DI MAMMA
LANCELLOTTI**

**6 TO 8
SERVINGS**

I was in the kitchen with Ida Lancellotti at her restaurant, Ristorante Lancellotti, while she made this sauce, a mixture of this and that in the kitchen crowned with the glory of fresh borlotti beans.

Ida looks a bit frail and is treated like porcelain by her three handsome sons, but she could probably work me under the table. She hauled out a large prosciutto from the cooler and cut meat away from

it before dicing it carefully for the sauce. She methodically prepared the remaining ingredients and tipped them into a battered saucepan—no fancy kitchen equipment here—then proceeded to cook them together slowly, checking the mixture often, not rushing it.

The sauce made, she led me to the restaurant dining room (closed until evening), where space had been made for her pasta-making table. She proceeded to make the tagliatelle that would provide the base for this sauce, kneading and rolling with an energy that belied her more than seventy years. Within an hour, bright yellow clumps of tagliatelle rested on the flour-covered table—not a fleck of flour had migrated elsewhere. Camillo, Ida's husband, walked through the dining room with a *"Ciao"* and into the kitchen, where I followed to watch him turn on the heat under the sauce and heat a big pan of salted water for pasta. Ida brought in enough pasta for the family and me, and Camillo dropped it into the boiling water, calculating just the right amount. He stirred the sauce, removed the pasta at the perfect moment, and arranged it on a platter.

I have rarely had a more satisfying pasta sauce, with such depth of flavor from such simple ingredients. As Ida's son Angelo reminded me, "This isn't a fancy dish; it's a farmer's dish, but it is made with the best there is."

I raise a glass of fizzy Lambrusco—the most appropriate wine to accompany this—to farmers like Ida and Camillo, who make this kind of dish daily from the simplest of ingredients!

Storing Pasta

A few of the recipes in this book call for preparing more pasta than is necessary for completing the dish. If you don't use all that you've made, let it dry completely—it should be brittle—then carefully store it in an airtight tin or plastic container. It will keep for several weeks.

Cook homemade dried pasta as you would any commercial dried pasta, in plenty of boiling salted water, until al dente (tender but still firm to the bite). It will cook more quickly than commercial dried pasta.

Segreti

• The secret to the success of this sauce is slow, slow cooking. It should just be at a simmer, no more, so that the beans cook without bursting and everything blends into a wonderful, rich flavor.

• Ask for an end piece of prosciutto, which is hard for a butcher to sell and therefore usually much less expensive than slices from the prime part of the prosciutto.

• To cut the pork fat and the prosciutto in the required tiny dice, chill them in the freezer first. They shouldn't freeze but should be hardened enough that the knife cuts through easily.

2 pounds fresh shell beans, such as
    borlotti, cranberry, or coco blanc,
    shelled (scant 3 cups) or
    2 cups dried borlotti beans
1 small onion, diced
4 ounces pork fat, cut into tiny
    (1/16-inch) dice
5½ ounces prosciutto, cut into
    tiny dice
4 medium-size firm tomatoes, cored,
    peeled, and coarsely chopped
Fine sea salt

Tiny bit of freshly ground black
    pepper
1 recipe Fresh Pasta Dough (page
    434), cut into tagliatelle, or
    1 pound dried tagliatelle
½ cup fresh flat-leaf
    parsley leaves
    (optional)

1. Bring a large pot of water to a boil over high heat. Add the fresh beans, return to a boil, lower the heat to medium, and cook, uncovered, until they are tender but not soft or mushy, about 15 minutes. Using a slotted spoon, transfer the beans to a bowl and reserve them and the cooking liquid separately. (If using dried beans, place them in a large pot, cover with water, and bring to a boil over high heat. Remove from the heat, cover, and let sit for 1 hour. Drain the beans and add enough fresh water to cover by 2 inches. Bring to a boil, reduce the heat so the water is boiling gently, and cook until the beans are just tender but not cooked through, about 35 minutes. Transfer the beans to a bowl and reserve them and the cooking liquid separately.)

2. Place the onion and pork fat in a medium-size saucepan over low to medium-low heat and cook very slowly until the onions are golden, about 15 minutes, being careful not to let them brown. Add the prosciutto, stir, and cook until it turns slightly dark at the edges and appears cooked, about 8 minutes. Add the tomatoes, stirring and crushing them slightly, the beans, and enough of the bean cooking liquid to just cover the beans. Season lightly with salt. Bring to a boil, reduce the heat

to low, and cook at a slow simmer until the liquid has reduced by about one-third (the mixture should still be very liquid and not dry), the tomatoes are softened, and the beans are completely tender but retain their shape, 40 to 50 minutes. Season to taste with salt and a bit of pepper. Remove from the heat and keep warm.

3. Bring a large pot of salted water to a boil over high heat. Add the pasta, stir, and cook until it is al dente (tender but still

firm to the bite), about 1½ minutes for fresh and about 7 minutes for dried. Drain the pasta and transfer to a warmed platter. Reheat the sauce if necessary and pour it over the pasta. If garnishing with parsley, mince the leaves and sprinkle them over all. Serve immediately.

NOTE: The recipe calls for pork fat—not lard. It is an important ingredient not only because it adds flavor, but because the tiny dice, which keep their shape, add a wonderful texture.

Massimo's Lasagne al Forno

LASAGNE AL FORNO ALLA MASSIMO

6 SERVINGS

Massimo Gangeni, whose tiny plot of terraced land overlooks the Leira River valley above Genoa (see essay, page 258), makes a living farming everything from tomatoes to fava beans and raising chickens and rabbits. This is a favorite recipe of his, which he bakes in a wood-burning oven. Like all the food Massimo prepares, it is light, simple, and fresh.

Massimo uses either fresh ripe tomatoes or his own tomato sauce, depending on the season, but either way, this dish is a refreshingly light take on lasagne.

This is delightful with a rich red wine, like Rossese di Dolceacqua.

1 recipe Mamma Lancellotti's Pasta
    Variation (see box, page 436)
    (see Note)
4 cups Light and Lively Tomato
    Sauce (page 423)

4 cups Béchamel Sauce (page 426)
1¾ cups (about 4 ounces)
    Parmigiano-Reggiano
2 cups (gently packed) fresh
    basil leaves

1. Preheat the oven to 375°F. Brush a 14 x 10-inch heavy baking dish with oil.

2. Follow the pasta dough directions, steps 1 through 5, reserving half for the lasagne. Cut the remaining pasta into tagliatelle, dry, and store for future use (see Note).

3. Bring a large pot of salted water to a boil. Fill a large bowl with cold water. Cut the reserved pasta strips into manageable 14-inch lengths and add them to the boiling water one or two at a time. Cook just until they are al dente (tender but still firm to the bite), about 2 minutes. Transfer the noodles from the boiling water to the cold water and let cool for less than a minute, then lift and gently squeeze the noodles to remove as much of the water as possible. Lay the noodles on a tea towel spread on a work surface and pat them dry.

4. Cover the bottom of the baking dish with a layer of the pasta, overlapping the noodles slightly if necessary and letting the pasta crawl slightly up the sides of the pan. Spread with one-third of the tomato sauce, then one-third of the béchamel, and finally one-third of the cheese. Tear half of the basil leaves in small pieces and sprinkle them over all. Repeat twice more with all the ingredients except the basil, which stays in the inner layers.

5. Bake in the center of the oven until the cheese on top is golden and the lasagne is bubbling, about 40 minutes. Remove from the oven and let sit for about 15 minutes before serving.

NOTE: You will use just slightly less than half the lasagne pasta the recipe makes. I recommend making the whole recipe and simply drying the pasta you don't use for future use (see box, page 137).

A LOOK AT PARMIGIANO-REGGIANO

Luciano Catellani says he fought Goliath before he was able to raise the cows he wanted to raise and produce the quality of Parmigiano-Reggiano cheese he loved.

When he was little, working alongside his grandfather, it all seemed so simple—milking the *vacche rosse*—red cows from the Razza Reggiana breed—on the family farm and later watching huge wheels of Parmigiano-Reggiano cheese being made with their rich yellow milk. He loved running among the stocky cows with their distinctively long, straight noses and horns that tipped up toward the sun. They were gentle, their milk was sweet, and the cheese it produced was unlike any other.

But by the time Luciano was a young man, things had changed. Milking machines had become commonplace, as were Frisian cattle, referred to locally as simply *neri,* or black cows, and practically no one raised the *vacche rosse* anymore. "The *nero* gave more milk than the *rossa,* though not a lot," Luciano explained. "But since they were better adapted to the milking machines, everyone started raising them."

When Luciano graduated from agricultural school, where he specialized in animal husbandry, he, too, invested in the *nero.* "But when I really tasted the cheese made with their milk, I realized it was totally dif-

ferent from the cheese made with milk from my grandfather's cows," he said. While milk from the *nero* cattle is considered quite good, it lacks a certain finesse and richness found in milk from the *vacche rossa.*

He got rid of his Frisians and began a campaign to bring back the Reggiana breed. "No one believed that cheese made from their milk was better. No one remembered," he said. "For the farmers around here, the Reggiana was antiquated."

He says he worked alone against everyone for more than a decade to keep the race alive. Eventually the Universities of Bologna and Parma got involved with him through their agricultural departments, and the community of Cavriago, near Parma, offered land and a dairy for his experiment.

"But there were many other industries that wanted the land and the buildings, and I had to fight for them," he said, sweeping his hand to include the modest low-slung buildings set in the middle of pasture.

In 1991 financing came through, and Luciano started the Azienda Agricola Grano d'Oro, the cooperative he runs with his brother, Matteo, and six other workers. By 1993 the cooperative had a small herd of sixty Razza Reggiana cows and buildings and equipment on loan from the community of Cavriago.

The cattle live in airy barns, eat fresh grass and hay, and produce milk of astonishing creaminess. This milk is transformed into about eight hundred wheels of Parmigiano-Reggiano (each seventy-two pounds) a year. Each is stamped with the distinctive mark of the *vacche rosse,* two cows pulling an old-fashioned cart, in addition to the distinctive marks of Parmigiano-Reggiano. For the moment, most of their cheese is sold right at the *caseificio,* or dairy, though some goes to local restaurants.

Luciano hasn't lost a bit of the conviction that propelled him this far. "The *rossa* is a great animal. They're easier and cheaper to keep," he says. "They don't get sick. They're very strong."

Besides the sturdiness of the *vacca rossa,* its milk has a higher protein content, better consistency, and more elasticity, which accounts for richer, smoother flavor and texture in the cheese and more cheese per quart of milk.

Luciano took me to the store, where huge wheels of the cooperative's cheese sat, ready to be cut for the line of customers that stretched out the door. Luciano cut off a sliver for me to taste, and I savored the buttery, sharp, salty, creamy cheese. It was, indeed, the best Parmigiano-Reggiano I had ever tasted.

A Different Kettle of Milk

The following day I visited the *Caseificio San Giovanni,* a family-owned dairy in the small farming town of Soliera where Parmigiano-Reggiano is made with milk from *neri.* Its owner, Silvano Bergianti, refers to the Frisians as "American" cattle. He admits there is a difference between their milk and that of the Razza Reggiana, but what matters to him after more than forty years in the business is one thing—production. He's loyal to the *nero* because it gives more milk and is more comfortable with the milking machine than the *vacca rossa.* And he's very proud of the cheese he makes.

Bergianti showed me through his dairy, explaining the process as we went. "Parmigiano-Reggiano is a semicooked cheese. After we add some whey we collected last night to the skimmed and whole milk from this morning, we heat the mixture gently over gas burners and constantly stir it until it reaches body temperature," he said. He then adds rennet made with the enzymes of calves that have eaten only plants and flowers, and leaves the mixture for eighteen minutes. "One of the reasons the price of the cheese has risen is because the rennet is so expensive and hard to find," Bergianti explained.

The waiting period signaled the coffee break, and we walked over with the two dairy workers to the family kitchen next door, where Bergianti's wife, Alma Arletti, had coffee made and on the table alongside bags of commercial biscotti and fat homemade sausages with bread.

Since the milk coagulates rapidly, it was a hurried affair. The employees ate bowlsful of coffee, milk, and biscotti softened to a sort of mush, then rushed back to work.

When I returned from my more leisurely

break, they were standing over a large cauldron cutting the coagulated cheese into chunks, then mixing it with a huge oversized whisk to break it apart.

The cauldron tipped slightly, and the curdled cheese slid into a large square of cotton that the two workers tied to a wooden pole so it formed a sack, then carried it—each holding one end of the pole, whey gushing out onto their boots and the floor—to a table. There they turned out the curdled cheese and cut it in half, then fit each half into a round plastic mold that gives the cheese its initial shape. The whey remaining in the cauldrons was poured into huge glass bottles that were set in baskets insulated with straw, to be saved for making ricotta or for fermenting overnight and adding to the next day's cheese.

In the evening the cheeses are transferred to round wooden molds with tiny teeth inside that imprint the familiar Parmigiano-Reggiano name and the number of the *caseificio* on the outside of the cheese so it can be identified. The cheeses stay in the mold for up to seventy-two hours, then they go into a metal mold where they get their final shape, for up to seventy-two additional hours.

The next step for the cheeses, which weigh upwards of eighty pounds each at this point, is to sit in a brine of sea salt and water for twenty-two to twenty-four days. The brine soaks into the cheese and later, as it ages, will help the cheese expel moisture. It also has conserving and antibacterial effects.

When the cheeses come out of the brine, they go into an aging room, where they are stacked from floor to ceiling. It is in this cooled room that they slowly take on the characteristic golden rind with its rusty colored markings and the buttery, sharp flavor characteristic of Parmigiano-Reggiano cheese.

Each cheese is washed regularly with brine. After about a year Bergianti tests the cheese using a tool that looks like an old-fashioned corkscrew, which he forcefully inserts into each one and pulls out, bits of cheese clinging to it. These he rubs between his fingers to feel its texture and sniffs to check aroma. He also taps the cheeses, determining their state from the sound.

At San Giovanni the cheeses are sold as young as eighteen months and as old as thirty months, with the best being twenty-four months old, according to Bergianti. At Azienda Agricola Grano d'Oro, Catellani says the optimal age for his cheese is between twenty-two and twenty-four months.

I would be proud to serve either cheese, for I know each is made with the utmost care and respect. But I think the Parmigiano-Reggiano made with milk from the *vacca rossa* superior, its flavor and texture richer, more buttery, less granular.

I found while in Parmigiano-Reggiano country that each cheesemaker works with the milk he prefers and makes with it the best possible cheese he can. There are subtle shades of flavor difference, to be sure, but as long as the cheese has been carefully made, aged, and transported, it is all simply delicious.

Chestnut Pasta with Wild Mushrooms

**PASTA DI FARINA
DI CASTAGNE
CON I FUNGHI**

6 SERVINGS

I first discovered chestnut pasta in Tuscany, at the Frateria di Padre Eligio of Mondo X, in Cetona (see essay, page 146), where I had it tossed with artichokes. Some time later, when I was in Basilicata, I discovered that the regional tradition called for serving chestnut pasta with dusky fresh or dried porcini. So when a friend there gave me a jar of this his own dried porcini, I couldn't wait to get home to try the combination. It was perfect, the heady flavor of the mushrooms blending well with the rich, slightly sweet pasta.

When porcini are sold fresh in markets, a handful of *nepitella,* a wild mintlike herb that we call pennyroyal, is always stuffed into the bag with them, for they grow in the woods together and are considered natural culinary companions. I've added mint to this recipe to replicate the intense flavor of *nepitella.*

Serve this rich, earthy, seductive dish with an equally earthy wine, like a fruity Chianti dei Colli Senesi.

2 ounces dried porcini mushrooms
2 tablespoons extra-virgin olive oil
1 clove garlic, green germ removed,
  minced
Fine sea salt
Hot paprika (optional)
⅓ cup (gently packed) fresh flat-leaf
  parsley leaves

¼ cup (gently packed) fresh
  mint leaves
1 recipe fresh Chestnut Pasta
  (page 437), cut into tagliatelle,
  or 12 ounces dried chestnut
  tagliatelle

1. Place the mushrooms in a medium-size bowl. Bring 2 cups of water to a boil in a small saucepan over high heat and pour it over the mushrooms. Cover the bowl with a plate and let the mushrooms soak until they are tender, about 30 min-

utes. Drain, reserving the soaking liquid and mushrooms separately. Strain the soaking liquid through several layers of cheesecloth, if needed, to remove any particles of soil or sand. Coarsely chop the mushrooms.

2. Bring a large pot of salted water to a boil over high heat.

3. Meanwhile, heat the oil with the garlic in a large heavy skillet over medium heat until the garlic sizzles and becomes translucent, about 4 minutes. Add the mushrooms, stir to coat with the oil, and cook until they are hot and tender, about 3 minutes. Add the soaking liquid, stir, increase the heat, and boil until the liquid is reduced by half, about 10 minutes more. Season well with salt and with hot paprika if desired. Keep the sauce warm.

4. Mince the parsley and the mint.

5. Add the pasta to the boiling water, stir, and cook just until it is al dente (tender but still firm to the bite); fresh will take less than 1 minute and dried about 7 minutes. Drain the pasta, reserving about ½ cup of the cooking water.

6. Transfer the mushroom sauce to a warmed large bowl. Add the pasta and toss until it is coated with the sauce and the mushrooms are distributed evenly throughout. Season to taste. If the pasta seems dry, add the pasta cooking water, 1 tablespoon at a time, tossing as you add it, until it is the consistency you prefer. Add the parsley and mint, toss to combine, and serve immediately.

Colored Pasta—We Think It's New, But It's Not

In Abruzzo, where the Rustichella d'Abruzzo pasta company has its headquarters, dried pasta used to be considered a valuable specialty. Gianluigi Peduzzi, a member of the family who owns the company, remembers that his grandmother often flavored and colored fresh pasta dough with tomatoes, sometimes spinach, and occasionally peppers before drying it. These colored pastas were often offered as hostess gifts, and people came to choose their favorite colors and shapes, which the Peduzzis packaged in gaily colored paper cones. Colored dried pasta was also considered a perfect gift for nursing mothers because, cooked in chicken broth, it was reputed to stimulate milk production.

MONDO X

I arrived midmorning at the Convento San Francesco, located in Cetona, south of Siena in Tuscany, and home to part of a dynamic community called Mondo X, or World X. I'd heard intriguing stories about it and its founder, Padre Eligio, a Franciscan monk. What intrigued me most was that he'd fostered an organization for young people in need that claimed agriculture as a healing force.

The Convento itself is not a farm but a luxurious restaurant and hotel, with lush gardens that include an *orto* (vegetable and herb garden) that supplies the restaurant. I was met there by Maria Grazia Daolio, director of the community, who both lives and works at the Convento. As we met it took me a moment to focus, for I was enthralled with the spatial arrangement of the centuries-old building, the warmth of its golden stone, and the beauty of its manicured grounds. The cool interior where we went to talk was luxurious and peaceful, yet simple and unadorned.

Maria Grazia explained that Padre Eligio had founded Mondo X in 1961 as an organization to defend young people. The organization is based, she explained, on the precepts of Saint Francis of Assisi, who both loved Jesus Christ and had a passionate concern for mankind.

One of the first things Padre Eligio did was establish a toll-free drug help line in Milan in 1964, which attracted hundreds of volunteers and exposed a tremendous need in Italy's young people. In 1974 Padre Eligio established the first Mondo X, an open community for people in crisis. Today there are more than thirty Mondo X communities around Italy, and most of them run working farms. Its members are part of the Frateria di Padre Eligio, the Brotherhood of Father Eligio.

Maria Grazia pointed out that Mondo X is neither a therapeutic nor a religious community. "Mondo X doesn't exist to spread any religion," she said. "Its members come together to help themselves and each other and, ideally, the rest of the world. If someone wants to join us, we suggest they stay for at least three years. Most stay four or five and some stay forever."

The communities are self-sufficient, as is this one at the Convento. The members live on what they make from the restaurant and hotel and from a small gift shop that sells the olive oil, honey, and hand-crafted toys produced by other Mondo X communities.

I asked how Mondo X came to possess this large and luxurious property. "This building, the Convento di San Francesco, was the first convent established by Saint Francis of Assisi, and it remained a convent until 1975, when the Franciscans donated it to Mondo X," Maria Grazia explained. "Where we are sitting, which is now the hall of the hotel, was once the friars' meeting hall."

Many donors have been inspired by the success of Mondo X and the legendary charm of its founder and have given farms and villas in various states of disrepair to the community, which restores and returns them to productivity. Padre Eligio often supervises the work himself, with the help of experts, as he did at the Convento.

Maria Grazia, who joined Mondo X in 1971, worked on the restoration of the Convento, which took eleven years. "Padre Eligio and two masons directed us," she said. The work, from rebuilt walls to carefully laid tiles, is extremely fine and detailed.

The community at the Convento opened the restaurant in 1984 and the hotel in 1989.

The restaurant serves a light formal cuisine. The hotel includes a handful of exquisite rooms, with a helipad for guests in a hurry. The gardens are lovely and restful, and like everything at the Convento, they emanate calm and joy.

Maria Grazia, graciously excusing herself, turned me over to Paolo Metri, a community member and waiter at the restaurant, who offered me a tour of the Convento and the community nearby.

We walked through the Convento grounds, stopping at a chapel where Saint Francis once prayed and which now holds an ancient Buddha as well as a crucifix. "This was a gift to Padre Eligio," Paolo said, pointing to the Buddha. "It is here to show that this is not only for Catholics."

He showed me the weaving and metal- and stone-working studios, the wood-fired bread oven where all the community's bread is baked, and the gardens. It looked to me like there was plenty of work to keep all thirty-six members of this community very busy.

Our tour finished, we drove several miles to the beautifully restored villa Eremo di Belverde, or Belverde Hermitage, which has a view of the valley below. Another Mondo X community, it is Paolo's home, though he goes to work each day at the Convento.

"Thirteen of us live here and raise rabbits and boar, as well as the olives to make our own olive oil," he said as we wandered down to see the cages and the stalls. "These animals supply us with meat once a week. Otherwise, we follow the Mediterranean diet and eat mostly vegetables and grains."

Paolo pointed out where work was underway and what work the community had already completed as we strolled the peaceful grounds. We looked into the state-of-the-art olive mill, dormant at this season, which produces a wonderfully fruity cold-pressed extra-virgin oil from the community's twelve hundred olive trees.

Further on we entered a small, very old chapel. "This was built in 1377 by a noble from Orvieto who gave money to build three chapels. This is in the style of Giotto," Paolo said, pointing to a characteristic, and very beautiful, fresco of the Virgin nursing the baby Jesus. There was also a fourteenth-century image of Christ on one wall, some of it vivid blue from lapis dust.

Once a month a priest still comes to say a public mass at the chapel. Other than that, the Eremo is solely for the community, which is bringing all the land around it into cultivation.

We drove a short distance to another farm called Montarioso, once a stop on the road where travelers and messengers changed horses. It has belonged to Mondo X since 1985 and is home to fifteen community members. They cultivate eighty acres of corn, both for animal and human consumption, plus other forage for animals and a variety of crops that includes artichokes, chestnuts (which grow on five-hundred-year-old trees), beans, peas, and chickpeas. There are also apple, pear, apricot, plum, and cherry trees. All cultivation is done organically, without synthetic chemicals, and the crops go to the community and to supply the restaurant.

I mentioned how impressed I was that Mondo X had revived all this farmland, turning it into something not only productive but also beautiful. "We are not lazy here, and we believe that farming is good work," Paolo said with a laugh. "But we are not horses either. We work carefully but not frantically."

As we drove back to the Convento, he told me about several other Mondo X farms throughout the country, as well as one on an island off Sicily where capers were just coming into production. He was thinking about moving to one of them. "It depends on where I'm needed," he said.

We returned to the Convento, where a table had been set for me in the restaurant.

Like all the menus, mine had been specially designed for me and watercolored by an artist in the community. Maria Grazia joined me for a while. "Your menu has been entered into a computer so that the next time you come to eat here we can pull it up and make sure that we don't serve you anything you've had before," she said.

I leisurely sampled the chestnut pasta with artichokes (see recipe, page 149), the subtle red pepper risotto, a whole trout smoked over six different woods, a timbale of porcini and mint, and a half dozen other dishes, each prepared with infinite care.

I later met Walter Tripodi, the chef, and thanked him. "My cuisine isn't really Tuscan," he said almost apologetically. "I am from Milan, so my cooking reflects northern Italy, but all the products I use are from here." I told him what a pleasure it had been to sample his food and asked him for his recipe for chestnut pasta with artichoke sauce, which he willingly shared.

My last stop was the gift shop, where I purchased some of the community's olive oil and their delicate wildflower honey. I carefully packed these in the car and turned to thank Paolo and Maria Grazia, both of whom had accompanied me outside.

I left with warm good-byes, very satisfied not only with the meal I'd eaten but also with the people I'd met. How lovely and how right, I thought, to open up the world of agriculture and food to so many and such varied people, both members of the community of Mondo X and their guests.

Rich Chestnut Pasta with Fresh Artichokes

Segreti

Briefly soaking artichokes in lemon water not only prevents them from darkening but also removes any bitterness.

This chestnut pasta recipe comes from the Convento San Francesco, which is home to one of the more unusual farms I visited in Italy and is run by the Frateria di Padre Eligio (Brotherhood of Father Eligio) of Mondo X (see essay, page 146). Chef Walter Tripodi uses ingredients raised on the community's farms for this elegant rendition of a peasant dish.

Try a rich Grattamacco Rosso as an accompaniment.

1 lemon, cut in half

5 large artichokes (each about 1 pound), or 5 pounds small artichokes

3 tablespoons extra-virgin olive oil

¾ cup dry white wine, such as Frascati

1 cup (gently packed) fresh flat-leaf parsley leaves

½ small red bell pepper, stemmed, seeds and pith removed, minced

2 cloves garlic, green germ removed, minced

Fine sea salt

1 pound fresh Chestnut Pasta (page 437), cut into tagliatelle, or 12 ounces dried chestnut tagliatelle

⅓ cup (gently packed) fresh mint leaves

Flat-Leaf Parsley

1. Squeeze the juice from the lemon into a large bowl of cold water. Trim the artichokes to the hearts (see box, page 42) and drop them into the water as they are trimmed. Once they are all prepared, leave them in the water for about 15 minutes.

2. Meanwhile, bring a large

pot of salted water to a boil over high heat.

3. Drain the artichoke hearts, pat dry, and slice ⅛ inch thick. Heat the oil in a medium-size heavy skillet over medium heat. Add the artichoke hearts, stir to coat with oil, and sauté just until they begin to cook, 2 to 3 minutes. Add ¾ cup water and the wine, stir, and bring to a boil. Partially cover, reduce the heat to medium, and cook until the artichoke hearts begin to get tender and about half the liquid has evaporated, about 10 minutes. Coarsely chop the parsley and add it with the bell pepper and garlic; stir, cover, and cook until the artichokes and pepper are tender, about 20 minutes. The vegetables should cook gently, so you may need to reduce the

heat to low. Check about halfway through the cooking time to be sure the artichokes aren't sticking and browning. Add more water if necessary; the mixture should be moist but not wet. Remove from the heat, season with salt, and keep warm.

4. Add the pasta to the boiling water, stir, and cook just until it is al dente (tender but still firm to the bite); fresh will take less than 1 minute and dried about 7 minutes. Drain the pasta, reserving some of the cooking liquid, and transfer the pasta to a warmed large serving bowl. Add the sauce and toss to combine with enough of the cooking water to moisten the dish to your liking.

5. Mince the mint and toss it with the pasta. Adjust the seasoning and serve immediately.

Stuffed Zucchini Blossoms

As late as the end of October, gardens and fields in Puglia, the most southeastern region of Italy, are ablaze with zucchini plants, valued as much for their cheery blossoms as for their long, narrow green fruit. Stuffed zucchini blossoms are a natural dividend of the seasonal bounty.

Although the dish is common throughout Italy, these stuffed blossoms from Dora Ricci, chef and owner of Al Fornello da Ricci outside Ceglie Messapico, near Ostuni, are extra special, mostly for what is not in them, for they are a study in simplicity.

For thirty years Signora Ricci has been charming diners with traditional Pugliese farm-style dishes with a subtle, light difference. She is painstakingly restrained. When she gave me this recipe, for instance, she insisted that it include the "aroma of garlic," and by that she meant very little. "Too much garlic kills other flavors," she said knowingly.

To gather ingredients for these stuffed blossoms, Dora's daughter, Antonella, goes out early in the morning to a neighboring farm for the blossoms, then to a local dairy for still-warm cow's milk ricotta. The blossoms are kept cool so they won't open until the filling is made and ready to be piped into them. They emerge from the oil almost translucent, hot, crisp, delicately delicious.

Serve an excellent Salice Salentino alongside.

8 good-size zucchini flowers, pistils removed, with a tiny zucchini attached if possible
1 cup very fresh ricotta

1 large egg
¼ cup (½ ounce) grated Parmigiano-Reggiano
1 small clove garlic, green germ removed, minced
Pinch of freshly grated nutmeg
Fine sea salt
⅔ cup all-purpose flour
1 cup carbonated mineral water or seltzer
6 cups very mild olive oil

Blossom Tips

Beautiful zucchini flowers seem delicate, but they are surprisingly sturdy. They easily accommodate the stuffing and stay closed without breaking. The amount of stuffing per flower will depend on the number and size of flowers you have. The amount given here fills eight flowers full. If you've got more blossoms, simply stuff them with less filling.

Zucchini blossoms should be used within a few hours after they are picked. Until then, keep them in a cool spot, with their stems either in water or wrapped in a damp paper towel. Check them over carefully for insects, but don't rinse them if you can avoid it; gently wipe them clean if necessary. Before the flowers are stuffed, pinch out the pistil from each center.

Stuffing zucchini blossoms is easy if you use a pastry bag fitted with a ¼-inch tip. Otherwise, use a teaspoon. Fry them in very mild olive oil, or half olive oil and half good-quality but mild vegetable oil, such as canola, so the flavor of the blossoms isn't overpowered by the oil.

1. Very gently wipe the zucchini blossoms clean if necessary. If a small zucchini is attached, slice it lengthwise in thirds, leaving it attached to the blossom.

2. Whisk together the ricotta, egg, Parmigiano, garlic, nutmeg, and a pinch of salt in a medium-size bowl.

3. Fit a pastry bag with a ¼-inch round tip. Spoon the filling into the bag, then pipe the stuffing into the zucchini flow-

ers, handling them gently. Each flower should have 2 generous tablespoons of filling.

4. Preheat the oven to very low.

5. Place the flour in a large bowl and whisk in the carbonated water until smooth. Line a baking sheet with clean plain brown paper or paper towels.

6. Heat the oil in a deep heavy saucepan over medium-high heat to 375°F. Test the heat by dropping in a teaspoon of batter; it should float quickly to the surface and turn golden.

7. Dip one of the flowers in the batter, making sure it is evenly and thoroughly coated. If it has a small zucchini attached, make sure it is coated as well. Hold the flower over the bowl to let any excess batter drip off, then lower it gently into the oil and cook just until the batter is crisp and golden, 4 to 5 minutes. You may do up to 3 flowers at a time. Use a slotted spoon to remove the flowers from the oil and transfer them to the prepared baking sheet. Place the baking sheet in the oven with the door slightly ajar to keep the finished flowers warm while you prepare the rest.

8. Arrange 2 flowers on each of 4 warmed small plates. Dust them lightly with fine sea salt and serve.

Frothy Fontina Sauce or Soup

FONDUTA VALDOSTANA

4 CUPS FONDUTA; ABOUT 6 SERVINGS

Italy's smallest region, the Val d'Aosta, is in the heart of the Alps, and because it sits on the French border, it is almost as French as it is Italian. Natives speak both languages and a dialect as well, and their friendly openness is infectious. *Fonduta,* a frothy cheese soup that can also be served as a sauce, is to the Val d'Aosta of northern Italy what clam chowder is to New England, for it is omnipresent.

Fonduta is made with fontina, the mild, creamy cheese made

Fonduta Tips

*F*onduta is not difficult to make, though there can be some potholes on the road to success. Make sure the bowl you use for the *fonduta* is large enough to hold all the ingredients and allow for vigorous whisking. The fontina is so creamy that it melts well and easily, but should you remove it from the heat and find that it has reverted to a ball within the milk, simply return it to the water bath and whisk until it has melted again. This is true even after you've added the egg yolks, which means this can be served the following day for delicious left-overs. The final whisking is essential to *fonduta,* for it needs to be frothy.

Be sure to have a peppermill filled with Tellicherry peppercorns close by, for grinding pepper over the steaming hot *fonduta* right before eating!

with milk from the brown-and-white cattle that forage on the dramatic slopes in the Val d'Aosta. Before leaving the area, I bought a whole fontina from cheesemaker Giuseppe Jeantet, who made it with late-spring milk, from cattle that had foraged on early-spring mountain flowers.

I took the cheese home and aged it for a few weeks in my own wine cellar, as Giuseppe urged me to do, then cut into it and tasted a thin slice. It was richly fla-vored and creamy indeed, reminiscent of the lovely air in the Val d'Aosta. I cut more to use in a *fonduta* that, as long as that cheese lasted, was a regular part of my repertoire. I still make it, but only when I can get fontina that resembles the one I bought at Giuseppe's *malga.*

Recipes for *fonduta* abound, but this one is best simply because of the balance of ingredients. It was given to me by the owner of a wonderful mountain restaurant called Locanda La Clusaz, tucked into the Valle del Gran San Bernardo, not far from Aosta. There the Grange family makes their own fontina as well. Grange, the restaurant chef, serves light and frothy *fonduta* over squares of freshly grilled polenta made from corn grown in his own fields across the road from his restaurant. Stone ground and nutty, his polenta was the perfect foil for *fonduta,* and this is the way I prefer to serve it.

Try this with Chambave Rouge from the cooperative la Ciotta di Vegneron in the Valle d'Aosta, or with Barbera d'Asti.

1 pound Italian fontina, rind trimmed, cheese cut into ½-inch cubes
2 cups whole milk

1 tablespoon unsalted butter
4 large egg yolks
1 recipe Polenta, grilled (page 428, optional)

1. Place the fontina in a large bowl, pour the milk over it, and let sit at room temperature for at least 2 hours.

2. Place another large bowl in a larger flameproof pan. Pour enough water in the pan to come partially up the sides of the bowl. Bring the water to a steady, though not tumultuous, boil over medium heat. Place the butter in the bowl and melt it. Add the cheese with the milk and stir constantly with a wooden spoon until the cheese is melted and the ingredients are blended. This will take up to 10 minutes. When it is nearly melted, exchange your spoon for a whisk to help the process along.

3. When the mixture is smooth, add the egg yolks, one at a time, and whisk until each is thoroughly combined. Continue whisking until the *fonduta* is very foamy on top, 3 to 4 minutes. Remove from the heat and ladle into warmed shallow soup bowls, preferably over polenta.

THE BEST ON THE MOUNTAIN

Right outside the mountain village of Cogne in the Val d'Aosta, where France melts into Italy, the Jeantet family raises a lively herd of thirty milk cows. The road to the Jeantets' small alpine home passes through pasture and woods, then up a steep and rocky climb until it stops in front of their barn. It is an ideal setting, framed by the spiky, snow-covered Gran Paradiso mountains and surrounded by national parkland.

Brothers Bruno and Geppino Jeantet and Bruno's wife, Mirella, are one of the few farm families who still make fontina, the flat, creamy golden rounds of cheese for which the region is famous. Most fontina is now made in cooperatives with milk that is gathered from local farms, but the Jeantets prefer to maintain the shepherd's lifestyle, spending summers "up the mountain" with their cows and the winter in Cogne.

Each spring the Jeantets, along with others who still live this way, walk their cows from the central pasture in Cogne up to the mountain, a journey of about five steep miles, in a pageant known as the *transhumence.* It is a festive occasion; the cows are decorated with flowers and boughs, and many townspeople join, picnicking along the way.

For four to five months the Jeantets live on their mountain farm, a comfortable chalet-style building with a barn and artisanal dairy out back, where Geppino makes fontina and *brossa,* a thick cream made from the fontina whey. He also makes a smaller, tall round of aged cheese from skimmed milk called *fromage,* and ricotta from the whey of *fromage.*

Having made an appointment to watch Geppino make cheese, I walked into the welcome warmth of the dairy early one August dawn and found him standing near a huge copper kettle set over a wood fire. Smoke hugged the ceiling of the small, white-tiled room. Soot from decades of use covered the outside of the copper kettle, which originally belonged to Geppino's grandfather. A rough, thick wooden lid with a door in it sat atop the kettle, and when Geppino opened it I saw the shiny copper gleam against the white, creamy milk inside.

Near the fire was a long table upon which sat one round wooden cheese mold. After saying hello—in French, which all residents of Val d'Aosta speak, along with Italian and a local patois—Geppino returned to the kettle, removed the lid, and began methodically scooping out curds with a copper strainer and packing them into the mold as whey rushed over the wooden table and onto the floor. He said nothing until he'd scooped the very last curd; then he turned, wiped his forehead, and leaned against the table.

"We're at the end of our season here," he

said. "The cows' milk supply is falling off. Usually I make four cheeses a day, but now I'm down to two. Pretty soon we'll all head down the mountain, but we try to stay up here as long as we can."

Geppino and Bruno are up before the sun each day to milk the cows and turn them out to pasture. Geppino goes immediately into the dairy to make his first cheese, which, once it is molded, he will turn ten to twelve times during the day so it settles evenly. The cheese is then put in the cellar where it is salted and aged. He will make his second cheese midafternoon and treat it just as carefully, finally turning it around midnight, the day's work done.

Geppino turned back to the copper pot to make *brossa*. He stoked the fire just enough to gently heat the whey, bringing the cream left in it to the top. This he scooped into a waiting sieve lined with cloth to drain and settle.

"We are just about the last people to make *brossa*," Geppino explained. "It's a byproduct that has become too expensive for big dairies to bother with." Geppino persists because they all love it poured over hot polenta, and he also likes being able to supply it to elderly people in the village who remember when *brossa* was common.

Mirella stepped into the small, smoky dairy to get cheese for hikers who had stopped by. She beckoned me to follow her down a cramped stairway into the aging room, where I had to crouch so as not to hit my head on the low doorway. Inside was a universe of sweet-smelling cheeses, all carefully lined up on red pine shelves. Mirella showed me how the younger cheeses deepen in color from pale ivory to gold as they age, and explained that each is wiped with brine once a day to prevent mold from forming, a task she shares with Geppino. She chose a two-month-old cheese and took it upstairs. "The best fontina is between seventy and ninety days." She said. "Older than that and the cheese can become bitter."

The Jeantets are among the youngest of the fontina makers in the region. "The average cheesemaker here is sixty years old," said Bruno, who is in his thirties, while Geppino is in his forties. According to Bruno, young people aren't attracted to the kind of life they have chosen, which offers lots of hard work and scanty remuneration.

"We love it, though," Bruno said. "We did this with our father, and my best memories are the summers we spent up in the mountains. For three months at a time we saw no one else, and we never had to take a bath. We just took care of the cows and made cheese right up in the pastures. By comparison, our life is luxurious now."

All fontina made in the Val d'Aosta is creamy and delicious, but the Jeantets' is exceptional. It tastes sweet and floral and as rich as if it had an extra pitcher of cream in it. I mention this to Bruno, complimenting him.

"It's because we do it on the farm," he said. "If we took the cows up higher, the cheese would be even better. Up there the cows eat only wildflowers, which makes their milk even better, more creamy."

They don't do that anymore because Bruno doesn't want to leave his family and Geppino is comfortable making cheese on the farm. Besides, the rent for the mountain pasture would be too expensive. Bruno wonders aloud if perhaps his memories are more nostalgia than reality anyway.

"What I really miss about our life then is the rhythm, when everyone on the mountain lived according to the sun," he said, chuckling at the memory. "Of course, we were always late because we didn't wear watches, but that never seemed to matter."

Mirella poked her head back in the dairy to ask if I'd like to stay for lunch, an invitation I accepted without hesitation. We emerged into a gorgeous blue-sky day and walked across the courtyard toward the house, admiring the dramatic peak of the Gran St. Pietro mountain that rose behind the trees. We stepped into the living room, and Mirella went to the woodstove and began to prepare polenta, setting the pot right on the coals. Framed against the window, she stirred it with a long, sturdy wooden stick for more than an hour. Occasionally Bruno added thin branches to the fire, and he and Geppino both teased her about her style. "I wasn't born here," she said good-naturedly. "I'm a city girl, and I learned to make polenta from their mother. I let them think they're the experts."

Just before the polenta was cooked, Bruno added a bunch of juniper branches to the fire. "It gives the polenta a special flavor," he said, winking.

Mirella turned the polenta onto a board in traditional fashion, where it sat in a large, firm, golden lump, steam curling from it. Geppino brought in his fresh *brossa,* and a friend of theirs, Elizabetta Allera, had brought spicy goat stew and *mocetta,* a dried beef sausage, to have with the polenta.

Geppino and Bruno both cut slabs of polenta and drowned them with *brossa.* I copied them and ate my first spoonful, reveling in the subtle flavors of corn, smoke, and rich, slightly tart cream. We spent the afternoon at the table talking, telling jokes, having a friendly time as we finished the mound of polenta, which went as well with the stew and sausage as it had with the *brossa.*

Before the last crumb was gone the sun had started to set, and the hired cowherd was bringing in the cattle. We stepped outside to watch as they lumbered calmly into their places in the barn. "They remember where to go from season to season," Mirella said.

She pointed out a chunky brown cow. "She gave the most milk last year, and we decorated her with a pine bough and white flowers for the return to winter pasture," she said, referring to their trip back down the mountain to Cogne after the summer season.

I bid them good-bye, admiring their strong nostalgia for the past and their insistence on indulging it. They are lucky to be able to do so, and village residents and the tourists who crowd Cogne each summer are lucky too, for they get the Jeantets' handmade cheeses, considered the best on the mountain.

Pine Nuts and Beans

PINOLI E FAGIOLI

6 TO 8 SERVINGS

Da Delfina may well be the most beautiful restaurant I have ever had the pleasure of visiting. Situated in the town of Carmigniano, west of Florence, it is one of those magical places that transports you from the moment you enter it. It is also one of the finest and best-known restaurants in the Tuscan countryside.

Although owner Carlo Cioni buys from local producers, he produces a fair amount himself, including his own olive oil, many of his own vegetables, which thrive in the garden outside the restaurant, his own vinegar, which sits in demijohns outside the kitchen door at the mercy of the atmosphere (which he claims is the key to a good vinegar), and his own black peppercorns.

Black peppercorns? Yes. Cioni is very proud of them too. His pepper tree doesn't produce a huge quantity, but enough to support the claim that he produces his own black pepper.

My husband, son, and I went to Da Delfina to sample certain local dishes we wouldn't have been able to find elsewhere. Signore Cioni knew we wanted the simplest dishes, and he began our meal with cool cherries and aged salami, a blessed peasant combination. When the diners at the table next to us saw what we were having, they requested the same, and soon every table in the restaurant was enjoying cherries and salami. I believe that day Cioni's entire stock of cherries was depleted.

Everything we tasted at Da Delfina was delicious and extraordinarily flavorful, but this dish of pine nuts and beans stood out. As Cioni said, it is the simplest of the simple, made with what farmers had at hand. Serve a delicious Chianti Classico alongside.

*3 pounds fresh shell beans, such as
    cranberry, borlotti, or Jacob's
    cattle, shelled (about 4 cups), or
    3¼ cups dried beans*
2 tablespoons extra-virgin olive oil
*1 medium-size ripe tomato, cored
    and diced*

*¼ cup (gently packed) fresh
    basil leaves, plus additional
    for garnish*
*Fine sea salt and freshly ground
    black pepper*
⅔ cup pine nuts (see Note)

1. Bring a large pot of salted water to a boil over high heat. Add the fresh beans, return to a boil, and cook, uncovered, until they are tender but not mushy, 20 to 25 minutes. Drain, reserving 1½ cups of the cooking liquid. (If using dried beans, place them in a saucepan with cold water and bring to a boil over high heat. Remove from the heat, cover, and let sit for 1 hour. Drain the beans and cover them with fresh water. Bring to a boil, reduce the heat so the beans are simmering merrily, and cook until they are tender but not entirely cooked through, about 50 minutes. Drain, reserving 1½ cups of the cooking liquid.)

2. Heat the oil, tomato, and basil leaves in a medium-size heavy skillet over medium-high heat. Cook, stirring, until the tomato begins to sizzle, 4 to 5 minutes. Reduce the heat to medium and stir in the beans and 1 cup (250ml) of the cooking liquid. Cover and cook until the beans are very tender and the tomatoes and basil have melted into them, about 30 minutes. Check often to be sure the beans aren't cooking too fast or sticking; you may need to reduce the heat and/or add the remaining cooking liquid.

3. Season to taste with salt and pepper. Add the pine nuts, stir, cover, and cook just until everything is heated through, 3 to 5 minutes. Adjust the seasoning and transfer to a warmed serving bowl. Garnish with fresh basil leaves and serve.

NOTE: The success of this recipe rests on the quality of the pine nuts. The best come from Italy, and they are long and thin. Flooding the market, however, are short, fat pine nuts from China, which are inferior. The Italian variety is more expensive but much more rewarding.

Taste before you buy pine nuts in bulk; they should have a good, sweet, nutty flavor. And only buy nuts that have been refrigerated. Once they're home, keep them refrigerated, or if you plan to keep them for a while, freeze them. They won't suffer and will keep well for about a month in the freezer.

Potato Dumplings as You Like Them

GNOCCHI COME VUOI

4 SERVINGS

Adriano del Fabro was an invaluable friend to me during my stay in Friuli, where he lives. Adriano is a journalist, or at least that's how he supports himself and his family. He writes for local publications and produces an amazing number of books each year on subjects ranging from folktales to food.

But at heart he is a farmer, and I was lucky enough to spend some time with him at his small farm where he, with his parents, raises fruit, vegetables, chickens, and a variety of other things. He is passionate about agriculture and keeps abreast of agricultural developments in Friuli and elsewhere in Italy. "Friuli is a contemporary region with its eyes on the future," he said. "Our neighbor to the north is Austria, and Austrians are very environmentally aware. They have created a huge demand for organic produce. Because of the European Union (EU), they can import easily from Friuli, and farmers are responding by producing organically with that huge market in mind."

Segreti

Letting the riced
potatoes cool on a
wooden work surface
(both the surface and
the air can absorb
moisture) makes for
drier potatoes, which
are necessary for
light gnocchi.

Adriano is always planting new and different crops, all of which he cultivates organically. He's recently planted varieties of antique apples, and he has a crop of blueberries that he is very proud of. His bushes produce so well that he puts out a small hand-lettered sign at his gate advertising blueberries for sale.

One evening he served me a typically Friulana farm meal that included these delicious gnocchi, sausages braised in milk, *frico* (a toasted cake of finely grated cheese), and his own blueberry grappa. It was a sumptuous repast.

Adriano served the gnocchi bathed in butter and sage, though they are also served with a rich, creamy cheese sauce. I've given both choices here.

FOR THE GNOCCHI
1 pound russet potatoes, peeled and
    quartered
1 large egg
½ teaspoon fine sea salt
½ cup plus 2 tablespoons
    all-purpose flour
¼ cup semolina, for dusting the
    baking sheet

FOR THE SAGE BUTTER
6 tablespoons (¾ stick) unsalted
    butter
15 fresh medium sage leaves
Pinch of fine sea salt

FOR THE CHEESE SAUCE
⅔ cup milk
1 tablespoon unsalted butter
4 ounces Italian fontina, grated

1. Bring 3 cups of water to a boil in a large pot over high heat. Place the potatoes in a steamer and set it over the boiling water. Cover, reduce the heat to medium, and cook until the potatoes are tender, about 20 minutes. Remove the potatoes from the heat. Push them through a ricer or a food mill or mash them lightly but well with a fork, then gently spread them out on a clean work surface to cool completely and give up as much moisture as possible.

2. When they are completely cool, transfer the potatoes to a bowl and mix in the egg with a fork until it is thoroughly combined. Add the salt and a scant ½ cup flour to make a dough that holds together, isn't sticky, and is very light and almost fluffy. Add more flour, 1 tablespoon at a time, until the desired consistency is achieved.

3. Lightly flour a clean work surface. Generously dust 2 baking sheets with an even layer of semolina flour. Cut the dough into quarters and roll each quarter into a rope that is about 17 inches long and ½ inch thick. Cut each rope into ½-inch-long pieces and transfer them to the prepared baking sheets. You should have around 136 gnocchi.

4. Bring a large pot of salted water to a boil over high heat.

5. Meanwhile, place a regular fork so that the tips of its tines are resting on the work surface. Roll the gnocchi down the tines of the fork so that each is striated. Return the finished gnocchi to the prepared baking sheets in one layer.

6. When all the gnocchi are formed, make the sage butter or cheese sauce. If making the sage butter, melt the butter in a small pan over low heat. Add the sage leaves and salt and keep warm over very low heat. If making the cheese sauce, place the milk and butter in the top of a double boiler set over simmering water. When the milk is hot, stir in the cheese and continue stirring until the cheese is melted and has formed a smooth sauce. Keep warm.

7. Drop about 15 gnocchi (or enough to cover the surface of the water in one layer) into the boiling water, stir, and cook just until they rise to the surface, 1 to 2 minutes. Using a slotted spoon or strainer, transfer the gnocchi to a warmed shallow serving bowl and repeat until all the gnocchi are cooked. Pour the butter or sauce over the gnocchi, stirring gently as you pour so the gnocchi are coated. There will be abundant sauce, but this is the way it is intended. Serve the gnocchi immediately.

Segreti

After you've cut the gnocchi, roll them down the back of the tines of a fork to striate them. The indentations left by the fork will catch the sauce, making each bite twice as savory.

Tender Spinach Dumplings with Cheese

**STRANGOLA-
PRETI AL
FORMAGGIO**

10 SERVINGS

This recipe comes from *agriturismo* Otto Marzo, near Sant' Ambrogio di Valpolicella, in the Veneto region of northern Italy. My husband and I visited this farming cooperative, which also offers lodging and meals to paying guests, to find out how they raise their goats and make the cheeses they're known for. The bonus was several hearty country meals and the discovery of these dumplings, a subtle blend of nutmeg, spinach, and Gorgonzola cheese.

Strangolapreti are a sort of pasta. The name literally translates "strangles the priest," and different versions of it are found in many regions of Italy, particularly in the north. Why do they have such an evocative name? Some think it refers to the heaviness of the dish, so heavy it would "strangle a priest"; others, to the legendary gluttony of priests in Italian history, who were known to visit even the poorest of families and eat through their entire larder.

Strangolapreti are the simplest of farm fare, sometimes made only with flour, bread crumbs, and water, sometimes with nettles instead of spinach. This particular recipe is lighter and more flavorful than other versions I've tasted, and the Gorgonzola sauce is a delicious inspiration. Make them on a chilly winter night, and serve a lovely bottle of Valpolicella alongside.

FOR THE STRANGOLAPRETI
1 pound day-old Italian-style bread, preferably a mixture of whole wheat and white, cut in small chunks
4 cups whole milk
1 pound fresh spinach, trimmed and well rinsed

3 large eggs
1½ to 2½ cups all-purpose flour
2 teaspoons fine sea salt, plus additional for the cooking water
1 teaspoon freshly grated nutmeg, or to taste

Segreti

• Place the *strangolapreti* as they are formed on a plate that has been rinsed with water (so they don't stick). When you've completed about 15, tip them into the water all at once rather than adding them singly, so they will cook evenly.

• This recipe is large, serving 10 people; for 4 generous servings, halve all the ingredients.

FOR THE SAUCE
¾ to 1 cup heavy (whipping) cream, preferably not ultrapasteurized
12 ounces Gorgonzola or other
good-quality blue cheese, such as Oregon blue, Maytag blue, bleu d'Auvergne, or Danish blue
Freshly ground black pepper

1. Place the bread and milk in a large bowl and soak, turning the bread occasionally, until all the milk is absorbed; this will take anywhere from 1½ to 2½ hours. Transfer the bread and milk to a food processor and purée.

2. Preheat the oven to very low.

3. Bring 3 cups of water to a boil in a large pot over high heat. Place the spinach in a steamer and set it over the boiling water. Cover, reduce the heat to medium, and steam the spinach until it is completely tender but still bright green, about 6 minutes. Remove from the steamer, transfer to a tea towel, and twist to remove as much liquid as possible. Mince the spinach; you should have a rounded ½ cup.

4. Place the bread purée and spinach in a large bowl and mix until thoroughly combined. Mix in the eggs, one at a time. Add 1½ cups flour and mix together. Then add more flour, 2 tablespoons at a time, until you have a thick dough that holds together well. Blend in the salt and nutmeg.

5. Bring a very large pot of generously salted water to a boil over high heat. Reduce the heat so the water is at a rolling boil and cook one *strangolapreti* as a test: Scoop out a heaping teaspoon of dough, round it off with another teaspoon, and drop it into the water. Cook until it is firm throughout, 3 to 4 minutes. Remove and taste for seasoning and texture. If it is too soft, add a bit more flour.

6. When the dough is to your liking, cook the *strangolapreti*, forming each one as directed above, about 15 at a time. Cook until they are tender and have no flour taste, 3 to 3½ minutes. If cooked too long, they will be tough.

7. Using a wire strainer, transfer the *strangolapreti* to a warmed serving bowl, cover loosely, and keep warm in a low oven. It can take up to an hour to cook all the dough, but you may

refrigerate part of it and continue cooking the following day.

8. While the *strangolapreti* are cooking, place ¾ cup cream and the cheese in a heavy saucepan and melt them together over very low heat until blended. If you've left the rind on the cheese, it may not melt as easily as the rest, but don't be con-

cerned if there are some small lumps. Taste the sauce and add the remaining cream if desired. Season to taste with pepper.

9. To serve, evenly divide the *strangolapreti* among 10 warmed soup bowls. Top each with an equal amount of sauce and a sprinkling of black pepper. Serve immediately.

Spinach and Ricotta Dumplings

**MALFATTI
DI SPINACI E
RICOTTA**

6 SERVINGS

These dumplings are called *malfatti*, which means poorly made, because they are very irregular in shape. A rustic peasant dish, they are delicate and pleasing nonetheless.

I learned about them when visiting Lisa Bonacossi, who is a woman of contrasts herself. Born into one noble family and married into another, she is the doyenne of the internationally known Cappezzana wine and olive oil estate in the Chianti region west of Florence, near the town of Pistoia. Yet she is as down-to-earth as a woman can be. Mother of seven children, four of whom are actively involved in the winery, she loves to cook, garden, make her own

Segreti

If you like a slight "crunch" to your *malfatti*, preheat the broiler, place the *malfatti* in a flameproof baking dish, and pour the sage butter over them. Broil just until they are golden and slightly crisp on top.

jams and marmalade, and talk about food. A small vegetable garden, or *orto,* within steps of the estate's inner courtyard produces pounds of tomatoes and bushels of beans, peas, eggplants, and peppers, as well as huge bunches of basil, sage, and flat-leaf parsley, the cornerstones of Tuscan cooking. A plot of garlic provides enough for the year, and plots of onions, carrots, and celery—called *odori*—go into the traditional Tuscan peasant dishes that issue from the Cappezzana kitchen.

This dish, from one of the *contadini,* or farmworkers, at Cappezzana, is a favorite, and Lisa Bonacossi insists that it can't be found in other parts of Tuscany. "It comes from Pistoia and Prato, not those more southern parts," she said. "You might find pasta there, but you find this up here." I offer this humble but delectable dish to you as Lisa Bonacossi offered it to me. Serve it with a fine glass of her estate's simple red wine, Barco Reale Chianti.

1 pound ricotta
1 cup all-purpose flour, for rolling
   the malfatti
1 pound fresh spinach, trimmed
   and well rinsed
2 large eggs
1 large egg yolk
2½ cups (about 4 ounces) grated
   Parmigiano-Reggiano

Heaping ¼ teaspoon freshly
   grated nutmeg
Fine sea salt and freshly ground
   black pepper
5 tablespoons unsalted butter
3 tablespoons extra-virgin
   olive oil

1. Place the ricotta in a nonreactive sieve set over a bowl and let it drain for about 4 hours. (Some ricotta does not contain any liquid, but some contains quite a bit. Judge the draining time by the variety of ricotta you purchase.

The drained ricotta should be soft but not at all wet or dripping.)

2. Place the flour on a large plate.

3. Bring 3 cups of water to a boil over high heat. Place the spinach in a steamer and set it

over the boiling water. Cover, reduce the heat to medium, and steam the spinach until it is limp and deep green, about 8 minutes. Remove from the heat, drain, and let sit until it is cool enough to handle. Place it in a cotton tea towel and squeeze it as dry as you can, then mince it.

4. Bring a large pot of salted water to a boil.

5. Meanwhile, place the spinach, ricotta, eggs, egg yolk, and 2 cups of the Parmigiano in a large bowl and stir to thoroughly mix. Season with the nutmeg, and salt and pepper to taste.

6. Shape the mixture into three 20-inch-long ropes, each one the width of your thumb. Cut the ropes into ¾-inch lengths and roll them quickly in the flour so they take on a very light dusting.

7. Add just enough of the *malfatti* to the boiling water to

Rice for Risotto

Arborio is widely considered the best rice for risotto, for it absorbs a great deal of liquid without losing its fine texture, and its high starch content accounts for the creamy sauce it creates during cooking.

But at the Principato di Lucedio, an estate in Piedmont that dates from before the thirteenth century, both the owner, Contessa Rosetta Clara Cavalli d'Olivola, and the farmer who cultivates the rice grown there, Varalda Annibile, recommend Carnaroli, a relatively new rice they have cultivated for the past twenty years.

Carnaroli has a higher starch content than Arborio and lends risotto an even richer creaminess. "It's what we all use around here," Annibile said. "It has better flavor and texture, even if everyone else thinks Arborio is the best."

Rice from the Principato di Lucedio is available from:

Zingerman's, 422 Detroit Street, Ann Arbor, MI 48106-1868; tel: (313) 769-1625

Larry's Markets, 10008 Aurora Avenue, Seattle, WA 98133

cover the surface without crowding the pan, and boil just until they rise to the top, less than 2 minutes. Remove them from the water with a slotted spoon and place in a bowl. Repeat until all the *malfatti* are cooked.

8. Heat the butter and oil in a large skillet over medium heat until they are sizzling. Add the *malfatti* and toss so that the pieces are moistened with the butter and oil and heated through. This will take just a minute or two. Sprinkle them with the remaining ½ cup Parmigiano, transfer to a warmed serving dish, and serve immediately.

NOTE: The sauce may be too buttery for some. Adjust the amount according to your own tastes.

Risotto with Asparagus—Da Mino

RISOTTO AGLI ASPARAGI

6   S E R V I N G S

This dish is virtually a spring rite in Lombardy near the Piedmont border. Verdant rice fields blanket the area, asparagus grows well in the sandy soil, and the two make a wonderful classic combination. Risotto is elegant prepared in dozens of ways, but here the asparagus melts into the rice, which absorbs its gentle grassy flavor.

I first tasted this risotto at Da Mino, a restaurant in the rice-farming town of Robbio. There I also learned the etiquette for serving—and eating—the dish. Using a large serving spoon, scoop a spoonful out of the pan and gently lay it on the center of a plate—it should retain the shape of the spoon's bowl. Follow this scoop with two others, placing one on either side of the first scoop. When you eat the risotto, move it out toward the edge of the plate so it cools, leaving the rest in a scoop where it will stay hot.

Serve *risotto agli asparagi* with a light, feisty red wine, such as Il Monello from Braida, in Piedmont.

1¼ pounds asparagus, trimmed, sliced ¼ inch thick, stalks and tips separated (see Notes)

2 cups Beef Broth (page 422) or canned low-salt chicken broth

2 tablespoons extra-virgin olive oil

1 small onion, minced

1½ cups Arborio, Carnaroli, or Viale Nano rice

3 tablespoons (½ ounce) grated Parmigiano-Reggiano

2 tablespoons unsalted butter

Fine sea salt

1. Bring 5 cups of water to a boil in a large heavy saucepan over high heat. Add the sliced asparagus stalks and return to a boil. Cook until the asparagus is tender but not mushy, about 6 minutes. Remove the stalks from the water with a slotted spoon. Add the tips and cook just until they've lost their initial crispness but are not really tender, about 1 minute. Remove them with a slotted spoon as well.

2. Measure 3½ cups of the cooking water and transfer it to a medium-size heavy pan. Add the broth and bring to a simmer over medium heat. Reduce the heat to low, cover, and keep warm.

3. Heat the oil with the onion in a medium-size heavy saucepan over medium heat. Cook, stirring, until the onion is softened but not browned, about 5 minutes. Add the cooked as- paragus stalks, stir, and add the rice. Cook the rice with the asparagus and onion until it begins to turn translucent, 2 to 3 minutes, stirring all the while to make sure it is completely coated with oil.

4. Stir enough of the broth mixture (about ½ cup) into the rice to almost cover it and cook, stirring, until the rice has absorbed nearly all of the liquid. You may need to adjust the heat under the pan; the broth should sizzle when it hits the bottom of the pan, but it shouldn't boil nor should it be inert. Continue to add the broth, a scant ½ cup at a time, and cook, stirring slowly but constantly. Let the rice absorb all but just the slightest bit of the broth before adding more. The rice should never be dry but should not be soupy either. After cooking for about 14 minutes,

the rice will approach ideal doneness. From that time on, add the broth 1 to 2 tablespoons at a time so that you are sure not to add too much. Continue adding broth and stirring until the rice is puffed slightly and tender except for right in the center, where it should be just firm, not hard or crisp. Most of the time the risotto will be perfectly cooked and blended with the asparagus after 17 minutes (see Notes). Stir in the cheese, then add the butter, and stir until it has melted into the rice. Season with salt to taste and remove from the heat. Stir in the aspara-gus tips, let the risotto sit for about 2 minutes to allow the flavors to blend, then serve.

NOTES: If your asparagus stalks are delicate and thin, cut off the tips in a whole piece. Cook them along with the stalks, removing them from the boiling water when they are just crisp-tender. Stir them into the risotto once it is fully cooked and seasoned, right before serving.

• The cooking time of rice varies depending on its age, so pay careful attention. You want the rice cooked but not completely tender all the way through.

How to Store Rice

Rice will keep well for about one year from harvest. Although that sounds like a generous length of time, in fact, most of us don't have any idea when our rice was harvested, so it's impossible to gauge freshness correctly. Therefore, it's best to buy rice from a reputable source and use it as soon as possible. If you don't eat rice often, it is really a waste of money to buy it in huge amounts. Instead, buy smaller quantities or as you need it.

Rice will keep on a cupboard shelf stored in an airtight container. You may freeze it, but do so for no longer than three months.

A LIVING RELIC

The Principato di Lucedio must be seen to be believed. This medieval villa in Piedmont, for centuries the center of a large rice farm, rises golden and magnificent out of the thousand acres of rice fields that surround it, like the setting for a rich epic novel.

At Trino, near Vercelli in the heart of Italy's rice-growing region, the Principato is a major player in the rice industry. Built between the eleventh and thirteenth centuries, it was once an enclosed, independent, and thriving village with two churches—one for the noble owners, the other for the peasants—and its own hall of justice, where the Principato's laws were administered.

Attracted by the rice produced there, I arranged a visit. I had first noticed the white cotton bags stamped with the Principato coat of arms, but it was the flavor and texture of its three specialty rice varieties—Arborio, Baldo, and Carnaroli—that captured my interest.

I hadn't been forewarned about the vastness of the property, and when I drove through the arched gateway, I was astonished to find myself in a courtyard the size of a football field, surrounded by majestic, though crumbling, buildings. From one of them emerged a stylish, attractively dressed woman, Contessa Rosetta Clara Cavalli d'Olivola, the owner I had come to meet.

I found the Contessa, as she is called, as tiny and delicate as the dimensions of the property were large. She greeted me warmly, and we walked slowly across the courtyard to the building housing her quarters, our footsteps echoing. She pointed out the chapel reserved for the nobility, built tall and high and currently in desperate need of repair. "Eventually there will be money to restore it," she said. "The state will help—they want to preserve it."

Using a set of ancient keys, she opened a tiny heavy wooden door and led me through the inner courtyard to the front door to her quarters. She opened that door and guided me up a gracious wide staircase of highly polished marble that swooped as it turned to end in a grand hall. I could imagine a throng of nobles and servants in it, their robes matching its grandeur.

The walls, which have aged to rich tones of sepia, gold, and olive, were hung with dour portraits and dark landscapes, and the long windows looked out on the inner courtyard I'd already glimpsed. The Contessa showed me the old kitchen, where almost an entire wall was taken up with an ornate woodstove that had functioned daily until five years before, when a modern stove was installed next to it.

We retired to a comfortably furnished sitting room, where the Contessa told me how it was that she came to own this relic.

"Centuries ago, the Principato belonged to my father's family, who lost it in battle or through inheritance to someone else," she said. "We don't know which."

Her father, who worked on the Italian stock exchange, dreamed of getting it back and devoted considerable energy to doing so, finally procuring it just a few years before he died. His wife then took over its administration and supervised the rice cultivation.

The Contessa inherited the great estate and moved there part-time from Turin to run it with her husband. In the early 1990s her son, Paolo, stepped in when his father died, and now mother and son keep it going with the help of five full-time workers. Elvira Padovan keeps house for the Contessa and Paolo, and she and her son, Pieroangelo, who works in the rice fields, are the only people who live full-time at the Principato, in dramatic contrast to the hundreds who once lived and worked there.

Along with the three varieties of specialty rices, the Principato's fields produce what the Contessa calls *riso comune,* a simple rice used for cakes and pudding. "*Riso comune* is the bulk of our production, which totals

twenty-five hundred tons a year," she told me. "It's a good-size production compared with others in the area, but it's not enough. We should produce more to keep this place going, but we've got all the work we can handle as it is."

The Contessa finds herself in a situation common in Italy. Historically, nobles owned enormous tracts of farmland, most of which have gradually been dispersed either through inheritance or government programs. But some large plots, like the Principato, still remain in the hands of a single family. With the liberation of peasant workers, who were either tenant farmers or some form of indentured servant until the 1960s, owners find it difficult to keep their estates productive. In the case of the Principato, earnings keep it functioning, but just barely.

That is why there are so many gracious and crumbling villas in Italy. They give a faded dignity to the landscape, but as I gathered from the Contessa, who desperately wants to see the Principato returned to some state of elegance and productivity, the situation is extremely frustrating. In her case some state funds may become available to repair certain parts of the Principato, as has happened for one of the churches. But when it comes to anything more, she must use her wits.

She has dreams. She'd like to turn the Principato into a luxurious hotel or a conference center, but for now she's busy with the rice-exporting business.

The following morning I met Varalda Annibile, a fifth-generation rice grower and the Principato's agricultural supervisor, and together we drove out to look at the rice fields. It was thrilling to be surrounded by the vivid blankets of green rice plants in what is considered to be the heart of Italy's best rice country.

We pulled off the single-lane road that runs outside the Principato onto one of the very narrow dikes that separate one field from another. Beneath the blanket of green is shallow water, without which the rice would die "like a flower wilts," according to Annibile. Though the Po River is close—it runs nearby, up against the Monferrato hills—they are obliged to buy

water from the state, which comes in through the Canal Cavour. "It's very expensive," Annibile said. "It's one of our major expenses."

As he explained the surprisingly labor-intensive process of rice cultivation, I slapped mosquitoes. He laughed heartily. "I'm out here so much I've built up a tolerance," he said. "They don't even come near me, but they love you."

Annibile explained that the landscape looks very different at the end of May, when the fields are drained and cleaned to prepare for planting, the weeds destroyed. Before mechanization, until the middle of this century, the fields were hand weeded by women who came from the Veneto area. Called *mondine* (rice weeders), they worked long and hard and under strict supervision. "The *mondine* weren't allowed to raise their heads when they worked," Annibile explained. "They were arranged in a triangle in the fields with the field captain behind them. If they raised their heads, they were punished." The work was brutal, the workday long. When they returned to their quarters behind the principal residence, however, they somehow still had the energy left to sing, and Annibile remembers hearing them. "I couldn't imagine how they could sing, with such hard lives," he said. "But there they would be, cooking and singing together well into the night."

"The *mondine* only got fifty percent of the weeds, though," he said. "With modern methods, the fields are much cleaner."

Once the fields are clean of weeds, they are leveled with the help of lasers and then filled with water until the rice is mature, sometime in August. Annibile checks the fields constantly, pinching rice kernels to see if they are developing properly. If they are, he leaves the fields alone. If the kernels are small, he fertilizes. He knows from experience and from keeping his eye on the land.

We passed a spot where the rice plants were weak and sparse. "The shade from this tree prevents the water from heating up so the rice can grow," Annibile said. "And sometimes algae forms on the water and the rice can't grow through it."

His biggest problem is the *dodo*, or wild brown rice, that dominates the cultivated rice if it isn't pulled out. Annibile sees no option but to treat the fields with synthetic chemicals in hopes of getting rid of it.

He sighed as we finished our tour. "Yes," he said. "I love it out here, but the land is so much weaker than it used to be."

He explained that cattle were once a vital link in the agricultural chain and that even though he rotates rice with soybeans to strengthen the soil, nothing can replace the cows. "No one can make money with cows, so the farmers got rid of them. Now we all push the land to produce as much rice as it can. But it suffers in the mean-

time," he said.

We returned to the Principato, and Annibile took me to the back courtyard, which was full of tractors and miscellaneous farm machinery that looked completely out of place amidst the old buildings. He wanted me to see the hall of justice, and we stepped inside.

"There used to be a crucifix here with a movable head," Annibile told me, pointing to the front of the room. "A monk stood hidden behind it, and when someone was pronounced guilty, he pulled a string so the head would nod."

He pointed to a column at the back of the church. "Go look at it," he said. "It's dry on the top and bottom and wet in the center. People here believe that the column has seen so much injustice in this room that it weeps."

We walked back into the sunlight, where trucks were being loaded with rice, which they would take to a nearby refinery to be hulled, then sold. A large portion of the specialty rices are sold in the United States. The *riso comune* stays in Europe.

The Contessa works hard marketing her specialty rices. She travels constantly, and her goal is to sell every single grain produced so she can expand, hire more workers, and eventually undertake the necessary restorations. She's not about to let this land slip away again.

Garlicky Cheese Polenta

**POLENTA
TARAGNA**

8 SERVINGS

Polenta is good, but *polenta taragna,* a specialty of northern Italy, particularly in Lombardy around Lake Garda, is divine. Rural farmworkers from a hundred years ago might roll their eyes to hear me say such a thing, for they practically lived on this dish, as there wasn't a huge variety of other foods to eat.

Polenta, with and without the buckwheat of *polenta taragna,* is still a staple in northern Italy, what pasta is to the southern part of the country. In this version it is a substantial and stick-to-your-ribs dish that is particularly satisfying on a cold winter evening with a blazing fire in the background. Serve it before or with a simple grilled steak, a green salad, and a good, hearty, rustic wine such as Valtellina Superiore.

5 teaspoons fine sea salt
3¾ cups (1 pound) mixed coarsely
   ground cornmeal and buck-
   wheat, or all coarsely ground
   cornmeal, preferably stone
   ground

16 tablespoons (2 sticks) unsalted
   butter
6 cloves garlic, green germ removed,
   cut crosswise into very thin slices
8 ounces Italian fontina, cut into
   thin slices

1. Bring 3 quarts of water and the salt to a boil in a large saucepan over medium-high heat. Slowly sprinkle in the meal, whisking as it falls into the water. When it has all been added, reduce the heat to medium-low. Continue whisking until the mixture begins to thicken; small lumps may form—be sure to whisk them out. After about 5 minutes, lumps will no longer form, and you may switch to stirring with a wooden spoon. Cook, stirring the polenta and scraping down the sides of the pan, until the polenta has thickened to the consistency of thick mashed potatoes and is quite

But it Tasted so Good!

Corn, brought from the New World, was a common crop in northern Italy by the mid-1500s. It was a godsend, for it was simple to cultivate and didn't compete with existing crops. Dried, ground, and cooked to a golden mush, it provided starving rural peoples with ample sustenance.

For centuries this mush, called polenta, remained the bulk of the rural northern Italian diet, so important that it took on almost mystical significance. But all was not well. Peasants ate their polenta, filling their stomachs, but they suffered from a variety of ills that remained undiagnosed until sometime in the eighteenth century, when they were determined to be the result of a severe nutritional deficiency called pellagra. It wasn't until around 1905, however, that the cause of pellagra was identified, and it all pointed back to corn. To obtain vital nutrients from corn, it must be processed with mineral salts (such as lime), and the peasants didn't know this.

Once the cause was determined, immediate steps were taken, among them properly processing corn. Pellagra virtually disappeared, and polenta retained its vital significance. Anyone who has ever visited northern Italy knows how delicious polenta is and how integral to the cuisine. One finds it combined with cheese and garlic, grilled and drizzled with olive oil, as a base for a fresh tomato sauce. Polenta, with its satisfying nutty taste and texture, has prevailed.

smooth, about 1 hour. Remove from the heat and keep warm.

2. Preheat the broiler.

3. Melt the butter in a small pan over medium heat. Add the garlic, stir, and cook until it turns golden and toasty, about 5 minutes (the milk solids in the butter will also turn golden, which is not a problem). Remove from the heat.

4. Evenly divide the polenta among 8 warmed shallow flame-proof bowls. Drizzle 1 to 2 tablespoons of the butter and garlic on top of the polenta, then cover with equal amounts of cheese. Broil about 5 inches from the heat until the cheese is melted and bubbling slightly, about 4 minutes. Serve immediately.

Filomena's Eggs with Peppers and Sausages

This spicy, full-flavored dish of fresh farm eggs, tomatoes, and peppers is a rustic specialty from the mountain town of Terranova di Pollina, in Basilicata. There farmers raise their own food in soil that is so rocky it doesn't look like it could produce a thing. Careful husbandry works its miracles, however, so that farm gardens yield a rich bounty, and a handful of healthy-looking chickens peck around every house.

While I was visiting the Lufrano farm just outside Terranova, the family's youngest daughter, Filomena, made this for me. She ran to the garden to get the peppers, onions, and tomatoes, reached into a special basket in the kitchen to pull out the homemade sausages, carefully cut slabs of her mother's home-baked bread, assembling all the ingredients before cooking them. As she worked, she related some of the dreams of a seventeen-year-old farm girl from Terranova and the pull she feels from both farm and town.

When the *ciambutella* was ready, Filomena proudly carried it into the dining room. It was richly flavored and delicious, and we ate it over homemade bread until it was gone.

Ciambutella can be served either as an antipasto or a main course. Serve a round, full-flavored red, such as Salento Rosso, alongside.

3 tablespoons extra-virgin olive oil

5 to 6 Italian frying peppers (about 1 pound), coarsely chopped, seeds and all

1 Hungarian hot wax pepper, or ½ fresh jalapeño pepper, finely chopped

1 small onion, coarsely chopped

2 medium-size ripe tomatoes (about 4 ounces), cored and coarsely chopped

Fine sea salt

4 uncooked fennel-spiced Italian pork sausages (each 3 to 4 ounces), cut into 1-inch lengths

4 large eggs

1. Heat the oil in a large heavy skillet over medium-high heat until hot but not smoking. Add the peppers, stir, and cook until the skins begin to brown. Reduce the heat to medium, add the onion, stir, and cook just until it begins to soften, about 4 minutes. Stir in the tomatoes with their juice, then stir in 1 cup water. Season with salt, reduce the heat so the liquid is gently simmering, and cook, stirring occasionally, until the vegetables are softened, about 20 minutes. Stir in the chunks of sausages and simmer until they are cooked through, about 15 minutes. If the mixture dries out, add a bit more water; it should be moist but not wet, and it shouldn't be dry enough to stick to the pan.

2. Whisk the eggs with a pinch of salt just to break them up. Pour them over the sausage mixture, stirring as you pour. Cook, stirring, just until the eggs are cooked but not dry, 3 to 4 minutes. Adjust the seasoning and serve with plenty of fresh bread alongside.

Artichoke Frittata

FRITTATA DI CARCIOFI

4 TO 6 SERVINGS

When artichoke season arrives in Tuscany, concurrent with the newly green hills and soft breezes of spring and early summer, this frittata arrives on tables, usually with fresh lemon wedges served alongside, so diners can squeeze lemon juice on it as they like.

Giovanni Ceretelli, an expert in Tuscan heirloom vegetable varieties, took me for a walk through the artichoke patch on his farm right outside Florence. Although it was near the end of the artichoke season, I walked away with a bouquet of fragrant purple Nespoli artichokes, which are considered the best and richest in flavor. As we climbed the hill back to the farmhouse he shares with his wife,

Luna, and their two children, Giovanni gave me this recipe, one of his favorites. I went right back to the apartment I was renting and made the frittata for my family, using not only Giovanni's heirloom artichokes but eggs from Luna's heirloom chickens as well! The marriage of artichokes and eggs is unexpectedly harmonious, the drizzle of lemon juice a lovely complement.

Artichokes and wine aren't the happiest of marriages, but if you are determined, try a fresh, light white, such as Lunaia Bianco di Pitigliano.

6 large eggs
½ teaspoon fine
    sea salt
2 tablespoons extra-
    virgin olive oil

4 small artichokes (about 13 ounces;
    see Note), leaves removed to the
    soft core of leaves, very thinly
    sliced lengthwise
1 lemon, cut into wedges,
    for serving

1. Preheat the broiler.

2. Whisk the eggs in a large bowl just until they are broken up but not frothy. Whisk in the salt.

3. Heat the oil in a 9-inch cast-iron skillet over medium-high heat. Add the artichokes and cook, stirring constantly, until they are golden and somewhat crisp, 2 to 3 minutes. Add the eggs, reduce the heat to medium, and cook without stirring until the bottom is set, bubbles come up through the top of the eggs, and only about ¼ inch of the top of the eggs is still liquid. This will take 2 to 3 minutes.

4. Place the pan 5 inches from the broiler element and cook just until the top is set and puffed, about 1 minute. Be very careful not to overcook the frittata; it should still be very tender in the center.

5. Flip the frittata out onto a serving platter and serve immediately, or let it cool and serve it at room temperature. Either way, serve it with lemon wedges for squeezing fresh juice over the top.

NOTE: If you can't find baby artichokes (which really aren't babies but either the secondary flowers from plants that produce large artichokes or simply a variety of artichoke that stays small), use the bottom of a large artichoke, which is also called the heart (see box, page 42).

Zucchini Frittata

FRITTATA DI
ZUCCHINI

6
APPETIZER
OR 2 TO 4
MAIN-
COURSE
SERVINGS

Segreti

For a good frittata, whisk the eggs together just until they are broken up and no further.

Elvira Padovan is housekeeper at the Principato di Lucedio, an ancient estate of houses, barns, and churches that forms a grand square out in the middle of rice-farming country, near the tiny town of Trino, in Piedmont (see essay, page 172).

Elvira lives a quiet life, tends a garden, and can be found on a fine early summer afternoon under a huge old apple tree right outside her front door, sorting vegetables, mending clothing, or pursuing her various duties.

This is her recipe for zucchini frittata, a common farm dish throughout Italy, which she makes with small zucchini from her garden. It tastes simply of the ingredients that go into it—fresh garden zucchini and fresh farm eggs. You may serve it as an appetizer or as a full meal along with salad, crusty bread, and a lovely Dolcetto d'Alba.

2 tablespoons extra-virgin olive oil
1 pound small zucchini, trimmed
    and diced
Fine sea salt

6 large eggs
⅓ cup (generous ½ ounce) grated
    Parmigiano-Reggiano
Freshly ground black pepper

1. Preheat the broiler.
2. Heat 1 tablespoon of the oil in a 9-inch nonstick flameproof skillet over medium heat. Add the zucchini and stir to coat it with oil. Season lightly with salt, cover, and cook until the zucchini is tender and slightly

golden, about 8 minutes. Check occasionally and adjust the heat if necessary to prevent the zucchini from burning. As you stir the zucchini, crush it with the spatula so that some of it is crushed and some is still in dice.

3. Add the remaining 1 tablespoon oil to the zucchini and stir so it is evenly distributed.

4. Whisk the eggs in a large bowl just until they are broken up, then whisk in the cheese and season lightly with salt and pepper. Pour the egg mixture over the zucchini and shake the pan to evenly distribute the eggs.

Cook without stirring until the bottom is set, bubbles come up through the top of the eggs, and only about ¼ inch of the top of the eggs is still liquid. This will take 2 to 3 minutes.

5. Place the pan 5 inches from the broiler element and cook just until the top is set and puffed, about 1 minute. Be very careful not to overcook the frittata; it should still be very tender in the center.

6. Flip the frittata out onto a serving platter. Serve hot or at room temperature.

Deep Green Frittata

FRITTATA ALLE ERBE

6 SERVINGS

This frittata is inspired by one I had at La Subida, in the hills just above Cormons in Friuli, a most special and unusual restaurant. La Subida's owner, Josko Sirk, and his wife, Loredana, are Slovenian. They speak Slovenian at home, send their two daughters to a Slovenian school across the border, celebrate Slovenian holidays, and serve mostly Slovenian food in their restaurant. They were born and live in Italy by political accident, when borders were redrawn after the Second World War and the village of Cormons became Italian. Now Slovenia proper is less than four miles away. The Sirks, like most of the people who live in this interesting and unusual border-land, make the most of the situation by maintaining their traditional customs while enjoying the advantages of living in Italy.

When Josko, who comes from a family of hoteliers, and his wife were married, her parents first made him sign a paper that guaranteed their daughter would never work in a hotel, for they didn't want her to work twenty-four hours a day. Josko has honored the agreement, sort of. La Subida is strictly a restaurant, but several hundred yards away, across the road and up a hill, he has built a series of lovely guesthouses that are tucked into the mountainside. The way he gets around breaking the agreement is that he doesn't ask his wife to help with the guesthouses.

Josko is a strong proponent of country ways. He serves typical farm food in his restaurant, and the guesthouses he designed are modeled after typical farmhouses, each with its own *fagolar*, or central cooking fireplace, in the kitchen. He has just completed more guesthouses whose arrangement around a central square replicates a typical peasant village. "I want people to honor the peasant ways, not to forget what is real, rich, vital to our heritage and our way of life," he said passionately. "If they come here and have a wonderful time amidst these simple surroundings, they will have a feeling for our lives, our ways, our traditions." From the simple peasant cooking served at La Subida to the design and materials used in the guesthouses, quality and comfort are foremost.

When I asked Josko for a recipe that he felt was most typical of the farms of his region, this is the one he gave me. His instructions for making it went like this: "Find yourself an Italian-Slovenian grandmother and go with her into the fields. Follow her and pick everything that she picks. When she is finished, go home, cook the greens of the field, and mix them with eggs for this frittata."

The *frittata con erbe*, which is a typical Easter season dish, must be very dark green and richer with vegetables than with eggs, for eggs were a precious ingredient on the Slovenian (now Italian) farm table. The greens you use are a matter of preference.

Serve this either hot or at room temperature—it is delicious both ways—and don't omit a lightly chilled fruity Tocai Friulano to serve alongside.

3 tablespoons extra-virgin olive oil

1 medium fennel bulb, trimmed and sliced paper thin

1 medium onion, sliced paper thin

2 large leeks, white part and 2 inches green, well rinsed, and diced

6 ounces Swiss chard or dandelion greens, trimmed, well rinsed, and diced

8 ounces fresh spinach or stinging nettles, trimmed and well rinsed

4 large eggs

½ teaspoon sea salt

6 fresh mint leaves

1. Heat 2 tablespoons of the oil in a large heavy skillet over medium heat until it is hot but not smoking. Add the fennel, onion, and leeks and cook, stirring occasionally, just until the onions are softened slightly, about 5 minutes. Add the chard and stir to combine. Cover and cook until the chard has softened and wilted into the onion mixture, about 8 minutes. Add the spinach, stir, and cook, covered, until the vegetables come together in a homogeneous mixture, 15 to 16 minutes more. The total cooking time for the greens is 30 minutes.

2. Preheat the broiler.

3. Whisk the eggs with the salt in a medium-size bowl just until they are broken up. Stack the mint leaves, slice them crosswise into very fine strips, and whisk immediately into the eggs. Stir the cooked vegetables into the eggs.

No Broiler Needed

There has never been a broiler on the Italian farm, so frittatas were finished by carefully sliding them out of the pan onto a flat plate, then placing the pan over the plate and turning the frittata into it to cook on the other side. The broiler is more efficent, but it is a non-Italian conceit!

Mint

4. Heat the remaining 1 tablespoon oil in a 9-inch flame-proof skillet over medium-high heat until it is fairly hot but not smoking. Add the egg mixture, flatten it out in the pan, and cook without stirring until the eggs are set but still liquid on top, about 5 minutes.

5. Place the pan about 5 inches from the broiler element and cook just until the top is set, about 4 minutes. Be very careful not to overcook the frittata; it should still be very tender in the center.

6. Flip the frittata out onto a warmed serving platter, cut into wedges, and serve immediately.

NOTE: You can use a combination of wild greens if you like, including dandelion, lamb's quarters, stinging nettles, wild fennel, or other wild edibles. Just be sure if you harvest them yourself that you do so from areas that have not been treated with chemicals, and if you can't tell lamb's quarters from nightshade, take along someone who can.

Light Green Frittata with Herbs

FRITTATA ALLE ERBE

6 FIRST-COURSE SERVINGS

This recipe is a modern rendition of the traditional *frittata alle erbe* of Friuli (see page 182). Light, aromatic, and heavier on eggs than the traditional, it makes a wonderful first course.

Use a wide variety of herbs, keeping in mind their strength; use mint and sage judiciously, for example, because the intensity of their flavors will overtake the others.

Try this with a light and fruity white, such as one of the Colli Orientali del Friuli, Tocai Friulano.

6 large eggs
Generous ¼ teaspoon fine sea salt
12 chives
½ cup (loosely packed) fresh herb
    leaves, including tarragon, basil,

fennel fronds, mint, sage, thyme,
    lemon thyme, salad burnet, and
    oregano, rinsed and patted dry
1 tablespoon extra-virgin olive oil

1. Preheat the broiler.

2. Whisk together the eggs and salt in a large bowl just until they are broken up. Mince the chives and finely chop (it isn't necessary to mince) the remaining herbs, then whisk them immediately into the eggs.

3. Heat the oil in a 9-inch flameproof skillet over medium-high heat until it is fairly hot but not smoking. Add the eggs, which will puff up, and cook without

stirring until the bottom is set but ¼ inch of the top is still liquid. This will take 2 to 3 minutes.

4. Place the pan 5 inches from the broiler element and cook just until the top is set, about 1 minute. Be very careful not to overcook the frittata; it should still be very tender in the center.

5. Flip the frittata out onto a warmed serving platter, cut into wedges, and serve immediately.

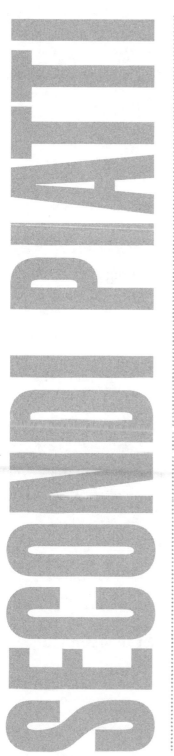

SECONDI PIATTI

SECOND COURSES

The foundation of the Italian farm diet has always been starches and vegetables. In certain regions—Tuscany, Basilicata, Piedmont, and Emilia-Romagna—meats were less of a rarity than in other regions, where they were reserved for a festive event. Poultry was raised to be sold, and it took a rare special occasion to merit serving it at the farm table. A farm meal that included seafood, however, was almost nonexistent, for until the middle of the twentieth century the coastlines of Italy were swampy, largely uninhabited, and impossible to cultivate. Farming was done in the hills that rise from the coastlines, and transporting anything to them was practically impossible. Anyone who has ever traveled through Italy knows that, even today, roads are often dicey and many rural areas have only recently become accessible.

Transportation has improved, of course, and products do travel, but seafood remains a food of the city or the fishing village or the island. The farm table in Sicily, for example, heavily features seafood, with swordfish figuring largely (it is the most common of foods, the "canned tuna" of the Sicilian table), along with fresh sardines and wonderfully fleshy octopus, which are boiled and sold at the markets.

All of that said, the Italian farm cook still treats a second course of meat, poultry, or seafood with infinite care. Lamb predominates, for sheep still graze the hillsides, feeding on wild herbs and grasses. Pork is omnipresent too, with pigs providing many of the cornerstones of Italian cuisine, including prosciutto, pancetta, bresaeola, and speck. And as for beef, in the Chianti area of Tuscany you can't drive a mile without seeing the little Chianina cattle grazing quietly in rolling pastureland; the Pugliese, too, would be bereft without their dairy and beef cattle. Chickens, guinea hens, turkeys, and rabbits are fixtures in the Italian *orto,* or vegetable garden, and on the farm, kicking up a racket whenever any human or other animal passes by.

Cook your way through dishes like Herb-Marinated Leg of Lamb, hearty Tuscan Wild Boar Stew, and fragrant Chicken with Sage, and you will find that the farmhouse approach provides aromatic, tender, satisfying dishes that take their nourishing place as the *secondo.*

Grilled Steak with Fresh Herbs

**BISTECCA DI
MANZO CON
ERBE**

4 SERVINGS

'd been invited for lunch in the private dining room at the Avignonese winery in Tuscany, near Montepulciano. Before we sat down, Alberto, one of the three Falvo brothers who own the winery, wanted me to take a look at their vast herb garden. Just about every culinary herb known to the contemporary world was there, planted in a large and tidy plot right outside the dining room. I brushed past chocolate mint and rue, several different types of basil, sages, rosemary, tarragon, and hyssop, an oregano called *persa,* and thin shoots of new garlic.

The owners of Avignonese are noted for going the extra mile in everything they do. They fertilize their vineyards with fava bean plants, and coddle an heirloom grape they planted, called Aleatico, which apparently originated with the Etruscans and yields a deliciously brazen red wine.

A No-Grill Cuisine

Emilio Lancellotti, one of the three Lancellotti brothers who own and run the Lancellotti Hotel and Restaurant in Soliera, outside Modena in Emilia-Romagna, pointed out to me something significant about fat. "People come to Emilia-Romagna wondering why meats aren't grilled in this region. People here were very poor. They couldn't cook over coals the way we do now, for when you do that, the fat drips away from the meat. In the old days, when the cuisine of this area was evolving, people needed every drop of fat they could get for calories. They couldn't afford to lose anything. Our cooking evolved to retain calories, not waste them." That is why grilling is as rare in the cuisine of Emilia-Romagna as it is common in Tuscan cuisine, where people were less in need—it must be assumed—of calories.

Segreti

Mince the herbs right before the meat comes off the grill or out of the pan so they don't lose any of their precious and flavorful oils.

They are fanatical about the quality of their wine and the food served to complement it. They also insist that all ingredients be local, from the herbs and vegetables that grow outside the dining room to the flavorful Tuscan Chianina beef that grazes in surrounding fields and is noted for its rich, marbled meat.

The day I visited, this delicious steak (from Chianina beef, of course) was on the menu, along with Stewed Fresh Favas (page 262). I found it a refreshingly simple way to serve uncommonly savory beef, and I highly recommend it. Use a mix of herbs, with mint as a strong component. I like mint and basil together, about half and half, but if you have sweet cicely, be sure to make that a generous third of the mix.

Serve this with a rich red wine, such as Avignonese Pinot Nero from Valdicapraia.

*4 beef rib or porterhouse steaks
(each 1 inch thick and
6 ounces)*
*⅔ cup (gently packed) mixed fresh
herb leaves, including mint,
anise hyssop, and basil*

*1 teaspoon best-quality red wine
vinegar*
4 teaspoons extra-virgin olive oil
Fine sea salt
*Freshly ground black pepper
(optional)*

1. Preheat a barbecue grill to medium-high. If using charcoal, when the coals are red and dusted with ash, spread them out and place the rack on the barbecue. When the rack is hot (after 1 to 2 minutes), place the steaks on the grill and cook them to your liking. A rare steak will take just 2 minutes on each side; medium-rare will take about 3 minutes per side.

2. Just before the steaks are cooked, mince the herbs.

3. Transfer the steaks to a serving platter. Drizzle each with ¼ teaspoon vinegar and 1 teaspoon oil; sprinkle lightly with salt and generously with the herbs. Season with pepper as well if using. Serve immediately.

Grilled Steak Morandi

**FILETTO ALLA
MORANDI**

4 SERVINGS

This is so simple it can hardly be called a recipe, but I include it in this book in honor of Nano Morandi. Nano is a force of nature, and the small grocery he owns in Modena—Giusti's—a living museum. It looks just the way you want an Italian grocery to look. Burnished surfaces are jam-packed with foods that lend the air their tempting aromas: garlic, tomatoes, the finest Parmigiano-Reggiano, olive oil, rich *aceto balsamico,* deep red wine, a bit of truffle. Dishes made by Nano's wife, Laura—a force in her own right—look so appealing behind sparkling glass counters that it's hard to resist ordering a portion to take home.

Nano kindly invited me for lunch and took me through the store into the tiny trattoria behind it. A handful of tables in a spot that looks as though it has been there forever, it was empty when I sat down at noon and jammed by the time my first course of puffy, hot *gnocci fritti* (page 39), prepared, as is all the food, by Laura, arrived at the table.

Though I sat by myself I wasn't alone; both Nano and Laura were constantly at the table, tempting me with glasses of wine and tastes of Laura's best dishes, like this one, Nano's favorite. To make it, she sears the best steak Nano can find on each side, drizzles it while blistering hot with aged *aceto balsamico,* and serves it with pasta and a fine red wine. I add a bit of ground bay leaf, pepper, and salt—an addition I'm sure Nano would applaud—and the combination, with the final drizzle of the aged vinegar, is ethereal—slightly sweet, a bit salty, highly aromatic. I recommend this when a simple, elegant dish is called for. Serve it alone on a plate with a salad to precede or follow it and plenty of fresh bread. To drink? The finest red Barolo you can lay your hands on. This dish merits nothing less.

Be sure to use the best-quality balsamic vinegar you can find, preferably that imported by Manicaretti Inc., whose source is a farm just a few miles from Nano's tiny, savory empire. Also, this deserves the finest meat you can find—don't stint. Consider this a special-occasion dish.

4 beef tenderloin steaks or other well-marbled steaks (8 ounces each)
8 imported dried bay leaves
1 teaspoon finely ground black pepper

Fine sea salt
4 teaspoons fine aged aceto balsamico

1. Heat a cast-iron skillet or grill pan over medium-high heat until it is hot but not smoking.

2. Finely grind the bay leaves in a spice mill and mix with the pepper in a small bowl. Press equal amounts of the mixture onto both sides of each steak and place the steaks in the hot pan. Cook the steaks to your liking; a steak that is about ½ inch thick will still be quite rare after about 2 minutes per side.

3. Transfer each steak to a very warm plate. Season lightly with salt and drizzle each as evenly as possible with 1 teaspoon of the *aceto balsamico*. Serve immediately. The steaks must be piping hot when they arrive at the table.

Succulent Herbed Roast Beef

ARROSTO ALLE ERBE CON E LARDO

6 SERVINGS

In Italy's northern regions, meat is traditionally roasted to perfection. My travels there inspired this fine beef tenderloin rubbed with rosemary and garlic, tied with lightly salted pork, and roasted with bay leaves tucked right under the pork.

I like to serve this with Potatoes in a Frying Pan (page 279), a simple green salad, and fresh bread. Drink an elegant red wine alongside, such as Brunello di Montalcino.

8 ounces thinly sliced salt pork or
    lightly salted unsmoked bacon
1 tablespoon fresh rosemary leaves
2 cloves garlic, cut in half, green
    germ removed

1½ pounds beef tenderloin or top
    loin roast
4 imported dried bay leaves
1 tablespoon extra-virgin olive oil
Fine sea salt

1. Preheat the oven to 450°F.

2. To rid the salt pork of some of its salt, bring a medium-size pan of water to a boil. Carefully drop in the salt pork, and when the water returns to a boil, remove it and pat it dry. Using a meat tenderizer (or the flat bottom of a heavy glass), gently pound on each slice of salt pork to flatten it slightly.

3. Mince the rosemary with the garlic, spread the mixture on the beef, and rub it into the meat. Lay 2 bay leaves about an inch apart on top of the roast and cover with slices of salt pork, laying them along the length of the roast so they completely cover it. Holding

the pork in place, carefully turn the roast. Lay the remaining 2 bay leaves on top and cover with the remaining salt pork. Using kitchen twine, tie the roast at 1-inch intervals around the width of the beef.

4. Heat the oil in a roasting pan over medium heat. Add the roast and brown on all sides, about 2 minutes per side. Pour about ½ cup water around the roast and place it in the oven. Roast until the pork is golden and crisp and the beef is cooked to your liking, about 20 minutes for medium-rare. Remove the roast from the oven and sprinkle it evenly with salt. Let it sit for at least 10 minutes or up to 20 minutes before slicing so the juices have a chance to retreat back into the meat.

5. Remove the twine from the beef and thinly slice it. Arrange the beef on warmed dinner plates and drizzle with the juices that have collected in the roasting pan.

Veal Stew from the Val d'Aosta

The Val d'Aosta is gorgeous with its snow-covered peaks and hidden little villages that look like something out of the *Sound of Music.* Traditions are strong and the people I met there are determined, young and old alike, to keep it that way. Shepherds still move to the mountains in summer where they make creamy fontina, *brossa,* and ricotta cheeses. Young women learn to make lace the old way. Culinary traditions remain the same.

Villagers still come together once a year to bake their rustic rye bread in the village bread oven, each family making enough for the year. Although tender when it is first baked, it turns rock hard with time, and they eat it then by breaking chunks from it with a special heavy knife, then serving it with butter and honey. Fresh, it tastes like a simple rye bread. Dry, it is like a light, crisp cracker.

Val d'Aosta is right across the border from France, and it has a dual heritage. Natives speak French and Italian interchangeably, as well as a local dialect, and the cuisine is a blend of influences from the two countries. This dish, which was traditionally made with mountain goat and is now more often made with veal, is like a culinary anthem; although the serving style is Italian, the preparation technique is decidedly French.

I tasted this with the Jeantet family (see essay, page 156) in their mountain home. Elizabetta Allera, whose family owns the restaurant Lou Ressignon in Cogne, had brought the stew, claiming that of everything served at their cozy alpine restaurant it is among the most typical of the dishes and the richest in flavor. The Jeantets added that it is a festive dish rather than something they, as a typical dairying family, would eat every day.

To honor this dish, drink a full-flavored red wine, such as Barbaresco.

1 tablespoon exta-virgin olive oil
1 large onion, cut into ½-inch dice
1½ pounds veal roast, cut into
  ¾-inch pieces
Fine sea salt
1 bottle hearty red wine, such as
  Cabernet Sauvignon

6 juniper berries
2 imported dried bay leaves
8 black peppercorns
2 tablespoons all-purpose flour
1 recipe Polenta (page 428)

1. Heat the oil and onion in a large heavy saucepan or Dutch oven over medium heat. Cook, stirring, until the onion turns translucent and begins to soften, about 7 minutes. Add the veal and sauté until slightly golden, about 4 minutes. Season with salt, then pour in the wine. The meat should be nearly covered with wine.

2. Place the juniper berries, bay leaves, and peppercorns in a large tea ball or tie them together in a square of cheesecloth, and place it in the pot, pushing it down under the wine. Bring the wine to a gentle boil, reduce the heat so it is sim-mering, and cook, uncovered, until the meat is tender and the sauce is rich in flavor, about 1½ hours.

3. In a small bowl, mix the flour with 2 tablespoons of water to form a liquid paste. Whisk ½ cup of the sauce from the stew into the flour mixture, then whisk that mixture back into the sauce. Continue cooking until the sauce is thickened and the meat is very tender, 20 to 30 minutes more.

4. To serve, transfer the stew to a warmed serving bowl, discarding the tea ball of spices. Serve with the polenta alongside.

Oxtails with Dominic's Sauce

CODA DI BUE CON SALSA ALLA DOMINIC

4 SERVINGS

This succulent recipe was inspired by Dominic Tufaro, whom I met in Terranova di Pollino, Basilicata. What actually inspired me was the traditional sauce he described to me, which is a staple in the cooking of the area. It makes good use of the wild fennel that grows on the hills around Terranova, as well as the distinctive fruity olive oil that comes from more distant parts of Basilicata.

Oxtail, a much underused cut of beef, offers an enormous amount of flavor and a beguiling elastic texture, all for pennies a pound. It requires lengthy cooking, usually at a lower temperature than called for here. But do as I suggest and you'll find yourself with oxtail that is both succulent and crisp, so dark it is almost black but falling from the bone. The fennel comes through clearly, and it all makes for a simply sublime multilayered dish.

You may serve this with al dente pasta that has been tossed with olive oil, or with Simple Country Potatoes (page 280). Drink a very hearty red wine, such as Aglianico dei Colli Lucani, from the Pugliese side of Basilicata.

5 teaspoons fennel seeds, preferably wild, but cultivated will do
1 tablespoon best-quality red wine vinegar
¼ cup extra-virgin olive oil
About 2½ pounds beef oxtail, cut into 2-inch lengths

2 medium onions, each cut into 8 wedges
2 imported dried bay leaves
Fine sea salt and freshly ground black pepper
2½ cups hearty red wine, such as Cabernet Sauvignon

1. Crush the fennel seeds in a mortar with a pestle. In a large bowl, whisk together the vinegar and oil, then add the fennel seeds. Stir, add the oxtail, and toss until the pieces are coated with

the mixture. Cover and refrigerate for 24 hours, stirring at least 4 times during that period so the oxtail marinates evenly.

2. Preheat the oven to 400°F.

3. Add the onions, bay leaves, and a small amount of salt and pepper to the oxtail and marinade; toss so all the ingredients are thoroughly combined. Transfer to an earthenware baking dish large enough to hold the pieces of oxtail in a single layer and pour 2 cups of the wine over the oxtail. Bake in the center of the oven until the meat on the oxtail is deeply browned and so tender it falls from the bone, about 3 hours. Stir the oxtail frequently and add the remaining wine if necessary to keep the oxtail very moist.

4. Remove the oxtail from the oven and let sit for at least 10 minutes or up to 20 before serving. Adjust the seasoning before serving.

Peppery Pork Stew

CIF-CIAF

6 SERVINGS

This Abruzzese dish is always made in January, when the farmer kills his pig for the year. After butchering, choice pieces from each part of the animal go into *cif-ciaf*, which is cooked long and slowly with tomatoes and peppers, to emerge deeply flavorful and a glistening rust color.

When I was in the Abruzzo to visit the Peduzzi family, creators of Rustichella pasta, Stefania Peduzzi told me about *cif-ciaf*, the very mention of it evoking a smile and glint in her eyes. "There is always a huge celebration, and everyone eats as much *cif-ciaf* as they possibly can," she said. She told me that it is traditionally cooked in a *tegame di coccio*, or fireproof earthenware skillet, which she feels is important to its richness, along with good-quality meat and long, slow cooking.

Serve this as they do in Abruzzo, with crusty bread and a bit of the ubiquitous sauce of crushed peppers cooked in oil (see recipe, page 391).

2 pounds pork shoulder meat, cut
    into ¾-inch pieces
1 teaspoon fine sea salt, plus addi-
    tional to taste
3 tablespoons extra-virgin olive oil
6 cloves garlic, unpeeled, slightly
    crushed
2 teaspoons sweet paprika
½ teaspoon hot paprika or cayenne
    pepper, or to taste

½ cup dry white wine, such as
    Trebbiano d'Abruzzo
4 sprigs fresh rosemary, or 1 tablespoon
    dried leaves, crumbled
1 pound fresh ripe tomatoes or
    canned plum tomatoes,
    preferably DiNapoli brand,
    coarsely chopped

1. Place the meat in a large bowl, sprinkle it with 1 teaspoon salt, and toss so it is evenly salted.

2. Place the oil and garlic in a large heavy skillet over medium heat. Stir and cook until the garlic is evenly golden on all sides, 7 to 8 minutes.

3. Add the meat, sweet paprika, and hot paprika or cayenne to the garlic, stir until they are combined, then cook, stirring occasionally, until the meat is golden on all sides, about 5 minutes.

4. When the meat is browned, add the wine and rosemary, pushing the sprigs down into the meat. Cook, stirring,

until the wine has evaporated, 7 to 8 minutes. Add the tomatoes and stir to incorporate them. Reduce the heat to medium-low, cover, and cook until the tomatoes have melted and the meat is tender, about 50 minutes. The mixture should be moist, not soupy; you may want to remove the cover for the last several minutes of cooking so that the liquid has a chance to reduce and intensify.

5. Remove the *cif-ciaf* from the heat, season to taste with salt, and serve. (Don't worry about the garlic skins; they will have disappeared.)

Dario Cecchine's Macerated Pork

**BRACIOLE DI
MAIALE ALLA
DARIO CECCHINE**

4 TO 6
SERVINGS

Segreti

Pounding the meat will tenderize it and allow the vinegar and spices to penetrate.

D ario Cecchine is known throughout Tuscany for his skill as a butcher and for his obvious energetic charm. He picked up his knowledge of the ancient ways of treating meat from his father and grandfather and from the research he's done. He considers himself an Etruscan (thought to be one of the first groups to settle Tuscany), and he uses what he calls Etruscan flavor combinations of herbs, vinegar, and honey.

I had the good fortune of watching as he prepared pork for a customer. He sliced it into smooth wide strips, drizzled it with his homemade vinegar, then sprinkled on herbs that he took from attractive jars and a huge basket that surrounded his workspace. These he crushed carefully into the pork, then wrapped it up like a gift. Before he handed it to the customer, he gave the package a powerful whack on each side, "To help the vinegar and spices penetrate," he said.

Dario's macerated pork is redolent with aromatic herbs and a hint of acidity from the vinegar. Make and enjoy it, for it embodies the flavor of the Tuscan countryside.

I like to serve this pork with Green Beans with Tomatoes (page 271) and an accommodating red wine, such as Brunello di Montalcino.

2 pounds boneless pork shoulder, cut
   into ⅜-inch-thick slices
1 teaspoon best-quality red wine
   vinegar
2 tablespoons fresh thyme leaves

½ teaspoon crushed red pepper flakes
2 imported dried bay leaves, broken
   into small pieces
2 teaspoons fennel seeds
½ teaspoon fine sea salt

1. Lay the pork slices in a single layer on a sheet of parchment or waxed paper placed on a work surface. Cover them with another sheet of parchment or waxed paper. Gently pound each

slice several times with a meat mallet or rolling pin, moving the instrument away from you as it hits the meat so as to encourage the meat to flatten, rather than just pulverizing it. Uncover the meat and sprinkle the vinegar evenly over one side of each slice.

2. Crush the herbs, spices, and salt together in a mortar with a pestle, then sprinkle them evenly over one side of the slices. Stack the slices of pork in 2 equal-size stacks, wrap them in parchment or waxed paper, and refrigerate for 24 hours.

3. Preheat a barbecue grill to medium-high. If using charcoal, when the coals are red and dusted with ash, spread them out and place the rack on the barbecue. When the rack is hot (after 1 to 2 minutes), lay the slices of pork on the rack and grill until the pork is cooked through and crisp, about 2 minutes per side.

4. Remove from the fire and serve while blistering hot.

Butchering the Law

Dario Cecchine is a butcher who works in the tiny hillside village of Panzano, in Tuscany, about an hour outside Florence. He's in his early forties, but he works as butchers did one hundred years ago, in his family's *macelleria,* or butcher shop, which looks as though it hasn't changed in the several hundred years that it has existed. There in spotless order, he carefully cuts, brines, air-dries, and hand tends all the meat in his shop.

Powerfully built and cheerful, Dario goes about his daily work with impressive energy. He was in the middle of cutting up some pork while I was visiting, when two men entered lugging a wild boar, bristles and all. After haggling quietly with Dario, they left it, and he lost no time in butchering it. Within an hour it was a collection of loins, roasts, ribs, and stew meat. When I asked if it was legal to buy an animal like that, he simply looked at me. "Well, I won't say it is," he finally replied. "But the two hunters who just sold it to me are the local policemen."

Tuscan Wild Boar Stew

**SCOTTIGLIA DI
CINGHIALE**

6   S E R V I N G S

cottiglia is a very typical Tuscan dish, particularly around Mon-talcino, traditionally made during the grain harvest for the peasant workers, who needed substantial food to fuel their hard work. During hunting season it was made with wild boar, at other times with stewing hen or rabbit, and it was served in the fields at midday on "plates" of Tuscan Bread cut in thick slabs.

Wild boar run rampant in much of Italy, as they do almost everywhere in Europe, rooting up agricultural crops on the one hand and providing sustenance for rural populations on the other. The boar's meat is akin to pork, though heartier and less tender. If you can get boar, then use it to make this dish; otherwise, make it with pork. The results will be succulent, with the wine giving the pork a depth of flavor that is similar to wild boar.

Serve a hearty red Rosso di Montalcino alongside.

Segreti

If using wild boar for this dish, marinate it first for 24 hours in red wine to cover with a bay leaf, juniper berries, carrots, and onions. Drain it, throwing away the marinade, which will have absorbed any "high" or gamy flavor from the boar. Add extra water as you cook the wild boar, for it absorbs more than pork.

2 tablespoons extra-virgin olive oil
1 medium onion, diced
3 cloves garlic, green germ removed, minced
2 pounds pork leg or shoulder meat, cut into 1½-inch cubes (see Note)
1 cup fresh flat-leaf parsley leaves
1 cup hearty red wine

1 can (28 ounces) peeled tomatoes
2 branches fresh rosemary
12 good-size fresh sage leaves
4 small dried bird's-eye peppers, crushed, or hot paprika to taste
6 thick slices Tuscan Bread (page 311) or other country bread
1 to 2 cloves garlic, peeled

1. Place the oil, onion, and minced garlic in a large heavy skillet over medium heat and cook until the onion is golden at the edges, about 10 minutes. Add the meat, stir, and cook until it has taken on a slight golden edge, about 5 minutes. Add the parsley

and wine, stir, and bring the wine to a boil. Reduce the heat so that the wine is simmering and cook, stirring occasionally, until the meat has absorbed most of the wine, about 25 minutes.

2. When the meat has "drunk" all but just a slight bit of the wine, add the tomatoes and cut them into quarters with a spatula once they are in the pan. Stir to combine the tomatoes and meat, then add the rosemary and sage, nestling them down into the tomato juices, and stir in the peppers. Bring the juices to a boil, reduce the heat, cover, and cook until the meat is very, very tender and has absorbed almost all the tomato liquid, resulting in a sparse but rather thick sauce, about 2 hours. Check the meat occasionally and stir so that it doesn't stick, breaking up the tomatoes into smaller pieces.

3. About 15 minutes before serving, stir in ½ cup water, just to moisten the dish.

4. Preheat the broiler.

5. While the *scottiglia* finishes cooking, toast the bread under the broiler and rub each piece with a garlic clove.

6. To serve, place a slice of garlic toast on each of 6 warmed plates and top with the *scottiglia*. Serve immediately.

NOTE: Use good-quality pork shoulder, checking to be sure it is without an excess of gristle and fat. You may also use boned fresh ham.

Aromatic Boar Ragù

**STUFATO DI
CINGHIALE**

**ABOUT 6
SERVINGS**

Roberta Camboule runs Zia Maria, an *agriturismo* near Alghero, on Sardinia, with her mother, the Maria for whom the *agriturismo* is named, and her father. Her father is the head chef, while Roberta helps him and takes over whenever he is away.

Roberta served this ragù on my first night at the farm, and I

Segreti

Cayenne pepper tends to add heat without flavor. Use hot paprika, as Roberta does in her cooking, for a nice round flavor with plenty of heat.

believe I finished every morsel on the platter. I loved its toothiness, its slightly exotic appeal from the blend of vinegar and grappa. The next day in the kitchen, when Roberta asked which recipes I wanted to learn, this was my first request.

Roberta makes the ragù with domesticated boar that her brothers raise out in back of the farm. I make it with pork, which is equally flavorful and much easier to find. Domesticated boar tastes like pork but with a slightly deeper flavor.

This is not a juicy dish but rather just moist enough to be pleasant. Be sure to serve it with lots of hearty, crusty bread and a rousing red, such as Cannonau from Sardinia.

2 tablespoons extra-virgin
   olive oil
1 large onion, diced
2½ pounds pork shoulder meat,
   cut into ¾-inch cubes
Fine sea salt
⅓ cup red wine vinegar

2 cups hearty red wine, such as
   Cannonau or Cabernet
   Sauvignon
¼ teaspoon hot paprika, or
   to taste
3 tablespoons grappa

1. Heat the oil and onion in a large skillet over medium-high heat. Cook, stirring occasionally, until the onion begins to brown on the edges and turn translucent in the center, about 6 minutes.

2. Add the pork, stir, season lightly with salt, and cook until the liquid it gives up has evaporated, 4 to 5 minutes. It isn't necessary that the pork brown. Stir in the vinegar and cook until it has been absorbed into the meat, about 8 minutes. Gradually stir in the red wine, then season with the hot paprika. Bring to a boil, then reduce the heat so the wine is simmering. Partially cover and cook, stirring occasionally, until the pork is tender, about 1 hour 20 minutes.

3. About 10 minutes before serving, stir in the grappa. Adjust the seasoning, remove from the heat, and serve.

Pork and Chicken Skewers with Lemon Rosemary Salt

SPIEDINI

4 SERVINGS

Segreti

The pieces of meat on the ends of the skewers will cook faster than those on the interior, so I suggest putting pork or sausage on the ends rather than chicken.

Alfredo Cavalli, a gardener by profession, is the volunteer chef, or *capo*, of the San Giovanni cooking crew, the same group of men who cook for all town occasions. *Spiedini* are his specialty. They are ideal for large feasts because they can be assembled in advance, grilled quickly, and have universal appeal. After one citrusy, garlicky bite I had to agree with him.

Served at home, *spiedini* are often accompanied by polenta, which in Emilia-Romagna is always drizzled with melted butter. Try a light red Lambrusco di Sorbara alongside.

8 ounces pork loin or shoulder, cut into 1-inch cubes

1 large red or green bell pepper, stemmed, seeds and pith removed, cut into 1-inch chunks

1 good-size onion, cut into 1-inch chunks

8 ounces boneless chicken or turkey breast, cut into 1-inch cubes

About 5 ounces pancetta, cut into 1½ inch cubes, trimmed if desired (see Note)

8 ounces thin, long pork sausages, cut into 1-inch lengths

2 tablespoons fresh lemon juice

4 to 6 teaspoons extra-virgin olive oil

1 to 2 tablespoons Lemon Rosemary Salt (page 394)

1. Preheat a barbecue grill to medium-high.

2. Assemble the brochettes: Skewer alternating pieces of pork, pepper, onion, chicken, pancetta, and sausage on 8 long skewers, beginning and ending with chunks of either pork or sausage. When all the *spiedini* are assembled, place the skewers on a platter and drizzle them evenly with the lemon juice.

3. If using charcoal, when the coals are red and dusted with ash, spread them out and place the rack on the barbecue. When the rack is hot (after 1 to 2 minutes),

place the *spiedini* on the grill and cook, turning until the meat and sausages are cooked through and golden and the vegetables are crisp-tender, 10 to 14 minutes, depending on the size of your fire.

4. Remove the skewers from the grill, drizzle them with the olive oil, and sprinkle generously with the lemon salt. Serve immediately.

NOTE: You may wish to trim some of the fat from the pancetta, as it tends to drip on the coals and cause flare-ups, or you may substitute prosciutto or any good-quality air-cured ham.

The Feast of San Giovanni

Every year in June, the tiny farming town of San Giovanni, about forty minutes from Modena in Emilia-Romagna, celebrates the feast of its patron saint. A huge three-sided white tent is put up in a field behind the church, whose steeple and surrounding linden trees are strung with small lights.

Most of the 750 town residents go to mass in the warm evening, overflowing out the church door and into the parking lot. Once the bells ring at the end of the mass, people stream from the church and head for the tent specially set up for a feast-day meal.

Those men who aren't at mass are already at work tending the fires in huge grills. As soon as the service is over, they set out the *spiedini*—small skewers of marinated meats and vegetables—to cook. Women bustle out from the church to arrange cakes and breads they've made on long tables draped with white cloths. Other cooks are heating up oil to fry the *gnocchi fritti,* pillows of fried dough, and *patate fritte,* or french-fried potatoes. For those who don't want *spiedini,* there are *panini alle salsicce,* or sausage sandwiches on freshly baked bread. Families and friends hurry to reserve places at the tables set up in rows, for everyone wants a seat for the festivities.

I stood with the cooking crew until the entertainment began on a small stage set up in front of the tent. Then I took my plate of *spiedini* and *gnocchi fritti* and sat down to enjoy the show, as town residents from age six to sixty-five entertained with songs. I was surprised by the beauty of their voices. My friend Anna Passatempi, who is married to a local farmer, explained that San Giovanni and the area around it is known for singers, including Pavarotti, who is from nearby Modena.

Herb-Marinated Leg of Lamb

This delicately crisp and flavorful leg of lamb, which is packed in fresh herbs to marinate overnight before it is cooked, is a typical shepherd's dish of the mountainous region of Gran Sasso d'Italia, in Abruzzo between Pescara and Rome. I first tasted it at La Bandiera, a restaurant owned by Marcello and Bruna Spadone and Marcello's mother, Anna Andrea, which is known for its carefully prepared, authentic regional specialties.

La Bandiera has an interesting history. Anna Andrea grew up on the farmland where the restaurant is now established. She left it to live in Rome, where she had a restaurant. She tired of the city, however, and wanted to return to her remote farm to establish an eatery of some sort. She began with a tiny, inviting little *osteria,* or pub, that served mostly wine by the glass and little snacks like the skewers of lamb drizzled with hot pepper sauce and wrapped in bread that are so typical to the Abruzzo mountains. Local farmers and tradespeople were her clients, and they came so regularly and often that she expanded. Today the restaurant is still a very country affair, and it still caters primarily to locals, but like so many country restaurants in Italy it sprawls, offering huge dining rooms for the frequent family celebrations like baptisms, weddings, and first communions that are such an integral part of Italian rural life.

According to the friends who brought me to the restaurant, one reason it has been such a success is that it serves the traditional farm and country dishes people no longer make for themselves at home. One of the best and a local favorite, according to Marcello, is this roast lamb, inspired by the shepherds who went into the mountains for months at a time and subsisted on grilled meat seasoned with wild herbs.

I think that lamb is delicious just about any way it is served, but this is truly something special. Marcello both grills and roasts the meat to give it a crisp exterior and moist interior with a smoky overlay of flavor. Serve it with the traditional accompaniment of Cherry Tomato and Arugula Salad (page 50) and drink a hearty red wine with it, preferably the wonderful Montepulciano d'Abruzzo from Valentino.

FOR MARINATING THE LAMB
1 butterflied small leg of lamb
  (about 3½ pounds) (see Note)
1 tablespoon extra-virgin olive oil
⅓ cup (gently packed) mixed fresh
  herb leaves, including savory,
  thyme, marjoram, and flat-leaf
  parsley

FOR ROASTING THE LAMB
Fine sea salt
3 tablespoons white or red wine

1 tablespoon extra-virgin
  olive oil
¼ cup mixed fresh herb leaves,
  including savory, thyme,
  marjoram, and flat-leaf
  parsley

FOR SERVING THE LAMB
2 tablespoons extra-virgin
  olive oil
1 teaspoon fresh lemon juice
Zest of ½ lemon, minced

1. To marinate the lamb, rub the meat all over with olive oil. Mince the herbs. Spread them on the inside of the leg and fold the leg together. Wrap it first in waxed paper, then in aluminum foil. Refrigerate for 24 hours.

2. Preheat a barbecue grill to medium-high. Preheat the oven to 450°F.

3. If using charcoal, when the coals are red and dusted with ash, spread them out and place the rack on the barbecue. Remove the lamb from its wrap-

ping and place it, still folded, on the rack and grill until it is golden on one side, 10 to 12 minutes. Turn it and grill the other side until it is browned and crisp, 10 to 12 minutes more.

4. To roast the lamb, lightly salt it all over and transfer it to a large baking dish. Whisk together the wine and olive oil. Mince the herbs and whisk them into the wine mixture, then pour it over the lamb. Place the lamb in the oven and roast it to your liking. For medium-rare, that will take

no longer than 10 minutes.

5. Remove the lamb from the oven and let it rest for 10 to 20 minutes so the juices can retreat back into the meat.

6. Just before serving, whisk together the oil, lemon juice, and lemon zest and drizzle it over the lamb. Slice the lamb and serve.

NOTE: Make this with American lamb, preferably 4 to 6 months old.

Slow-Roasted Shoulder of Lamb

ARROSTO D'AGNELLO

4 TO 6 SERVINGS

This recipe comes from Luna Rossa, a small restaurant high in the mountains of Basilicata, the region that forms the instep of Italy's boot. Luna Rossa is so hidden in the town of Terranova di Pollino that it's a miracle people even find it. But they do find it—attracted by its simple, traditional farmhouse fare. There I found specialties one would usually expect to find only on the farm, like this comforting dish of lamb seasoned with herbs. Simple, delicious, and flavorful, it meets the demands of those who work in the fields around Terranova.

Be sure to use the best lamb shoulder you can get, preferably from American lamb. And drink a robust red wine, like the kind they make in Terranova from vines that grow on the scrabbly, bushy hillsides and produce surprisingly flavorful grapes, which go into the rich and robust Aglianico del Vulture Riserva.

2 imported dried bay leaves
2 cloves garlic, cut in half, green germ removed
2 tablespoons lard
Freshly ground black pepper

1 lamb shoulder (3 to 3½ pounds)
2 tablespoons extra-virgin olive oil
Fine sea salt
Bay leaves or flat-leaf parsley sprigs, for garnish

1. Preheat the oven to 350°F.

2. Crush the bay leaves in your fingers, then mince them with the garlic cloves. Either mash the garlic mixture and lard together with a fork on a work surface or process to a paste in a food processor. The bay leaves should be in crumbs, not powdered. Transfer the mixture to a small bowl, grind black pepper to taste over it, and mix well.

3. Using a small sharp knife, make slits evenly throughout the lamb shoulder and fill the slits with the seasoned lard. Place the lamb in a baking dish. Pour ½ cup water and the oil around it.

4. Bake the lamb in the cen-

ter of the oven until it is crisp on the outside, 1½ hours. Cover the lamb with aluminum foil and continue baking until it is tender and nearly falling from the bone, about 1½ hours more.

5. Remove the lamb from the oven and the foil from the lamb. Sprinkle the lamb evenly with salt and let rest for at least 15 minutes so the cooking juices have a chance to retreat back into the meat. To serve, pull the meat from the bone and arrange it on a warmed platter. Garnish with bay leaves or fresh parsley. Bring the cooking juices to a simmer and either pour them over the lamb or serve them separately.

Bay leaves

Herbed Farmhouse Lamb Chops

**COSTOLETTE DI
AGNELLO ALLE
ERBE**

6 SERVINGS

Lamb is typical to Abruzzo, particularly in the mountains, where it is usually grilled no matter what the cut. This preparation, which comes from Marcello Spadone, whose restaurant La Bandiera offers traditional regional fare like this, is particularly flavorful and simple to prepare.

The breading dusted on the lamb chops offers delicate but distinct herbal seasoning while allowing the flavor of the tender lamb to come through. These chops cook very quickly, so watch them carefully!

Try a hearty, rich Montepulciano d'Abruzzo alongside.

Heaping ¼ cup (loosely packed)
   fresh rosemary leaves
Heaping ¼ cup (loosely packed)
   fresh sage leaves
1 tablespoon fresh thyme leaves
⅓ cup dried bread crumbs

Fine sea salt
6 medium lamb loin chops (each
   about 8 ounces)
2 tablespoons extra-virgin
   olive oil
Freshly ground black pepper

1. Preheat a barbecue grill to medium-high.

2. Mince together the herbs and place them in a small bowl. Add the bread crumbs and a good pinch of salt and toss until they are thoroughly blended with the herbs.

3. Brush the lamb chops on both sides with the oil and season slightly on both sides with salt and pepper.

4. Using half the herb mixture, press an equal amount onto one side of the lamb chops. Turn the chops and press the remaining herb mixture on the other side of the chops.

5. If using charcoal, when the coals are red and dusted with ash, spread them out and place the rack on the barbecue. When the rack is hot (after 1 to 2 minutes), place the lamb chops on the grill and cook until they are golden and slightly crisp on one side, about 4 minutes. Turn and repeat on the other side. The amount of time you grill the chops will depend on how rare you like them. After 4 minutes per side, they are usually done all the way through but still moist and juicy. For rare lamb chops, reduce the cooking time by 1 minute per side.

6. Remove from the grill and serve immediately.

Olive Oil: Less Expensive Than You Thought

If you think olive oil is expensive, consider this: A bottle of good wine costs between $12 and $20. A bottle of olive oil costs the same. However, a bottle of wine is generally drunk in an evening, while a bottle of olive oil generally lasts a month.

Gesuina's Roasted Chicken

**POLLO ARROSTO
ALLA GESUINA**

4 SERVINGS

This comes from Gesuina Pesce, a tiny woman who lives on the Masiero farm outside Florence, in a part of the Chianti hills that is often referred to as the Conca d'Oro, the golden spoon, because of the quality of the golden olive oil produced there.

Until the mid-1960s, Gesuina and her husband, Alfredo, were *mezzadri*, or tenant farmers, who worked the farm in exchange for their house and a percentage of the food they produced. When the tenant farming system was abolished, the Pesces continued to work the farm but as paid employees. In the early 1970s the Masiero family, restaurateurs from Florence, bought it. Although they weren't obligated do so, the Masieros continued the former owners' arrangement with the Pesces.

The Pesces retired in the 1980s and decided to spend the winters in the nearby town of Pontassieve, where they purchased an apartment. They use the farm as their spring and summer residence, raising the same crops in their garden, the same chickens, guinea hens, and rabbits they've always raised. It's comfortable for everyone.

Alfredo is an old-fashioned gardener, steeped in the use of compost and crop rotation. No synthetic chemicals make their way into his garden. He explained how one year he plants favas in one area, and the next year in another, so his soil stays balanced and rich. He spends all day in the garden, planting, trimming, harvesting, and caring for everything, from the fig tree laden with figs as big as baseballs to the rabbits he jealously guards, fearful that foxes will get in and steal them.

Gesuina's kitchen on the farm is large and dark, its one window overlooking the garden and the valley, letting in light so bright it looks like a television screen. Like many farm wives of her generation—she is in her late sixties—she never became accustomed to turning on lights, for electricity came late in her life.

The day I visited, Gesuina had several things going on the stove—fresh tomato sauce, fish that she'd sautéed and was planning to serve with the sauce, and a chicken she was preparing to roast. When I asked her how she roasted her chicken, she led me out her front door and there picked rosemary and sage from bushes growing outside it. For the garlic she turned to a braid Alfredo had made, which hung on the wall. She deftly chopped some and stuffed it and the herbs in the cavity of the chicken. "It roasts with those inside," she said shyly. "It's nothing, just a simple dish."

It is a simple dish, but the herbs add a great deal of subtle flavor as their aromas penetrate the bird from within.

Try the chicken with a lively Chianti Rufina.

1 chicken (3½ to 4 pounds), with
    giblets
Fine sea salt and freshly ground
    black pepper
2 long sprigs (12 inches each) fresh
    rosemary

¾ cup (gently packed) fresh sage
    leaves, or 3 tablespoons dried
    leaves, crumbled
4 cloves garlic, green germ removed,
    coarsely chopped

1. Preheat the oven 450°F.

2. Remove the giblets from the cavity of the chicken. Rinse the cavity quickly under cold running water, removing any excess pieces of fat. Pat the chicken dry. Sprinkle the cavity well with salt and pepper, then stuff the herbs and garlic inside. Add the giblets, truss the chicken, and place it in a roasting pan.

3. Roast until the skin of the chicken is puffed and golden and the juices run clear from the thigh joint when it is pierced with a fork, about 1 hour.

4. Remove from the oven, salt the chicken all over, and flip it on its breast, slightly tilted toward the head end. Let it rest for 20 to 40 minutes before carving and serving.

Chicken with Lemon Salt

POLLO AROMATIZZATO

4 TO 6 SERVINGS

This is one of those easy, inspired dishes that you can put together in a moment, yet the result is so flavorful it tastes as if you'd labored over it. I made this one day when I had a chicken, no time, and a jar of Lemon Rosemary Salt on hand, one of my favorite Italian seasoning blends which I picked up from Alfredo Cavalli, a full-time gardener and sometimes cook in the small farming town of San Giovanni in Emilia-Romagna (see recipe for *spiedini*, page 204).

I love the flavor of the salt, and when I looked at my robust but naked chicken it seemed the perfect seasoning. It is, as you'll see, for it gives the chicken a light but impressive lemon and rosemary fragrance. Try this with a round, full red wine, such as San Giovese di Romagna.

1 chicken (3½ to 4 pounds), with
    giblets
3½ teaspoons Lemon Rosemary
    Salt (page 394), plus additional for serving

½ lemon
1 tablespoon extra-virgin
    olive oil

1. Preheat the oven to 450°F.

2. Remove the giblets from the cavity of the chicken. Rinse the cavity quickly under cold running water, removing any excess pieces of fat. Pat the chicken dry. Season the cavity with 2 teaspoons of the lemon salt, squeeze the juice of the lemon half inside, and place the squeezed lemon rind inside the cavity along with the giblets. Truss the chicken.

3. Rub the chicken all over with the olive oil. Place it in a roasting pan and roast in the center of the oven until the chicken is golden and the juice runs golden from the thigh joint when it is pierced with a fork, about 1 hour.

4. Remove the chicken from

the oven and quickly sprinkle it on the breast side with 1 teaspoon of the remaining salt. Turn the chicken onto its breast, with its feet end slightly higher than the head end, and sprinkle with the remaining ½ teaspoon salt. Let the chicken rest for 20 to 40 minutes.

5. To serve, remove the trussing string from the chicken and drain any juices in the cavity into the roasting pan. Remove the giblets from the cavity. Transfer the chicken and giblets to a warmed serving platter (you may want to cut the chicken into serving pieces before placing it on the platter). Heat the juices over medium-high heat, scraping up any browned bits from the bottom of the pan. If there aren't ample juices, add ½ cup water to the juices in the pan and stir until combined. Either pour the juices over the chicken or serve them separately. Serve immediately, with additional lemon salt alongside.

Chicken with Sage

POLLO ALLA SALVIA

6 SERVINGS

Ghiselda Bini and her husband, Bruno, live on two acres of prime land right outside Radda in Chianti, a picture-perfect little Tuscan town. Former tenant farmers, they bought an old farmhouse of their own several years ago after working since the 1960s to save the money. They've completely remodeled and modernized it, retaining nothing but the dimensions of the old rooms. They proudly showed it to me from top to bottom.

Bruno works at a neighboring winery, but his real love is farming, and that's what he does with each spare minute—working their large and productive garden, caring for his own vines, making his own wine. Ghiselda is renowned as a fine cook whose repertoire includes classic Tuscan dishes like this one. In fact, this dish could be a sort of culinary flag for Tuscany, since it contains many of the most typical regional ingredients, from ubiquitous sage to Chianti to fruity green olive oil. The result is deep herb-flavored chicken with the delightful counterpoint of cured black olives. I like to serve pasta as a first course and a Chianti dei Colli Senesi alongside.

2 tablespoons extra-virgin olive oil
1 chicken (3½ to 4 pounds), cut
    into 8 serving pieces
Fine sea salt
⅓ cup fresh sage leaves
1 clove garlic, green germ removed,
    cut crosswise into thin slices

2 cups hearty Chianti or other
    good-quality red table wine
1 cup black olives cured in brine,
    preferably from Liguria or
    Nyons, unpitted
1 cup fresh flat-leaf parsley leaves,
    for garnish

1. Heat the oil in a large skillet over medium-high heat. Add the chicken and sauté until browned on all sides, about 5 minutes per side. Work in batches if necessary to avoid overcrowding the pan. Return all the chicken to the pan and season with salt. Add the sage leaves and garlic to the pan, pushing them down among the chicken pieces to make contact with the bottom of the pan. The sage will curl and turn dark.

2. Add the wine to the pan and stir as best as you can, scraping up any browned bits from the bottom of the pan. Bring the wine to a boil, then reduce the heat so the wine simmers merrily. Partially cover the pan and cook for about 10 minutes. Turn the chicken and continue cooking for 10 minutes more. Add the olives and cook, uncovered, until the chicken is done, about 15 minutes more, turning the chicken once.

3. Remove the chicken from the pan and place it on a serving platter. Bring the sauce to a boil and cook until it is reduced by half, about 10 minutes.

4. Mince the parsley. When the sauce is reduced, pour it over the chicken. Garnish with the parsley and serve immediately.

ALCALA

Though mid-February it was already hot in Catania, on the eastern side of Sicily, when I arrived there from Naples. Hot, sunny, and completely alluring. I was thrilled to be on this island I'd heard and dreamed about, and happier still to be with my friend, Susan Lord, who knows and loves it well. Our combined interest and passion presaged an exciting visit.

We drove immediately out of Catania into the countryside, which was lush with citrus groves and presided over by Mount Etna, a living, percolating force that resembles a majestic wild animal in repose. Its presence creates uncertainty, for it regularly belches steam into the atmosphere, which may explain the verve and intensity of the local population. They must live with its unpredictability.

Our attention turned from Mount Etna as we drove up the long dirt road leading to Alcala, a forty-four-acre farm where we were to stay for several days. The road was bordered by trees heavy with large, juicy oranges and small mandarin oranges and a shrub the Sicilians call *asparagi di barbera* (*Ruscus hypogossum*) because its new shoots look like wild asparagus.

We pulled up in front of a long, pinkish farmhouse that was shaded by jasmine and huge old cyprus trees. On hearing our car,

owner Anna Sapuppo emerged from the house to greet us. A dynamic young woman educated in Milan, she runs the farm with her brother, Giovanni, an agronomist. About ten years ago she decided to take in paying guests and has tastefully turned several small farm buildings into apartments, each with its own terrace, woodstove, and kitchen. The modest sum she charges for room and board helps ensure the farm stays in the family.

After setting down our bags we rejoined Anna, who took us up on one of the apartment terraces for the view's full impact. I simply stared at the mountain, the citrus groves with their splotches of vivid orange and yellow, the white stone town of Misterbianco off in the distance. It was lovely, lush, vivid.

Anna explained that when her grandfather, a minor member of Sicilian nobility, owned the farm it was planted with wine grapes. "It was a small *colonia,* or estate, run by indentured farmworkers, called *coloni,*" she said. "I remember watching my grandfather make the wine with his *coloni.* First, the men would go out into the vineyards to test the grapes. They would confer and my grandfather would decide what to do based on the collective opinion. He couldn't do it without them, and they couldn't do it without him."

She took us to the farm's *palmento,* or

winery, and explained how the grapes were delivered by wagon on one level and crushed there by men wearing huge wooden shoes. The juice sluiced into stone vats below and sat for one night. The skins were pressed separately, and their juice was mixed with the rest using a special container called a *salma*. "The *salma* contains thirty-three *quartara*," Anna said. "A *quartara* is about ten liters, and thirty-three was the age of Christ when he was crucified. There's a lot of symbolism in Sicily, even in winemaking." The wine was sold to local people who came with their demijohns, or large wicker-covered bottles, to pick it up.

In 1955 Anna's grandfather realized his grapes would never be granted a DOC, or Denominazione di Origine Controllata, a pedigree guaranteeing them a place on the market, because they didn't grow within the designated zone. Rather than continue to produce wine that would never be of much economic value, he pulled out most of his vines and planted citrus—oranges, lemons, and mandarin oranges—ideal crops for the climate and the market.

The farm still produces some wine grapes, and the juice is still sold to a local cooperative where it is turned into a very drinkable wine. The family is paid in wine, which they drink and serve to guests. They also have enough olive trees to produce their own oil and a handful of fruit varieties—other than citrus—to make their own jams.

In the intervening years, however, the citrus market changed dramatically. Now,

with the blended borders resulting from the European Union (EU), inexpensive citrus from countries where wages and benefits are lower than in Italy is flooding the Italian market, creating a crisis for Sicilian growers. "My father raised three children with the money he made growing citrus on this farm, something I could never do now," Anna said. "He was paid roughly the same price for citrus that I'm paid now, but I pay farmworkers three times what he paid them."

But Anna and her brother are determined—and creative. She has developed a mail-order citrus business that ships boxes of seasonal fruit to subscribers each month. That, along with renting rooms and providing meals, helps. But she gazes out over the citrus orchards with regret. "It's very complicated," she said. "I try with other farmers here to create businesses related to the farm."

I asked if the local authorities were encouraging. She laughed, rolled her eyes upward, and said, "We won't really talk about that. You've probably heard how complicated and difficult it is to understand Sicily. But none of us will give up."

The Mystery Cook

Our first night at Alcala we enjoyed one of several wonderful, very simple meals, which were accompanied by the local cooperative's wine. When I quizzed Anna about the dishes, she knew the recipes by heart but gave them to me with little passion. Finally she admitted she didn't like to cook and that she did it only when her cook, a man named Nunzio San Filippo, wasn't on duty in the kitchen.

The following day I went off in search of Nunzio and eventually found him picking shoots of the *asparagi di barbera* for the evening meal. A bachelor in his late sixties, he talked about how he came to prepare meals for Anna's family and her guests.

The Sapuppos were members of Sicily's noble class, and they had a large staff to work their land and keep their house. At first a field worker on the farm, Nunzio befriended the family cook, Tino, who eventually brought him into the kitchen as an apprentice. At eighteen, Nunzio renounced field work to become a full-time cook and waiter for the Sapuppos. "Those were the days," Nunzio said as I sat in the tiny family kitchen one morning, watching him work. "We wore white gloves and jackets to serve the family and their guests. It was all very formal."

Nunzio explained that Tino had been trained by a *Monsu,* a French-trained chef that all noble Sicilian families employed at one time. Tino learned a very formal style of cooking from the *Monsu,* which he adapted and passed along to Nunzio. Nunzio's cooking style is much more casual than the formal *Monsu* tradition, but it bears many of its formal, classical hallmarks, as I noted when he prepared *aglassado,* braised beef, a dish with little relation to the local climate or flavors.

Other dishes he prepared were much more exciting and much more in the Sicilian peasant tradition. He carefully, even methodically, moved about the kitchen, which contained nary a modern convenience except for running water, producing a rich tomato sauce (page 424), braised cauliflower, wild greens with toasted bread crumbs, and many other dishes that burst with hearty Sicilian flavor.

I had planned to stay and watch him for an hour, but three hours later we were still talking as he cut up cabbage for a simple salad. When he felt he could take a break, he set a place at the kitchen table and served up a bit of everything he'd made, motioning me to sit down. I was touched but reluctant to sit and eat while he was working. I asked if he wasn't going to eat too. "Oh no, I don't eat until 3 P.M.," he said. "Here, let me get you some bread."

I felt spoiled and pampered sitting there in the kitchen, Nunzio puttering around me, filling my water glass, making sure all was fine. He let no detail pass, and it didn't take much to imagine him in a different era, in the formal dining room next door, dressed in his finery as he hovered.

I had a delicious meal in Nunzio's kitchen. When I was finished I tried to clear the table, but Nunzio would have none of it. Instead he wished me well and sent me on my way with a handful of oranges. "In case you get hungry this afternoon," he said.

Chicken with Pasta and Potatoes

Pollo con pasta e patate is a "bastard" recipe, a blend of French and Sicilian, which does the very un-Italian thing of mixing chicken and pasta together in a single dish. Unusual, but delicious.

This is a favorite dish of Nunzio San Filippo, the cook at the Sapuppo farm, near Catania in Sicily (see essay page 216). Semiretired now, Nunzio spends three days cooking at the farm and the other days at his own home cooking for his nieces and nephews, who visit often. This is their favorite dish, a meal-in-a-pot that is typical to the Sicilian farm and needs no other accompaniment. There are dozens of recipes available for *pasta e patate*, and each cook makes his or her own. This is extra delicious, I think, for it includes Nunzio's Tomato Sauce and lots of parsley, which deliver added spice, flavor, and color. Open a bottle of Regaleali Bianco to serve alongside.

3 tablespoons extra-virgin olive oil
4 cloves garlic, crushed slightly
1 chicken (3½ to 4 pounds), cut
  into 8 serving pieces
1 pound waxy potatoes, peeled and
  cut into quarters
2 medium carrots, cut into
  ¼-inch-thick rounds

1½ cups fresh flat-leaf parsley leaves
  (about 1 medium bunch)
1 cup Nunzio's Tomato Sauce
  (page 424)
Fine sea salt
8 ounces small dried pasta, such
  as orecchiette
½ cup fresh basil leaves

1. Heat the oil and garlic in a large skillet over medium heat. Stir and cook until the garlic is lightly browned on all sides, 6 minutes. Remove it from the pan and set aside. Add the chicken to the oil and sauté it on both sides until it is a deep golden brown, about 5 minutes per side. Remove the chicken from the pan, add the potatoes and carrots, and sauté them until the potatoes are golden, 5 minutes more. Add water to cover by about 3 inches and return the chicken and garlic to the pan. Add the parsley and tomato sauce,

stir, and season to taste with salt. Cover and bring to a boil, then reduce the heat so the liquid is simmering merrily and cook until the potatoes and chicken are cooked through, 35 to 40 minutes.

2. Check the level of the liquids. If necessary, add water to bring it at least 2 inches above the ingredients. Cover and bring to a boil. Add the pasta, stir, return the water to a boil, and cook just until the pasta is al dente (tender but still firm to the bite), 7 to 10 minutes.

3. Remove from the heat and adjust the seasoning. Tear the basil leaves into small pieces and sprinkle over the chicken and pasta, then serve.

NOTE: This is a cross between a soup and a stew, so you may either leave it soupy (similar in consistency to the other *pasta e patate,* in the chapter on soups, page 73) or cook it a bit longer to evaporate the liquid to the consistency you like.

Mita's Roast Guinea Hen

**FARAONA AL
FORNO ALLA
MITA**

**4 OR 5
SERVINGS**

This recipe is a favorite of Mita Antonini, a farmer near Cortona, in Tuscany. Mita uses a handful of sage and a lot of garlic to season a guinea hen to perfection, making it a dish fit for the finest company. The flavor combination is a good one to remember for other fowl too, from turkey to Cornish hens.

Serve a wonderful rich red, such as Chianti Rufina from Selvapiana, alongside.

*1 guinea hen (3 to 3½ pounds),
   with giblets (see Note)*
*1 cup (gently packed) fresh sage
   leaves*
*4 large cloves garlic, cut in half,
   green germ removed*

1 teaspoon coarse sea salt
1 teaspoon extra-virgin olive oil
Fine sea salt
*Freshly ground black pepper
   (optional)*

1. Preheat the oven to 450°F. Remove the giblets from the guinea hen and set aside.

2. Mince the sage, garlic, and coarse salt together and stuff the mixture in the hen's cavity. Add the giblets. Truss the guinea hen, place it in a roasting pan, and rub it all over with the oil. Roast the hen until it is golden, the leg and thigh joint moves easily in the socket, and the juice from the thigh joint runs clear when pierced with a fork, 45 to 50 minutes.

3. Remove the bird from the oven, salt it all over with sea salt, then turn it on its back and let rest for 20 minutes.

4. Scrape the stuffing and giblets from the guinea hen into the roasting pan. Cut the heart and gizzard into tiny pieces. Cut the guinea hen into serving pieces and arrange them on a platter. Place the roasting pan over medium-high heat, add ½ cup water to the pan, and stir, crushing the liver into the liquid and scraping up any browned bits on the bottom of the pan. Cook, stirring, until the liquid is reduced by about one-third. Adjust the seasoning and pour the sauce over the hen. Season with pepper if desired and serve immediately.

NOTE: Try to find a guinea hen, but if you can't, prepare this with a full-flavored farm-raised chicken.

Braised Guinea Hen

SALMÌ DI
FARAONA DI
MALVARINA

4 OR 5
SERVINGS

Though called a *salmĭ,* which generally refers to a game bird cooked in red or white wine, or a rabbit cooked in its own blood, this dish isn't either. Perhaps it was once a more rugged peasant dish, but today it is bright and fresh, redolent of lemon and capers.

Maria Maurillo, who cooks for guests at her family's farm, Malvarina, made this *salmĭ* the second night I stayed with them. As I watched—and occasionally helped—her make the accompanying *peperoni fritti* (page 274) and *tortichilion di mele* (page 365) for dinner, the *salmĭ* simmered away, sending its heavenly aroma into the air.

Maria uses guinea hen, which is very common to the Italian farm, almost more than chickens. When I asked her why, she didn't know, except to say that perhaps it was because their dark meat is more full flavored and rich than that of a chicken. I think she's probably right. It certainly isn't because they are easier to raise than chickens. A guinea hen doesn't adapt to crowded conditions and literally won't survive unless it has space to run. This is why when you walk through an Italian vegetable and herb garden, the guinea fowl squawk and holler and are always running in the other direction, leaving a wake of their little designer feathers, which are gray to black, with tiny white spots.

Guinea hen is rich in flavor and holds up particularly well in this robust preparation that includes lemon juice, cloves, sage, and capers. Make it a day in advance to allow the flavors to mellow and deepen. If guinea hens are unavailable, chicken can be easily substituted.

A lovely red wine, such as a Torgiano red, is ideal for this assertive dish.

Rural Italian Wine Wisdom

In rural Italy it is believed foolhardy to drink red and white wine at the same meal, for it is thought to be poor for the health, to *fare male allo stomaco.*

Segreti

• If you pass the sauce through a food mill, follow it with a fresh piece of bread, which will clean out the mill. Discard the bread once it's been through the mill.

• Try to find a guinea hen, but if you can't, prepare this with a full-flavored farm-raised chicken.

1 tablespoon extra-virgin olive oil

1 guinea hen or chicken (3 to 4 pounds), with giblets (see Notes)

Fine sea salt

1 medium carrot, cut into ¼-inch dice

2 small onions, cut into ¼-inch dice

2 cloves garlic, cut in half, green germ removed

5 strips lemon zest (each about ½ x 3 inch)

3 whole cloves

10 fresh sage leaves

½ cup chicken stock

¼ cup fresh lemon juice (see Note)

Freshly ground black pepper

⅓ cup capers (2 ounces), preferably preserved in salt (see box, page 66)

1. Heat the oil in a Dutch oven or other heavy pan over medium heat. Add the poultry and brown it on both sides, seasoning lightly with salt, about 7 minutes per side. Remove the poultry from the pan. Add the vegetables and garlic, stir, and cook until the onions turn translucent and soften, 10 to 12 minutes. Stir in the lemon zest, cloves, sage, chicken broth, and lemon juice. Return the poultry to the pan along with the giblets and turn so it is completely moistened. Season lightly with salt and pepper, cover, and cook over low heat until the poultry is so tender it falls from the bone, about 1 hour. Check the poultry halfway through and turn it if necessary to cook it evenly.

2. Remove the pan from the heat. Transfer the meat, most of which will have fallen from the bone, to a warmed serving platter. Include any pieces on which the meat still clings to the bone and discard any excess bones. Stir the capers into the sauce and skim off any excess fat if desired. Coarsely purée the sauce, using a wand mixer, blender, or food mill. Adjust the seasoning and pour the sauce over the poultry. Serve immediately.

NOTES: Have a bit of extra lemon juice on hand in case you want to heighten the seasoning. The amount of juice you will need depends on the lemons and the chicken stock you use.

MALVARINA

It doesn't seem as if a real farm could be so close to Assisi, I thought as I wandered narrow roads trying to find Agriturismo Malvarina, a farm that takes paying guests. I had the shadow of an address, and although I'd called for directions, the phone connection was so bad I could hardly understand them. I finally stopped at a gas station, and the owner knew where I was headed. "Rivotorto is what you want," he said, pointing the way.

Just two miles outside Assisi and up the slopes of Mount Subasio, it started to feel rural. There were lush green fields across the road on one side, and I spied olive trees climbing the hill in the other. I followed signs to the farm up a long gravel road until I reached a tall house completely covered with ivy.

Rain was pouring down and a gray-haired woman under a huge umbrella came out to greet me and show me to the comfortable, simple room I had reserved in a long, low former stable. It looked out through a jumble of Scotch broom and low pine trees to the plain, which shimmered in the remainder of the light.

The woman was Maria Maurillo. She was the "mama" of Malvarina and, it turned out, a good part of its heart and soul as well. She left me with the welcome information that dinner would be in an hour.

As I strolled to dinner, I inhaled the wet and fragrant air. The enormous dining room, installed in the farm's former *cantina,* or wine cellar, had a huge fire blazing at one end and three long tables. Since I was alone, I was invited to sit at the family table, a round one tucked in the corner.

Three plates were stacked at each place. On the top plate sat a round of fried dough spread with a rich tomato and tuna sauce and sprinkled with cheese. A young woman bustled about putting spoonfuls of eggs scrambled with zucchini, zucchini blossoms, and olive oil alongside.

Claudio Fabrizzi, a handsome, heavy-set man and Maria's eldest son, sat next to me. He is the host at Malvarina, and the fact that his family farm welcomes up to thirty people a night is, according to his mother, a result of his capriciousness.

"Claudio, Claudio," she said with a smile playing at the corners of her mouth. "He was a banker, and before that he was in real estate. But there is something you should know about Claudio. If he isn't with horses, he isn't happy." He raises riding horses on the farm, sponsors trekking trips, and welcomes trekkers at Agriturismo Malvarina.

Claudio shrugged and added that while he'd been in real estate he'd managed other people's farms as a sort of consultant. His own family's farm wasn't making any money, and as he looked around at the possibilities, it seemed to him a good idea to turn it into an *agriturismo.*

Aside from making the farm economically viable, Claudio considered it a matter of family pride, for Malvarina has an unusual history. Claudio's grandparents lived there, cultivated olives, operated an olive mill, and made their own oil. By 1929 times had gotten tough and they had to sell the farm.

When Claudio's father grew up, he became obsessed with trying to get the farm back. It took him until the 1960s, but he did it. The family moved to the farm and together they kept it alive, if not completely economically viable.

Fast forward to the 1980s and the idea of the *agriturismo.* "We couldn't have survived just farming," Claudio said. "If we'd tried, I'd be sixty pounds thinner though!"

Claudio and his father started restoring the farm. They turned the granary and chicken house into lovely private apartments. The former stable, where I stayed, included several other bedrooms and a bright, pleasant dining room where breakfast was served. When Claudio's father died, the *agriturismo* was just beginning to take root.

Farming and horses are the major activities at Malvarina. The Fabrizzis have thirty-eight acres planted in about three thousand olive trees. They have apples, figs, pears, and beehives. Maria makes all the jam served in the *agriturismo,* and they have a friend who comes and makes their honey. Claudio's wife, Patrizia, and Maria tend a vegetable garden,

and Patrizia's mother and a few other neighbors supply them with other greens and vegetables for the restaurant.

When Claudio first launched the *agriturismo,* he wasn't sure which direction it would take. He didn't know that the restaurant would become so successful, nor did Maria realize that she would become a full-time cook.

She takes it in stride, though. When asked if it is a lot of work, she says simply, "No. My husband always brought colleagues home, my sons always had their friends in, I cooked all the time anyway," she said. "This isn't that much different."

Because Maria's roots are Sicilian, her food is rife with heady tomato sauce, citrus zest, hot peppers, and richly sautéed vegetables, evident in her Braised Guinea Hen (page 222) and Fried Bell Peppers (page 274). Desserts are simple and delicious, from Maria Maurillo's Amazing Apple Cake (page 365) to her Anise Cookies (page 366).

"We've made huge investments and are gradually paying them off," Claudio said. "It's all happening slowly but it's working. Now I want to establish a trekking business."

Meanwhile, Claudio is happy to take those guests who are interested on short rides around the property. As for Malvarina, with its gentle breezes that carry the scent of Scotch broom and *petali di angeli,* or mock orange, its simple comforts and ready humor, and Maria's food, which sustains long after you've left, it looks like it will endure for a long time to come.

Guinea Hen in Vin Santo

FARAONA AL VIN SANTO

4 TO 6 SERVINGS

This recipe, redolent with the rich flavors of guinea hen and Vin Santo, is a true Tuscan specialty, for though Vin Santo is made in a few other Italian regions, it is best known and most common in Tuscany. Vin Santo can be either very sweet or quite dry (see box, page 227), but what remains constant is its deep floral flavor, which gives this dish a "sweetness" that doesn't have anything to do with sugar. Since the Vin Santo is added right before serving, all of its flavor remains. This recipe is elegant and richly flavored, and while guinea hen is best, a good farm-raised chicken would be excellent too.

Try this with a Chianti dei Colli Fiorentini.

2 tablespoons extra-virgin olive oil
1 tablespoon unsalted butter
1 guinea hen (3½ to 4 pounds),
    cut into 8 serving pieces (see
    Note)
Fine sea salt
1 pound white onions, cut length-
    wise in half, then cut into ¼-
    inch-thick slices
3 cloves garlic, green germ removed,
    minced

¾ cup fruity white wine, such as
    Pinot Grigio
¼ cup Vin Santo or Sauternes

1. Heat the oil and butter in a Dutch oven over medium heat. Add the guinea hen and brown it, about 5 minutes on each side. You may want to do this in two batches to avoid crowding the pan. Lightly salt the guinea hen and remove it from the pan. Add the onions and garlic to the pan, reduce the heat to medium-low, and cook the onions until they are golden and tender, 15 to 20

minutes. Check them to be sure they don't brown and adjust the heat as necessary.

2. Return the guinea hen to the pan. Add the white wine, stir, and season lightly with salt. Bring the wine to a boil, then reduce the heat to low and cook until the guinea hen is tender and cooked through and the juices run golden from the thigh when it is pierced with a knife, about 45 minutes. Just before serving, add the Vin Santo, stir, and let it heat through without boiling for 3 to 5 minutes so its flavor remains intact. Serve immediately.

NOTE: Try to find a guinea hen, but if you can't, prepare this with a full-flavored farm-raised chicken.

The Holy Wine of Tuscany—Vin Santo

Vin Santo, or holy wine, is the well-known flowery sweet dessert wine of Tuscany that is made from grapes left on the stem to dry for several months in a cool, airy room somewhere on the farm. Rooms dedicated to the drying of these grapes are unheated. If it is terribly cold and damp, the windows are closed. If it is warm, the windows are open to allow the cool air to flow over the grapes.

When the grapes are pressed, the juice with its highly concentrated sugars is put in small barrels, which are sealed with a plug of concrete that has the date marked on it. The wine ages undisturbed for at least three years, and the day of the Vin Santo tasting is an important one, for the results are anticipated by everyone. The vintner must trust that the alchemy occurring in the barrel is positive—because it is sealed, it is impossible to check. Most vintners who make Vin Santo, however, have few worries about their product, for years of experience have taught them what they need to know to make a good Vin Santo.

Dina's Roasted Rabbit

**CONIGLIO
ARROSTO ALLA
DINA**

6 SERVINGS

Dina Beni is a pretty woman with skin so brown and wrinkled she could only have done one thing all her life—work outside. And she still does, though she was well into her seventies when I met her, scurrying around her farm tending the rabbits and chickens, raising beautiful vegetables, going inside just to prepare and eat meals.

Dina lives in Massa dei Sabbioni, in Tuscany, in a gorgeous old farmhouse that dominates the valley. The inner courtyard has a view that overlooks first her garden, where flowers, vegetables, and herbs grow in equal profusion, then the valley and hills beyond. When I stopped to pick up a rabbit she had dressed for me, we walked up a narrow stone stairway to reach her kitchen, which was nearly as big as the courtyard. Windows were small and it was quite dark inside, but she didn't turn on the lights, a common practice in Italy, where eyes are more accustomed to working in the dark.

I admired the enormous fireplace, which was literally large enough to sit in, as Dina and her husband do every night. At either side of the grate, tucked back under the mantelpiece, was a narrow bench, each with cushions on the seat and slippers underneath. Dina followed my gaze and laughed. "That's where we live in winter when we're inside," she said. It looked so cozy I wanted to crawl in.

A room with a comfortable, well-used feel, this kitchen emanated flavor. I could almost taste the many meals Dina had prepared here for her extended family. She handed me my rabbit and we went out to the garden where she cut me an armful of rosemary, some basil, and a bouquet of roses and gave me this aromatic recipe for braising the rabbit. I went right back to the charming little apartment my husband, son, and I were staying in to prepare it. We enjoyed it sitting on the terrace, sipping a full red Tignanello alongside.

2 tablespoons extra-virgin olive oil
1 rabbit (about 3 pounds) cut into
  6 serving pieces
1 large clove garlic, green germ
  removed, minced
Fine sea salt and freshly ground
  black pepper

2 medium-size tomatoes (each
  about 4 ounces), cored and cut
  crosswise in half
1 cup (gently packed) fresh
  basil leaves
6 long branches fresh rosemary

1. Heat the oil in a large heavy skillet over medium-high heat. Add the rabbit pieces and sauté until golden, about 5 minutes per side. Brown the rabbit in two batches if necessary to avoid overcrowding the pan. Rub the rabbit pieces with the minced garlic; there will be just enough to lightly season each piece. Return all the rabbit pieces to the pan in one layer. Don't add more garlic; 1 clove gives just the right amount of flavor to the dish. Season the rabbit generously with salt and sparsely with pepper.

2. Squeeze the tomato halves gently over the rabbit, then push them down among the rabbit pieces. Coarsely chop the basil and sprinkle the leaves over the rabbit. Lay the rosemary branches over all. Cover and cook over medium heat until the rabbit is cooked through, about 1 hour, turning the pieces at least twice to be sure they cook evenly. Adjust the heat if necessary, for the rabbit should cook slowly, and any liquids given up by the tomato and the rabbit should simmer gently.

3. Remove the rabbit from the heat. Adjust the seasoning if necessary and serve.

Tuscan Baked Rabbit

Alfredo Pesce gave me this recipe while standing in his *orto,* or vegetable garden, on the side of a hill near the town of Pontassieve, outside Florence. A former *mezzadri,* or tenant farmer, he is now retired, and at seventy-five years of age he contents himself with keeping a substantial vegetable garden where fava beans, tomatoes, melons, raspberries, and rabbits all grow in profusion. Because his little patch of land is tucked in the hills, his vegetables are later than those in Florence. When I visited him in mid-May, his fava beans were not quite ripe, while the Florentine markets were full of the fat-podded beans.

Though Alfredo's wife, Gesuina, does the family cooking, Alfredo seems to be the keeper of the recipes, and he cited this tender, earthy rabbit dish as one the couple eats often, either with Swiss chard as here, or with roasted potatoes. In Alfredo's case the ingredients come, naturally, from his *orto.* The olive oil he uses comes from the trees that stretch down the hill in front of him.

Try a lively red, such as Rosso di Montepulciano, with this.

*1 young rabbit (about 3 pounds),
    cut into 6 serving pieces*
*3 cloves garlic, cut lengthwise
    into quarters, green germ
    removed*
2 tablespoons extra-virgin olive oil
Fine sea salt
3 small red onions coarsely chopped

*2 pounds Swiss chard, stems
    trimmed, well rinsed, and
    coarsely chopped*
Freshly ground black pepper
*½ cup dry white wine, such as
    Pinot Grigio*
*2 long branches (6 inches each)
    rosemary*

1. Make 12 small slits in the meatiest parts of the rabbit and insert the garlic quarters in the slits. The breast pieces have thin flaps of meat that extend from them; fold the flaps of meat back,

and attach them to the breast with a piece of garlic. This will prevent them from cooking too quickly. If the flaps don't seem solidly attached, use a small skewer or tie some kitchen string around the pieces to keep the garlic and flaps in place.

2. Heat the oil in a large heavy skillet over medium heat. Add the rabbit and brown on both sides, about 8 minutes, salting it lightly on each side once browned. You may need to brown the rabbit in two batches to avoid crowding the pan.

3. Remove the rabbit from the pan and add the onions. Stir and cook until they begin to turn translucent, 3 to 5 minutes. Add

the Swiss chard, stir, cover, and cook until it is tender and dark green, about 30 minutes. Season to taste with salt and pepper.

4. Nestle the rabbit pieces among the chard leaves, pour the wine over all, and tuck the rosemary between the rabbit pieces. Sprinkle lightly with salt, cover, and cook over medium-low heat until the rabbit is tender and the juices run golden from the thigh when it is pierced with a sharp knife, about 35 minutes.

5. To serve, either carry the cooking vessel to the table or transfer the chard and onions to a warmed platter, top with the rabbit, and pour the cooking juices over all.

Roast Rabbit with Salmoriglio

ARROSTO DI CONIGLIO CON SALMORIGLIO

4 TO 6 SERVINGS

Salmoriglio, a blend of lemon juice, olive oil, garlic, and dried oregano, originated in Sicily and is a staple in many farm homes. There it is used to flavor everything from fish to rabbit to vegetables. I learned about it from Nunzio San Filippo (see essay, page 216), a farm cook near Catania, and have used it regularly since. I add more oregano to the dish itself—dried oregano, that is, for the fresh leaf is parsimonious with its flavor. Try to find dried Sicilian oregano, which grows wild on the rocky interior slopes of the island and is, after harvesting, carefully sorted so that you get only the intensely flavored leaves, no buds or stems. If you can't find it, use Greek oregano.

A well-chilled white such as Regaleali Bianco is ideal with this dish.

1 rabbit, (about 3½ pounds), cut
   into 8 serving pieces (see Note)
2 cloves garlic, green germ removed,
   minced

1 tablespoon dried oregano
1 recipe Herb and Lemon Sauce
   (page 425)

1. Place the rabbit in a baking dish large enough to hold the pieces in one layer. Rub on all sides with the garlic, then sprinkle with the oregano, crushing it between your fingers to release its flavor. Turn the pieces so they are evenly covered with the garlic and oregano. Cover and refrigerate for at least 3 hours or overnight.

2. Remove the rabbit or chicken from the refrigerator at least 30 minutes before you plan to cook it but preferably 1 hour before. Drizzle half the herb sauce over the meat, turn the pieces so they are coated, and let warm to room temperature.

3. Preheat the oven to 500°F or preheat a barbecue grill to medium-high.

4. If you are baking the meat, place it in the center of the oven and bake until it is beginning to turn golden, about 20 minutes. Drizzle half the remaining sauce over the meat and continue cooking until it is golden and crisp, 20 to 30 minutes more, depending on the meat and the size of the pieces. If you are grilling the meat over charcoal, when the coals are red and dusted with ash, spread them out and place the rack on the barbecue. When the rack is hot (after 1 to 2 minutes), place the meat on the rack, spreading out the pieces so there is plenty of room between them. Cook until they are golden on one side, about 10 minutes, brushing occasionally with the sauce that was used to marinate the meat and pressing the garlic and oregano into the meat. Turn the

meat, drizzle any remaining marinade over it, and cook until it turns golden on the second side, about 15 minutes. Turn the pieces once more so the meat cooks evenly and the marinade that you've put over it is thoroughly cooked as well, 5 to 8 minutes more.

5. To test for doneness, cut into the thickest piece of meat all the way to the bone and pull back the knife. If the meat is pink, continue cooking. If it is opaque, it is cooked. (Chicken will take about 5 minutes longer to cook than rabbit.)

6. Remove from the oven or grill and drizzle with the remaining sauce. Let sit for 10 minutes so it is not blistering hot, then serve.

NOTE: If you can't find rabbit, use a chicken with its giblets.

Fish in Sicilian Herb and Lemon Sauce

PESCE CON SALMORIGLIO

4 SERVINGS

Sicily is the only Italian region where seafood regularly makes its way to the farm table because tomatoes, peppers, and citrus are raised there within sight of the rolling waves of the Golfo del Noto in the southeast or the Golfo del Gela in the south. Seafood is common on the Sicilian farm table, and this is a simple, and deliciously Sicilian, way to prepare it. The sauce, called *salmoriglio,* in Italian, with its high notes of lemon and oregano, brightens the flavor of the fish, and since it can be made and kept for a day or two, it makes for a quick, easy meal.

Unlike other herbs, oregano is always used dried in Italy. When fresh, oregano has a flavor that is too mild and fleeting; when dried, it becomes concentrated and intense. This is the flavor the Italians prefer.

Serve this with a well-chilled and fruity white, such as Regaleali Bianco.

1½ pounds tuna steaks, about ½
   inch thick
2 cloves garlic, green germ removed,
   minced

1½ teaspoons dried oregano
1 recipe Herb and Lemon Sauce
   (page 425)

1. Preheat a barbecue grill to medium-high.

2. Rinse the fish and pat it dry. Rub the minced garlic on one side of the fish steaks. Crush the oregano and rub it on the other side of the steaks. Place the fish in one layer on a platter, cover, and refrigerate for 30 minutes.

3. Pour all but ¼ cup of the sauce over the fish, moistening both sides of each piece.

4. If you are using charcoal, when the coals are red and dusted with ash, spread them out. Oil the rack and place it on the barbecue. When the rack is hot (after 1 to 2 minutes), place the fish steaks on the rack and grill until they are golden, 3 to 4 minutes. Carefully turn them and cook until they are golden on the second side and cooked to your liking. For fish that is cooked all the way through, another 4 minutes will be sufficient.

5. Transfer the fish from the grill to a serving platter or serving plates. Drizzle with the remaining sauce and serve.

Baked Fish alla Salina

Maria Francesca Bongiorno, who lives amidst a field of caper plants on the island of Salina, in the Eolian archipelago off the west coast of Sicily (see essay, page 67), and whose terrace is almost obscured by the cherry tomatoes she hangs there so she has them handy until spring, gave me this recipe when I was visiting her family's caper farm. Simple and bright, the dish speaks volumes about the typical cuisine of Salina, which is based on seafood, fresh garden vegetables, and lots of capers.

Try with a lightly chilled simple white wine, such as Bianco di Salina.

1 whole mild white fish (2 to 3 pounds), such as redfish or red snapper

¼ cup capers, preferably preserved in salt (see box, page 66)

1 large onion, thinly sliced

1 pound cherry tomatoes, stemmed and halved

1 red or green bell pepper, stemmed, seeds and pith removed, cut into paper-thin rings

⅓ cup extra-virgin olive oil

Fine sea salt and freshly ground black pepper

½ cup dry white wine, such as Bianco di Salina or Frascati

½ cup fresh basil leaves, for garnish

1. Preheat the oven to 400°F. Rinse the fish well, cleaning the cavity, and make sure the gills are removed. Pat dry and refrigerate until ready to bake.

2. In a large bowl, combine the capers, onion, tomatoes, bell pepper, and olive oil, tossing to thoroughly coat the vegetables with the oil.

3. Place the fish in a baking dish large enough to hold it and

the vegetables with plenty of room to spare. Sprinkle the fish inside and out with salt and pepper, then cover it with the vegetable mixture. Season again with salt and pepper and pour the wine around the fish.

4. Bake in the center of the oven until the fish is opaque throughout, 30 to 40 minutes. To test for doneness, insert the point of a sharp knife into the fish behind the head, and pull back. If the meat is still very translucent, continue baking just until it is opaque.

5. Remove the fish from the oven, garnish with the basil leaves, and either serve from the baking dish or transfer the fish and vegetables to a serving platter.

capers

Grilled Fish from Salina

**PESCE ALLA
GRIGLIA
ALL'EOLIANA**

4   S E R V I N G S

Salina is a magical place, a rocky, mountainous island in the Tyrrhenian Sea as subject to tempestuous weather as it is to languid, sunny days. It's never too hot, for subtle sea breezes keep the air moving, and though harsh, the land is arable. Every spot that can be cultivated is, it seems, with everything from capers to flavorful cherry tomatoes.

Small fishing boats come in regularly, and residents crowd around to buy what is fresh. In summer particularly, this recipe is a typical way to prepare the catch. It is then served with a Caper and Potato Salad (page 65) and enjoyed, as often as not, outdoors.

Serve this with a lightly chilled Regaleali Bianco.

4 tuna or shark steaks (each about
    6 ounces)
2 tablespoons extra-virgin olive oil

¼ cup fresh flat-leaf parsley leaves
4 teaspoons fresh lemon juice

1. Preheat a barbecue grill to medium-high. If using charcoal, when the coals are red and dusted with ash, spread them out. Lightly oil the rack and place on the barbecue.

2. Massage each tuna or shark steak lightly with 1 tablespoon of the olive oil.

3. When the rack is hot (after 1 to 2 minutes), place the fish steaks on the grill and cook until the fish is opaque throughout, 2 to 3 minutes per side, depending on the thickness and variety of fish steaks.

4. Mince the parsley.

5. Transfer the fish to warmed plates. Drizzle each steak with 1 teaspoon lemon juice, then sprinkle with the parsley. Serve immediately.

Brilliant Swordfish Steak

**RUOTA DI PESCE
SPADA**

**4 TO 6
SERVINGS**

Going to a fish market in Sicily is like going to a swordfish convention, for swordfish are everywhere. Fish markets abound in city and countryside alike (though in the countryside a "fish market" is likely to be the boat from which the fish was caught, pulled in to dock), and it goes without saying that recipes for swordfish abound. This is one of my favorite farm recipes. Robust and colorful, it is quick to assemble and is served at room temperature, making it perfect for company, since it is ready in advance.

Try this with a lightly chilled Bianco di Alcamo, a white wine from Sicily.

2 pounds swordfish in one thick
(4- to 5-inch) piece, with skin if
possible (see Note)
5 cloves garlic, cut lengthwise into
quarters, green germ removed
Fine sea salt and freshly ground
black pepper

¼ cup Nunzio's Tomato Sauce
(page 424)
1 teaspoon dried oregano
1 cup (loosely packed) fresh
basil leaves
2 tablespoons extra-virgin
olive oil

1. Preheat the oven to 350°F.

2. Rinse and pat the fish dry. Make shallow slits in the swordfish on top and stick half the garlic quarters in so the point is barely sticking out. Repeat on the other side. Lightly sprinkle both surfaces of the fish with salt and pepper and place the fish in a baking dish. Spread the tomato sauce over the top of the fish. Crushing the oregano with your fingers, sprinkle it over the tomato sauce, then coarsely chop the basil and sprinkle it on top. Finally, drizzle the fish with the oil and sprinkle 2 table-

spoons of water around the fish.

3. Bake the fish in the center of the oven until it is cooked through, about 1 hour 10 minutes. The best way to check for doneness is to stick a knife point halfway down into the fish, bend it back, and peer in with a flashlight. It should be opaque at the center. Or stick the knife point in and hold it there for at least 30 seconds, then touch the knife blade to your tongue. If the blade feels hot, the fish is cooked through.

4. Remove the fish from the oven and let it cool to room temperature. Before serving, cut away the skin and cut the fish into wedges.

NOTE: If you can't find swordfish, try this with tuna, marlin, black-tip shark, or another meaty fish. You want a round of fish, preferably cut from the center of the fish, though that

will depend on its size. Generally, swordfish landed in the United States or destined for that market are much larger than those found in Sicily; in that case, buy half a steak that is cut 4 to 5 inches thick, as called for in the recipe, and tie it to form a round.

Glutton's Swordfish

**PESCE SPADA
ALLA GHIOTTA**

**6 TO 8
SERVINGS**

In early spring the quantity of swordfish at markets throughout Sicily is astonishing. Their beautiful torpedo-shaped bodies—always cut through so a cross-section of the meat is visible to show off quality—and long swords sit regally on tables, shelves, in mounds of ice.

There are many ways to prepare swordfish on the Sicilian farm, and this is inspired by a recipe from the Messina area, along the northwest coast. Rich with the typical Sicilian blend of pine nuts and raisins, it is flavorful with onions and garlic and gutsy with ripe tomatoes. I choose to use canned tomatoes, finding them generally most flavorful, unless I happen to be making this dish at the height of summer, when tomatoes are juicy and ripe. In that case, I simply substitute the weight of ripe tomatoes for canned.

Try this with a Falerno del Massico.

¼ cup raisins

½ cup all-purpose flour

½ teaspoon fine sea salt, plus
   additional to taste

4 swordfish, black-tip shark, marlin,
   tuna, or other meaty fish steaks
   (each 8 ounces)

½ cup extra-virgin olive oil

1 medium onion, diced

2 cloves garlic, lightly crushed

1 rib celery, strings removed, diced

¼ cup pine nuts

1 tablespoon capers preserved in salt,
   rinsed

15 oil-cured black olives, pitted

1 can (28 ounces) plum tomatoes

Freshly ground black pepper

2 imported dried bay leaves

The Italian word for tomato, "pomodoro," was coined by the Italian botanist Piero Andrea Maltoli, who first mentioned the fruits in 1544, calling them "pomi d'oro," golden apples.

1. Place the raisins in a heat-proof bowl, cover with boiling water, and let them plump for 15 minutes. Drain.

2. Sift the flour and salt onto a piece of waxed paper, and coat the fish steaks with it.

3. Heat the oil in a large heavy skillet over medium-high heat until hot but not smoking. Add the fish steaks and brown for about 1½ minutes per side. Place the browned steaks in one layer in a large baking dish.

4. Preheat the oven to 400°F.

5. In the same oil, which will have a bit of browned flour in it from the steaks, cook the onion, garlic, and celery until the onion is transparent, about 4 minutes. Add the raisins, pine nuts, capers, and olives; continue cooking until the onion and celery are tender, about 4 minutes more. You may need to reduce the heat so the onion doesn't burn.

6. Add the tomatoes with their juices to the onion mixture and break them up with the spatula. Bring to a boil, season to taste with salt and pepper, and cook until the tomatoes have softened and are hot, about 7 minutes.

7. Pour the sauce over the fish, making sure the juices run down between the steaks. Add the bay leaves and push them down into the sauce. Bake until the sauce is sizzling and the fish is cooked through, about 15 minutes. To check for doneness, pierce one of the steaks with a sharp knife and pull back on it. The meat should be opaque throughout.

8. Remove from the oven and serve immediately. This is also delicious at room temperature.

Salt Cod with Marinated Peppers

**BACCALA
MARINATO**

4 SERVINGS

S alt cod is the most commonly eaten fish on the Italian farm, but it appears only rarely. When it does, it is combined with lively local flavors, as in this simple, delicious dish, which originated in the mountains of Basilicata. There peppers in every form—dried, fresh, preserved in oil—are a mainstay of the cuisine, and they are a perfect foil to this succulent, toothsome form of cod.

I've adapted this recipe slightly to include roasted peppers, and I like it so much that I often marinate a batch of peppers just so I can make it.

Serve the cod and peppers with a full-bodied, richly flavored red, such as Basilicata's Aglianico del Vulture or a Taurasi from Campania.

1 pound salt cod
⅓ cup all-purpose flour
½ teaspoon fine sea salt, or to taste
2 tablespoons oil from Preserved
    Roasted Bell Peppers (page 404)
2 tablespoons extra-virgin olive oil

1 cup Preserved Roasted Bell Peppers
Hot Pepper Oil (page 289) or
    crushed red pepper flakes, to
    taste (optional)
½ cup (gently packed) fresh
    basil leaves

1. Thirty-six hours before you plan to make this dish, place the salt cod in a large nonreactive bowl or pan and cover it with a generous amount of water. Soak at room temperature, changing the water at least 4 times over the 36-hour period. This will remove much of the salt. Drain the salt cod, pat dry, and cut it into 4 pieces. Remove any bones and bits of skin from the fish.

2. Place the flour on a plate or piece of waxed paper. Add ½ teaspoon salt and stir to combine. Dredge both sides of the

salt cod pieces in the mixture and set aside.

3. Heat the oil from the marinated peppers and the olive oil in a large skillet over medium-high heat until hot but not smoking. Add the salt cod and cook until it is golden and crisp, 3 to 4 minutes per side. Add the peppers to the cod and cook, stirring occasionally, just until they are heated through, 4 to 5 minutes. Taste and adjust the seasoning with additional salt and hot pepper oil if desired. Transfer the fish and peppers to a warmed serving platter.

4. Tear the basil into large pieces and shower it over the cod. Serve immediately.

L'ORTO

THE VEGETABLE GARDEN

The *orto* is the epicenter of all that appears on the Italian farmhouse table. It is a market garden, a truck garden, or simply someone's personal garden where vegetables, herbs, and occasionally flowers thrive. Often an *orto* will include olive trees, fruit trees, and grapevines too.

In Italy there is always an *orto* near the farmhouse so the farm cook has only to walk a short way to choose what is ripe, mature, ready to cook. Signature to the Italian *orto* are tomatoes, small purple or green artichokes, red and yellow bell peppers, tiny little hot peppers, cardoons (always a tease, for until they're mature they have an uncanny resemblance to artichokes), garlic, onions, and many leafy greens, including chard, spinach, and dozens of traditional lettuce varieties. On my farm visits I often saw unfamiliar greens as well—wild or semiwild varieties like *asparagi di barbera,* a wild asparagus—all of which go into a panoply of vegetable dishes.

Herbs are vital to the *orto,* from sage with its silvery green leaves, to rosemary, bay, basil, and thyme. Parsley—which develops into huge, bushlike plants—and chives are essential. Occasionally wild marjoram creeps in, a welcome invader.

All this freshness results in the intensely flavored and easy-to-make vegetable dishes that are the essence of the Italian farm table. There they are prepared with love and eaten with enjoyment.

Tiny Artichokes with Parmigiano-Reggiano

CARCIOFI CON PARMIGIANO

2 TO 4 SERVINGS

Giannola Nonino is the charming and worldwise matriarch of the Nonino family, who make grappa in Friuli (see essay, page 246). She has a quick wit and a fierce determination that shows through in just about everything, even her desire to share her favorite recipes with me. This is one of them, and it's a favorite of mine as well when small artichokes are in season, which is spring to early summer in most of Italy.

But the dish has little to do with Friuli. It is part of what I refer to as "Italian" cooking, rather than linked to a specific region.

Small, or baby, artichokes are often referred to in Italy as "figli," or children.

Giannola has a huge garden, but artichokes don't grow in it. They are a more southern vegetable, and she buys them at a local market. The inspiration is hers, however, and like all her food, simple to put together and simply delicious.

To tie it to Friuli, that varied and alluring northern region, serve it with a lightly chilled Pinot Bianco Colli Orientali del Friuli and follow the meal with a small glass of Ué, Nonino's light and fruity grappa.

1 lemon, cut in half
10 baby artichokes (about 3
    pounds)
2 tablespoons extra-virgin olive oil

Fine sea salt
¾ cup (1½ ounces) grated
    Parmigiano-Reggiano

1. Squeeze the juice of the lemon into a large bowl of cold water. Remove all the tough outer leaves of the artichokes right down to the inner golden leaves. If they are dark or tough all the way to the heart, simply remove them all, leaving the heart. (Don't be concerned about the choke; it is so tender that it won't present a problem). Place the artichokes in the acidulated water as they are prepared.

2. Just before cooking, cut all the hearts lengthwise into ⅛-inch-thick slices and pat them dry.

3. Heat the oil in a medium-size heavy skillet over medium-high heat until it is

quite hot. Add the artichokes (which should sizzle gently), toss, and cook until they are golden on both sides and tender in the center, 7 to 8 minutes. As the oil and the artichokes heat up, the sizzling will become more pronounced. You want to cook these fast until they are cooked through but without burning them, so shake the pan and toss them, keeping them moving at all times.

4. Remove the artichoke slices from the heat with a slotted spatula, season with salt, and transfer to a warmed serving dish. Pass the cheese for sprinkling over the artichokes.

GORGEOUS GRAPPA: THE NONINOS OF FRIULI

Grappa is to Italy what Cognac is to France, though Cognac is dressed in rich golden robes, while grappa generally has on its used, work-worn clothes.

Grappa is strong alcohol—90 proof and more—distilled primarily from the seeds and skins of grapes crushed for wine. Until about forty years ago it was considered a peasant drink in Italy. Farmers made grappa at home and brought it out after a long Sunday lunch, or took a warming shot early in the morning with coffee before going off to work. It was also made and sold in bulk, but the quality was usually questionable.

In the 1930s the Italian government decreed that grappa could no longer be sold in bulk but had to be bottled and labeled. That was its first step toward general acceptance, though it wasn't until the 1960s that grappa became a drink that could be brought out and served to polite company.

The Nonino family have been grappa distillers in Friuli, in the north of Italy on the Slovenian border, for four generations. In the late nineteenth century, the great-grandfather of current owner Benito Nonino began distilling alcohol, traveling among vineyards with his mobile still to make small quality batches. Then Benito's mother took over and became the first female grappa distiller in Italy. She continued to distill in small batches, carrying on the good name of Nonino.

When Benito and his wife, Giannola, took over the family business, they wanted to expand. In researching different production methods, they discovered that Benito's great-grandfather had distilled grappa from single grape varieties rather than from the blends that were currently the norm. Intrigued, they decided to try the original method. But the custom at the Friuli wineries was to blend all varieties of crushed grapes and sell the blend to distillers.

The Noninos went to the best local wine-makers and asked if they would set aside crushed grapes of a single variety. "The grapes had to be sorted for us, and we knew that would cost money," Antonella Nonino, one of Giannola and Benito's three daughters, said. "So we offered them a premium. They agreed and hired local women to sort the grapes."

The first batch of single-variety grappa Benito made was from Picolit grapes, a tiny, sparsely producing variety that gives the characteristic and lovely floral aroma to much of Friuli's white wine. He and Giannola were very pleased with the result.

"It gave a light, smooth grappa," Antonella said.

The Noninos searched for an appropriate

bottle for their grappa and settled on one that resembled a perfume bottle. Giannola tried to sell it but repeatedly came up against the rough-and-ready reputation of traditional grappa.

"When we were invited to dinner, I'd take it as a gift and it wouldn't be served," Giannola said, remembering her embarrassment. "People thought it was a peasant drink, something the farmer drank when he came home at night. They were right, it was, but if they'd tried ours, they would have seen that it was different."

Giannola has a strong personality—it has been compared to a tornado—and the more she was confronted with lack of interest in her grappa, the harder she tried to sell it. She got herself invited to press functions and dinners and brought along Nonino grappa for the table. Finally it started getting good notices, and from there to nationwide distribution and international recognition was a mere handful of years. Today Nonino grappa is exported throughout the world, and the entire Nonino family works full-time to make sure the market continues to expand. Benito stays home and distills the grappa, helped occasionally by one of his three daughters, all of whom grew up around the distillery. Giannola travels to promote it, also often in the company of one or more of her daughters.

As the Nonino distillery grew, Benito and Giannola realized that traditional Friulana grape varieties like Ribolla, Schioppettino, Tazzelenghe, and Pignolo, used for both wine and grappa, were becoming increasingly scarce. Local vintners were pulling them out in favor of more productive and marketable varieties. Staunch promoters of local agricultural traditions, the Noninos instituted an award that they give each year to vintners who cultivate local grape varieties.

Today the Nonino name is a household word in Italy, for the family is also unendingly self-promoting. One of their most successful campaigns has been a black-and-white family photograph in which the three lovely daughters surround their handsome parents. Splashed all over Italy, it has turned them into mascots of a sort—symbols of Italian success.

Not everyone in Italy, or even in Friuli, thinks Nonino grappa is anywhere near the best in the country. It is often sneeringly called a grappa for women, for it is approachable and light, without the throat-ripping heat of many grappas. That broad appeal has been the key to its success, however, and whatever people say about it, everyone agrees that the Noninos have done much for the overall reputation of grappa. "They've brought it from the farm to the public, put it in beautiful bottles, and kept the quality high," a rival grappa producer told me. "It's made it better for all of us."

The Noninos are aware of their critics, but they go their own way. "We're from Friuli and when we travel for business, we can never wait to return," said Antonella. "We want Friuli and agriculture in Friuli to be successful. And if we succeed right along with it, that's fine too."

Braised Artichokes from Massa Lubrense

CARCIOFI DI MASSA LUBRENSE IN UMIDO

4 SERVINGS

Segreti

Try to find artichokes with stems on them, for the stem is like the heart—once peeled, it is succulent and offers up a great deal of flavor. Remove the stem and look at its cut end—you will notice the interior is a pale green color. Peel the stem right down to that pale core, for the outer layer of the stem is stringy and impossible to chew.

This rustic version of a classic Roman dish comes from a small vegetable market in the town of Massa Lubrense, on the Amalfi peninsula. I was staying with my family in Marina del Cantone and had stopped to buy vegetables for supper. The grocer asked what I planned to do with the artichokes I'd chosen, then without missing a beat, gave me this recipe along with a head of garlic because he was sure I had none. I drove the winding road back to Cantone, where our apartment overlooked the sea, and set to preparing what has come to be a favorite dish. The gentle moist cooking method blends together the flavors of the onions, garlic, parsley, and potatoes, enhancing the delicately delicious, slightly tart, and slightly nutty flavor of the artichoke.

4 good-size whole artichokes, leaf tips trimmed, rinsed

6 cloves garlic, cut in half, green germ removed

3 cups (gently packed) fresh flat-leaf parsley leaves

4 tablespoons extra-virgin olive oil

12 small new onions or yellow onions, about the size of golf balls, peeled and cut in half

3 medium new potatoes (about 6 ounces each), peeled and cut into 1½-inch chunks

Fine sea salt and freshly ground black pepper

1. Trim the stem of each artichoke flush with the bottom and reserve the stems. Turn over each artichoke so the stem end is up, place it on a hard surface, and press firmly on the artichoke so it flattens slightly, and the leaves open. Arrange the artichokes, right-side up, in a single layer in a stockpot or Dutch oven.

2. Mince together the garlic and parsley. Open the artichokes enough (if they haven't already opened enough from being

pressed) so that you can easily divide the parsley mixture among them, placing it in the center of each artichoke. Pour 1 tablespoon oil into each artichoke.

3. Peel the artichoke stems, cut them into ¾-inch lengths, and scatter them among the artichokes along with the onions and the potatoes.

4. Pour ¼ cup water around the artichokes. Sprinkle with a liberal amount of salt and pepper, cover, and bring to a boil over medium-high heat. Reduce the heat to medium-low and cook, covered, until the artichokes are tender, about 40 minutes. Add additional water if

necessary; this depends largely on the type and season of the artichoke (at different times of year they tend to release more water). Check reasonably often to be sure nothing is burning and sticking to the bottom of the pan. To test for doneness, pierce the heart of the artichoke with a knife. The heart should be tender but not mushy.

5. To serve, place the artichokes on warmed plates and divide the accompanying vegetables among the plates, spooning them around the base of the artichokes. Use your hands to remove and enjoy the artichoke leaves.

A Garden for Health?

In Italy vegetable gardens are everywhere—squeezed up against a railroad track, tucked to the side of an urban back door, in front or in back of just about every house you see that has even the smallest amount of land around it. There the garden keeps the family alive, though according to the proverb *L'orto vuole uomo morto* (The garden wants the man dead), it doesn't do much for the man who works it. I must have heard this proverb a hundred times, always in a joking tone, as I spoke with farmers and gardeners. It was explained to me as a reference to the hard work involved in cultivating the often poor Italian soil, not in eating the wonderful products that grow there!

The Italian Orto

The Italian *orto* varies from region to region, depending on climate and soil. But there are many plants that thrive just about everywhere, and most of them are included in the following list, which will help you create your own Italian *orto*.

Seasons blur a great deal, depending on the region, but I've listed the vegetables and herbs for the seasons in which they are generally at their best.

Seasonal Vegetables:

SUMMER TO FALL:
Aglio (garlic)
Cipolle rosse (red onions)
Fagiolini (green beans)
Melanzane (eggplant)
Meloni (melons)
Peperoncini (Hungarian hot wax chilies)
Pomodori (tomatoes, such as Costaluto Genovese large)
Zucchini (zucchini)

FALL AND WINTER INTO SPRING:
Bietola (Swiss chard)
Carciofi (artichokes)
Cardi (cardoons)
Radicchio (radicchio; Chioggia and Treviso)
Scarola (escarole)
Spinaci (spinach)

SPRING TO EARLY SUMMER:
Asparagi (asparagus)
Fave (fava beans)
Finocchi (fennel)
Piselli (peas)
Patate (potatoes)

Herbs and Lettuces:

Basilico (basil): Genovese, spicy bush basil, Italian large-leaf varieties; summer and fall; loves warmth and sun
Borragine (borage): Spring, summer, early fall
Menta (several varieties of mint): Spring, summer, fall
Misticanza (mixed greens or mesclun): Best in cool temperatures of autumn, winter, spring
Origano (oregano): Year-round in mild climates; dies back in cold winters

Prezzemolo (flat-leaf parsley): Year-round in most climates; can die in cold winters
Rosmarino (rosemary): Year-round in most climates
Rucola (arugula): Best in cool temperatures of autumn, winter, spring
Rucola selvatica (wild arugula; also called *sylvetta*): Best in cool temperatures of autumn, winter, spring
Salvia (sage): Year-round in mild climates; dies back in cold winters
Timo (thyme): Year-round in most climates

For high-quality seeds, write to:

Seeds of Change,
PO Box 15700, Santa Fe, NM, 87506-5700;
(800) 762-7333;
www.seedsofchange.com;
and
Johnny's Selected Seeds,
Foss Hill Road, Albion, ME 04910-9731;
(207) 437-4301

Asparagus with Parmesan

ASPARAGI ALLA PARMIGIANA

4 SERVINGS

Segreti

White asparagus requires less trimming than the green stalks, probably because the ends are trimmed before it gets to market. You must peel it, however, removing a fairly thick layer so no strings will be left to haunt you. A vegetable peeler will do the job. If using green asparagus, get the fattest spears you can find, snap them at the base, and don't peel them.

D a Domenico, a lovely restaurant in the region of Piave, not far from Treviso in the Veneto, was once a small family trattoria. Now it is more grand and imposing, the vineyard on the land exchanged for a lush green park. Part of it is set aside for a vegetable garden, and the woods that encroach provide wild mushrooms and greens at various times during the year.

The Veneto is well known for its asparagus, and fields of fat white spears are sprinkled throughout the area. Chef Domenico Camerotto takes full advantage during spring and serves asparagus in dozens of ways. Until I tasted this dish, my favorite way with asparagus was to eat it unadorned and hot from the steamer with my fingers. I was happy to have my habits changed by this recipe, in which cheese and a drizzle of butter add a lovely dimension.

1 pound fat asparagus, white or green, trimmed and peeled if necessary
½ cup Parmigiano-Reggiano (1 ounce) grated

1 to 2 tablespoons unsalted butter, melted (see Note)

1. Preheat the broiler.
2. Bring about 3 inches of water to a boil in the bottom half of a steamer. Lay the asparagus flat in the top half of the steamer and cook until it is tender but not mushy, about 10 minutes. Remove the asparagus from the steamer and arrange on a heatproof serving plate.

3. Sprinkle the cheese evenly over the asparagus stems, leaving the tips bare. Drizzle the butter over the cheese as evenly as you can.
4. Place the asparagus about 3 inches from the broiler element and broil until the cheese is golden, 3 to 5 minutes. Remove from the oven and serve immediately.

NOTE: The amount of butter you use depends on your taste. If you use the larger amount, it blends with the cheese and makes it more of a unified garnish, even though much of the butter will end up on the plate, to be sopped up with fresh bread. The smaller amount means less on the plate but less unity as well.

Luna's Cauliflower Sautéed in Garlic and Oil

CAVOLFIORE, AGLIO E OLIO

6 TO 8 SERVINGS

Luna Lattarulo, a writer and part-time assistant to her husband, agronomist and organic farming consultant Giovanni Ceretelli (see essay, page 36), loves to cook but doesn't like to complicate things. Giovanni has an enormous garden that wanders over the hillside in front of the old Tuscan farmhouse where they live, and from it Luna gets vegetables that taste of brilliant sun and herb-scented air.

This simple recipe is a perfect example of Luna's style. It will win you over, and you'll find yourself serving cauliflower more than you ever thought possible.

1 large head cauliflower, cut into florets (about 8 cups)
2 tablespoons extra-virgin olive oil

2 cloves garlic, green germ removed, minced
Fine sea salt and freshly ground black pepper

1. Bring about 3 inches of water to a boil in the bottom half of a steamer. Place the cauliflower florets in the top half and steam until they are tender but still somewhat crisp, about 9 minutes.

Remove from the steamer.

2. Heat the oil and garlic in a large skillet over medium-high heat until the garlic begins to sizzle. Stir and add the steamed cauliflower. Sauté the cauliflower until it is golden, 2 to 3 minutes, adjusting the heat as necessary to keep the garlic from burning.

3. Remove from the heat, season to taste with salt and pepper, and serve.

Smothered Cauliflower

CAVOLFIORE
AFFOGATO

8 TO 10
SERVINGS

When you taste this smothered cauliflower, you'll think you've never before had cauliflower that tasted so unusual or so good. I ate this at Anna Sapuppo's lovely farm just outside Catania, Sicily. There it was prepared by Nunzio San Filippo, her cook, who learned his profession from a *Monsu,* or French-trained cook of the sort that was very common in the noble homes of Palermo and other parts of Sicily in the eighteenth, nineteenth, and early twentieth centuries.

Earthy and unusual with its tinge of sweet and sour, this dish is wonderfully satisfying. It is not an easy one to translate, for the cauliflower of Catania is different from the cauliflower Americans know. Large, velvety green, and compact, it has a very mild flavor and is so dense it gives up little liquid during cooking. I'm happy to say this recipe produces a *cavolfiore affogato* that is almost identical to Nunzio's; it has a similar rich flavor and that same quality that has people going back for yet another serving.

Segreti

If you have any smothered cauliflower left over, do as Nunzio does and serve it over pasta. Heat the leftovers in a skillet over medium heat (4 cups cauliflower to 1 pound pasta is a good ratio). Cook the pasta until just al dente, about 7 minutes, and drain it. Add the cauliflower to the pasta and toss, adding some pasta cooking liquid if necessary to slightly moisten the pasta. You may also toss in some *mollica,* or toasted bread crumbs (page 427) if you like. Serve this to a standing ovation!

Nunzio advises making it several hours before serving so the flavors have a chance to mellow, and serving it at room temperature.

I follow another of Nunzio's suggestions by tossing leftovers with pasta (see the *Segreti*). Serve a deep, round red, such as Cerasuolo di Vittoria, with this hallmark of Sicilian cooking.

1 large onion, thinly sliced
2 large heads cauliflower, cut into
    florets with stems
4 anchovy fillets, minced
¾ cup raisins
12 oil-cured black olives, pitted and
    coarsely chopped

4 tablespoons extra-virgin olive oil
Fine sea salt
½ cup hearty red wine, such as
    Cerasuolo di Vittoria
½ cup (gently packed) fresh flat-leaf
    parsley leaves

1. Scatter half the onion slices over the bottom of a medium-size deep skillet. Arrange half the cauliflower florets over the onion, stems toward the center, so that when you look in the pan you see simply florets. Sprinkle the anchovies, raisins, olives, and 3 tablespoons of the oil over the cauliflower.

2. Arrange the remaining cauliflower, stems down, over the top, pressing the florets down firmly atop the filling. The cauliflower will mound up over the sides of the pan. Scatter the remaining onion over the cauliflower; drizzle with the remaining 1 tablespoon oil, ¼ cup water, and salt to taste.

3. Loosely cover the skillet with aluminum foil, place over medium heat, and cook, checking often to be sure the cauliflower isn't sticking. If it is, add water a tablespoon at a time. As it cooks, press on it so that it sinks down slightly into the pan. As soon as you can, remove the foil, cover with a pan or lid that fits over the cauliflower and inside the skillet, and add 4 pounds of weight to that to press the cauliflower as it cooks.

4. Adjust the heat to medium-low and continue cooking, checking the cauliflower occasionally until it is soft and nearly cooked through, about

1¼ hours. Remove the weight and cover. Pour the wine over the cauliflower and cook until the cauliflower is completely tender and the cooking liquid is reduced by about two-thirds and darkened to a deep caramel color, about 40 minutes more.

5. Place a large shallow serving bowl, top side down, over the skillet and quickly invert it so that the cauliflower and its juices drop into the bowl. Let the cauliflower cool to room temperature.

6. Just before serving, mince the parsley and sprinkle it over the cauliflower.

Massimo's Eggplant Parmigiana

**MELANZANE
ALLA
PARMIGIANA DI
MASSIMO**

6 SERVINGS

Massimo Gangeni was the first farmer I talked with when I drove from my home in Louviers (Normandy) to begin a long research trip for this book. A young man dedicated to organic farming, he willingly spent time with me on a day in early spring when his fava plants were so laden that it was particularly generous of him to take a break from harvesting the beans (see essay, page 258).

We talked agriculture, then cooking, and he shyly revealed his favorite recipes. It turned out he loves baking in a wood-fired oven—and that he never eats meat. This recipe for eggplant parmigiana is one Massimo particularly favors. The eggplant slices are broiled rather than dipped in batter and fried, then combined with Massimo's light, fresh-flavored sauce and plenty of Parmigiano-Reggiano to yield an herb-scented dish in which each ingredient is pronounced yet contributes to a deliciously harmonious blend.

Serve this with a lovely dry white Vermentino.

FOR THE TOMATO SAUCE
4 pounds ripe tomatoes, peeled,
    cored, and cut horizontally in
    half, or 2 cans (28 ounces each)
    whole plum tomatoes, drained
1 teaspoon fine sea salt, plus
    additional to taste
1 tablespoon extra-virgin olive oil
1 medium onion, diced
2 cloves garlic, green germ
    removed, minced

½ cup (gently packed) fresh
    basil leaves

FOR THE EGGPLANT PARMIGIANA
2 pounds eggplant, trimmed
3 tablespoons plus 1 teaspoon
    extra-virgin olive oil
1½ cups (about 3 ounces) grated
    Parmigiano-Reggiano
1 tablespoon extra-virgin
    olive oil

1. Sprinkle the cut side of the fresh tomatoes with 1 teaspoon salt and turn them over to drain on a rack or in a colander for 30 minutes so they can give up some of their juice. Coarsely chop the fresh tomatoes.

2. Place the oil, onion, and garlic in a medium-size saucepan over medium heat and cook, stirring occasionally, until the onion turns translucent but doesn't brown, 5 to 6 minutes. Add the tomatoes, crushing the canned tomatoes (if using) with a spoon after you add them. Stir and bring to a boil, then reduce the heat and simmer the sauce for 15 minutes.

3. Coarsely chop the basil and stir it into the tomatoes.

Continue cooking until the tomatoes soften, though they will still be in chunks and taste fresh, about 15 minutes. If using canned tomatoes, cook them for 15 minutes as well. Remove from the heat and season to taste with salt.

4. Preheat the broiler.

5. Cut the eggplant into ½-inch-thick slices and brush each slice on both sides lightly with olive oil. Place the slices on a baking sheet. Broil about 5 inches from the broiler element until the slices are golden and tender, 2 to 4 minutes per side. Watch them carefully; some slices may cook faster than others. Remove them with a spatula as they finish cooking.

6. Preheat the oven to 400°F.

7. Oil a 14 x 10-inch oval baking dish with 1 teaspoon oil. Arrange a layer of eggplant slices in the dish, crowding them just slightly if necessary so they cover the bottom of the dish. Pour one-third of the tomato sauce over the eggplant and sprinkle with one-third of the cheese. Repeat, making 2 more layers.

8. Bake until the sauce is bubbling merrily, the cheese is golden, and it all smells so deli-cious you can't wait to eat it, about 40 minutes. Remove from the oven and drizzle the extra-virgin olive oil over the dish. Bring it immediately to the table with the aroma, to tempt your guests, but wait about 10 minutes before serving so nobody winds up with a burned tongue.

The Truth About Olive Oil

"Virgin olive oil is obtained from the fruit of the olive tree solely by mechanical or other physical means under conditions, particularly thermal conditions, that do not lead to the deterioration of the oil. It has not undergone any treatment other than washing, decantation, centrifugation, and filtration. Virgin olive oil is therefore the oily juice of a fruit (the olive). It is virtually the only oil that can be consumed as it is obtained from the fruit and when properly processed maintains unchanged the flavor, aroma, and vitamins of the fruit.

"Extra-virgin olive oil is virgin olive oil that has an organoleptic rating of 6.5 or more and a free acidity, expressed as oleic acid, of not more than 1 gram per 100 grams."

—From *The Olive Tree, the Oil, the Olive,* **International Oil Council**

In other words, good-quality extra-virgin olive oil is the best oil there is!

ON A LIGURIAN SLOPE

It was May and I was driving all the way from northern France to Liguria, Italy. My first stop was to see Massimo Gangeni in the hills of Voltri above Genoa.

Since entering Italy on the *autostrada,* I'd driven less steadily, absorbed as I was with looking at the hills that were heavy with cultivation. Steep, dropping right to the Ligurian sea, they were terraced to a fare-thee-well. There were even terraced greenhouses, some of their glass panels open on this warm and sunny day to reveal pale pink tomatoes. The further I drove, the more excited I became.

I'd agreed to meet up with my friend Fabio "Buzzi" Pucinelli, who coincidentally happened to be in Liguria at the time. We arrived at our rendezvous location, a café at the first exit into Italy from France, and when I mentioned to Buzzi where I was headed, he offered to lead me there. He seemed convinced that I, a non-Italian, would never find it on my own.

We exited the *autostrada* at Voltri, which held little promise as far as agriculture

was concerned. Genoa stretches along the Ligurian sea, its outskirts as gray and dusty as a donkey's back. I found myself driving through hair-raising urban traffic past busy neighborhoods, and when we turned off onto the Via Aquasanta, the address of Massimo's farm, though it was calmer, I was perplexed. I hadn't expected an urban farm.

I didn't get one.

I followed Buzzi up the Via, which was really one lane but served as two, brushing side-view mirrors with cars hurtling down the hillside. A rickety bridge took us across the Leira River, and there we found Massimo's mailbox.

"How did you find this?" I asked Buzzi.

"I just knew where it was," he said, shrugging, as if to say one had to be Italian to do such things. I had a feeling I was going to get that response often in my wanderings.

We continued up a steep dirt road that clung to the hill until we rounded a bend and came upon a tanned, dark-haired, lean young man filling a basket with fat fava beans. He looked up, smiled, and continued his work. This was Massimo, working against the clock to harvest his beans. "I don't usually deliver," he said apologetically. "But this request I couldn't deny, and it's got to be ready by five o'clock. I'll be back in half an hour."

With that he jumped in a tiny old van

and raced down the hill. Our lot was to wait, look out over the valley at the terraced lush green hills, and marvel that organic agriculture thrived this close to a metropolis.

Massimo returned, ready to talk. His fields, which cover a mere acre, climb many feet up the side of a steep hill and were originally terraced hundreds of years ago. Calling them fields gives them a status they don't deserve, for they are more like wide notches in the hillside. But proliferating within them is everything from favas to zucchini, tomatoes, eggplant, carrots and onions, gorgeous fat, purple asparagus, fennel, rosemary, apricots, peaches, and cherries. All organically cultivated, they provide a living for Massimo.

Massimo scampers like a mountain goat among the plots, occasionally hopping into the toylike three-wheeled pickup truck he uses to get to the highest of his fields. A serious, intense young man, he considers his life paradise.

"I was a sailor before this," he said. "I trained in marine engine repair at school, and I went out on boats to fish and do repairs." He didn't like the sea as well as he'd thought he would and didn't like the chance involved in fishing, but he loved working outdoors. On the long days at sea, he found himself thinking of the childhood days he'd spent each year with his uncle on a farm in Sardinia, where his family is from.

He returned to port in Genoa and started looking for land. A friend of his who'd been farming was about to quit.

Massimo took a look at his friend's farm, loved the space, the view, the impression of being far away from everything, and signed up for a fifteen-year lease.

Committed to organic farming and possessed only with the knowledge he'd gained from his uncle and his grandmother, who kept a huge garden in Sardinia, he set to building up the soil and planting crops. He bought a bull and a handful of sheep to keep the bull company, his goal a ready supply of compost. He tried to ignore the bull's temper, hoping it would stop trying to tear down the barn with its horns. Finally he realized that he and the bull—and the sheep, for that matter—were incompatible, so he sold them. Now he buys compost from a neighbor.

Massimo is a vegetarian, but as he put it, a farm has to have some animals. So he does keep chickens, whose eggs he sells, and a few rabbits for atmosphere, which he will

sell if someone requests one. Four dogs complete the picture—they live in the bull's former quarters.

Massimo goes twice a week to a market in central Genoa to sell his produce and eggs. He has worked hard over the years to cultivate a clientele of connoisseurs.

"I've moved from market to market and was eventually offered a spot in the city center not too long ago," he explained. "It's perfect because the customers are well-to-do and appreciate organic vegetables. Not only that, but they tell their friends and that helps most of all."

Though he may not do it consciously, Massimo, with the help of a retired neighbor, Salvatore, has created a work of art on his hillside. His fields are beautifully arranged, and all are oriented to catch the maximum amount of water as it trickles down the hillside. "Water may be my biggest problem," Massimo said, "and erosion. We're always fighting that, but we arrange things to minimize it as much as possible."

Some of his fields are lined with raised beds of borage and lettuce. In others graceful bamboo tepees provide a framework for climbing tomatoes, and in yet another potato plants, white flowers in bloom, thrive with a border of artichokes and cardoons.

The faded-pink stucco two-hundred-year-old farmhouse, which sits about halfway up the hill, looks out over the vertical patchwork. Up a narrow, winding path behind the house is a series of newly plowed terraces waiting for seed. Massimo has been busy with his hand-held tiller, the only mechanical tool he can use on these tiny fields.

Because of the mild Mediterranean climate of the farm, which is located so close to the sea that its rumble is almost audible, Massimo can work year-round. The greenhouse allows him to harvest zucchini in April, tomatoes in early June. He's also got lush and hearty fennel, cabbage, and lettuces throughout the winter. It's a job that allows him no time off, but for this young zealot, his fervor matched only by his generosity, time off is not what he yearns for.

He simply wants to farm. He's very happy with his choice, expressing only one frustration. "I don't own this land," he said. "The original landlord lived here and let out part of the house and land to his farmworkers. The house is still divided in three parts, and my partner, Christina, and I occupy the second floor. I've got ten years more on my lease, so we'll see. I'm going to keep on working at it."

Grazia's Stuffed Escarole

**SCAROLA
IMBOTTITA ALLA
GRAZIA**

4 SERVINGS

Escarole must be one of the best lettuces ever created, for it is the perfect mix of sweet and bitter and its fleshy leaves stand up well to a rousing vinaigrette. It is versatile too, as I learned while on the Amalfi peninsula, south of Naples, where escarole is as common as the lemons that hang from the trees. There it is often stuffed with a blend of capers, anchovies, pine nuts, and raisins, then braised to a delicate tenderness. Garlic and peppers give it a delightful little spark.

There are many versions of this dish. This simple one comes from Grazia Caso, a lovely woman who lives on the south side of the peninsula in the fishing village of Marina del Cantone, where she and her family run a seaside restaurant, Taverna del Capitano.

Grazia prepares many of the dishes at the restaurant that she remembers from her childhood, often dressing them up with a contemporary touch. Her stuffed escarole maintains its peasant origins, however; serve it as a first course with a chilled full-flavored white, like Greco di Tufo.

4 large escarole hearts (about 8
   ounces each) (see Note)
12 oil-cured black olives, pitted
1 tablespoon capers, rinsed if they
   are preserved in salt
4 anchovy fillets

2 tablespoons pine nuts
2 tablespoons raisins
3 tablespoons extra-virgin olive oil
3 cloves garlic, peeled
1 dried hot chili pepper

1. Rinse the escarole hearts and drain. You may need to gently press the escarole with your hands to remove excess water, but it should remain slightly damp.

2. Mince together the olives, capers, anchovies, pine nuts, and raisins. Place one-quarter of the mixture in the center of one of the escarole hearts and bring the leaves

up and around it. Wrap kitchen string around the leaves and tie it closed to make a small packet. Repeat with the remaining escarole.

3. Heat the oil, garlic, and hot pepper in a large heavy saucepan over medium heat. Gently brown the garlic on both sides, 3 to 5 minutes. Remove the garlic from the oil and add the escarole packets, stem end down. Cover and cook, checking and turning them frequently, until they are golden on both sides, about 12 minutes. Reduce the heat if the escarole begins over-browning, and continue cooking, checking frequently, until the escarole is limp and translucent, about 35 minutes. The escarole will give up liquid as it cooks, preventing it from sticking to the pan.

4. Transfer the packets to a warmed serving platter, being careful not to take the hot pepper with them. Remove the strings and pour the cooking juices, if there are any, over the escarole. Serve immediately.

NOTE: The heart of the escarole is the inner core of pale green leaves with pure white stems.

Stewed Fresh Favas

STUFATO DI BACCELLI

4 SERVINGS

I first tasted this spring ragù at the Avignonese winery, near Cortona in Tuscany. It was made from favas that grew right outside the windows of the main house. Keeping company with the favas were more than a dozen types of rare herbs including chocolate mint, Persian (a type of oregano), hyssop, and rue, which not only keeps flies away but is cooked with sugar, puréed, and fed to colicky babies (and at the winery, sometimes minced and strewn across grilled

Chianina beef). There are also artichokes and spring peas, lettuces, peppers, and eggplants, and all go into the cooking at Avignonese.

Not all the favas are in the vegetable garden. At Avignonese, a winery with an eye toward improving its growing techniques, favas are also planted between rows of vines to fertilize the soil. These are not harvested but left to bloom and then dug under, their nitrogen adding to the richness of the soil.

On a warm spring day Massimiliano Mariotti, the winery chef at Avignonese, prepared a lovely meal for me using fresh garden produce and the succulent Chianina beef that grazes on the rich pastureland in the Chiana valley of Tuscany. My first course was homemade pasta with a simple meat and tomato sauce, followed by an oven-roasted steak surrounded with this simple ragù. The beef was delicious, but it was the fava bean ragù that caught my attention. At the end of the meal, there wasn't a morsel left on my plate.

Serve an Avignonese Pinot Noir alongside.

Spring Onions— What Are They?

Spring onions are those that are the very earliest of the season. In fact, they are white or yellow onions harvested when they are young and tiny—usually about the size of a golf ball. In Europe these young onions are sold from spring through early summer, tied in bunches with their tender greens attached. They already have a pronounced flavor, yet it is less intense than that of more mature onions, and their flesh is juicier.

If you can't find spring onions—the most likely place to look would be a farmers' market or a supermarket supplied by local farmers—then use the freshest, youngest onions you can find.

2 tablespoons extra-virgin olive oil, plus additional for serving

4 spring onions (see box, left), cut into very thin rounds

3 pounds fresh fava beans in their pods, shelled and skinned, (about 3 cups; see Note)

¼ teaspoon dried oregano

Fine sea salt and freshly ground black pepper

1. Gently warm the oil in a medium-size skillet over low

heat. Add the onions, increase the heat to medium, and cook until the onions are translucent but not at all golden, about 3 minutes. Add the fava beans. If the favas are of different sizes, add the big ones first. Stir them into the onions and add ¾ cup water. Cook, covered, until they are soft and tender, 15 to 20 minutes. When the larger beans are almost soft, add the smaller beans, stir, and add an additional ¼ cup water if needed to keep them from sticking to the pan. Continue cooking until all the beans are tender and still in one piece, not mushy, an additional 10 to 12 minutes.

2. Remove from the heat. Mince the fresh herbs or crush the dried herbs, add them to the favas, and stir. Season to taste with salt, and if this is to be served on its own, with pepper as well. Transfer to a warmed serving dish, drizzle with additional olive oil if desired, and serve.

NOTE: If your fava beans are very fresh, you may be able to leave on the inner peel. Sample one and see. If the peel is bitter, the favas will be better off without it (see box, page 91).

Fritter of Spring Favas, Artichokes, and Peas

FRITTELLA DI FAVE, CARCIOFI, E PISELLI

6 SERVINGS

It would be difficult to imagine a fresher, greener, more delicately pleasing dish than this combination of tender vegetables. Flavored with onions and fennel, it is an ode to spring and all that is best during that season.

The combination is called a "fritter," but it is really a light vegetable stew. I got the recipe from Gina di Stefano Monteleone di Petralia Sottana, the grandmother of my friend Gabriella Monteleone. Gabriella's family comes from the Madonie mountains, a rolling and lovely rural area about an hour and a half south of Palermo. Once the fields were dotted with cattle, and the country villages had close social fabric; now many of the field workers have moved to the larger towns, selling their houses to city folk for summer homes. However, those who still live on the land have gardens that produce the ingredients necessary for this dish.

This is generally served as a first course over pasta or rice, or with toast or even hard-cooked eggs alongside, but I prefer it either as a first course by itself or as a vegetable course along with roast poultry or fish. Try a lively refined red, such as Etna Rosso, alongside.

1 lemon, cut in half

10 small or 5 large artichokes

2 tablespoons extra-virgin olive oil

1 medium onion, minced

3 cloves garlic, green germ removed, minced

1 small fennel bulb (about 6 ounces), diced

1½ cups (gently packed) fennel fronds (optional but desirable)

2 pounds fresh small fava beans in their pods, shelled and skinned (see box, page 91)

2 pounds fresh peas in their pods, shelled (about 3 cups)

1 teaspoon sugar

Fine sea salt

Extra-virgin olive oil, for serving

1. Squeeze the juice from the lemon into a large bowl of cold water. If using small artichokes, remove all the tough outer leaves right down to the inner golden leaves. If they are dark or tough all the way to the heart, simply remove them all, leaving the heart. (Don't be concerned about the choke; it is so tender that it won't present a problem.) If using large artichokes, trim them to the hearts (see box, page 42). Drop the artichokes into the acidulated water as they are prepared and let soak for 15 to 30 minutes before cooking.

2. Heat the oil in a

medium-size heavy skillet with deep sides. Add the onion, garlic, and diced fennel, cover and cook, stirring occasionally, until the onion turns translucent, about 7 minutes.

3. Drain the artichokes and pat them dry. Cut the small artichokes into eighths or slice the large artichoke hearts ¼ inch thick. Mince the fennel fronds. Add the artichokes, fennel fronds, favas, and peas to the onion mixture and stir. Add enough water to not quite cover the vegetables and sprinkle with the sugar and a generous seasoning of salt. Stir, cover, and bring to a boil. Reduce the heat and simmer until the vegetables are

tender but still have some texture, about 20 minutes. Remove the cover and continue cooking until about two-thirds of the liquid has evaporated and the vegetables are completely tender, about 15 minutes more. Remove from the heat and adjust the seasoning. Either serve immediately or let cool to room temperature (see Note). Serve extra-virgin olive oil alongside for drizzling over the vegetables.

NOTE: Once cooked, these vegetables tend to turn a bit gray as they cool. Just before serving, stir them so that the vegetables under the surface layer, which have kept their gorgeous green color, will present themselves.

Luna's Fava Beans and Potatoes

**FAVE E PATATE
ALLA LUNA**

4 SERVINGS

Here's another recipe from Luna Lattarulo (see essay, page 36), who had me laughing with her tales of being buried under fava beans from the kitchen garden outside their old Tuscan farmhouse. Fortunately, the Lattarulo-Ceretelli family loves favas, and Luna thinks of dozens of things to do with them. Her simplest recipe calls for fresh favas tossed with garlic and oil. I embellished on

Fava beans are often called "La carne dei poveri," the meat of the poor.

the idea, adding small chunks of new potatoes from the market and tiny-leafed basil grown from Italian seeds, which I picked outside my front door.

This goes very well with a quickly grilled steak or lamb chop, but it is also simply delicious on its own with a flask of wonderful Tuscan olive oil to drizzle over it right before eating.

2 medium new potatoes (about 4 ounces each), peeled and cut into ½-inch cubes
2 tablespoons extra-virgin olive oil
1 clove garlic, green germ removed, minced
Fine sea salt

4 pounds fresh fava beans in their pods, shelled and skinned (see Note)
1 tablespoon extra-virgin olive oil (optional)
¼ cup (very loosely packed) fresh basil leaves

1. Bring about 3 inches of water to a boil in the bottom half of a steamer. Add the potatoes to the top half and steam until they are tender, about 10 minutes. Remove from the heat.

2. Heat 1 tablespoon of olive oil and garlic in a large skillet over medium heat. Cook until the garlic is sizzling and begins to turn golden, 1 to 2 minutes. Pat the potatoes dry if necessary and add them to the pan. Stir, season lightly with salt, and let cook until the potatoes are golden on one side, 4 to 5 minutes. Stir the potatoes, add the favas and stir again. Cover and cook just until the favas have turned a brighter shade of green, are tender, and have lost their raw taste, 3 to 4 minutes. Adjust the seasoning and transfer to a warmed serving bowl.

3. Drizzle with the remaining 1 tablespoon extra-virgin olive oil if desired. Tear the basil leaves into small pieces, sprinkle over the potatoes and favas, and serve.

NOTE: If your fava beans are very fresh, you may be able to leave on the inner peel. Sample one and see. If the peel is bitter, the favas will be better off without it (see box, page 91).

Fava Beans with Curly Endive

I first tasted this fava and endive dish at Al Fornello da Ricci, a country restaurant in Puglia, near the town of Ceglie Messapico. The food served there, prepared by Dora Ricci and her daughter Antonella, is as typical to the region as are the *trulli*—small cone-roofed stone homes that once housed the farmworkers of the region.

Pugliese food is earthy yet delicate, like this dish, which is one of the region's best. Here dried favas, whose almost nutty flavor and creamy texture still sustain the local rural population, are paired with potatoes and complemented by the light oil of the region. The endive and onions with vinegar provide a flavorful foil. Every Pugliese cook has her own recipe for this dish—some go heavier on the favas, others on the potatoes. Guided by Dora and Antonella, I offer this version, which is so good you'll have to control yourself not to eat it all.

At Al Fornello da Ricci, this dish is served as an antipasto, but I find it makes a wonderful meal all on its own. Serve this with the suggested accompaniments and a rich Rosso del Saleno from Taurino alongside.

1 pound dried fava beans
4 medium russet potatoes
    (about 1¼ pounds),
    peeled
1 medium red onion, sliced
    paper thin
¼ cup white or red wine vinegar
2 good-size heads curly endive
    (about 2 pounds), leaves
    separated, rinsed, and dried

½ cup plus 3 tablespoons extra-virgin
    olive oil
Fine sea salt
2 good-size green bell peppers,
    stemmed, seeds and pith removed,
    cut into thin strips
2 small fresh hot peppers, such as
    Hungarian hot wax peppers, cut
    into very thin strips with seeds

Segreti

Puglia produces more oil than any other region in Italy, and it is full-bodied yet delicately flavored. You must use a good-quality olive oil for blending into the bean purée, for its flavor is an essential part of this dish. Also, the peppers must be hot to offset the other flavors—you'll find they add a lot to the dish!

1. Place the favas in a large pot, cover with water, and bring to a boil over high heat. Remove from the heat and let sit for 1 hour. Leaving the favas in the warm water, remove them one at a time and peel each by making a slit on the side of the bean and squeezing gently so the inner bean pops out of its skin. Discard the cooking water and return the favas to the pan.

2. Add the potatoes to the favas and cover with cold water by about 2 inches. Bring to a boil over high heat, reduce the heat so the water is boiling gently, and cook, partially covered, until the favas are completely tender and the potatoes are falling apart, about 1 hour. Check the beans and potatoes often, skimming any impurities that rise to the surface of the water. If they seem to be sticking to the bottom of the pan, add a small amount of water.

3. While the potatoes and beans are cooking, combine the onion and vinegar in a small serving bowl and stir so they are blended. I like to refrigerate these so they are chilled when served.

4. Bring a large pot of salted water to a boil and add the curly endive. Return to a boil and cook just until the endive is tender, about 5 minutes. You may have to cook it in batches. Drain in a colander until as much water as possible drains away, then squeeze the endive gently to remove more water. It doesn't have to be perfectly dry but shouldn't be swimming either.

5. Heat 2 tablespoons of the oil in a large skillet over low heat, add the endive, and stir until it is coated with the oil. Season to taste with salt. (If the endive is still piping hot after it has drained, heating the oil isn't necessary; simply toss the endive with oil and season with salt.)

6. Heat 1 tablespoon of the oil in a large heavy skillet over medium-high heat. Add the bell peppers and hot peppers and sauté quickly until they are softened and browned and almost crisp on the edges, 6 to 8 minutes. Season with salt and remove from the heat. Keep warm.

7. When the beans and potatoes are soft and all the water is cooked away, stir them vigorously

with a wooden spoon, always working in the same direction, until they are mostly smooth. Some small lumps are fine. Vigorously stir in the remaining ½ cup oil, again working in the same direction, until it is completely incorporated, then season to taste—generously—with salt.

8. Place the bean purée in a warmed shallow serving bowl. Surround it with the curly endive and serve with the fried peppers and the marinated onion alongside. (You may also mix the endive into the bean purée.) Serve immediately.

fava beans

Green Beans with Pancetta

FAGIOLINI CON
PANCETTA

6 TO 8
SERVINGS

I had just spent the morning in Cormons, Friuli, with Lorenzo d'Osvaldo and his wife, Lucia, touring their cured-meat production, their small vineyard out behind their huge house, and the winery downstairs in its roomy basement (see essay, page 299). We concluded my visit in the winery sipping Osvaldo's light Cabernet and sampling thin slices of his luscious, lightly herbal pancetta, which he uses in the following recipe, a substantial meal in itself. The fresh green taste of the beans is heightened by the farm pancetta cooked in vinegar, which gives a marvelous, pleasing "edge" to the dish.

Segreti

I buy pancetta ends to use in this recipe. They keep for a long while and are often sold for considerably less than slices from the prime part of the meat.

1½ pounds green beans, trimmed, strings removed if necessary
6 ounces pancetta, sliced about ⅛ inch thick, cut into thin strips

¼ cup best-quality red or white wine vinegar

1. Bring about 3 inches of water to a boil in the bottom half of a steamer. Add the green beans to the top half and steam until they are crisp-tender (or to your liking), 8 to 10 minutes. Transfer them to a serving platter. (If you want to serve them warm, warm the platter and time the steaming of the beans so they emerge cooked while the vinegar and pancetta are cooking together.)

2. Place the pancetta in a large skillet (nonstick is preferable) over medium heat and heat until the fat melts, about 3 minutes.

Add the vinegar and shake the pan to evenly distribute it. Cover and cook for about 2 minutes to allow the meat to absorb some of the vinegar. Remove the pan from the heat, pour the pancetta and vinegar over the beans, and toss to combine. Or you may just leave the pancetta on top, and as you serve make sure everyone gets an equal amount of pancetta, beans, and vinegar. Serve immediately.

NOTE: There is no salt and pepper called for here, and none is necessary. However, let your palate be your guide!

Green Beans with Tomatoes

FAGIOLINI UCCELLINI

4 SERVINGS

It was a very hot day in mid-June, and I was sitting on a small bench on the terrace at the Lattarulo-Ceretelli home, near Poggibonsi in Tuscany. Luna Lattarulo, whose recipes are featured throughout this chapter, my husband, Michael, and I were watching our children roller-skate on the rough concrete in front of us, all wondering how they managed to stay upright. Luna and I talked recipes, and she mentioned this as one of her family's favorites. Now I make it often in summer, for beans and tomatoes are a perfect summer pair, ripe at the same time. I like to serve the dish alongside simple roast chicken, but it is also wonderful with polenta or a simple bowl of pasta. You can also prepare it in advance—these beans are as good (or even better) several hours after they are made. (For more on Luna and her husband, Giovanni Ceretelli, see the essay on page 36.)

1 small sprig fresh sage (about 5 leaves)
1 pound green beans, trimmed, strings removed if necessary

2 tablespoons extra-virgin olive oil
Generous ½ cup (loosely packed) sage leaves
Fine sea salt and freshly ground black pepper
2 small ripe tomatoes (each about 3 ounces), cored, peeled, and cut into ½-inch chunks
1 clove garlic, green germ removed, minced

1. Bring a large pot of salted water to a boil with the sprig of sage. Add the beans, return to a boil, and cook until the beans are tender but not mushy, about 12 minutes. Drain the beans and discard the sage sprig.

2. Heat the oil and half the sage leaves in a large skillet over medium-high heat until the leaves are sizzling. Add the beans and season with salt and pepper. Sauté the beans just until they are coated with oil, then add the tomatoes. Cover and cook until the beans are tender and the tomatoes have nearly melted, 8 to 10 minutes.

3. Mince the remaining sage leaves and the garlic together. Add to the vegetables, stir, and cook just until the aroma of the garlic begins to waft through the kitchen, about 1 minute. Transfer to a serving dish and serve.

Wild Greens with Bread Crumbs and Capers

GIRI CON MOLLICA E CAPPERI

4 SERVINGS (WITH PASTA SERVES 6)

Feudo Tudio is a working farm and *agriturismo* about two hours east of Palermo, in Sicily. There Rita Farinella, a local woman who grew up with a gift for cooking the traditional Sicilian dishes she ate at home, prepares meals composed of many simple dishes, most of them made with ingredients raised on the farm. Depending on the season, one of Rita's meals might include the same green prepared two or three different ways, which was the case when I was there and *giri* were in season. Rita served them in a frittata, as a stuffing for pork, or more simply, as here, which was my favorite preparation.

Like Swiss chard, only wild, a bit bitter, and less tender, *giri* have a rich green flavor that I fell in love with. When I returned home, I gathered a variety of different greens from my garden, steamed and prepared them as Rita had prepared the *giri,* and this is the result, which is delicious. You may use just about any mix of greens, but be sure to include bitter ones like curly endive or dandelion greens. Arugula is wonderful as well, particularly when its leaves are large and have taken on some heat—it adds an alluring depth.

I like to serve this with a simple pasta dish, such as tagliatelle dressed with Nunzio's Tomato Sauce (page 424). You may also coarsely chop and toss the greens with the pasta.

1 pound mixed greens, such as
   Swiss chard, dandelion greens,
   spinach, arugula, curly endive,
   and escarole, trimmed, well
   rinsed, and coarsely chopped
2 tablespoons capers, preferably
   preserved in salt (see box,
   page 66)

2 tablespoons extra-virgin olive oil
1 large clove garlic, green germ
   removed, minced
2 tablespoons Toasted Bread Crumbs
   (page 427)
Fine sea salt and freshly ground
   black pepper

1. Bring about 3 inches of water to a boil in the bottom half of a steamer. Add the greens to the top half and steam until they are tender and wilted, 3 to 4 minutes. Remove from the steamer, transfer to a colander to drain, and cool to room temperature.

2. Mince the capers.

3. Heat the oil and garlic in a large heavy skillet over medium heat. Add the *mollica* and capers and mix well. Add the drained greens and cook, stirring constantly, until the greens are heated through and all the ingredients are thoroughly combined. Season to taste with salt and pepper and serve.

Fried Bell Peppers

PEPERONI FRITTI

4 TO 6
SERVINGS

This dish was served one night at Malvarina, an *agriturismo,* or farm turned inn, near Assisi, where Maria Maurillo produces meals of astonishing flavor and quality. The peppers, fried to a sweet darkness, were served alongside her fried tomatoes and puffy, olive-oil-rich pizza dough, which resembled focaccia.

I like the peppers so much I always make enough to have leftovers, for they are a terrific snack, as delicious cold as they are hot. Serve them with Tuscan Bread (page 311) or pizza dough and sip a glass of Chianti.

3 to 4 tablespoons extra-virgin olive
   oil
2 pounds red bell peppers, stemmed,
   seeds and pith removed, cut into
   2-inch-wide strips

Fine sea salt
½ cup (gently packed) flat-leaf
   parsley leaves
2 cloves garlic, cut in half, green
   germ removed

1. Heat half the oil in a large heavy skillet over medium-high heat until it is shimmering but not smoking. Add enough peppers to cover the bottom of the pan and cook until they darken to a rich color on one side, 2 to 3 minutes. They will not cook evenly but will color in splotches, which is fine. Turn the peppers and cook until they are colored on the other side, 3 to 4 minutes more. Reduce the heat to medium and continue cooking until they are softened and more evenly colored—

they should be tender without being completely limp. The whole process will take between 11 and 15 minutes, depending on the thickness of the peppers. Adjust the heat under the peppers to keep them from burning.

2. As the peppers cook, transfer them to a serving platter and sprinkle lightly with salt. Continue cooking the peppers, adding more oil when necessary.

3. Let the peppers cool. Just before serving, mince the parsley and garlic together and sprinkle over the peppers.

FABIO'S BABBO—
THE URBAN PEPPER FARMER

Fabio Picchi, chef and owner of one of Florence's best and most renowned restaurants, Il Cibrèo, zipped through the Florentine traffic like a honeybee on its way to the hive, making turns so fast I gave up trying to figure out where we were going. Our destination was the home of Fabio's parents where I was to meet his father, Enzo Picchi, who is known in and around Florence for the chili peppers he grows on his balcony. Gardening is Enzo's hobby, chilies his particular passion. I first heard about him when visiting Dario Cecchini, a friend of Fabio's and one of Tuscany's best butchers. He gets all his peppers from Fabio's father.

Outside a contemporary apartment building, Fabio set the scene. "This is one of the better neighborhoods of Florence, between the Via Mazza and the Viale Mazzini," he said. We took the elevator upstairs and Enzo, a handsome man with a friendly grin and a very full head of bushy white hair—the kind that seems to grow only on Italian heads—opened the door with a smile.

"*Piacere*" (Pleased to meet you), he said with a strong handshake. He ushered us into the dining room, where the table was covered with baskets holding dried red peppers, from tiny, fairy-sized ones to those as long and wide as a finger. Placing a necklace of dried peppers strung on gold thread around my neck, he said, "I made it for you, so don't forget it." Thus began one of the funniest and fastest-paced afternoons of my life. I soon found that I was in the company of a father and son who take tremendous enjoyment from out-joking each other as they talk, careening from one subject to another, managing to disseminate information at the same time. They got their practice many years ago when they had a very popular and controversial television talk show.

Standing near the peppers, whose aroma filled the room, Enzo waved a recent newspaper article in my face touting the pepper's contribution as a cure for heart disease. "I've got other stories about the virtues of peppers," he said with an intense look. "I had a hurt shoulder once, and the doctor told me to rest, to quit working. Well, of course, I didn't. Instead, I worked in the garden, trimming pepper plants. I rubbed some trimmings on my shoulder, forgot about it, and soon afterward the shoulder was just fine." He looked at me, raised his eyebrows, and shrugged. "Let's go to the garden," he said.

We stepped out onto the balcony, which held a simple bay tree and a couple of herbs in pots. I was crestfallen until I realized we hadn't arrived yet. Enzo led the way up a narrow spiral staircase and we emerged onto a 650-square-foot terra-cotta–tiled terrace with a 360-degree view of Florence. My eyes strained to take it all in, but there was simply too much to look at, between the stunning view and what was right at my feet. This was an urban terrace literally turned into a small farm.

Fabio tapped my arm and said, "Look here," as he showed me a lemon tree in a pot, its branches heavy with fruit, then pointed to a bougainvillea, onions planted at its roots. Dozens of tomato plants were in pots to one side, and the sprouts of Enzo's chili pepper plantation sat inside a small greenhouse. Since it was late spring and early for vegetables, many other plants had just been started including tomatoes, zucchini, and bell peppers. Tables held pots of fully grown parsley and chives, and huge urns in one corner held a bay tree and various combinations of marjoram, basil, oregano, and bushy thyme. Lettuces poked out everywhere, their leaves lush and rich.

I mentioned how healthy all his plants looked; and Enzo likened his terrace garden to the fertile land around Naples. "There is dirt, water, sun, and lava—everything they need," he laughed. His lava is the terra-cotta tiles of the terrace, which throw heat right back at the plants.

"Taste this," Fabio said, tearing off a leaf from a lettuce that looked like a giant burnished-red rose. It was succulent and, combined with the basil leaf he next held out to me, filled my mouth with the flavor of the Tuscan sun.

Enzo hasn't always grown vegetables on a terrace. Until about twenty years ago he was a tennis champion and part-time fisherman. An accident put an end to that. When he emerged from the hospital, he started puttering on the terrace. That, and a request from Fabio to grow peppers for Il Cibrèo, led to this astounding enterprise, which he considers a hobby but which occupies him full-time.

The terrace next door was completely bare; not even a potted flower graced its surface, as though to scold Enzo's lush enterprise. "It's sad over there, sad, sad," Fabio said, laughing.

We stopped for a moment to look out at the Duomo and the faraway Piazza of San Michele. "That's where he goes to get his soil," Fabio said, pointing to the piazza. "At night he digs it up and brings it back here. Not long ago the street collapsed over there, and he and I are the only ones who know why." He and his father laughed together, but I honestly couldn't tell whether or not they were joking.

We strolled the narrow paths of the terrace, brushing by herbs that emitted fragrant aromas, passing potted olive trees, the fruit of which Enzo cures. There were plum trees, trays of cabbages, garlic, more lettuce, and peppers started everywhere. "I harvested ten thousand peppers last year," Enzo said. "I take them inside to dry in a drafty spot away from the sun, so they keep their flavor. You should smell our apartment."

He ducked inside a fully equipped toolshed to get a container filled with the pepper seeds he saves each year, the varieties carefully labeled. "It's these seeds that, once broken, can prevent heart attacks," he said with certainty.

With every step my amazement increased. I turned to Enzo. "All you're missing is a cow," I said.

He grabbed my arm. "Come here."

We came to two gas-fired burners on a stand, with a big kettle sitting on one of them. Enzo Picchi lifted the lid. "This is my cow," he said. He buys sheep manure, mixes it with the composted clippings from his garden and water, then simmers it. He uses the cooled liquid for fertilizer. I shook my head. Incredible. He'd thought of everything, and his efforts yielded enough vegetables for his family, their friends and their families, and when the need arises, for Il Cibrèo as well.

We walked over to the railing of the terrace and looked across the railroad tracks at a soccer field. "In summer all the big games are played there, and helicopters hover overhead filming the games," Fabio said. "At least once a summer a photographer catches a glimpse of my father's terrace, which is bright red with peppers then, and makes the airplane fly over it so he can film it."

Enzo turned to me. "All the geniuses gardened. Look at Leonardo da Vinci. Why not me?" he laughed and headed down the staircase.

We cooled off in the kitchen with a glass of chilled pineapple juice. Then Enzo pulled down an electric coffee grinder, its edges turned red from years of grinding chilies. "Today is a perfect day to grind peppers, not too humid," he said.

He turned the results of his grinding over to me so I could spice up my cooking. "Not just with the peppers but with the memory of this visit," he said with a wink.

Potatoes in a Frying Pan

PATATE IN TECIA

4 GENEROUS
SERVINGS

Potatoes fried toasty golden are a typical farm side dish in Friuli. A humble blend of ingredients, this dish can easily go upscale, as it did when I tasted it at the charming Ristorante La Taverna in the hills near Gorizia, on the border of Friuli and Slovenia.

I've incorporated this into our family repertoire and usually serve it as a main dish along with a mixed green salad, for a meal that is extremely simple and satisfying.

If you'd like to serve this as a side dish, it goes well alongside roast rabbit or chicken. You may also want to serve it alongside Chicken with Sage (page 214).

Serve with a light and velvety Merlot del Collio.

4 ounces slab bacon, rind removed, diced
1 medium onion, diced
4 ounces prosciutto or speck (see Note), diced
1½ pounds waxy potatoes, peeled
and cut into ¾-inch cubes
1 tablespoon extra-virgin olive oil (optional)
Fine sea salt and freshly ground black pepper

1. Place the bacon in a large heavy skillet over medium heat and cook, stirring occasionally, until the fat turns translucent, 2 to 3 minutes.

2. Add the onion and cook until it begins to turn translucent and softens, about 10 minutes. Add the prosciutto, stir, and add the potatoes. You may need to add the olive oil at this point if the meat hasn't given up enough fat.

3. Stir the ingredients to coat them with fat or oil, season with salt and a bit of pepper, cover, and cook until the potatoes are tender, about 30 minutes. Stir them every 5 to 8 minutes so they cook and brown evenly; they won't turn very crisp

but will have lovely golden edges. Uncover the pan, raise the heat just slightly, and cook, stirring and scraping the bottom of the pan, just to brown the potatoes over all. This final step will take just 3 to 4 minutes.

4. Transfer the potatoes and meat to a warmed serving dish and serve.

NOTE: Speck, originally from Austria, is pork that is smoked and air-cured. It resembles a smoky prosciutto.

Simple Country Potatoes

PATATE SEMPLICI

4 TO 6 SERVINGS

Potatoes are delicious just about any way, and one of the ways I enjoy them best is like this, with plenty of hot pepper and a zing of vinegar. That's how they do it on the farms in Basilicata, a mountainous region that makes up the instep of the Italian boot. There the soil is hard and rocky, the climate rude, and coaxing food, including peppers and potatoes, from the earth isn't easy. But the farmers of Basilicata, many of whom still use donkeys to help them work the soil, manage well.

In Basilicata they serve this alongside roast or baked lamb, though it also makes a good main dish with a salad or plate of greens, such as Wild Greens with Bread Crumbs and Capers (page 273), alongside.

3 pounds flavorful potatoes, such as
   Yellow Finn, Yukon Gold, or
   Norland, peeled
1 tablespoon best-quality red wine
   vinegar
Fine sea salt

Hot paprika or crushed red pepper
   flakes
¼ cup extra-virgin olive oil
1½ cups (loosely packed) fresh flat-
   leaf parsley leaves

1. Bring about 3 inches of water to a boil in the bottom half of a steamer. Add the potatoes to the top half and steam until they are tender, about 20 minutes.

2. While the potatoes are steaming, whisk the vinegar with salt and paprika to taste in a large serving bowl. Whisk in the olive oil, adding it in a thin stream, until it is emulsified with the vinegar.

3. Mince the parsley and add it to the vinaigrette.

4. When the potatoes are cooked through, transfer them to the bowl, toss well with the vinaigrette, and adjust the seasoning. Serve piping hot.

Pumpkin with Fresh Tomato Sauce

ZUCCA CON SALSA DI POMODORI

4 TO 6 SERVINGS

Luna Lattarulo, who lives in Tuscany, is one of my favorite Italian cooks, particularly when it comes to vegetables. A vegetarian, she works wonders with the vegetables from her family's organic garden. So rich were her recipe suggestions that I was tempted to use her as the sole source for the vegetable chapter of this book, but I limited myself to a few, featured throughout this chapter. This one I love as much for its flavor as for its delightful play of colors on the plate.

The best pumpkin variety for this dish is the Cinderella, Rogue d'Etamples, or Kuri variety, which are available at farmers' markets and specialty produce stores. They each have a firm texture and pleasantly sweet, nutty flavor.

Serve with a lightly chilled richly flavored white, such as Vernaccia di San Giminiano, made in the old style, flavored with the grape skins.

In the late 16th century, Italians thought that the potato was a truffle and called it *tartufo*.

⅓ cup all-purpose flour
Fine sea salt and freshly ground
    black pepper
1½ pounds pumpkin, peeled and
    cleaned (see Note), cut into
    ¼-inch-thick slices
5 tablespoons extra-virgin olive oil

¼ cup (gently packed) fresh
    basil leaves
3 ½ cups Light and Lively Tomato
    Sauce (page 423)
½ cup (about 1 ounce) finely grated
    Parmigiano-Reggiano

1. Sift the flour, ½ teaspoon salt, and pepper to taste onto a piece of waxed paper or a plate; mix together. Coat the pumpkin slices with the flour mixture.

2. Heat half the oil in a large heavy skillet over medium heat. Add as many pieces of pumpkin as will fit in a single layer. Cook until the pumpkin is golden on one side, about 2 minutes, then turn and cook until the second side is golden and the pumpkin is tender, 1½ to 2 minutes more. Transfer the slices as they cook to a warmed serving platter with sides or a shallow bowl. Repeat with the remaining pumpkin, adding oil to the pan between batches as necessary.

3. When the pumpkin is cooked, mince the basil.

4. Heat the tomato sauce, add the basil, stir, and season to taste with salt and pepper if necessary. Pour the sauce over the pumpkin, sprinkle with the cheese, and serve.

NOTE: To "clean" pumpkin, simply cut in half and scrape out the seeds and all of the stringy material inside using a large spoon. Scrape away any stubborn strings with a sharp knife. Use a vegetable peeler to remove the skin; a sharp knife may be necessary too for getting at hard-to-reach areas.

Spinach Hearts

CUORI DI SPINACI

4 TO 6 SERVINGS

Segreti

When rinsing vegetables that have a great deal of soil or sand clinging to them, place them in a large sink filled with water, swish them around, and carefully lift them out. Empty and rinse the sink, then refill it with clear water. Repeat the process as many times as necessary until the water is completely clean and there is no grit at the bottom of the sink.

Nunzio San Filippo, resident cook at Alcala, a farm in Sicily, prepares delicate spinach hearts this way. They were a revelation to me, almost like a different vegetable, for I'd never isolated just the tiny, pale greenish yellow, wrinkled leaves at the heart of the spinach plant.

Nunzio was careful to urge me to season lightly. "The flavor of the spinach is so elusive, you must taste before you add each seasoning to be sure you're not overpowering it," he said.

2 tablespoons extra-virgin olive oil
1 pound spinach hearts (see Note), well rinsed, drained, and finely chopped

Fine sea salt
1 to 2 tablespoons fresh lemon juice
½ cup (about 1 ounce) finely grated Parmigiano-Reggiano

1. Heat the oil in a large heavy skillet over medium-high heat. Add as much spinach as will comfortably fit into the pan—it can mound over the top—and cook, stirring constantly, until it begins to wilt. Continue adding spinach and stirring, until it is all in the pan. Cook, stirring, until all of the spinach is wilted; this will take about 7 minutes in all. Continue cooking until the spinach is very tender but not soft and mushy, about 10 minutes more. Season to taste with salt and lemon juice.

2. Transfer the spinach to a warmed serving bowl and serve with the cheese alongside.

NOTE: To trim the spinach to just the heart, remove all the large leaves on the outside of the plant, leaving the bunch of small leaves that are at the center of the plant. They are usually pale green to yellow and tightly curled, a sign of their immaturity. Trim the root end of the stem. Reserve the larger leaves for salad or other spinach dishes. You will need about 3 pounds of spinach to get 1 pound of hearts.

BIODYNAMIC AND ORGANIC FARMING

Biodynamic farmers follow principles outlined in 1924 by Rudolf Steiner, a German scientist and reputed clairvoyant. The term "biodynamic" comes from the Greek *bios,* which means life, and *dynamis,* which means energy. Steiner believed in a "farm organism," the farm as an entity in itself. He was convinced that everything crops need in terms of fertilizer and soil nutrients should be generated on the farm through natural methods.

Steiner developed several preparations that he felt would regenerate nutrients, minerals, enzymes, and natural growth hormones in the soil to create and maintain its fertility and health. These preparations remain highly suspect to those who practice "conventional" farming based on synthetic soil additives. Indeed, they do at first sound bizarre. One such preparation calls for stuffing cow manure into cows' horns, burying them in September, and digging them up six months later. The manure and horns are transformed into a remarkably sweet-smelling soil, tiny portions of which are carefully hand blended into water. The resulting "tea" is sprayed on fields to regenerate their strength.

Another principle is attentiveness. Farmers who practice biodynamic farming remain closely involved with the soil—walking it daily, touching it, smelling it. They watch the skies for weather, heed the lunar calendar, often celebrating significant lunar dates, and otherwise maintain an interest in all the elements that go into growing a living organism. Because of this and the preparations they use, they are rarely surprised at what occurs on the farm, for it is usually a result of their husbandry.

Organic farming is similar to biodynamic farming but without the rituals. It is farming without inacceptable chemicals, either for fertilizer or for pest or weed control. Instead, organic cultivation relies on crop rotation, plant residues, and manure to keep soil rich; biological pest controls; botanical pesticides (made from plants); and as much attentiveness as is required by biodynamic farming. Though both biodynamic and organic farming rely on soil additives, all the additives are deemed acceptable by organic inspection organizations.

Arguments exist for and against these "alternative" or "organic" farming methods. Can they produce enough food, fast enough, for the world? That is a complex question, but the answer is probably yes. Organic agriculture would mean that land would be infinitely healthy and productive, which would guarantee both a place for farmers and good food for the table. But for rural economies to be viable, another part of the puzzle, more than healthy soil, must come into play. The public must be willing to return to eating locally grown foods during their peak season of ripeness. In that way, local farmers would have a local market. And rural inhabitants must continue to want their life of socializing in cafés, meeting friends in the village *piazza,* buying from small family-owned *negozi,* or shops.

I thought about these related issues a great deal during my trips through Italy, where organic and biodynamic farming are widely practiced and where the tradition of eating seasonal foods produced locally is as old as the artwork and monuments that sprinkle the land. In Italy there is a reverence for seasonal foods, an excitement generated by the first artichokes, the wild greens and vegetables, the true and sweet flavor of seasonal fruit. An active village life is vital in Italy, and rural communities are more alive than they are in either the United States or France, which is comforting to see.

But Italy is changing as it steps further into the twenty-first century and does what everyone seems to—imitate the United States. Changing food habits are evident everywhere, from strawberries on a plate in December to long-conservation milk and pasteurized cheese on grocery shelves. Italian food magazines tout out-of-season foods, as well as mass-produced ingredients like artificial sugar and low-fat prepared foods. More people work outside the home than ever before, which means there is less time for everything at home.

I hope and believe the traditions of eating locally grown seasonal foods will prevail in Italy, and that traditional farming techniques that respect the land will as well. I think that organic and biodynamic methods will become even more firmly established, in part because Italians are accustomed to fresh food that has big flavor, which comes not from spices but from the ingredients themselves raised in a healthy environment. I know that being social is integral to the Italian character, rural or otherwise, which bodes well for rural communities.

It may well be that the habit of having full-flavored food and the need for social discourse and company will save agriculture in Italy, keep it from becoming too industrial, too reliant on inacceptable chemicals, too distant and impersonal. Let us hope it does and that Italy becomes a model for the rest of the developed and developing world.

Maria's Fried Tomatoes

**I POMODORI
FRITTI DI MARIA**

**6 TO 8
SERVINGS**

Segreti

Use any firm, slightly underripe, but wonderfully flavorful tomato for the best results. Soft tomatoes tend to dissolve during cooking.

Maria Maurillo of Malvarina, near Assisi, fries the living daylights out of her tomatoes, so that their skins are nearly blackened, their flesh wonderfully sweet. She uses whatever tomatoes are most flavorful, and the day I watched her she was slicing plum tomatoes in half lengthwise, frying, and talking to me all the while. I kept thinking the heat was too high as the skins got darker and darker, but of course I said nothing. And later, as I ate the sublime, sweet, and aromatic tomatoes, I was glad I hadn't. They were perfect. I make these often in summer when tomatoes flood the vines and am always reminded of Maria.

Serve a crisp, fragrant white wine here, such as the excellent Torre di Giano Bianco.

4 tablespoons extra-virgin olive oil
3 pounds (about 8 medium) firm,
    flavorful tomatoes, cored and cut
    lengthwise in half
Fine sea salt

¼ cup (loosely packed) fresh thyme
    leaves
2 cloves garlic, cut in half, green
    germ removed

1. Pour enough of the oil into a heavy skillet to make a thin but even layer on the bottom of the pan (for a 10-inch skillet, use half the oil) and heat over medium-high heat until it is hot but not smoking. Add as many tomatoes, skin side down, as will easily fit into the pan without crowding. Cook until the skin is spotted very dark brown to black, about 4 minutes. Turn the tomatoes and cook until the cut side is very dark brown as well, 4 to 5 minutes more. Reduce the heat to medium and continue cooking, turning the tomatoes regularly, until they are very dark around the edges and have almost melted but still keep their shape, 16 to 20 minutes. Adjust the heat so the tomatoes brown but don't burn.

2. Transfer the tomatoes to a serving dish. Repeat the process with the remaining tomatoes, adding more oil to the pan as necessary. Sprinkle the cooked

tomatoes lightly with salt.

3. Just before serving, very finely mince the thyme and garlic together and sprinkle it over the tomatoes.

Antonella's Zucchini

GLI ZUCCHINI ALLA ANTONELLA

4 SERVINGS

Antonella Di Rosolini is a doctor in the town of Modica, in southeast Sicily. She and her husband, Giuseppe Cicero, an organic farming consultant with the government, have farmland in their hometown of Rosolini, about ten miles east of Modica, where they go on weekends. There Giuseppe, a farmer at heart, raises everything from olives for his own oil to flowers for his honey-producing bees. He also grows vegetables, and each weekend they cart back enough produce to last them the week.

Giuseppe and Antonella both love to cook, and watching them together in the kitchen is a pleasure—she is very precise, he more of a poet. Together they produce simple, wonderful dishes like this, which is perfumed with their homegrown rosemary.

This can be a side dish, or it can be tossed with pasta.

Zucchini

2 tablespoons extra-virgin olive oil
1¾ pounds very fresh small zucchini, trimmed and cut into ¼-inch-thick rounds

2 heaping tablespoons (loosely packed) fresh rosemary leaves, or to taste
Fine sea salt

1. Heat the oil in a large skillet over medium-high heat until it is hot but not smoking. Add the zucchini and stir to separate the rounds.

2. Mince the rosemary and add it to the zucchini. Season with salt, stir, and cover. Cook just until the zucchini is tender but still has some body, shaking the pan and tossing the zucchini so the slices brown lightly but don't burn, about 8 minutes.

3. Remove from the heat, adjust the seasoning, and serve.

DAL FORNO

FROM THE BREAD OVEN

The term *forno* conjures up the loveliest, warmest, and most fragrant images of the rural Italian baker or farm cook kneading dough in his or her *madia,* a troughlike dough table, then forming and setting out loaves—long or round, small or huge—to rise, covered with a heavy cloth to protect them. When the twigs or almond husks or grapevine trimmings that are fuel have burned to coals in the oven, the baker pushes them aside and slides the prepared loaves into the oven in a precise choreography. All is done with a rhythm that begins before dawn and continues on well into the night.

An hour is usually enough time to bake good crisp-crusted loaves, and when they are removed from the oven, into its residual heat go *torte,* or cakes; *scacce,* double-crusted pizzas; *empanate,* double-crusted savory pies; *focacce,* flavored flat breads; *biscotti,* and other simple cookies, most of which you will find in this chapter.

While much baking still occurs on the farm, each rural village has its *fornai,* or bakeries, too. These simple buildings are often indistinguishable from the houses around them except for the fresh, warm aromas that issue from the door. These village bakeries offer traditional specialties, from breads to biscotti—sweet and savory—to very simple cakes. If a farmer doesn't have his own oven, the village *fornaio* is a daily destination. It was for me too, no matter where I stayed. Once I discovered that all the baked goods I love best in Italy come from the *fornaio,* I made a beeline to the nearest one each morning and often again in the evening.

The farther south one travels in Italy, the better the bread, for in the south the flour is made from hard wheat, which gives springy, chewy loaves. Southern baked goods—from *focacce* to *empanate*—are studded with olives and herbs and are delightfully savory. I think the full flavors are due to the prominence breads and savory pastries have in most southern Italian farm meals, staples intended to fill and to satisfy.

Baked goods from the Italian farmhouse are one of the riches of Italian farmhouse cooking. I predict you will make your way through this chapter with delight, experimenting and enjoying as you go.

Spicy Flatbread

I ate this tasty pillowy bread several times while in the area around Modica, in southeast Sicily, and loved it each time. A simple yeast dough brushed with oil and sprinkled with oregano (and hot peppers if you like), it came to the table once everyone was seated, a perfect accompaniment to the country rosé wine that was already running freely. It is a simple farm appetizer that quells even the mightiest hunger.

2 tablespoons cornmeal or semolina
½ recipe Simple Dough (page 433)
2 tablespoons dried oregano

2 tablespoons extra-virgin olive oil
⅛ teaspoon crushed red pepper
   flakes, or to taste

1. Sprinkle a large baking sheet with the cornmeal.

2. Roll out the dough to a 17 x 10-inch rectangle and fit it on the prepared baking sheet. Sprinkle the dough with the oregano, drizzle with the oil, then sprinkle with the pepper flakes.

Let rise until the dough has almost doubled, 30 to 40 minutes.

3. Preheat the oven to 425°.

4. Bake the bread in the center of the oven until it is golden and puffed, about 25 minutes. Remove from the heat, cut in squares, and serve hot.

Crisp Sardinian Bread

Carta da musica, literally translated as music paper, is the remarkable crisp bread of Sardinia. The other Sardinian crisp bread is *pane carasan* or *pane carasatu,* which leads to some confusion for the visitor who may not be aware of two versions of this crisp bread on the rugged island. It is only in the touch that you can tell them apart, for *pane carasan* is much thinner and more brittle than *carta da musica*. However, both thin breads originated with the Sardinian shepherds who made them to take—in round baskets specially woven for the purpose—to the mountains to sustain them during long months of shepherding.

The best *carta da musica* in Sardinia is reputedly made in Bitti, a rough mountain town tucked way up in the hills, at the Giulio Bulloni Panificio. After driving through some of the wildest, most remote country I've ever experienced (apparently used as a hideout for Sardinian kidnappers), I spent several hours watching *carta da musica* being made at Bulloni Panificio in an amazingly complex process.

There the flat bread is made with leavened dough left to rise for several hours before being shaped into flat rounds. These rounds are put on a conveyor belt and run slowly through an extremely hot oven, where they emerge puffed, like pillows. A woman stands at the oven exit and tosses the "pillows" onto a large round table surrounded by other women who deftly cut them horizontally in half. The two halves go on another conveyor belt and are run through a second oven to bake crisp. The shatteringly crisp halves are stacked, left to cool, and then wrapped in coarse paper and either sold right at the bakery or shipped around the world. How they stand up to the voyage I'll never know, for the package I took away with me was much the worse for wear when I arrived at my destination!

This is a simplified but deliciously satisfying version of Bulloni's *carta da musica*. Serve it warm from the oven drizzled with extra-virgin olive oil and sprinkled with sea salt. I also like it with the very untraditional addition of Lemon Rosemary Salt (page 394).

FOR THE BREADS
2 cups semolina, plus additional
for dusting the baking sheets
2 cups whole-wheat
pastry flour
1½ teaspoons fine sea salt
1 to 1¼ cups lukewarm
water

FOR GARNISHING
3 tablespoons extra-virgin
extra-virgin
olive oil
Fine sea salt

Segreti

Semolina is finely ground hard wheat, ideal for breads and pastas.

1. Preheat the oven to 450° F. Lightly dust 2 baking sheets with semolina.

2. Mix both flours and the salt together in a large bowl. Gradually work in enough lukewarm water to make a soft dough. Turn the dough out onto a lightly floured surface and knead for just a minute or two until it is smooth. Let it rest for 20 minutes at room temperature. It is not necessary to cover it.

3. Divide the dough into 8 equal pieces. Pat a piece into a disk, then roll it into a 12- to 14-inch round or rectangle that is as close to paper thin as you can get it, making sure that the edges are as thin as the center. If the shape isn't perfect, don't be concerned, for much of the charm of this bread is its rustic nature. Transfer the dough to a prepared baking sheet; it may rip slightly

or you may have rolled folds into it, but don't worry about it.

4. Bake the bread until it is beginning to harden and turn golden, 3 to 4 minutes. Using your fingers or a long spatula, flip it and bake it on the other side until it is completely crisp and unevenly golden, 3 to 4 minutes more. (The baking time is highly variable. Watch your first bread to figure how long you should bake the others.) It may bubble in spots, which is perfectly normal. Transfer the baked bread to a work surface or wire rack. Repeat with the remaining dough, cooling and flouring the baking sheets between batches.

5. Just before serving, warm the breads in the oven if necessary. Paint each bread generously with oil and sprinkle with sea salt to your liking.

Savory Biscotti from Maria Riccardi

Segreti

Boiling the biscotti requires no more than sliding them into the pot and waiting for them to bob to the surface. Be sure to let the excess water drip off before setting them on the baking sheet. They will still be damp when they go into the oven but will bake up wonderfully crisp and golden.

When I spent the day with Maria Riccardi and her family on their farm in the Terranova mountains of Basilicata (see essay, page 401), she brought a big tin of these biscotti out for me to have with her husband's slightly fizzy farm-made wine. I expected them to be sweet, but they weren't. They were crisp and savory instead, and completely intriguing. I ate one, then another, along with the cheese, sausages, and *ciambella* (page 342) Maria and her daughter, Filomena, served.

Maria puts no salt in her savory biscotti, but I have added some for balance. I find it brings out the flavor of the anise seeds. I like to serve the biscotti as Maria did, along with antipasti, which, depending on the season, might include fresh fava beans and radishes, hard sausages, or provolone cheese.

*1 cup lukewarm water
¼ teaspoon active dry yeast
4 to 4½ cups unbleached all-
    purpose flour*

*1 large egg
½ cup lard, at room temperature
2 teaspoons anise seeds
1 teaspoon fine sea salt*

1. In a large mixing bowl, whisk the water and yeast together. Add 2 cups of the flour, 1 cup at a time, and whisk until smooth. Whisk in the egg, then add the lard and whisk until it is incorporated into the dough. Add the anise seeds and salt, then mix in enough of the remaining flour to make a hearty dough that is firm but not hard. You will proba-

bly end up using just slightly more than 4 cups flour. Knead until all the ingredients are combined, 4 to 5 minutes.

2. Transfer to a clean (unoiled) large bowl and cover with plastic. Let the dough rise at room temperature (68° to 70°F) until it has increased in bulk by about one-third, about 1 hour.

3. Line 2 baking sheets with

parchment paper. Gently punch down the dough and divide it into 32 pieces, about 1 ounce each. Roll each piece of dough on an unfloured work surface into a 6-inch-long rope. Bring the two ends of the rope together and cross them as though you were going to tie a knot, but go no further. Set them on the baking sheets and let rise at room temperature until they have puffed slightly, about 15 minutes.

4. Preheat the oven to 350°F. Bring a large pot of salted water (1 tablespoon sea salt to every 2 quarts water) to a boil over high heat.

5. Slide several biscotti gently into the boiling water so they don't crowd the pot, and cook just until they rise to the top. Remove them with a slotted spoon and let the excess water drip from them. Return them to the paper-lined baking sheet and repeat with the remaining biscotti. Let them sit until they are dry on the surface, about 7 minutes.

6. Bake the biscotti in the center of the oven until they are pale gold and hard, about 55 minutes. Remove from the oven and serve warm or at room temperature. These will keep for at least a week in an airtight container.

Olive Oil Rolls

PANINI ALL'OLIO

3 6   R O L L S

These *panini* sat on the bar at Il Cibrèo Caffè in Florence early one morning. My husband, Michael, and I had just walked through the nearby Sant' Ambrogio market, where farmers come from the hills around Florence to offer the most wonderful and unusual wild and cultivated salad greens, heirloom vegetables (not heirlooms to the farmers but simply the varieties they and their forebears have always grown), and sharply seductive olive oil. We stood at the bar drinking coffee, and the *barista,* or barman, gave us each one of these rolls to enjoy alongside. Still warm—the way they should be eaten—they were redolent of Tuscan olive oil from the Conca d'Oro, an area in the hills right outside Florence that is considered the best in Tuscany for oil. We'd been up since dawn and our appetites were keen, and I still don't think I've ever had a better breakfast anywhere, anytime.

This is my interpretation of that magical *panino*—a citified version of the bread and olive oil eaten on Tuscan farms in the early morning, when chores are finished and the workday has yet to begin.

FOR THE ROLLS
1⅓ cups lukewarm water
2 teaspoons active dry yeast
½ cup extra-virgin olive oil
1 tablespoon fine sea salt
4 to 4½ cups all-purpose flour

FOR GARNISHING
3 to 4 tablespoons extra-virgin
*   olive oil*
Fine sea salt

1. In a large mixing bowl, whisk the water and the yeast together. Whisk in the olive oil. Add the salt and the flour, 1 cup at a time, mixing just until the dough comes together. Turn the dough out onto a work surface and knead until it is smooth and satiny, which will take about 4 minutes by hand. The dough should be soft and somewhat sticky, although a clean finger pressed into it should not stick.

2. Transfer the dough to a clean (unoiled) large bowl and cover with plastic. Let rise at room temperature (68° to 70°F) until it has nearly doubled in bulk, about 1½ hours.

3. Line 2 baking sheets with parchment paper. Turn the dough out onto a very lightly floured work surface and punch it down gently. Don't knead it, as it isn't necessary to further develop the gluten. Divide the dough into 36 equal pieces. Roll each piece into a 10-inch-long rope. Let rest for just a minute (long enough for them to pull back slightly, as they will,

from the developed gluten). Fold the rope of dough in half, bringing the two ends together. Twist the two strands over each other twice, and pinch the ends together to hold the twist so the rolls look like coiled logs. Lay the rolls at least 2 inches apart on the prepared baking sheets. Cover loosely with a tea towel and let rise until puffed, about 30 minutes.

4. Preheat the oven to 350°F.

5. Bake the rolls in the center of the oven until they are puffed and golden at the edges, about 25 minutes. The rolls should not be a deep golden but rather pale all over and gently golden at the edges. To test the rolls for doneness, rap one on the bottom with your knuckle. If it sounds hollow, it is baked.

6. To garnish the rolls, immediately brush them generously with oil, then brush them with oil again so they glisten and almost drip. Sprinkle them lightly with salt. These rolls are fabulous straight from the oven.

Golden Prosciutto and Parmesan Breads

PANE, PROSCIUTTO, E PARMIGIANO

84 ROLLS

These little spirals, which look like golden snails, were served to my husband, son, and me at Pomurlo Vecchio, an *agriturismo* not far from Orvieto, in Umbria. According to cook Eola Bianchi, who grew up cooking the country specialties of Umbria, they represent a typical farm snack of prosciutto, bread, and cheese. I was intrigued not only by their coiled snail shape but also by their fragrant cheese flavor punctuated by salty prosciutto. Signora Bianchi serves them at the beginning of a meal as part of an antipasti assortment, along with sausages, pickled vegetables, and assorted fresh vegetables.

Serve these satisfying appetizers with a simple white Orvieto. Arrange them on lettuce leaves to get the full effect of their snail-like appearance.

FOR THE ROLLS
1 recipe dough for Olive Oil Rolls
  (page 295 and step 1, below)
1½ cups (about 3 ounces)
  finely grated Parmigiano-
  Reggiano

3 ounces prosciutto, sliced about ⅛
  inch thick, minced

FOR THE EGG WASH
1 egg
1 teaspoon water

Segreti

Mince meat, such as the prosciutto in this recipe, with a very sharp knife rather than the food processor; it maintains a better texture.

1. Make the dough, adding the cheese after you've added 2 cups of the flour. Mix in another cup of the flour, then add the prosciutto and mix briefly. Incorporate as much of the remaining flour as is needed to make a soft but not sticky dough. Turn out the dough onto a lightly floured surface and knead until it is tender and elastic. It should be somewhat sticky but a clean finger should not stick to it.

2. Transfer the dough to a clean (unoiled) large bowl and cover with plastic. Let rise at room temperature (68° to 70°F) until it is nearly doubled in bulk, 1½ to 2 hours.

3. Line 3 baking sheets with parchment paper. Punch down the dough and divide it into 84 equal pieces (they should weigh about ½ ounce each). Roll each piece of dough into a 4- to 4½-inch-long rope and coil the rope around itself. Set the coils on the prepared baking sheets, leaving at least ½ inch between them. Let rise until they are puffed but not doubled in bulk, 15 to 20 minutes.

4. Preheat the oven to 450°F.

5. Whisk together the egg and water to make the egg wash and brush it over the coils.

6. Bake in the center of the oven until the coils are golden, puffed, and baked through, about 14 minutes. Transfer to wire racks to cool. These are best if eaten within 2 hours after being baked; however, they may be cooled, wrapped in aluminum foil, and stored in plastic bags for up to 1 month in the freezer.

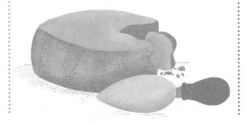

PROSCIUTTO WITH LOVE

Leonardo d'Osvaldo reminded me of Pan as he bounced rather than walked through his unusual and highly personal smokehouse in a residential neighborhood of Cormòns, north of Trieste in Friuli.

Wiry, energetic, endearingly positive, this young man prepares pork the old-fashioned way, smoking it over herb and wood fires, rubbing it with spices, tending it daily instead of rushing it the way large commercial producers do. He makes *pancetta* and speck (a spicy, smoky, air-dried pork), but he is best known for his delicately smoked and air-cured prosciutto.

Smoked, air-cured pork was once a specialty of Cormons. "There used to be four professionals here," Osvaldo said. "I'm the only one left." He maintains the tradition because he loves it and is wedded to the old way of doing things. He works at home with his family around him; his father lives close by; and he knows the farmers who produce most of his pigs. "Farmers here always raised three pigs, two for themselves and one to sell," he said. "Fortunately for me, some still do."

Osvaldo has trans-formed part of his lovely house, built in 1800 and the oldest in Cormòns, into the workrooms where he prepares and ages the pork. We walked into the salting room, which was completely tiled and outfitted with stainless-steel tables, the only modern part of the structure. "I don't like the tile because it doesn't breathe the way the old walls did," he said. "But I had to put it in. When I'm working with fresh meat, an inspector comes by once a week."

He produces twelve hundred prosciutti a year, working from November through February, when temperatures are ideally cool. He follows painstaking rituals learned from his father and grandfather, and his prosciutto is considered the best in Italy. All but the few he keeps for his extended family are sold before they are finished curing and shipped to exclusive accounts around the country.

For prosciutto the first step is salting the meat. He places hams in a trough filled with damp salt and slowly and carefully massages it into the skin. He then rubs in ground Tellicherry pepper, which he loves because it adds sweetness without heat. He puts a bag aside each year to dry for the following year so that he is always using well-dried pepper. "It's got to be perfectly dry to release flavor," he said. "I won't use the fresh pepper I get."

Five days later he massages the salt and pepper further into the meat, working at the same time to urge blood and water still inside it out. "The salt relaxes the meat," he said. "So when I massage, it has a real effect."

He rubs more salt into the ham, then lets it rest in a cool, moist room for about twelve days. As the salt seeps in, it simultaneously extracts more water from the ham and gives it a light seasoning as well.

He takes the salted hams outside and washes them, rubs in more pepper, and fits them into a press that applies substantial but gentle pressure to remove final traces of blood and water. Depending on the age of the pig, the ham will stay in the press for three to five days. "I do it by eye," Osvaldo said.

When the hams have been pressed to a thick flattened shape, he wipes them off and hangs them in a special room outside reserved for smoking. The fire is made of cherry and grape wood, which he prefers because they add aroma without sweetness, and a branch of fresh bay leaves. He hangs a big kettle of water over the fire and into that puts rosemary, sage, fennel, and lemon verbena for a gentle veneer of flavor.

Hams hang in the smoke and moisture for two to four days, depending on the outside temperature and the ham. When he

It's All in the Name—
Will the Real Prosciutto Please Come Forward?

In Italy if you ask for prosciutto, you in turn will be asked: *prosciutto cotto* or *prosciutto crudo,* the air-cured ham that we in America call prosciutto. If you want air-dried ham, ask for *prosciutto crudo.* The best known of these are prosciutto di Parma and prosciutto San Daniele, but there are others, including prosciutto d'Osvaldo, prosciutto di Siena, and prosciutto di Veneto, each of which you must ask for by name.

Prosciutto cotto, by the way, is simply cooked ham.

judges them perfectly smoked, he transports them upstairs in the house, where he has transformed a multitude of bedrooms into aging rooms. "Families here used to be huge," he said, laughing. "Every one of these rooms housed someone in my grandfather's family." How funny those people might feel if they were resurrected and came to visit, only to see fragrant prosciuttos hanging in bedrooms where they had once listened to lullabies!

He opens the windows at night so the moist air can enter and stall the aging process just slightly. "The hams must age slowly so their flavor develops," he said. The shutters are closed during the day to keep the hams in darkness, for light turns their fat yellow.

He checks the hams daily and after six months rubs the cut side of each with a blend of lard, pepper, paprika, and other spices—his secret mixture. "It softens the prosciutto," he said, "and lightly seasons it."

To test the quality of the ham, he takes a finely crafted tool made from a horse's bone and sticks it under the skin of the ham and into one of the veins. He can tell by its aroma how the aging is proceeding. "Maybe two percent of my hams don't mature properly," he said. "But since I eat and sleep with them during the twelve months they age, they are usually just fine."

Before he sells a prosciutto, he washes off any mold that may have formed on the outside,

trims it to a perfect smoothness, then wraps it with a label that carries his name.

"Come," he said, "let's try some speck and *pancetta*." Like the shoemaker with holes in his boots, he had no prosciutto to offer, for his family had finished their yearly supply.

We went downstairs to the cellar where he makes wine from vines that his father-in-law cultivates behind the house. He has just started bottling it and is hoping to build up a small wine business as well. He opened a bottle of Cabernet and sliced some meats. "Traditionally, our meats are sliced by hand, paper thin, but it's becoming a lost art," he said. "All the old ways are changing. I'm here to keep some of them alive."

There we sat in his cellar, enjoying the speck, which he cures with seven different spices, and the *pancetta*, which is lightly smoked. Both were delicious. I regretted missing his prosciutto but received a surprise at La Subida restaurant, on the outskirts of Cormons, some days later. Owner Josko Sirk seated me, then returned moments later with a plateful of carefully hand-sliced Osvaldo prosciutto. "I always have it here," he said. "And Leonardo told me you hadn't tasted it at his house, so here you go." Sweet, lightly smoky, so tender it almost melted on my tongue, it lived up to the quality and hard work that went into its making. And the cooperation between Osvaldo and Sirk lived up to the legendary generosity of the people of Friuli.

Bay leaves

Golden Artichoke Rolls

CARCIOFI POMINI

6 ROLLS

I was at Al Monte, a rustic farm and restaurant near Ragusa in southeast Sicily, with Carmelo Chiarmara, a young chef who was raised on a farm nearby. Carmelo insisted I come because he didn't think a visit to the area would be complete without the experience.

We entered a long, low farm building that had been transformed into the restaurant. The transformation was no more than the basics: The walls were painted white and hung with a few well-cared-for old farm implements. A simple kitchen had been built at one end. Long tables lined the room, and the atmosphere was bright and rich with tasty aromas.

The kitchen included a wood-burning oven so long that it took up the whole end wall, and a huge gas burner upon which sat a vat of steaming whey that was being stirred by farm owner and chief cook Maria Blandino. She was making the ricotta that serves as the basis for all meals served at Al Monte. "Fresher than this doesn't exist," I thought.

Maria Blandino explained that their principal business is raising cattle and making *caciocavallo* and provolone cheeses. So many of the people who came to the farm to buy cheese wanted to stay and eat that the Blandino family took up the challenge and has never looked back. Their restaurant is jammed most of the year with diners hungry for the simple farm fare they offer.

As I stood in the kitchen, I noticed these deep golden rolls, which looked like free-form artichokes—thus their name—cooling outside the door of the wood oven. I must have looked hungry, for Maria offered me one. It was delicious, filled with flavorful pork and olives and baked to a crisp.

When the ricotta was ready, she invited us to sit at one of the tables, and her grown children started scooping it out of the vat

Rosemary comes from the Latin rosmarius, "dew of the sea," so called because it is native to the area near the Mediterranean Sea.

into bowls, which were brought to us steaming. It was rich, creamy, and slightly salty. As we savored it, they brought platters of these artichoke rolls along with other savory breads and various double-crusted pizzas. All was washed down by a typical thirst-quenching Sicilian rosé, the kind of wine that is made on almost every farm on the island.

These rolls go together easily, and once baked they are very impressive to look at. But they are better still to eat, for the dough is tender-crisp, the pork succulent, the bit of cheese a tasty inspiration.

1 tablespoon fresh rosemary
8 ounces unseasoned ground pork
2 cloves garlic, green germ removed, minced
Fine sea salt
Hot paprika
2 tablespoons cornmeal or semolina

1 recipe Simple Dough (page 433)
25 oil or brine cured black olives, pitted
4 ounces provolone, caciocavallo, or sharp Cheddar, grated
2 tablespoons extra-virgin olive oil

1. Mince the rosemary and mix it with the pork and garlic. Season with salt and hot paprika. Pinch off a small portion of the meat mixture. Flatten it and cook it in a small pan over medium-high heat until cooked through. Taste for seasoning and adjust if necessary.

2. Sprinkle a baking sheet with the cornmeal. Roll out the dough to a 20 x 16-inch rectangle. Place heaping teaspoonfuls of the pork mixture on the dough at regular intervals about 2 inches apart. Intersperse the olives between the

little mounds of pork; cut the olives in half if necessary so there are as many pieces of olive as there are spaces to fit them. Evenly scatter the cheese over all, then drizzle with the olive oil.

3. Beginning at one narrow end, firmly roll up the dough until you have a fat roll. Gently press the roll so that it stays closed, then slice it crosswise into 6 equal pieces. Place the pieces, cut side down, on a baking sheet and gently flatten each one. Using a very sharp knife or razor blade, make a 1½-inch-deep X in the top, then make an-

other slash through the X so that the top is divided into sixths. Gently press the sections apart. Let the rolls rise at room temperature until they've increased in bulk by about one-third, 30 to 45 minutes.

4. Preheat the oven to 450°F.

5. Bake the rolls in the center of the oven until they are golden and baked through, about 30 minutes. Remove from the oven and let cool for at least 5 minutes before serving.

NOTE: These delicious rolls will delight you with their taste, but they will be maddeningly independent while they are in the oven, sometimes baking up in lovely regular shapes and sometimes baking up lazily. No matter their shape, they are appetizing to look at and delectable to eat!

Pork and Ricotta Rolls

TOMMASINI

ABOUT 24 ROLLS

These beautiful little rolls, which are flavored with fennel, pork, and fresh ricotta, are served around Modica in southeast Sicily and are a frequent prelude to a farm meal. Their one disadvantage is that they are so tasty it's far too easy to eat one too many before the full meal that follows.

I'd been invited to lunch at the *agriturismo* Al Monte, outside Ragusa in Siciliy. After an artichoke roll (page 302) and a warm slab of bread baked with olive oil and oregano, a platter of *tommasini* was brought to the table. One was good, but two were necessary to get the full effect of flavor and texture (and to satisfy a certain gluttony, it must be said). In Sicily, where farmworkers still do a lot by hand and have appetites as big as a house, such bread-based pastries are vital for satisfying hunger. Since the rolls and pizzas are seasoned with meat, cheese, vegetables, and olive oil, they make nutritious snacks and meals in themselves.

For those of us who aren't farmworkers, these rolls are just plain delicious. I like to make and serve them as a main course, along with a chilled Corvo Bianco and a big salad. It makes an unconventional meal but one that satisfies on every level.

12 ounces unseasoned ground pork
2½ teaspoons fine sea salt
2 teaspoons fennel seeds (optional)
Freshly ground black pepper

Hot paprika or cayenne pepper
3½ cups ricotta
1 large egg
2 tablespoons extra-virgin extra-virgin olive oil
1 recipe Simple Dough (page 433)

Segreti

If you plan to eat the Pork and Ricotta Rolls cold, you will need to add more salt to the pork mixture as its flavor will fade as it cools.

1. Mix the pork with 1½ teaspoons of the salt, the fennel seeds if using, and black pepper and hot paprika to taste. Flatten a pinch of the mixture and cook it in a small skillet over medium-high heat until it is cooked through. Taste and adjust the seasoning.

2. Whisk together the ricotta, egg, oil, and the remaining 1 teaspoon salt.

3. Line 2 baking sheets with parchment paper. Divide the dough in half. Roll out each half to a 19 x 10-inch rectangle. Evenly spread half the ricotta mixture on each rectangle to within ¼ inch of the edges. Pinch off heaping teaspoonsful of the pork mixture and evenly place

them about ¼ inch apart on top of the ricotta. Working gently but quickly, starting at one wider end, roll up each dough rectangle as tightly as you can. This can be a little tricky because the cheese has a tendency to ooze. Cut the rolls into 1½-inch-thick slices and set the slices, cut side down, on the prepared baking sheets. Pinch the top of each roll together, simultaneously pushing it gently down onto the baking sheet, so you are pinching and slightly flattening the rolls at the same time.

4. Cover the rolls loosely with a tea towel and let rise at room temperature until they expand by about one-half, about 30 minutes.

5. Preheat the oven to 400°F.

6. Bake the rolls in the center of the oven until they are golden, puffed, and baked through, about 25 minutes. Transfer to a warmed platter or serving basket and serve immediately.

NOTE: These are very good picnic fare too, though they don't keep more than about 8 hours.

Potato Bread

PANE CON PATATE

TWO 1½-POUND LOAVES

This bread recipe comes from Ceglie Messapico, a small country town in Puglia just above the heel of Italy's boot. I was visiting the Ricci family there, owners of Al Forno da Ricci, one of the best and most traditional restaurants in southern Italy. Their daughter, Antonella, had agreed to be my guide to the area, with the caveat that she would take me to the producers she found most interesting.

Our first stop was not a farm, however, but Lucia Urso's bakery where *focacce* (flat gorgeous loaves of bread), golden and sticky baked figs, and myriad sweet and savory *biscotti* filled the shelves. Antonella insisted that I meet the baker.

Lucia was in the back of her shop, up to her elbows in dough, but she greeted us with a smile, extracted herself, and came to talk. We stood in front of the huge oven that opens right into her shop, and I asked her the secret to the quality of her baked goods.

"The flour, of course," she said, referring to the hard-wheat flour of Puglia, which bursts with vitality. "And the almond shells." She explained that she fuels her oven with almond shells, and she feels they lend a sweetness to her bread. It is most likely a combination of these two things, as well as Lucia's light hand, for though her baked goods are rustic, they are delicate too. She makes one hundred pounds of bread dough twice a day and, according to Antonella, sells every single baked crumb.

She urged several slices of her *focaccia* made with this potato dough on us. I asked for the recipe and make it often. I love its chewy texture and fine crumb, as well as its alluring almost sour flavor.

This bread is best slightly warm from the oven.

8 ounces russet or other starchy
   potato, peeled
2 cups lukewarm water
1 teaspoon active dry yeast

5½ cups all-purpose flour
1 tablespoon coarse sea salt
Cornmeal or semolina, for dusting
   the baking pans

1. Bring 3 inches of water to boil in the bottom half of a steamer. Add the potato to the top half and steam until it is completely tender, about 25 minutes. Put the potato through a ricer or lightly but thoroughly mash it with a fork. Let it cool to room temperature.

2. In a large mixing bowl, whisk the lukewarm water and yeast together. Add 2 cups of the flour and whisk until smooth. Stir in the potato and salt, then continue to add flour until the dough is firm but tender. Turn the dough out onto a heavily floured surface and knead until it is very manageable, at least 10 minutes. It should be slightly sticky but come away from the work surface and from your hands easily.

3. Transfer the dough to a clean (unoiled) large bowl and cover it with a damp tea towel. Let rise at room temperature (68° to 70°F) until it has doubled in bulk and become quite light, 2½ to 3 hours.

4. Sprinkle two 9- to 9½-inch round cake pans with a thin, even layer of cornmeal. Punch down the dough and divide it in half. Form each piece into a round loaf by kneading it briefly, then bringing the outside edges of the dough to the center and pressing them firmly in place until the loaf holds a round shape. Place each loaf, smooth side up, in a prepared pan. Cover with a dry tea towel and let rise at room temperature

until the loaves expand by about one-third, about 1 hour.

5. Preheat the oven to 450°F.

6. Slash the tops of the loaves in several places with a razor blade or very sharp knife. Bake them in the center of the oven until they are golden, about 35 minutes. Remove from the oven, then turn out of the pans and let cool to room temperature on a wire rack. If storing the loaves, wrap them in aluminum foil, place in plastic bags, and freeze for up to 1 month.

Rich Farm Bread

GNOCCO INGRASSATO

TWO 2-POUND LOAVES

I first tasted this bread at Ristorante Lancellotti, which is run by the Lancellotti family (see essay, page 80), in Soliera, near Modena in Emilia-Romagna. It was traditionally made on the farm in the morning so that the workers who'd been out since dawn could eat it warm for their morning *merenda,* or snack, along with mortadella, a moist pork sausage that is the precursor of what we call bologna, and a glass of sparkling Lambrusco.

Ida Lancellotti made *gnocco ingrassato* on the farm when she and her husband, Camillo, still had milk cows. Now she or her daughter-in-law Szdena or her son Angelo, who is chef at the restaurant, share the responsibility, and they serve it as an *aperitivo* with each meal.

Segreti

if you have fat trimmed from prosciutto or other cured pork, use it here instead of the lard.

Still warm, it arrives at table cut into slabs along with healthy chunks of mortadella. I was so captivated by its gentle flavor and texture that I ate all three slices on the plate, completely ignoring the mortadella.

The bread was originally made with the yellow fat of prosciutto, and according to Emilio Lancellotti, maitre d'hotel and scholar, who has studied the traditional cuisine of his region in depth, the sour flavor of the fat mellowed in the bread. He remembers the weekly *gnocco* day—when the bread was fresh from the oven—as a great day indeed. "We loved it," he said. "I'll never forget as a kid coming into the kitchen and having a slice of warm *gnocco.*"

He explained that *gnocco* was a luxury for workers, who had no machinery to help them during their long, hard days in the fields and dairies and needed all the calories they could get. Every morsel of fat was used somewhere, as evidenced by this recipe.

According to Emilio, sliced onions were sometimes added to the dough right before the rising and baking. Angelo, always tweaking tradition just slightly, often adds a healthy handful of chives, freshly picked from his vegetable garden and chopped fine.

I sometimes follow Emilia-Romagna farm tradition and serve this before a meal with chunks of mortadella. It is also delicious along with a meal or toasted for breakfast.

2 cups lukewarm water
1 teaspoon active dry yeast
8 cups all-purpose flour
1 tablespoon fine sea salt
1 cup (8 ounces) lard, at room
*   temperature*

Cornmeal or semolina, for dusting
*   the baking pans*
2 big bunches chives, snipped into
*   ½-inch lengths (about 1 cup), or*
*   1 small onion, sliced paper thin*
*   and minced (optional)*

1. In a large mixing bowl, whisk the lukewarm water and yeast together. Whisk in 2 cups of the flour and then the salt. Add the lard in small chunks and whisk until the batter is smooth. Add enough of the remaining flour to make a soft dough. Turn

the dough out onto a lightly floured work surface and knead until it is elastic and satiny, at least 10 minutes. The surface of the dough won't be entirely smooth but will have shallow dimples.

2. Return the dough to the bowl and cover with plastic. Let rise at room temperature (68° to 70°F) until doubled in bulk, about 1½ hours.

3. Heavily dust the bottoms of two 9-inch round cake pans with cornmeal. Punch down the dough and knead either the chives or onion (if using) into it. Divide the dough in half. Knead each piece of dough two or three times, then shape each into a round loaf by pulling the outside edges in toward the center until the loaf keeps its round shape. Place each loaf, smooth side up, in one of the prepared pans and cover with a tea towel. Let rise at room temperature until almost doubled in bulk, about 45 minutes.

4. Preheat the oven to 400°F.

5. Just before baking, slash the top of each loaf several times with a sharp knife. Bake in the center of the oven for 20 minutes. Reverse the positions of the pans so they bake evenly and continue baking until the loaves are golden and sound hollow when tapped, an additional 20 minutes. Remove from the oven, then turn out of the pans and let cool to room temperature (if you can wait that long) on a wire rack. If storing the loaves, wrap in aluminum foil, place in plastic bags, and freeze for up to 1 month.

NOTES: The Lancellottis use fat from prosciutto or other cuts of pork to make *gnocco ingrassato.* With Angelo's blessing, I use lard because it is easier to find. The flavor differs from that of Angelo's bread but not so substantially that it can't be called by the same name.

Do not use both chives and onions in this recipe, just one or the other.

Tuscan Bread

PANE TOSCANO

TWO
2-POUND
LOAVES

I found this recipe during a visit to the Marini Salumeria in Tuscany, not far from Pistoia, where the Marini family produces incredibly pure-tasting sausages, salamis, and prosciutti. I spent the morning with the Marinis, a remarkably boisterous, talented, and fun-loving family, and toward lunchtime was offered a tasting of their flavorful products along with this delicious bread. When I asked Signora Marini where she got it, she took my hand and we ran across the street to meet Antonio Copini at the Fratelli Copini bakery. Copini was just pulling loaves from the oven, and the aroma was heavenly.

What made his bread so extraordinary? "I make bread the way the *contadini* did," he said, referring to the farmworkers who used to bake their own breads on the farm. He uses a *madre,* or mother (similar to a sourdough starter), which rises slowly, allowing the flavor of the flour and yeast to meld and the gluten to develop. "The *contadini* made it once a week," he said. "And they baked it in a wood-fired oven. I make it every day and bake it in a gas-fired oven, but it turns out just like theirs." We concluded the secret is probably the long, slow rise of the *madre,* which allows flavor and texture to develop.

Tuscan bread is delicious hot from the oven with a drizzle of fine olive oil, and it makes a fine base for *panzanella* (page 53) and for all the *crostini* in this book.

FOR THE MADRE
1 cup lukewarm water
1 rounded tablespoon active dry
  yeast
1¾ cups all-purpose flour

FOR THE BREAD
2⅓ cups lukewarm water
7¼ to 7¾ cups all-purpose flour
Cornmeal or semolina, for dusting
  the baking pans

1. At least 12 hours before you want to bake the bread, make the *madre*. In a large mixing bowl, whisk the lukewarm water and yeast together. Gradually whisk in the flour until you have a smooth batter. Cover loosely and let sit at room temperature (68° to 70°F) for at least 9 hours or up to 12. The *madre* will be bubbly, very elastic in texture, and will emit a seductive yeasty aroma.

2. To make the bread, whisk the lukewarm water into the *madre,* then gradually stir in enough flour to make a firm yet soft dough. Turn the dough out onto a lightly floured work surface and knead, adding more flour as needed, until the dough is smooth and satiny, about 5 minutes. The dough should be firm yet soft enough so that when you pinch it, it will still feel somewhat sticky. This dough is less elastic than other yeast doughs, and while it will feel dry on the surface, it will remain sticky inside. You may be tempted to continue adding flour, but don't go over the maximum amount given. To test the dough, touch it lightly with a clean finger. If it comes away clean, the dough is ready to form into loaves.

3. Heavily dust two 9-inch round cake pans with cornmeal.

4. Divide the dough in half and form into round loaves by bringing the outside edges of the dough to the center and pressing them firmly in place until the loaf holds a round shape. Place them, smooth side up, in the prepared pans and cover loosely with a tea towel. Let rise at room temperature until the bread increases in bulk by two-thirds, about 1½ hours.

5. Preheat the oven to 400°F.

6. Slash the tops of the loaves in a crosshatch pattern. Bake in the center of the oven until the loaves are golden and sound hollow when tapped, 45 to 50 minutes. Remove the bread from the oven, then turn out of the pans and let cool on a wire rack before cutting. If storing the loaves, wrap in aluminum foil, place in plastic bags, and freeze for up to 1 month.

Tuscan bread

NOTE: Tuscan bread differs in appearance from other bread because it has a matte crust.

When you see it, don't think there is anything wrong with the bread—it is perfectly normal.

Bruno Bini's Favorite Pizza

LA PIZZA DI BRUNO BINI

6 TO 8 SERVINGS

Like so many families in Italy, the Binis, a Tuscan farm family who live outside Radda, in Chianti, have a wood-burning oven that is the happy source of many pizza meals. Once the dough is made, just about anything from the Bini's garden is likely to find its way on top of it. Bruno Bini favors the traditional *rossa Fiorentina* variety of onion, sliced very thin, atop his thick pizza dough. These red onions are sweet and flavorful and becoming increasingly rare in Tuscany, although they are still to be found in farmers' markets.

When I prepare Bruno Bini's pizza, I use the freshest, firmest red onions I can find and mound them on. Those on top get a nice crisp edge, while those underneath melt into sweetness. Don't forget to sprinkle the pizza with salt as soon as it emerges from the oven. Also, if you're using Pizza Dough I, remember to begin making it the night or morning before you plan to serve it.

A lightly chilled Bianco Vergine della Valdichiana goes extremely well with this tasty pizza.

Cornmeal or semolina, for dusting the baking pan
1 recipe Maria's Pizza Dough (page 432) or Pizza Dough I (page 431)

1½ pounds red onions, cut lengthwise in half and sliced as thin as possible
2 tablespoons extra-virgin olive oil
Fine sea salt

1. Lightly sprinkle a 15 x 11-inch baking sheet with cornmeal. Roll out the pizza dough and fit it in the pan. Cover

loosely with a tea towel and let rise at room temperature (68° to 70°F) until the dough has increased in bulk by a generous one-third, about 1 hour.

2. Preheat the oven to 450°F.

3. Strew the onions over the prepared dough all the way to the edges and drizzle them with the oil. Bake in the center of the oven until the onions are softened and golden and the dough is baked and golden at the edges, 35 to 40 minutes.

4. Remove the pizza from the oven and sprinkle it all over with salt to taste. Let cool for about 5 minutes before cutting into serving pieces.

Pane e Cipolle

In the old days farmers in many parts of Italy were achingly poor and subsisted on onions. If they lived in Emilia-Romagna, they combined their onions with Parmesan cheese on a flat bread that was baked in the ashes of the fire. In Tuscany they simply ate saltless Tuscan bread and onions.

Today it is common to describe someone who has no sense of gastronomic adventure as an eater of *pane e cipolle,* or a bread-and-onion eater.

Francesca's Pepper Pizza

PIZZA CON PEPERONI DI FRANCESCA

6 TO 8 SERVINGS

This recipe is based on a wonderful pizza I ate in the Passatempi kitchen, not far from Bologna in Emilia-Romagna. The Passatempis do things a little differently in this region, where corn and wheat are king—they raise organic vegetables, which they sell at local markets, and they do very well, in part because their daughter, Francesca, and their son, Paolo, work with them.

Both young people admit that selling organic vegetables in their local markets isn't an easy thing to do. "People don't really under-

In Italy, peppers are described as peperoni quadrati (four-sided), peperoni a cuòre di bue (bull's heart), peperoni a pomodoro (tomato shaped), and peperoni a corno (ham shaped).

stand what organic vegetables are," said Paolo. "Then they taste them and they understand, but getting them to taste is the hardest part."

Francesca works all winter on a flower farm, but during the summer she is a lively part of the family, and she was there when I stayed with them. One day she made this pizza for lunch, after a backbreaking morning in the fields. I was impressed with the rapidity with which she put it together and with its rich, sweet flavor once baked. Of course, it had the Passatempi organic peppers piled on top, with their incomparable flavor. Use organic peppers if you can find them, for they have a better developed and more pronounced flavor than those raised conventionally.

Serve this with a Trebbiano di Romagna.

*Cornmeal or semolina, for dusting
   the baking pan
1 recipe Maria's Pizza Dough
   (page 432)
3 tablespoons extra-virgin
   olive oil*

*1½ pounds red and/or green bell
   peppers, stemmed, seeds and pith
   removed, cut lengthwise into
   2-inch-wide strips, then cut
   crosswise in half
Fine sea salt*

1. Lightly sprinkle a 15 x 11-inch baking sheet with cornmeal. Roll out the pizza dough and fit it in the pan. Cover loosely with a tea towel and let rise at room temperature (68° to 70°F) until the dough has puffed and almost doubled in bulk, 20 to 30 minutes.

2. Preheat the oven to 450°F.

3. Heat 1 tablespoon of the oil in a large skillet over medium-high heat. Add as many peppers as will fit in a single layer and sauté just until the peppers soften and their skins are slightly golden but still somewhat crisp, about 10 minutes. Transfer to a plate with a slotted spoon. Repeat with the remaining peppers.

4. Spread the peppers evenly over the dough. Bake in the center of the oven until the dough is golden and baked through, about 30 minutes. Drizzle with the remaining 2 tablespoons oil and sprinkle with salt to taste. Cut into serving pieces and serve immediately.

Pizza from Salina

PIZZA DI SALINA

**4 TO 6
SERVINGS**

The isle of Salina, in the Eolian archipelago off the western Sicilian coast, is a calm, remote paradise. Once completely rural and self-sufficient, it has been discovered by tourists, although it remains real, warm, and charming. Arable land in Salina is devoted largely to capers (see essay, page 67), Malvasia grapes, which go into the very sweet local wine of the same name, tomatoes, and other garden vegetables, including the escarole that shares the stage with capers here.

Pizza has worked its way into the local cuisine on Salina, and I sampled this sitting on a terrace overlooking the sea, after I'd spent the day on a caper farm. I loved it for the surprise of escarole and the bright flavor of the island capers.

Like other pizzas, it can serve as the prelude to a meal or the meal itself. Try it with a Rosato Dell'Etna, a surprisingly full-flavored rosé from the volcanic slopes of Mount Etna.

More About Capers

Use the best-quality capers you can find, preferably those cured in sea salt, which retain their texture and lovely perfumed flavor better than those cured in vinegar.

If using salt-preserved capers, see page 66 for how to prepare them. If you can't find capers cured in salt, go ahead and use those cured in vinegar, but drain, rinse, and pat them dry as soon as you get them home, then replace them in their jar and cover them completely with olive oil. Their flavor will blossom and they will flavor the oil at the same time, giving you two condiments in one.

Keep in mind that the ideal caper is the size of a plump raisin, for it had enough time on the caper plant to develop a full flavor, something tiny capers just don't offer.

½ recipe Simple Dough (page 433)
1 cup Nunzio's Tomato Sauce (page 424)
⅓ cup capers, preferably preserved in salt (see box, page 66)

8 cups escarole, rinsed, patted dry, and torn into bite-size pieces
3 tablespoons extra-virgin olive oil
Fine sea salt and freshly ground black pepper

capers

1. Preheat the oven to 400°F. Lightly sprinkle a 15 x 11-inch baking sheet with cornmeal.

2. Roll out the dough into a 15 x 11-inch rectangle and fit it in the prepared pan.

3. Spread the tomato sauce as evenly over the dough as possible. Pat dry the capers, then sprinkle them over the tomato sauce.

4. Toss the escarole with the olive oil in a large bowl until the leaves are coated. Season with salt and pepper to taste, toss again, and spread the greens evenly over the pizza.

5. Bake in the center of the oven until the dough is golden around the edges and the greens are wilted and golden (see Note), about 25 minutes. Let cool for about 5 minutes, then cut into serving pieces and serve.

NOTE: The escarole turns dark golden when cooked but retains a wonderful flavor.

Antonella Pizza

LA PIZZA DI ANTONELLA

10 TO 12 SERVINGS

Both Antonella DiRosolini and Giuseppe Cicero come from the town of Rosolino, about twenty-five miles south of Modica, in southeast Sicily. Although they now live in Modica, they have kept their house and property in Rosolino, where Giuseppe raises organic olives, vegetables, and fruits and makes his own honey. Each weekend finds them in Rosolino, where they harvest produce from their land to take back to Modica for a weeks' worth of fine meals.

They lead a hectic life—Antonella is a doctor and Giuseppe is an agricultural consultant specifically focused on organic cultivation (see essay, page 36). Because their time is limited, their meals are simple, revolving around dishes like this. It needs nothing more than a drizzle of extra-virgin olive oil once it's on your plate.

Try a full-bodied red, such as Regaleali Rosso, along with this.

Cornmeal or semolina, for dusting the baking pans
1 recipe Simple Dough (page 433)
1¾ pounds cherry tomatoes, stemmed and cut in half
6 cloves garlic, green germ removed, minced

8 anchovy fillets, drained, patted dry, and minced (optional; see Note)
2 tablespoons dried oregano
4 tablespoons extra-virgin olive oil
Fine sea salt

1. Preheat the oven to 400°F. Lightly sprinkle two 15 x 11-inch baking sheets with cornmeal.

2. Divide the dough in half, roll out each half into a 15 x 11-inch rectangle, and fit it into one of the prepared pans.

3. Place the cherry tomatoes, cut side down and evenly spread, on the rectangles of dough, then sprinkle evenly with the garlic, anchovies if using, and oregano, crushing it as you sprinkle it to release the most flavor. Drizzle each pizza, including the edges of the dough, with 2 tablespoons of the oil. Season with salt to taste.

4. Bake the pizza in the cen-ter of the oven until the dough is golden and the tomatoes are soft but not mushy, about 30 minutes. If baking the pizzas on separate racks, reverse their positions after 15 minutes so they bake evenly.

5. Let cool for about 5 minutes, as the tomatoes are blistering hot, then cut each pizza into 8 pieces and serve.

NOTE: I like to use half the amount of anchovies listed here and put them all on one pizza, so there is a pizza for those who like anchovies and one for those who don't. You may also cut the recipe in half to make just one pizza.

A MYSTERIOUS FLAVOR

The first bread I ate in Sicily was on the Sapuppo farm, right outside Catania (see essay, page 216). I was staying there with my friend Susan Lord, former food editor of the Italian cooking magazine *Gambero Rosso* and lively companion in culinary adventure. The bread was served at dinner, and I was immediately seduced by its beautiful, almost custardy texture, subtle ivory color, and thick, crisp crust. After my first bite, I looked quizzically at Susan, who was watching me intently.

"What's the flavor?" she asked.

"Cinnamon," I stated with certainty.

"No," she said, "there isn't any cinnamon in this bread, but I taste it too."

I didn't believe her and asked Anna Sapuppo. She looked at me like I was crazy. "This is simply *pane di casa,* daily bread, the simplest of breads. There is no cinnamon in it."

I still wasn't convinced.

"This is the flavor of bread here," Susan insisted. "I always notice it when I come to Sicily, which I've been doing three or four times a year for almost thirty years. I don't know what it is, but it's not cinnamon."

Still doubting like Thomas, I examined a slice under a bright light, hoping to find dark flecks of cinnamon in it, but I was disappointed. We ate our way through the entire basket—it went down like cake—savoring and wondering at each bite.

While our days in Sicily were already scheduled, that one loaf of bread launched a search that took us even further afield, into bakeries and flour mills throughout the island. We bought loaf after loaf, all of which had different degrees of the same haunting flavor. We encountered round, flat, and oval loaves that ranged from heavy to light, and fanciful loaves shaped like cockscombs and fishes, which symbolize things like good fortune.

It wasn't until we were in the office of Dr. Giuseppe Cicero, who works for the Sicilian agricultural and forestry department in Modica, in southeast Sicily, and is an expert on organic cultivation and olive oil, that some light was shed on our search, for Dr. Cicero is also a bread fanatic. When I asked him about the flavor of Sicilian bread, he knew instantly what I meant.

"I don't taste cinnamon," he said. "But I know the flavor you mean. It comes from the wheat."

He explained that the indigenous wheat around Modica is called *russello,* a hardy old variety that is falling out of favor. "It's a shame to see it disappear," he said. "It's a good wheat, and its growth pattern prevents weeds, so farmers don't have to use herbicides. It is also the only wheat here that gives the flavor you're talking about." He acknowledged that it yields less than contemporary hybrids, and mechanical harvesters designed for hybrid wheats don't work efficiently in fields planted with *russello.* But he is partial to *russello* because he loves the bread it produces.

The following day Dr. Cicero took us to a handful of organic farms in the area, and on the way back he offered to find us the best breads in the area. After visiting several bakeries, we ended up with four different loaves, and the best was the simplest—a *pane di casa* from Dr. Cicero's favorite bakery that was hard, twisted, and dense. Its cinnamon flavor was so intense that I searched it on the sly for the spice but to no avail. "It's made with pure *russello* flour," the doctor said, tearing off a hunk and eating it.

On our return to Modica, Dr. Cicero directed us to a small flour mill in Modica Bassa, the lower part of town, which specializes in milling *russello.* Right around the corner from the bustling business district, it is owned by Giorgio Rocasalva, whose family has been in the milling business for generations.

Susan and I walked into the floury din, where automated hulling machines danced and whirred, and met Mariucca Rocasalva, the owner's daughter, who was to be our guide. Bags of flour were stacked on pallets in the middle of the floor, marked with their destination. Workers supervised the cleaning machines, the flour mills, the shipping and receiving, while customers formed a line in front of Signore Rocasalva's small office,

which looked like a tollbooth. Its glass front was open partway so people could talk to him if they bent down, and through that opening passed currency, business cards, hands put out for a shake.

Stuck all over the walls of the mill were hand-lettered Modicana proverbs put there by Signore Rocasalva. My favorite was "When millers fight, the flour gets better." Mariucca explained that this was the most appropriate too, since her father and his three brothers, millers all, have plenty of issues among them.

On either side of the office were shelves stacked with rough-looking cheeses, olive oil, honeys. Sacks of borlotti, favas, lentils, and chickpeas crowded the floor around them. Mariucca explained that her father is always discovering delicious local products as he travels in search of *russello* for his mill, and he makes them available to his clients, which is why his mill resembles a country store. "He travels farther to find *russello* now. It's not as popular anymore because of its low gluten content," Mariucca explained. "And it's hard to cultivate, and its yield is low. Everyone wants puffier bread these days, and they don't want to have to work so hard to cultivate their wheat."

"Besides," as Signore Rocasalva told us when he finally emerged from the office

and directed Mariucca to take his place there, "farmers don't get government subsidies to grow *russello,* so most of them don't cultivate it."

He walked over to a sack and took out a handful of fat reddish wheat kernels. "This is *russello,*" he said. "It's twice as expensive as other wheat."

He took us upstairs past huge machines where the wheat is soaked in water, selected, and crushed, then past old-fashioned wood-and-screen sifters that vibrated noisily as they removed the chaff and the germ. The resulting kernels go downstairs to be milled into semolina, a coarse flour used primarily for pasta. Some is milled again into flour called *remacchinato,* which makes the remarkable bread that tastes of cinnamon.

Signore Rocasalva took us back downstairs, and we stood amidst the machinery as he talked about learning the art of milling from his father, whom he greatly admired. "My father was something else," Signore Rocasalva said. "He was always hungry to learn. He begged his parents to send him to school. 'I will learn to write,' he told his father, 'so that I can write to you and mother when I'm in the military.' But his father replied that if he wrote them letters they would be 'put in difficulty' because they couldn't read, so he refused."

Signore Rocasalva credits his father, who finally learned to read and write after the Second World War, with teaching him to value good food and good products, good wheat and good farmers, and good business. He does very well, sticking to his artisanally made products and his old wheat varieties, one of few local millers to be so dedicated. "There used to be ten or more varieties of wheat grown around here," he said. "Now there are three or four. We've got to keep the older varieties because they're strongest and they represent tradition."

A small knot of clients was waiting to talk with Signore Rocasalva despite the lateness of the hour, for it was almost 8 P.M. In most countries, I thought, the miller would have locked his door and gone home for supper long ago. But not Signore Rocasalva. He finished his sentence and left us with a firm handshake.

Though Dr. Cicero gave us a key, and the visit to the Rocasalva mill was rich and informative, neither was definitive in terms of the bread flavor question. Our sampling continued all across Sicily. We found the best breads were those made with the traditional wheat, and it always had the alluring cinnamon flavor in varying degrees of intensity. We eventually developed our own conclusion.

Like everything that is wonderful and edible in the world, it takes a delicate combination of soil, sun, atmosphere, and variety to produce flavor. There is also the human element to consider, the careful hand of quality. From our experience and research we deduced that it is the combination of such intangibles that gives bread in Sicily its alluring flavor.

This conclusion was not arrived at through scientific study but through another kind of study—that of seeing, listening, and finally, tasting.

Sicilian Double-Crusted Potato Pizza

SCACCIA CON PATATE

6 TO 8 SERVINGS

This is just one version of *scaccia,* the delicious and infinitely versatile Sicilian double-crusted pizza that comes from the area around Catania, in eastern Sicily. A typical farm lunch there might begin with hot *scaccia* filled with any number of things, primarily vegetables and herbs, for it is traditionally made with whatever is fresh in the *orto,* or farm garden, or with wild herbs gathered in nearby pastures.

Scaccia is an essential peasant dish, and like so much Sicilian—and Italian—farm cooking, it offers big flavor and satisfaction from the simplest ingredients. Here potatoes and a rich tomato sauce are seasoned with thin slices of onion and softened with olive oil, then braised inside the rich and tender dough. What could be simpler? Or better?

East this as Sicilians do, either as a midmorning *merenda,* or snack, or for lunch. You may also want to add a simple green salad, and you will certainly want to serve a tasty Regaleali Rosso alongside.

1 large russet potato (about 8 ounces)
½ recipe Simple Dough (page 433)
¾ cup Nunzio's Tomato Sauce (page 424)

1 small white onion, sliced very thin
Fine sea salt
1 tablespoon extra-virgin olive oil

1. Peel the potato and slice as thin as you possibly can, preferably using a vegetable peeler to get paper-thin slices.

2. Lightly oil a baking sheet. Roll out half the dough to a 24 x 12-inch rectangle. It will be quite thin but don't be concerned. Slip the oiled baking sheet under half of the rolled-out dough. Spread the dough on the baking sheet with the tomato sauce to within ¼ inch of the edge. Cover the sauce evenly with the potato, then with the

onion. Season with salt to taste.

3. Bring the dough resting on the work surface up and over the filling and press the edges firmly together, slightly rolling the edges of the dough toward the center so they are sure to stay together. Brush the top of the dough with the olive oil. Let the *scaccia* rise until the dough is slightly puffed, about 20 minutes.

4. Preheat the oven to 425°F.

5. Bake the *scaccia* in the center of the oven until the dough is golden, about 40 minutes. Let cool for about 5 minutes, then cut into 6 to 8 pieces and serve.

Double-Crusted Eggplant Pizza

SCACCIA DI MELANZANE

6 TO 8 SERVINGS

This *scaccia,* or double-crusted pizza, from the Modica area, in the southeastern sector of Sicily, makes good use of summer eggplant and the sweetly flavorful tomato sauce of Nunzio San Filippo, cook at the Sapuppo family farm, near Catania (see essay, page 216). Rich and mouthwatering, it can be served either as an appetizer or as a main meal along with a salad.

1 small eggplant (about 8 ounces), rinsed, cut into ¼-inch-thick rounds

3 tablespoons extra-virgin olive oil

½ recipe Simple Dough (page 433)

6 tablespoons Nunzio's Tomato Sauce (page 424)

Fine sea salt

1 clove garlic, green germ removed, minced

½ cup grated Parmigiano-Reggiano

1½ tablespoons salt-preserved capers, rinsed, soaked in hot water for 1 hour, drained, and patted dry (optional; see Note)

½ cup (gently packed) fresh basil leaves

1. Preheat the oven to 425°F. Lightly oil 2 baking sheets.

2. Evenly space the eggplant rounds on one of the baking sheets and brush the tops with 2 tablespoons of the oil. Bake in the center of the oven until the eggplant is tender and slightly golden, about 20 minutes. Remove from the oven and let cool. Leave the oven on.

3. Roll out the dough to a 24 x 12-inch rectangle. It will be quite thin but don't be concerned. Slip the remaining baking sheet under half of the rolled-out dough. Brush the dough that is on the baking sheet with the tomato sauce. Top with the eggplant and season with salt to taste. Sprinkle with the garlic, then with the cheese. Sprinkle with the capers if using. Mince the basil leaves and sprinkle over all.

4. Bring the dough resting on the work surface up and over the filling and press the edges firmly together, slightly rolling the edges of the dough toward the center so they are sure to stay together. Brush the top with the remaining 1 tablespoon olive oil. Let the *scaccia* rise until the dough is slightly puffed, about 20 minutes.

5. Preheat the oven to 425°F.

6. Bake the *scaccia* in the center of the oven until golden, about 30 minutes. Let cool for about 5 minutes, then cut into 6 or 8 pieces and serve.

NOTE: I have made this many times, and the caper question has arisen more than once. Should one add them or not? Well, in my family we like it both ways, though the preference is without, but others insist they are necessary. You will have to follow your own tastes.

Double-Crusted Basil Pizza

Who can resist basil in any form? This basil-rich *scaccia,* or double-crusted pizza, emerges from the oven golden, light, and satisfying—perfect for a summery evening. I recommend bush basil for this recipe, the variety most favored in Italy, for its intense and spicy flavor.

Serve this with a light, fruity red, such as Regaleali Rosso.

½ recipe Simple Dough (page 433)
4 tablespoons extra-virgin olive oil
¾ cup (about 2 ounces) grated
  Parmigiano-Reggiano, or sheep's
  milk cheese

4 cups (gently packed) basil leaves
½ cup capers (see box, page 66)
Fine sea salt and freshly ground
  black pepper

1. Lightly oil a baking sheet. Roll out the dough to a 24 x 12-inch rectangle. It will be quite thin but don't be concerned. Slip the oiled baking sheet under half of the rolled-out dough.

2. Brush the dough on the baking sheet with half the olive oil. Sprinkle half the cheese over the dough. Tear the basil leaves and spread them over the cheese. Scatter the capers over the basil, the remaining cheese over the capers, and finally drizzle with 1 tablespoon of the remaining oil. Season with salt and lightly with pepper.

3. Bring the dough resting on the work surface up and over the filling and press the edges firmly together, slightly rolling the edges of the dough toward the center so they are sure to stay together. Brush the top with the remaining 1 tablespoon olive oil. Let the *scaccia* rise until the dough is slightly puffed, about 20 minutes.

4. Preheat the oven to 425°F.

5. Bake the *scaccia* in the center of the oven until golden, about 30 minutes. Let cool for about 5 minutes, then cut into 6 or 8 pieces and serve.

Double-Crusted Sun-Dried Tomato Pizza

**SCACCIA ALLA
CAPULIATO**

**6 TO 8
SERVINGS**

Segreti

When working with dough for the double-crusted pizza, be sure not to roll it too thin and to lift rather than pull it to avoid making holes in it.

This is a perfect winter *scaccia,* or double-crusted pizza, from around Catania, in eastern Sicily. In the Sicilian dialect sun-dried tomatoes are called *chiappe,* or cheek, for that is what the dried halves resemble. When minced, the dried tomatoes are called *capuliato*—thus the name of this *scaccia.*

The onions in this *scaccia* are abundant, the better to lend a sweet sharpness. If you prefer fewer onions, simply adjust the quantity. This is delicious with a simple Regaleali Rosso.

½ *recipe Simple Dough (page 433)*
2 *medium onions, sliced very thin*
¾ *cup good-quality oil-packed sun-dried tomatoes, coarsely minced*

Fine sea salt
Hot paprika or cayenne pepper
1 *tablespoon dried oregano*
3 *tablespoons extra-virgin olive oil*

1. Lightly oil a baking sheet. Roll out the dough to a 24 x 12-inch rectangle. It will be quite thin but don't be concerned. Slip the oiled baking sheet under half of the rolled-out dough. Strew the dough on the baking sheet evenly with the onions and tomatoes to within ¼ inch of the edge. Season lightly with salt and with hot paprika to taste, then sprinkle with the oregano. Drizzle evenly with 2 tablespoons of the olive oil.

2. Bring the dough resting on the work surface up and over the filling and press the edges firmly together, slightly rolling the edges of the dough toward the center so they are sure to stay together. Brush the top with the remaining 1 tablespoon oil. Let the *scaccia* rise until the dough is slightly puffed, about 20 minutes.

3. Preheat the oven to 425°F.

4. Bake the *scaccia* in the center of the oven until golden, about 30 minutes. Let cool for about 5 minutes, then cut into 6 or 8 pieces and serve.

Double-Crusted Broccoli Pizza

SCACCIA AI BROCCOLI

8 SERVINGS

*S*cacce have migrated from the farms, where I tasted my favorites, to city bakeries, where I found others that I loved. No two were the same, and the fillings ranged from a simple slather of tomato sauce to a variety of vegetables, including broccoli, which I've used here.

The broccoli in this *scaccia* is well cooked by the time it emerges from the oven, for broccoli cooked al dente is too crisp for the pizza crust.

This is rich in flavor, texture, and just the tiniest little bite from *olio santo*, the peppery oil so typical to Sicily. Try it with a rich and robust Cerasuolo di Vittoria or a Regaleali Rosso. And *buon appetito!*

1 pound broccoli florets, trimmed
½ recipe Simple Dough (page 433)
8 ounces ricotta
1 clove garlic, green germ removed,
  minced

Fine sea salt and freshly ground
  black pepper
2 teaspoons Hot Pepper Oil
  (page 389)
1 tablespoon extra-virgin olive oil

1. Bring about 3 inches of water to a boil in the bottom half of a steamer over high heat. Add the broccoli to the top half and steam until it is tender, 6 to 8 minutes. Remove from the heat and let cool.

2. Lightly oil a baking sheet. Roll out the dough to a 24 x 12-inch rectangle. It will be quite thin but don't be concerned. Slip the oiled baking sheet under half of the rolled-out dough. Spread the dough on the baking sheet evenly with the ricotta, then sprinkle with the garlic and season with salt and pepper to taste. Break apart the broccoli florets if necessary so that they evenly cover the ricotta and are basically all the same size. Season with salt and pepper and drizzle evenly with the pepper oil.

4. Bring the dough resting on the work surface up and over

the filling and press the edges firmly together, slightly rolling the edges of the dough toward the center so they are sure to stay together. Brush the top of the dough with the olive oil. Let the *scaccia* rise until the dough is slightly puffed, about 20 minutes.

5. Preheat the oven to 425°F.

6. Bake the *scaccia* in the center of the oven until golden, about 30 minutes.

Double-Crusted Onion and Pepper Pizza

SCACCIA CON CIPOLLE E PEPERONI

8 SERVINGS

Fragrant fresh rosemary is a must for the filling in this *scaccia*. Dried rosemary just won't do, so beg, borrow, or—well, do what you must to procure it fresh.

Try a simple rich Regaleali Rosso alongside.

*½ recipe Simple Dough
    (page 433)
1 medium onion, sliced
    very thin
Fine sea salt
Hot paprika or cayenne pepper*

*1½ pounds green bell peppers or
    Italian peppers, stemmed, seeds
    and pith removed, cut into thin
    strips
3 tablespoons extra-virgin olive oil
3 tablespoons fresh rosemary leaves*

1. Lightly oil a baking sheet. Roll out the dough to a 24 x 12-inch rectangle. It will be quite thin but don't be concerned. Slip the oiled baking sheet under half the rolled-out dough. Arrange the onion in an even layer on the dough on the baking sheet to within ¼ inch of the edge. Season with salt and hot paprika to taste. (In Sicily this would have just enough heat to leave a pleasant tingling sensation on the back of your palate.) Sprinkle the pepper slices over the onion. Drizzle with 2 tablespoons of the olive oil, sea-

son with a bit more salt, and strew with the rosemary leaves.

2. Bring the dough resting on the work surface up and over the filling and press the edges firmly together, slightly rolling the edges of the dough toward the center so they are sure to stay together. Brush the top with the remaining 1 tablespoon oil. Let the *scaccia* rise until the dough is slightly puffed, about 20 minutes.

3. Preheat the oven to 425°F.

4. Bake the *scaccia* in the center of the oven until the dough is golden, about 30 minutes. Let cool for about 5 minutes, then cut into 8 pieces and serve.

Maria's Focaccia

FOCACCIA DI MARIA

1 THICK FOCACCIA; ABOUT 8 SERVINGS

Segreti

Brushing the dough with olive oil tenderizes the top and gives it a heady olive flavor.

Maria Maurillo, who owns Agriturismo Malvarina with her son Claudio (see essay, page 363) and does all the cooking there, prepared this simple focaccia and served it before supper with Cured Pork with Sage and Vinegar. The focaccia can be varied in innumerable ways—by sprinkling it with fresh rosemary, paper-thin slices of garlic, crushed hot pepper, or a thin wash of tomato sauce. Use your imagination with this dough, which is tender, golden, and satisfying.

Cornmeal or semolina, for dusting
   the baking pan and work surface
1 recipe Maria's Pizza Dough
   (page 432)

1 tablespoon extra-virgin olive oil
1 teaspoon coarse sea salt
Cured Pork with Sage and Vinegar,
   for serving (page 42) (optional)

1. Preheat the oven to 400°F. Sprinkle a 16 x 12-inch baking sheet with cornmeal.

2. On a work surface lightly sprinkled with cornmeal or semolina, roll out the dough to a

Sage

16 x 12-inch rectangle. Transfer the dough to the prepared baking sheet; it will shrink somewhat but simply press it to the edges of the baking sheet. Cover with a tea towel and set it atop the preheating oven (or in another warm spot). Let rise until it has increased by about one-third, which should take about 20 minutes.

3. Using a fork, poke the dough lightly several times on top. To garnish the dough, brush it with the olive oil and sprinkle it evenly with the salt.

4. Bake the focaccia in the center of the oven until it is puffed and pale golden, about 25 minutes. The dough should not be dark but light golden.

5. Remove from the oven and let cool for about 5 minutes. Using scissors or a sharp knife, cut into 8 equal pieces. Serve accompanied by the pork or the condiment or topping of your choice.

Sicilian Tuna Torte

EMPANATA DI TONNO

6 TO 8 SERVINGS

In Sicily many preparations are wrapped in bread dough, including this intriguing torte, a more dressed-up dish than most. This recipe was given to me by Corrado Assenza, arguably Sicily's finest baker and a passionate student of his culinary roots. We sat around the dinner table one evening, and he talked about traditional recipes of the area he is from, around Nuoto. Rich and varied, they include this *empanata,* which Corrado said is typical to the farm cuisine of southeastern coastal Sicily, where tuna is brought in by small fishing boats and landed at the town of Marzamemi on the southernmost tip of the island. Once landed, it is usually sold right from the boat.

Fresh tuna has a beguilingly mild yet distinctive flavor, and here it combines with the gutsiness of garlic, olives, parsley, and tomatoes in a dish that is not only lovely to look at but also substantially satisfying.

This makes a fine main course. I like to serve it after Tomatoes with Herb Sauce (page 24) and with a green salad as well. Try a rich, smooth, elegant red alongside, such as Cerasuolo di Vittoria.

1 large egg

2 pounds fresh tuna, skin and
    bones removed

3 tablespoons extra-virgin olive oil

2 medium onions, thinly sliced

3 cloves garlic, green germ removed,
    cut crosswise into thin slices

4 good-size very fresh tomatoes
    (about 3 ounces each), cored,
    peeled, and cut crosswise in half

1 recipe Simple Dough (page 433)

1½ cups (gently packed) fresh
    flat-leaf parsley leaves

Fine sea salt

2 tablespoons capers, preferably
    preserved in salt (see box, page 66)

½ cup good-quality black olives
    cured in brine, preferably from
    Liguria or Nyons, pitted and
    coarsely chopped

Flat-Leaf
Parsley

1. Preheat the oven to 400°F. Whisk together the egg and 2 teaspoons water in a small bowl to make an egg wash. Set aside.

2. Rinse the tuna with cold water, pat it dry, and cut it into ½-inch-thick slices. Refrigerate until ready to use.

3. Place 2 tablespoons of the oil, the onions, and garlic in a large skillet over medium heat and cook, stirring occasionally, until the onions are tender but still opaque, about 7 minutes. Remove from the heat and set aside.

4. Remove most but not all the seeds and juice from each tomato by gently squeezing each

half. Cut the tomatoes into ¼-inch-wide strips. Set aside.

5. Divide the dough in half. Roll half of the dough into a 15-inch round and fit it into a 9½-inch springform pan, letting the edges of the dough drape over the sides of the pan. Brush the bottom of the dough with the egg wash. Divide the remaining dough in half, and roll out one half into a 9½-inch round (see Note).

6. Coarsely chop the parsley.

7. Spread one-third of the onion mixture over the bottom of the dough and season lightly with salt. Top with half the tuna

and one-third of the parsley and season lightly with salt. Strew half the capers and half the olives over the tuna and layer half the tomatoes on top. Repeat, ending with the final third of the onions and parsley. Drizzle with the remaining 1 tablespoon olive oil.

8. Fit the smaller dough round on top of the filling and brush it with egg wash. Trim the overhanging dough to ½ inch and bring the edge over the top round of dough, gently pressing it onto the top. Brush the top and edges of the dough with egg wash. Make 8 evenly spaced slits in the dough to allow steam to escape.

9. Place the pan on a baking sheet and bake in the center of the oven until the dough is golden and slightly puffed, about 35 minutes. Remove the pan from the oven, then remove the sides of the pan, leaving the torte on the bottom. Transfer the torte to a serving platter with a rim to catch any juices that will spill when you cut it. Serve immediately or at room temperature.

NOTE: The recipe for dough makes a bit extra. I simply roll the extra dough into a ball, let it rise for 20 minutes, brush it with egg wash, and bake it. It makes a small loaf that can either be served warm along with the tuna torte or be kept for another meal.

Herbed Lamb Torte

EMPANATA D'AGNELLO

6 SERVINGS

This lamb and herb-rich *empanata* is a specialty of Modica and its environs in southeastern Sicily, not too far from Nuoto. There sheep graze in fields and pastures that are divided by lovely hand-built low stone walls, a hallmark of the area. Built by the farmers with rocks removed from their soil, they are feats of balance and gravity—simple works of art.

This dish is its own work of art, and it comes to the table golden and tantalizing. Be sure to cut it at the table so guests can enjoy the curls of herb-redolent steam that issue forth. Moist and hearty yet elegant, this is a typical farm dish that can be served hot, then eaten room temperature as an afternoon *merenda,* or snack, the next day.

I like to serve Antonella Dirosolini's Lush Tomato Salad (page 51) as an antipasto, then present this as the main course. It is a lovely combination.

I would pour a smooth and hearty red, like Cerasuolo di Vittoria or Corvo, both from Sicily, with this satisfying dish.

1 large egg
2 to 3 tablespoons extra-virgin
    olive oil
1½ pounds lamb shoulder meat,
    cut across the grain into ¼-inch-
    thick slices
1 medium onion, minced
2 cloves garlic, green germ removed,
    cut into thin slices
8 ounces starchy potatoes, peeled

and cut into ½-inch cubes
⅓ cup hearty red wine
1 tablespoon all-purpose flour
1½ cups (gently packed) fresh
    flat-leaf parsley leaves
1 tablespoon fresh rosemary leaves
1 recipe Simple Dough (page 433)
Fine sea salt
1 teaspoon Hot Pepper Oil (page
    389)

1. Preheat the oven to 425°F. Whisk together the egg and 2 teaspoons water in a small bowl to make an egg wash. Set aside.

2. Place 2 tablespoons of the olive oil in a large heavy skillet over medium-high heat and quickly brown the lamb on both sides. You may need to do this in batches to avoid crowding the pan. Remove the meat from the

pan. Add the onion and garlic to the pan and cook, stirring frequently, until the onion is softened, about 4 minutes. Add the potatoes, stir, and pour the wine over all. Cook, covered, until the potatoes are beginning to turn tender, about 4 minutes. Sprinkle with the flour, stir, cover, and cook until the potatoes are nearly tender and the cooking liquid has thickened, about 3 minutes. Remove from the heat. Set aside.

3. Coarsely chop the parsley, mince the rosemary, and combine.

4. Divide the dough in half. Roll half of the dough into a 15-inch round and fit it into a 9½-inch springform pan, letting the edges of the dough drape over the sides of the pan. Brush the bottom of the dough with the egg wash. Divide the remaining dough in half and roll out one half into a 9½-inch round (see Note).

5. Spread one-third of the onion mixture over the bottom of the dough and season lightly with salt. Top with one-third of the lamb and one-third of the herb mixture. Repeat twice more, ending with the final third of the herb mixture. Pour any juices from the lamb over the final layer of lamb and drizzle with the pepper oil.

6. Fit the smaller dough round on top of the filling and brush it with egg wash. Trim the overhanging dough to ½ inch and bring the edge over the top round of dough, gently pressing it onto the top. Brush the top and edges of the dough with egg wash. Make 8 evenly spaced slits in the dough to allow steam to escape.

7. Place the pan on a baking sheet and bake in the center of the oven until the dough is golden and slightly puffed, about 35 minutes. Remove the pan from the oven, then remove the sides of the pan, leaving the torte on the bottom. Let it cool for about 15 minutes. Transfer the torte to a serving platter with a rim to catch any juices that will spill when you cut it. Serve immediately or at room temperature.

NOTE: The recipe for dough makes a bit extra. I simply roll the extra dough into a ball, let it rise for 20 minutes, brush it with egg wash, and bake it. It makes a small loaf that can either be served warm along with the lamb torte or be kept for another meal.

DOLCE, DOLCE

SWEET, SWEET

The Italian farm table without its desserts would be a sad place indeed, for they are one of its most distinct and lively pleasures. Fortunes on the Italian farm haven't allowed for expensive, elaborate confections, and the result has been to the advantage of Italian farm desserts, for everything, from cakes to tarts, is simple, rustic, and intensely flavored.

Although times are better now than they once were, when a piece of fruit was the height of dessert, tradition holds, and a bowl of luscious seasonal fruits, like juicy figs just picked from the tree, cherries in their prime, oranges, and mandarins, often accented with dried fruits and fresh nuts, is always beautifully, baroquely presented. Now, however, they might be accompanied by a crumbly *pan di Spagna* (literally, "bread of Spain"), a richly flavored *torta di nocciole,* or hazelnut cake, any one of a number of *torte di mandorle,* or almond cakes, or *torte di mele,* apple cakes. *Crostate,* or tarts, are ubiquitous, filled with everything from lemon marmalade to fresh apricots, and always crisp crusted and bursting with flavor. And fruit and nut ices are common in summer, when the heat demands a cool finish to a meal. They are often accompanied by crisp, flavorful biscotti, or cookies.

What I love best about Italian farmhouse desserts, and what you will discover as you make your way through this chapter, is their unexpectedness, for they almost always offer more than meets the eye. There may be a sprinkling of cinnamon hiding in the *pastafrolla,* or sweet pastry, tiny bits of lemon zest folded into ricotta, a layer of sugar and almonds where least expected, a sudden burst of anise flavor. It makes for lively, spontaneous finishes to a meal.

Enjoy the recipes in this chapter—make them often and with abandon. You'll find them simple to prepare and lovely to present, real gifts from the Italian farm. Serve a lightly chilled Moscato d'Asti or Brachetto d'Acqui with them, both ideal dessert wines and those most commonly served on the farm.

Luna's Sponge Cake

**PAN DI SPAGNA
DI LUNA**

8 SERVINGS

Pan di Spagna is the universal cake of Italy. Like *biscuit de Savoie* or *genoise* in France, *pan di Spagna* (which means bread of Spain), is a basic cake that can be served as is, or cut and layered, soaked with syrup or alcohol and used to line a mold for *zuccotto* (page 354), or spread with jam for a snack. There are as many *pan di Spagna* recipes in Italy as there are cooks who make it, and of all those I tasted, this was my favorite. Slightly coarse and-grained and rustic, it is redolent of citrus and not too sweet, and I thank Luna Lattarulo, wife of agronomist and organic farming consultant Giovanni Ceretelli, for the recipe (and for the lovely afternoon when we ate it with a cup of espresso in her kitchen). At our house the preferred way to eat *pan di Spagna* is slathered with *marmellata di fragole* (page 411).

1¼ cups unbleached all-purpose
  flour
Pinch of fine sea salt

6 large eggs, at room temperature
¾ cup sugar
Zest of 1 lemon, minced

1. Preheat the oven to 350°F. Butter and lightly flour a 9½-inch springform pan and set it on a baking sheet.

2. Sift together the flour and salt onto a piece of waxed paper.

3. In the work bowl of an electric mixer fitted with a whisk, whisk the eggs and sugar, beginning at medium speed, until they are combined. Then raise the speed to high and continue whisking until they are pale yellow, fluffy, and thick-looking but not so thick that a ribbon forms when you lift the whisk from the bowl, about 4 minutes total.

4. Whisk in the lemon zest. Sprinkle one-third of the flour mixture over the egg mixture and gently fold it in; repeat with the remaining flour mixture in

Segreti

The trick here is folding the flour mixture into the lightened eggs and sugar. It's a little like mixing oil and water. I fold gently but thoroughly, then very gently whisk the batter once or twice for further insurance that all is well incorporated. When whisking the eggs and sugar, take them to the point where they are pale yellow and puffed, but not so far that the batter falls in a thick ribbon when you remove the whisk from the batter, or the cake will be too light and insubstantial.

two additions. Using a large whisk, gently whisk the batter once or twice just to be sure that the flour is fully incorporated. Turn the batter gently into the prepared pan.

5. Bake the cake in the center of the oven until it is puffed and golden and a finger gently pressed on the top leaves the slightest depression, 35 to 40 minutes.

6. Remove the cake from the oven and let cool on a wire rack for 15 minutes. Loosen and remove the sides of the spring-form pan and let the cake cool to room temperature. Remove the bottom of the pan from the cake and serve as you like.

NOTE: Because it has no baking powder in it, this cake can be mercurial. I have made it dozens of times, and I can honestly say it never quite looks the same way twice when it emerges from the oven. It is always golden and puffed, and it always fills the house with a wonderful citrus aroma. But if the weather is humid or damp, it rises less; if it is dry, the cake rises well but can have a slightly dry crumb. Sometimes it wrinkles a little more on top; sometimes it pulls in slightly more at the sides. Fortunately, it is always delicious and far superior to versions that contain baking powder, so I'm willing to accept the inconsistencies.

Sicilian Farmhouse Cake

**CIAMBELLA
SICILIANA**

**8 TO 10
SERVINGS**

The cuisine of Sicily is like the whole island, the result of *numerevoli contrasti,* or innumerable contrasts, as the Nobel Prize–winning poet Salvatore Quasimodo wrote. It is simple yet complex, earthy yet elegant, rustic yet sophisticated.

I enjoyed a simple country meal prepared by Giuseppina Morello, the mother of two olive growers, Gaetano and Giuseppe Morello (see essay, page 363), and it seemed to me to be all the tastes of Sicily on one table. There was a wonderfully uncomplicated, yet intriguingly flavored orange and onion salad; *sarde beca fico,* perhaps the island's signature dish of stuffed, folded, and fried fresh sardines; *pasta a' carrettiera,* a rich dish of pasta and sardines; and *giri,* or wild chard, pungent with garlic and *mollica,* dried bread crumbs.

This cake made with olive oil, which gives it a rich texture, was the finish, and it was perfect. Light and lovely, it was subtly veined with rich chocolate. Signora Morello gave me the recipe, and I've made it dozens of times, adapting and changing it as I go. This is an adaptation—the spices are my addition—and it is the best of all the versions I've tried. Giuseppe Morello, who lives near me in France, gave it his seal of approval, so I have no qualms about offering it here! It is a satisfying cake to end a simple meal, to serve at a birthday party, or to sample as an afternoon snack.

You may serve this plain or dusted lightly with homemade Confectioners' Vanilla Sugar (page 411). A fresh fruit salad alongside is a welcome addition as well.

Cinnamon was first brought from the East Indies to Sicily by the Saracens. It was the crusaders who took it to the rest of Europe.

1¾ cups cake flour
1¼ teaspoons baking powder
½ teaspoon ground cinnamon
¼ teaspoon ground cloves
Pinch of fine sea salt
4 large eggs, at room temperature

1½ cups granulated sugar
¼ cup milk
¼ cup extra-virgin olive oil
3 tablespoons unsweetened cocoa
2 tablespoons confectioners' sugar
(optional)

1. Preheat the oven to 350°F. Lightly oil and flour a 12-cup bundt pan, tapping out any excess flour.

2. Sift together the flour, baking powder, spices, and salt onto a piece of waxed paper.

3. In a large bowl or the work bowl of an electric mixer, whisk together the eggs and granulated sugar until they are light and pale yellow and have doubled in volume, about 4 minutes.

4. With the mixer running on low speed, evenly sprinkle the flour mixture over the egg mixture, alternating with the milk and olive oil and beginning and ending with the flour mixture. Mix just until blended (this step should be quick). Fold in any flour on the sides of the bowl by hand.

5. Transfer 1 cup of the batter to a medium-size bowl, sift the cocoa over it, and gently fold it into the batter.

6. Pour a thin layer of the white batter into the bottom of the prepared pan. Add all the chocolate batter as evenly as possible, then pour in the remaining white batter.

7. Bake the cake in the center of the oven until it has risen, is golden, and a finger gently pressed on the top leaves just the slightest depression, about 40 minutes.

8. Remove the cake from the oven and let cool on a wire rack until it pulls slightly away from the sides of the pan, about 15 minutes. Turn the cake out onto the rack and let cool to room temperature. Before serving, dust it with confectioners' sugar if desired.

THE TRAIN GOING 'ROUND THE MOUNTAIN
Circumetnea

Anna Sapuppo, proprietor of Alcala farm, outside Catania in Sicily, where a friend and I were staying, suggested we take the Circumetnea train up the slope of Mount Etna to Randazzo, a medieval town that bursts with activity each Sunday morning for its weekly market. We needed no urging and were waiting at the station in the nearby town of Misterbianco when the tiny, old-fashioned train puffed in.

We climbed on and settled into hard seats as the train lurched to a start. The train slowly, slowly made its way up the flank of Etna through many villages, including Paterno, Santa Maria di Licodia, Biancavilla, and Bronte. I was riveted to the window the entire trip, fascinated by the groves of strange, twisted, silvery gray trees that grew almost parallel to the ground, their roots disappearing into the lava that had swept down the mountainside hundreds of years ago. There wasn't a leaf on any of them, so it was impossible to discern what they were, but we decided they had to be fig trees.

We debarked at Randazzo, the end of the line, and searched out the market, a lively, rough-and-tumble affair. Stopping at a large truck whose side folded down to become a table, I found more varieties and preparations of olives than I had ever seen before. There were fleshy black ones that tasted richly and simply of olives, smaller ones marinated in lemon, and smooth-skinned brown to black ones dusted with dried hot peppers. Other trucks and stands sold mounds of oxblood red tomato paste and leathery sun-dried tomatoes that were puckery tart. Sacks of pistachios were stacked everywhere, picked, as it turned out, from all those twisted trees we'd seen on the way. Everything at this market was grown in Sicily.

The crowds were thick, there to haggle over vegetables and fruit, kitchen linens and toys, clothing and shoes. Though high on Mount Etna, the merchants were surprisingly diverse, ranging from a South American couple selling clothing from the Andes, to eastern Europeans with a wide array of pirated cassette tapes.

Suddenly *carabinieri* emerged from nowhere to clear the streets of cars and people. A silence fell, then from around a bend suddenly swooshed more than a hundred bicyclists, moving like a soundless horde of bees. The crowd standing on the sidewalk clapped and cheered, and in a moment they were gone.

Traffic resumed, vendors spread out their wares, the crowd melted back into the market. It was just another Sunday market day in Randazzo.

Farmhouse Orange Cake

CIAMBELLA
ALL' ARANCIA

8 TO 10
SERVINGS

Ciambella is found in most farm homes and rural bakeries throughout Italy. It is a lovely cake that suits just about any time of day, from breakfast on.

I sampled my first *ciambella* at a delicious impromptu lunch in Basilicata, on the Lufrano farm high in the Pollino mountains (see essay, page 40). I'd spent the afternoon with the Lufranos, and just as dusk was falling, Filomena, the daughter of the household, pulled out a *ciambella* with one piece missing and brought it to the table. "I made this yesterday," she said with shy pride. "I promise it's better today!"

After my visit with the Lufranos, I had many more occasions to taste *ciambella,* usually from rural bakeries where it was offered by the slice. Countless times as I waited in line, I saw farmers, truck drivers, mothers with small children buying a slice or two to eat on the spot or take to the nearest bar to enjoy with coffee.

There are many recipes for *ciambella,* all similar in that they produce a flavorful cake with a texture that is perfect for dunking in coffee or welcoming a mixture of cut-up fresh fruit. I believe the olive oil in the batter is responsible, for it helps create the dense, moist, dunkable texture of this cake. I prefer this recipe for its delicate flavor. Don't be alarmed at the batter's distinctive olive oil aroma; it will mellow in baking. And heed Filomena—this cake improves the day after it is baked.

2¼ cups cake flour
1¼ teaspoons baking powder
Pinch of fine sea salt
3 large eggs, at room temperature
1½ cups granulated sugar

¼ cup fresh orange juice
¼ cup extra-virgin olive oil
Zest of 2 oranges, minced
2 tablespoons confectioners' sugar
    (optional)

1. Preheat the oven to 350°F. Lightly oil and flour a 12-cup bundt pan, tapping out any excess flour.

2. Sift together the flour, baking powder, and salt onto a piece of waxed paper.

3. In the work bowl of an electric mixer, whisk together the eggs and granulated sugar until they are light and pale yellow and have doubled in volume, about 5 minutes.

4. With the mixer running on low speed, evenly sprinkle the flour mixture over the egg mixture alternately with the orange juice and olive oil, beginning and ending with the flour mixture. Mix just until blended (this step should be quick). Fold in the orange zest and any flour on the sides of the bowl. Turn the batter into the prepared pan.

Ciambella indicates a sweet cake with a hole in the middle of it. An old Italian saying holds that "not all the holes in *ciambella* will be round," a gentle warning that life does not always proceed as expected.

5. Bake the cake in the center of the oven until it has risen, is golden, and a finger gently pressed on the top leaves just the slightest depression, about 40 minutes.

6. Remove the cake from the oven and let cool on a wire rack until it pulls slightly away from the sides of the pan, about 15 minutes. Turn the cake out onto the rack and let cool to room temperature. Before serving, dust with confectioners' sugar if desired.

Trentino Christmas Cake

**ZELTEN
TRENTINO**

**15 TO 20
SERVINGS**

This is a traditional version of *zelten,* the Christmas cake from the Trentino region of northern Italy. The region was once part of Austria, which is evident in everything from the lacy mountain architecture to this buttery fruit- and nut-rich Christmas bread.

Zelten is made at home only around Christmastime, but commercial versions can be found year-round. Every home cook makes it a little differently. Some use more fruit; some use less. The blend of spices and aromatics varies, and so does the shape.

I collected several recipes for *zelten* from farm cooks, and this is my favorite. It is best made two to three days before slicing so the flavors have a chance to mellow. I make it for Christmas morning to dip in steaming coffee.

1 cup raisins
8 ounces dried figs, coarsely chopped
3 tablespoons grappa
¾ cup lukewarm milk
1½ teaspoons active dry yeast
¾ cup Vanilla Sugar (page 441)
4 large eggs, at room temperature
1 teaspoon vanilla extract

¾ teaspoon fine sea salt
Zest of 1 orange, minced
4¾ cups all-purpose flour
*7 tablespoons unsalted butter, at
    room temperature*
1 cup walnuts, coarsely chopped
⅔ cup pine nuts

1. Cover the raisins with boiling water in a small bowl and let soak for 15 to 20 minutes. Drain and pat dry.

2. Place the raisins, dried figs, and grappa in a large bowl, mix, and macerate, covered,

for at least 1 hour.

3. Blend the milk and yeast in a large bowl and let sit for about 5 minutes so the yeast can dissolve.

4. Add the vanilla sugar to the yeast and mix with an electric mixer. Add 3 of the eggs, one at a

Fertile Oranges

At first glance Sicily seems covered with orange groves, and in reality, a huge portion of its arable land is planted in oranges; even the ornamental trees planted along city sidewalks and boulevards produce fat oranges. The climate is propitious, and so is the superstition, for in Sicily oranges symbolize abundance and fertility.

time, mixing until they are thoroughly incorporated. Add the vanilla extract, salt, and orange zest and mix well. Add 4½ cups of the flour, 1 cup at a time, to form a soft dough, mixing well after each addition for a total of 5 minutes. The dough should be quite soft and somewhat sticky but not unmanageable.

5. Divide the butter into quarters and add it to the dough, a quarter at a time, incorporating it thoroughly into the dough either by kneading it or mixing it in with the electric mixer. The dough will be quite sticky, but don't add flour.

6. Cover the dough and let it rise at room temperature (68° to 70°F) until it has increased in bulk by about one-third, about 1½ hours. Punch the dough down and knead in the fruit and grappa until they are evenly distributed through the dough. Place the dough in a clean bowl, cover, and let rise until it has increased in bulk by a bit less than one-third, about 1 hour. Punch down the dough and knead in the nuts until they are evenly distributed.

7. Lightly oil a baking sheet. Turn out the dough onto a work surface covered with the remaining ¼ cup flour. Knead it a couple of times, working in the flour so that you can easily handle the dough. Shape the dough into a lozenge shape (a blunted diamond) that is about 2 inches thick and transfer it to the prepared baking sheet. Let rise, uncovered, at room temperature just until the dough has risen slightly, about 30 minutes.

8. Preheat the oven to 350°F.

9. Whisk together the remaining egg and 2 tablespoons water to make an egg wash and brush it all over the dough.

10. Bake the cake in the center of the oven until it is golden and puffed, about 1 hour.

Remove the cake from the oven and transfer to a wire rack to cool completely. When the cake is completely cool, serve it immediately or wrap it in parchment paper and aluminum foil (or place it in an airtight metal box). The cake will keep very well for 2 to 3 days.

Trentino Christmas Cake II

ZELTEN TRENTINO II

8 TO 10 SERVINGS

This quick version of *zelten*, leavened by baking powder instead of yeast, is available all year long. The recipe comes from Rosalba Montibeller, who runs a farm and restaurant with her husband, Valter, in Roncegno Terme, just outside Trento in the Alto-Adige. Rosalba, a wonderful cook and champion of local recipes, counts *zelten* and strudel as her favorite desserts. While she prefers to make *zelten* only around the holidays, if a guest specifically requests it, she will break with tradition.

This cake is very satisfying, and it will keep for several days in an airtight container, so you can make and have it ready for the holidays.

1½ cups raisins
8 ounces dried figs, coarsely chopped
¼ cup grappa
3⅔ cups all-purpose flour
2 teaspoons baking powder
¼ teaspoon fine sea salt
7 tablespoons unsalted butter, at room temperature

¾ cup Vanilla Sugar (page 441)
3 large eggs, at room temperature
¼ cup milk
1 cup walnuts, coarsely chopped
⅔ cup pine nuts
Zest of 1 orange, minced

1. Cover the raisins with boiling water in a small bowl and let soak for 15 to 20 minutes. Drain and pat dry.

2. Place the raisins, dried figs, and grappa in a large bowl, mix, and macerate, covered, for at least 1 hour.

3. Preheat the oven to 375°F. Lightly butter a 9-inch round cake pan.

4. Stir together the flour, baking powder, and salt onto a piece of waxed paper.

5. In a large bowl or the work bowl of an electric mixer, mix the butter and sugar until light and pale yellow. Whisk in the eggs, one at a time. Stir in the flour mixture alternately with the milk, beginning and ending with the flour mixture. Mix until the batter is very smooth, being careful not to overmix.

6. Fold in the dried fruit with the grappa, the nuts, and orange zest, working carefully until all of the ingredients are thoroughly combined. Turn the batter into the prepared pan.

7. Bake the cake in the center of the oven until it is puffed and golden and baked through, about 50 minutes. Remove the cake from the oven, then remove it immediately from the pan. Let cool on a wire rack.

Hazelnut Cake

TORTA DI NOCCIOLE

8 TO 10 SERVINGS

This is a signature cake of Piedmont, home of the *tonda gentile della Langa,* the incomparably tender and sweetly flavored hazelnut that grows there in profusion, or used to. Today the farmers in Langhe, a lush area of Piedmont known for its fine wine grapes, responding to a boom in the Barolo, Moscato, and Dolcetto wine markets, are gradually denuding the land of hazelnuts in favor of vineyards. With low-priced hazelnuts pouring into western Europe from Turkey, it's tough for Italian candy and cake makers to pay the high prices for Piedmont hazelnuts.

There are still enough hazelnut orchards left to supply homes and at least one chocolate maker in Torino, the venerable Peyrano, who insists on using only local nuts. I tasted the local hazelnuts at the Peyrano factory and found them crisp and light, not at all woody, like most hazelnuts. I tasted them again at the Manera home (see essay, page 27), where Barbara Manera, Luciano and Maria Manera's daughter, sat studiously cracking the nuts from a bowlful she'd picked from their trees. Barbara is the keeper of the Manera family recipe for hazelnut cake, and her afternoon plans included making one for me to try.

I also tried a hazelnut cake at a tiny trattoria down the road from the Maneras' farm, where Maria sometimes helps in the kitchen. Both were delicious, and this recipe combines the best of each of them. It is rich with the essence of hazelnuts, has just the right amount of sweetness, and is perfect with a cup of espresso for an afternoon *merenda,* or snack.

Toasting Nuts

For almonds or hazelnuts, preheat the oven to 350°F. Place the nuts on a baking sheet in a single layer and bake until they smell nice and toasty, usually about 10 minutes. Remove from the oven. For hazelnuts, immediately wrap them in a cotton tea towel, let them cool to room temperature, then rub them to remove their skins. For almonds, nothing more than letting them cool to room temperature is necessary.

For pine nuts, preheat the oven to 300°F and bake for 3 to 5 minutes, checking them often, as they can burn in an instant.

6 large eggs, separated, at room temperature
6 tablespoons Vanilla Sugar (page 441)
1⅔ cups whole hazelnuts, toasted and skins removed (see box, this page)
Pinch of fine sea salt
1 tablespoon confectioners' sugar (optional)

1. Preheat the oven to 350°F. Butter and lightly flour a 9-inch springform pan.

Segreti

• **Egg yolks at room temperature are much easier to incorporate into batters; and egg whites at room temperature are much easier to whisk to soft or stiff peaks.**

• **Always add a pinch of salt to egg whites before whisking to loosen them up.**

2. In a large bowl or the work bowl of an electric mixer, whisk the egg yolks and 4 tablespoons of the vanilla sugar until thick and pale yellow.

3. Process the hazelnuts in a food processor with 1 tablespoon of the vanilla sugar until they are finely ground.

4. Whisk the egg whites and salt in a large bowl or the work bowl of an electric mixer until foamy. Add the remaining 1 tablespoon vanilla sugar and whisk until they form soft peaks.

5. Mix the ground nuts into the egg yolk mixture, then fold in one-quarter of the egg whites. Carefully fold in the remaining egg whites and turn the batter into the prepared pan.

6. Bake the cake in the cen-

ter of the oven until it is puffed and golden, about 30 minutes. Let the cake cool for 10 minutes on a wire rack. Remove the side of the pan and let the cake cool completely before removing it from the bottom of the pan.

6. Just before serving, sift the confectioners' sugar over the cake if desired.

NOTES: If you are lucky enough to live in a region where wild hazelnuts grow, harvest them and use them in this cake, for they have an uncanny resemblance to the *tonda gentile* of the Langhe.

Believe what you read in this recipe! There is no flour, and none is needed, resulting in a very light cake. It will keep for several days in an airtight container.

Fabulous Almond Tart

TORTA DI MANDORLE

8 TO 10 SERVINGS

When you taste this delicate, crisp, almond-rich tart, you will swoon. It is a typical Sicilian country dessert made with richly flavored almonds and intensely scented lemons. There is a touch of cinnamon too, which reflects the years of Arab domination in Sicily.

Gabriella Monteleone, a friend who lives in Palermo, has family sprinkled throughout the rural Madonie mountains, and her grandmother is a renowned cook there. When Gabriella told her about the work I was doing, she said I must have this recipe. Nothing is more representative of the area, according to her, than this satisfying *torta*. Served with a cup of espresso, it is as good for breakfast as it is for a 10 A.M. or snack, or a 4 P.M. *merenda*. It makes a fine dessert, of course, particularly with fresh fruit alongside. However you decide to serve this, you will find it creates a very special occasion!

FOR THE PASTRY
3½ cups all-purpose flour
*4 large egg yolks, at room
    temperature*
1 cup sugar
*3 tablespoons unsalted butter, at
    room temperature*
*10 tablespoons lard, at room
    temperature*
Zest of 1 lemon, grated
Generous pinch of fine sea salt

*1 to 2 tablespoons white wine,
    such as Frascati, if needed*
1 large egg

FOR THE FILLING
1½ cups sugar
¼ teaspoon ground cinnamon
*1 pound almonds, skins removed
    (see box, page 351) and finely
    chopped*

1. For the pastry, place the flour in a mound in a wide, shallow bowl and make a well in the center. Place the egg yolks, sugar, butter, lard, lemon zest, and salt in the well and mix the ingredients in the well with your fingers. Gradually work in the flour from the sides of the well, bringing it in with your fingers. If the mixture feels very dry and you can see it is not going to come together easily, sprinkle as much white wine as needed over it. When the mixture is crumbly and begins to feel like it will come together, use the heel of your hand to push it gently down and away from you, as though you were smearing it across the bowl's surface, just until it is homogeneous. Do not work it too hard; you don't want to develop too

much gluten in the flour. This effectively blends all the ingredients together. When the dough holds together, divide it in half and pat each half into a flat disk. Cover with a bowl and let sit at room temperature for 30 minutes.

2. Whisk together the egg and 2 teaspoons water in a small bowl to make an egg wash.

3. Roll out half the pastry to a 12-inch round and fit it into a 10-inch tart pan with a removable bottom, letting the pastry hang over the edge of the pan. Brush the pastry all over with the egg wash. Roll out the other half of the pastry to an 11-inch round.

4. Preheat the oven to 350°F.

5. For the filling, place the sugar and 6 tablespoons water in a medium-size saucepan over low heat and cover. Do not stir it; if you want to blend the sugar and water together, shake the pan gently to do so. Heat until the sugar is completely dissolved. Add the cinnamon, swirl it around in the syrup, then add the almonds. Let the almonds cook just until you smell a toasty aroma, about 4 minutes. Immediately turn the almond mixture into the pastry-lined tart pan and smooth it out. Cover with the pastry round, pressing it onto the edge of the bottom pastry. Trim away any excess pastry, brush with the egg wash, and slip the pan onto a baking sheet.

6. Bake in the center of the oven until the pastry is golden, about 40 minutes. Remove the tart from the oven and immediately remove the ring from the tart pan (see box, page 352). Let cool to room temperature on a wire rack before serving. This tart is even better the day after it is made.

Skinning Almonds

Bring a medium-size pot of water to a boil over medium-high heat. Add the almonds and let the water return to a boil. Boil the almonds for about 30 seconds, then remove them from the water with a slotted spoon or ladle. Cover the water and set it aside. To remove the skins from the almonds, simply squeeze them at one end and they will slip out. (They come out so easily and fast that you need to aim them at a bowl or work surface, or you'll find yourself involved in an almond search.)

For stubborn skins, simply return the water to a boil, add the reluctant almonds, and boil them for an additional 30 to 60 seconds before draining and squeezing them.

How to Remove the Removable Tart Ring

Tart pans with removable bottoms and rings are an almost foolproof guarantee of a perfect tart, or *torta*. Occasionally, however, removing the ring may pose a problem, particularly when a filling is sugary and the sugar runs out of the pastry to glue the ring to the bottom of the pan. The solution is simple in most cases—before removing the tart from the oven, invert a bowl whose bottom is smaller than the tart pan, on a countertop. Immediately upon removing the tart from the oven, place it atop the inverted bowl. Gravity will usually cause the ring to drop from the bottom of the tart pan, then you can transfer the tart to a wire rack to cool. If caramelized sugar holds the ring to the bottom, use a small-bladed knife to gently and quickly work the ring away from the edges of the tart while the sugar is still hot and soft so you won't break the edges of the crust. Finally, run the knife blade between the ring and the bottom of the tart pan to further loosen it and let gravity do the rest.

Occasionally pastry is too fragile and insists on crumbling and breaking. In that case, place the tart on a wire cooling rack and run the knife blade between the pastry and the tart pan and on the outside seam between the tart ring and the bottom of the pan, once right after you've removed the tart from the oven and again five minutes later.

Corrado's Almond Cake

TORTA DI MANDORLE ALLA CORRADO

10 SERVINGS

This richly flavored and buttery cake comes from Corrado Assenza, one of the finest pastry chefs in Italy, certainly the best in Sicily. His Caffè Sicilia, in the small town of Noto, is known throughout Sicily and beyond, for he has fans as far away as Japan. Young people from all over the world beg to study with him, and he accommodates as many as he can.

A complex man strictly rooted to his land, he is a scientist by training, a pastry chef by passion. His father owned the bakery, and after his studies Corrado returned to the pastry shop, though his father urged him to make another life for himself. But Corrado's sentiments for his family and the pastry tradition were too strong.

Because he applies both the skills and flavors he learned from his father and his education as a scientist to what he does, his pastries have multiple layers of flavor and an incredible lightness. His approach is philosophical, intellectual. His results are sublime.

I sampled everything Corrado had in his pastry case the day I visited him, and some things in the backroom as well. His ladyfingers were the crispest and lightest—and best flavored—I've ever had, his tiny almond and pistachio cakes and cookies richly flavored and tender. All were so dependent on local ingredients that I didn't even ask for recipes; in any case, Corrado would have discouraged it, knowing how impossible it would be to recreate them elsewhere. He is adamant about using local ingredients and is, in fact, so insistent on top-quality that he grows many of the fruits and herbs that make their way into his pastries.

When I bit into this almond cake, however, I knew I'd found a recipe to honor him and his work, one that could be replicated. He agreed and willingly gave it to me. The cake is easy to make, but you must grind the almonds almost as fine as flour, for they replace flour here and provide the cake's substance and texture.

Follow Corrado's lead and offer this cake in the morning with coffee, in the afternoon with a glass of light white wine, or for dessert with fresh fruit. This cake keeps very well up to a week if stored in an airtight container in a cool spot.

4 heaping cups almonds,
    skins removed (see box,
    page 351)
1¼ cups sugar

8 tablespoons (1 stick) unsalted
    butter, at room temperature
Large pinch of fine sea salt
3 large eggs, at room temperature

1. Preheat the oven to 350°F. Butter and flour a 9-inch springform pan.

2. Grind the almonds with ½ cup of the sugar in a food processor until they are very, very finely ground, almost like flour.

3. In the work bowl of an electric mixer, whisk the butter and remaining ¾ cup sugar until pale yellow but not to the point that it becomes light like mousse. Add the salt and whisk, then add the eggs, one at a time, whisking briefly after you add each one. Once all the eggs are added, whisk quickly just until they are completely incorporated and the mixture is light, but not so long that the mixture separates.

4. Fold in the ground almond mixture with a rubber spatula to make a stiff batter. Turn it into the prepared pan and smooth the top.

5. Bake the cake in the center of the oven until it is puffed and golden on top and springs back when you touch it lightly, 30 to 40 minutes.

6. Remove the cake from the oven and let cool on a wire rack for 15 minutes. Remove the sides of the pan and let cool to room temperature. Remove the bottom of the pan and transfer the cake to a serving platter.

NOTE: Please don't be tempted to add almond extract to this cake. Its flavor is too harsh, too artificial, and will mask the gentle, sweet, and true flavor of the ground almonds.

Fruit- and Chocolate-Studded Pudding Cake

LO ZUCCOTTO

8 TO 10 SERVINGS

This dessert is typically Florentine, its shape thought to resemble Florence's Duomo. There are dozens of versions of *zuccotto,* the differences being mostly in the composition of the filling, and I got this one from Lisa Bonacossi, proprietor with her husband, Ugo, of the Capezzana winery near Pistoia.

Though Lisa has always had a chef in the house to make meals for her family of nine, she does a great deal of cooking herself, preferably typical Tuscan country dishes. This dessert is slightly more urban than the typical country dessert, but since Lisa included it in her repertoire as a favorite, I include it here. I happen to love everything about it, from assembly to presentation to savoring its multitude of flavors and textures.

You must plan ahead for the *zuccotto;* the sponge cake is best if it sits for twenty-four hours before being sliced and soaked, and once assembled, the *zuccotto* needs to ripen in the refrigerator overnight.

¼ cup granulated sugar

2 tablespoons maraschino liqueur, brandy, or grappa

1 recipe Luna's Sponge Cake (page 337)

4 cups ricotta

⅔ cup Confectioners' Vanilla Sugar (see box, page 356)

¾ teaspoon vanilla extract

4 ounces bittersweet chocolate, finely chopped

⅔ cup dried fruit (see Note), chopped

1. Place the granulated sugar and ¼ cup water in a small heavy saucepan and bring to a boil over medium heat, stirring constantly, until the sugar dissolves. Remove from the heat and let cool slightly. (If you have time, let it cool to room temperature.)

2. Whisk together the sugar syrup and liqueur. Cut the cake into ½-inch-thick slices, then line an 8-cup mold with a rounded bottom (a mixing bowl is the perfect choice) with the cake, cutting the cake to fit over the bottom and sides. Reserve enough of the remaining cake to cover the filling. Remove the cake slices from the bowl and place them on a platter. Brush the slices with the sugar syrup, then turn and brush the other side. Line the mold with the soaked cake slices. (You will need about two-thirds of the cake to line the mold and cover the filling.)

3. In the work bowl of an electric mixer, whisk the ricotta until it is light and smooth, almost like thick cream, 4 minutes with an electric mixer, 8 to 10 minutes by

Confectioners' Vanilla Sugar

Make your own confectioners' vanilla sugar by grinding vanilla sugar (page 441) in a clean coffee or spice grinder. It has excellent flavor and none of the stabilizers or starches found in commercial confectioners' sugar. (If your grinder is small, do the sugar in batches so you don't overtax the motor.)

hand. Whisk in the confectioners' sugar and vanilla extract. Fold in the chocolate and the dried fruit with a rubber spatula until thoroughly combined.

4. Fill the prepared mold with the ricotta mixture. Arrange the slices of cake intended to cover the filling in a layer on top.

Cover with parchment paper and aluminum foil, then place a plate that fits inside the bowl on top and weight it with three 1-pound weights. Refrigerate for at least 12 hours or up to 24.

5. To serve, remove the weights, plate, and paper from the mold. Place an inverted serving plate over the top and flip it; the *zucotto* will slide right out of the mold onto the plate. If necessary, shake the mold slightly to loosen it. Present the *zuccotto* whole. To serve, cut it in wedges.

NOTE: I've used various combinations of high-quality dried fruits, including citrus peel, cherries, citron, figs, and dates, and I've used simply raisins. The cake is wonderful no matter what fruit you use!

Lemon Marmalade Tart

CROSTATA DI MARMELLATA DI LIMONE

ABOUT 8 SERVINGS

Ghiselda Bini, from Chianti in Tuscany, is responsible for this tart recipe, which has become a favorite in our household. I sampled her bittersweet marmalade while sitting with her in the spacious kitchen of the home she and her husband, Bruno, recently built. When she mentioned that she uses her marmalade in *crostate,* well, I had to try it. The results are a wonderful, complex blend of flavors—tart and sweet, bitter and gentle, as good as its golden caramel looks promise.

1 recipe Franca's Sweet-Tart Pastry
   (page 439)
1½ cups Ghiselda's Lemon

Marmalade (page 414)
1 egg

1. Divide the pastry into 2 pieces, one twice as large as the other. Pat the smaller piece into a flat disk, wrap in plastic wrap, and let sit at room temperature for at least 30 minutes. Roll out or press the larger piece of pastry to a round 11½ inches in diameter. Fit it into a 9½-inch tart pan with a removable bottom, leaving the pastry rising above the edge of the pan.

2. Preheat the oven to 400°F.

3. Roll out the smaller piece of pastry on a lightly floured piece of parchment paper to a very thin 8-inch round. Cut the pastry into about 10 strips, ⅜ inch thick. If the pastry is very soft, refrigerate it for about 10 minutes to firm it up.

4. Spread the lemon marmalade evenly over the pastry in the tart pan. Fold the edges of

the pastry down over the marmalade; don't worry if it crumbles and breaks a bit, as it will all bake up nicely together.

5. Whisk together the egg and 2 teaspoons water for an egg wash and brush the edges of the pastry with it. Lay half the pastry strips across the filling in one direction and brush them lightly with egg wash. Lay the remaining strips across in the other direction and brush those with egg wash.

6. Transfer the tart pan to a baking sheet. Bake the tart in the center of the oven until the pastry is golden and the marmalade is slightly golden on top, 30 to 35 minutes. Remove from the oven and let cool for at least 15 minutes on a wire rack. Remove the ring of the pan and let cool completely before serving.

Apricot Tart

CROSTATA
ALL'ALBICOCCA

ABOUT 8
SERVINGS

Il Capricorno is a little inn high in the Italian Alps that serves fresh, rustic food made with ingredients grown on a family farm in the village below. I was particularly taken with this apricot tart, which emanated rich apricot aroma as it was set down in front of me. The sweet pastry lightly balances the slightly tart, inspired combination of fresh jam and fruit.

1 recipe Franca's Sweet-Tart Pastry
   (page 439)
½ cup best-quality apricot jam

1 pound apricots, cut in half
   and pitted
1 egg

1. Divide the pastry into 2 pieces, one twice as large as the other. Pat the smaller piece into a flat disk, wrap in plastic wrap, and let sit at room temperature for at least 30 minutes. Roll out or press the larger piece of pastry to a round 11½ inches in diameter. Fit into a 9½-inch tart pan with a removable bottom, leaving the pastry rising above the edge of the pan.

2. Preheat the oven to 350°F.

3. Roll out the smaller piece of pastry on a lightly floured piece of parchment paper to a very thin 8-inch round.

Cut the pastry into about 10 strips, ⅜ inch thick. If the pastry is very soft, refrigerate it for about 10 minutes to firm it up.

4. Spread the jam evenly over the pastry in the tart pan. Top with the apricot halves, cut side down, arranging them attractively atop the jam and overlapping up to 3 halves in the center if necessary. Fold the edges of the pastry down over the fruit; don't worry if it crumbles and breaks a bit, as it will all bake up nicely together.

5. Whisk together the egg and 1 teaspoon water for an egg wash and brush the edges of the pastry with it. Lay half the pastry strips

across the filling in one direction and brush them lightly with egg wash. Lay the remaining strips across in the other direction and brush those with egg wash.

6. Transfer the tart pan to a baking sheet. Bake the tart in the center of the oven until the fruit is bubbling and the pastry is

golden, 35 to 40 minutes. Remove from the oven, let cool for 10 minutes, then loosen the ring of the pan and remove it very carefully so that any filling that has bubbled over doesn't stick. Let cool on a wire rack to at least lukewarm before serving.

Ricotta Tart

CROSTATA CON RICOTTA

6 TO 8 SERVINGS

This is one of the more rustic dessert recipes I received from Filomena Lufrano, a lovely young woman who lives in Terranova di Pollino, Basilicata. She and her mother share the family cooking, as well as the work of raising chickens and sheep, growing the vegetables, and doing the other chores that make this family very nearly self-sufficient. They make their own sheep's milk cheese, and from the whey, they make luscious, creamy ricotta, which Filomena uses in this tart.

Sprightly and light, the combination of cinnamon, chocolate, and candied fruit goes together easily and makes for a very satisfying finish to a meal. If you don't have candied fruit, you may substitute currants or minced dates.

1 recipe Franca's Sweet-Tart Pastry
 (page 439)
1¼ cups whole-milk ricotta
1 large egg
1 cup sugar
¼ teaspoon ground cinnamon

2 ounces best-quality candied fruit,
 minced
½ ounce best-quality bittersweet
 chocolate, such as Lindt
 Excellence, minced

1. Preheat the oven to 375°F.

2. Roll out or press the pastry over the bottom and up the sides of a 9½-inch tart pan with a removable bottom. Line it with parchment paper or aluminum foil, fill with pastry weights, and bake until it is just golden, 15 to 20 minutes. Let cool to lukewarm and remove the paper and pie weights. Leave the oven on.

3. Meanwhile, make the filling. Place the ricotta in a medium-size bowl. Whisk in the egg, then the sugar, until well blended.

Whisk in the cin-namon, then stir in the candied fruit and the chocolate until all the ingredients are thoroughly combined. Turn the filling into the baked pastry shell and smooth the top.

4. Bake the tart in the center of the oven until the filling is set, about 30 minutes. Remove from the oven and let cool to room temperature on a wire rack, then remove the ring from the pan and serve.

NOTE: While this is best the day it is made, it will keep well for 24 hours.

Extraordinary Ricotta Torte

TORTA DI RICOTTA

8 TO 10 SERVINGS

The play of the flavors of this delicious torte—the creamy ricotta, tangy lemon, and hint of cinnamon—is soft yet dramatic and unlike anything I have ever tasted.

Any good-quality whole-milk ricotta makes a very rich, smooth filling and is what I recommend for luscious results.

What's in a Name?

Ricotta is made with the whey left after making cheese. It is reheated, then strained; thus its name: ricotta = re-cooked.

FOR THE PASTRY CREAM

2 cups milk

1 vanilla bean, split

6 large egg yolks, at room
    temperature

¾ cup sugar

6 tablespoons all-purpose flour

Generous pinch of fine sea salt

FOR THE PASTRY

1½ cups plus 1 tablespoon
    all-purpose flour

1 teaspoon ground cinnamon

Pinch of fine sea salt

7 tablespoons unsalted butter, at
    room temperature

2 large egg yolks, at room temperature

½ cup sugar

FOR THE FILLING

1½ cups best-quality whole-milk
    ricotta

½ cup sugar

1 large egg yolk, at room
    temperature

Zest of 2 lemons, minced

1. For the pastry, mix the flour, cinnamon, and salt in a wide, shallow bowl. Shape into a mound and make a well in the center. Place the butter, egg yolks, and sugar in the well and mix the ingredients in the well with your fingers. Gradually work in the flour from the sides of the well, bringing it in with your fingers. When the mixture is crumbly and begins to feel like it will come together, use the heel of your hand to push it gently down and away from you, as though you were smearing it across the bowl's surface, just until it is homogeneous. This effectively blends all the ingredients together. When the dough holds together, pat it into a small, flat disk, cover it, and let sit at room temperature for 30 minutes, which will allow the gluten in the pastry to relax.

2. Preheat the oven to 350°F.

3. Roll out the dough about ⅛ inch thick. Fit the dough (see Note)—in pieces if necessary— over the bottom and about 2 inches up the sides of a 9-inch springform pan. Alternatively, you

may press the dough with your fingers into the pan, making it as even as possible. Bake the dough, without lining it or filling it with pastry weights, until it is pale golden but not cooked through, about 15 minutes. Let cool to lukewarm. Leave the oven on.

4. For the pastry cream, reserve ¼ cup of the milk. Scald the remaining 1¾ cups milk with the vanilla bean in a medium-size heavy saucepan over medium heat. Remove from the heat, cover, and let sit for 10 minutes.

5. In the work bowl of an electric mixer, whisk the egg yolks and sugar together until they are thick and pale yellow and a ribbon forms when you lift the whisk from the bowl, about 5 minutes. Add the flour and salt and whisk until blended, then whisk in the reserved ¼ cup milk. Remove the vanilla bean from the hot milk and whisk the milk into the egg mixture, then pour the mixture into the saucepan. Bring to a boil and boil for 2 minutes over medium-high heat, whisking constantly. Remove from the heat and immediately transfer the pastry cream to a bowl to cool slightly.

6. For the filling, in a food processor, mix the ricotta, sugar, egg yolk, and lemon zest until blended. Add the pastry cream and mix until thoroughly combined. Pour the mixture into the pre-baked crust.

7. Bake the torte in the center of the oven until the top is golden and a knife inserted into the center comes out clean, about 70 minutes. Remove from the heat and let cool on a wire rack for 10 minutes. Remove the sides of the pan and continue cooling to room temperature. You may serve this at room temperature or slightly chilled.

NOTE: To fit the pastry into the pan requires a bit of engineering, but it is very simple. Roll out the dough until it is quite thin, about ⅛ inch. Cut a round to fit the bottom of the pan, then cut the remaining pastry into generous 2-inch-wide strips. Fit the strips around the sides of the pan, pressing them gently onto the bottom and each other so that they form one pastry shell. Patch when and where you need to, trying to keep the pastry as even as possible. Any seams will disappear during baking.

AN AFTERNOON WITH MARIA MAURILLO

I'd been on my own in a small apartment in the Tuscan countryside for two weeks, going out each day to interview farmers, winemakers, cheesemakers, and chefs. I'd decided to take a break and visit an *agriturismo,* a farm that offered rooms and meals.

Stepping into the dining room at Agriturismo Malvarina I found just the change I was looking for—an immediate entry into a circle of warmth and friendliness. I received a hearty greeting and handshake from host Claudio Fabrizzi, a place at the family table, a roaring fireplace, and food so flavorful and good my fatigue simply disappeared. Typical of so many of my experiences in Italy, I had to pinch myself to believe it was real.

The following day promised to be as lively as the evening, as I was to spend the afternoon in the kitchen with Claudio's mother, Maria Maurillo, the woman responsible for all the wonderful dishes I'd already sampled. When I arrived at the kitchen door, Maria was already busy sautéing and mixing, and she called for me to enter.

She quickly gave me a tour of the kitchen, which had been carved out of Mount Subasio so that its back wall was literally rock. It contained a big professional stove, two stacked ovens, a large, cool pastry counter positioned by a high window so it got plenty of light. Things were bubbling on the stove, and Maria was about to begin mixing pastry for her dessert.

"I always make dessert first," she said as she tossed flour into the mixer, along with butter and egg yolks. "That way I'm secure. If I'm behind on everything else, I know that dessert at least is ready."

She put me to work slicing apples as she browned two good-size guinea fowl, which she would stew with a vibrant mixture of lemon zest and capers (see Braised Guinea Hens, page 222). She returned to wrap the apples in pastry and roll the whole package cleverly in parchment paper. "Take this down," she said with a sly look. "It's one of my secrets."

Dessert in the oven, Maria returned to her guinea hens, adding onions, carrots, lemon juice, and lemon zest. Covering them, she moved on to slice her way through a mound of tomatoes. She then heated some oil and proceeded to sear the tomatoes until they were nearly black.

The tomatoes finished and on a serving platter, she mixed up pizza dough, which she left to rise in a big lump on the pastry board.

After a quick check of the guinea fowl, she glanced into a pot where an odd-looking legume was simmering. *"Cicerchie,"* she said. "They grow in Umbria. They're like chickpeas." Puréed with herbs and vegetables, these would be the first course that evening.

Back she went to the oven to check dessert, pulling me with her. Squinting from the heat, she unwrapped the parchment paper from the cake with a wary eye. "If I misjudge, it will burst," she said. Forty years of cooking experience held her in good stead; it was fine, and she returned the cake to the oven to finish baking.

She disappeared into the pantry and came out with a hunk of dried meat. *"Barbozza,"* she said. Air-dried pig jowl. She put it on the electric meat slicer (standard equipment in even the barest of Italian kitchens) and sliced away.

Maria, whose roots are in Sicily, has the fiery warmth of a Sicilian, which she transmits to her food as well. It is substantial and vivid, and flavors zing and pop in every extraordinary dish she makes. I'd hoped to learn a few of her secrets by spending an afternoon with her, but she generously gave me a small lifetime's worth of tips, hints, and recipes.

Maria's helper arrived in the kitchen and immediately took care of a mound of dirty dishes before conversing with Maria about the night's plan. They spent more time gossiping and laughing than talking food, yet Maria effectively communicated

her needs, for at a certain moment they went their separate ways to their appointed tasks.

Maria fried the sliced *barbozza* with sage leaves, then stood back as she poured in vinegar, which sent up an eye-searing cloud of vapor.

I watched and wrote furiously, trying to follow everything. Each time I asked for *le dosi,* or the quantity, Maria would roll her eyes. "I don't measure, I just cook," she said, though she tried to calculate how much flour or butter or oil or wine she dusted or splashed in for me.

When all was prepared, Maria stopped, pushed a strand of hair off her forehead, and looked at me intently. An hour remained before guests would begin to trickle into the dining room for dinner. "You like biscotti, right?" she asked, then proceeded to make the dough for Anise Cookies (page 368). I watched and wrote, then together we rolled them out.

Maria was called away, leaving me with a large mound of dough, which I rolled and pinched, twisted and baked as Maria had shown me. Still no Maria but a pile of biscotti to show for my efforts, I made my exit and dressed for dinner. That evening guests and the Fabrizzi family all sat at the same table. As food was served and someone asked Maria how to make something, she smiled and pointed at me. "Ask her," she said. "I think she knows more than I do."

Maria Maurillo's Amazing Apple Cake

TORTICHILION DI MELE

6 TO 8 SERVINGS

I loved watching Maria Maurillo at Agriturismo Malvarina near Assisi (see essay, page 363), put this dessert together. A combination of apples dusted lightly with sugar and enveloped in her unbeatable biscotti dough, it is a simple country treat, yet it has so much style when presented that everyone there to sample it was awed. Though born on a farm in the heart of Umbria, it makes a fine finale to a sophisticated meal.

2 pounds tart apples, such as Braeburn, Winesap, Criterion, Rhode Island Greening, or Mutsu, peeled, cored, and sliced paper thin

Scant 2 tablespoons Vanilla Sugar (page 441)
1 recipe dough for Maria's Biscotti (page 366), prepared through step 2

1. Preheat the oven to 400°F.
2. Toss the apple slices with the sugar and set aside.
3. Cut a 16 x 15-inch piece of parchment paper. Roll out the biscotti dough to a 16 x 13-inch rectangle on the paper. Trim the edges so they are nice and even, reserving the excess pastry.
4. Mound the apple mixture down the center of the dough in a strip, leaving a 1-inch border at either end and a 1-inch border on each side. Using the paper, gently bring the pastry together, overlapping the edges if possible or simply bringing the edges together. Press the edges into each other, patching where necessary. The pastry is so easy to work with that patching is a simple affair. The pastry doesn't have to look perfect—imperfections will bake out—but it should be solidly "welded." Press the ends together. Keeping the parchment paper around the pastry, bring the edges of the paper together and skewer them tightly shut with toothpicks so they act as a sort of

girdle, keeping the apples from pushing the pastry apart (see box, this page). Transfer the wrapped pastry to a baking sheet large enough to hold it and any juices that may run from it as it bakes.

5. Bake the pastry in the center of the oven until it is golden at the ends and nearly completely golden on top, about 40 minutes. (To check, ease open the parchment to have a look.) Remove the skewers from the paper and open it slightly, then continue baking until the pastry is completely golden and baked through, about 10 minutes more. Remove the pastry from the oven and let cool on the baking sheet on a wire rack until it is lukewarm, then remove the paper and transfer the pastry to a serving platter. Cut into thick slices and serve.

NOTE: This is wonderful the day it is made and even better the following day.

Pastry Tips

To seal the pastry, hold the parchment paper edges together with one hand (keeping the pastry together), and with the other hand press the dough on top, gently but firmly. If necessary, patch it to reinforce its strength, using leftover bits of pastry. Then, bringing the parchment paper together at the top of the cake, skewer its edges with toothpicks to hold them loosely in place. The paper acts as a sort of girdle for the pastry.

Should the top break open while baking, simply dust it with confectioners' sugar before serving or serve it as is—it's golden and lovely, and your guests will think it's meant to be that way!

Maria's Biscotti

BISCOTTI DI MARIA

ABOUT 70 BISCOTTI

Wonderful meals issue forth from Maria Maurillo's kitchen at Agriturismo Malvarina, near Assisi, like water from a mountain spring. I was lucky enough to spend a couple of afternoons with her in the kitchen (see essay, page 363), which was as much fun as it was instructive.

This light, friable, sweet dough is Maria's standby for her wonderful apple cake (page 365) and also for biscotti. It is very, very easy to work with, and one afternoon I played around with it, forming it into dozens of fanciful shapes. Tiny little braids were my favorite, but one must have the better part of an afternoon to make those!

These buttery cookies will keep for a week in an airtight container, though I doubt you'll have them around that long.

3¼ cups all-purpose flour
½ teaspoon baking powder
¼ teaspoon fine sea salt

13 tablespoons unsalted butter, at
    room temperature
1 cup Vanilla Sugar (page 441)
2 large eggs, at room temperature
1 recipe Baked Almonds and Sugar
    (page 440; optional)

1. Sift together the flour, baking powder, and salt onto a sheet of waxed or parchment paper.

2. In the work bowl of an electric mixer, mix the butter and sugar until light and pale yellow. Add the eggs, one at a time, mixing well after each addition. Gradually add the flour mixture, mixing until you have a soft dough. Turn the dough out onto a generously floured work surface and knead very gently until it is smooth and tender, with no air holes, about 2 minutes. Let the dough rest, uncovered, for 30 minutes. If making Maria's Amazing Apple Cake, proceed after this step.

3. Preheat the oven to 375°F. Line 2 or 3 baking sheets with parchment paper.

4. You may do several different things with the dough, as Maria does. Using about 1 tablespoon dough, make a little ball and press a sugared almond into it, flattening it slightly. Or roll out the dough on a floured surface so it is less than ⅛ inch thick but not as thin as 1⁄16 inch. Cut out 2-inch squares, fold one corner to the center, pressing it gently so it sticks, and press a candied almond onto the point of the dough. Or roll the dough into ¼-inch-thick ropes and form them into rounds, knots, or braids. Place the biscotti

about ½ inch apart on the prepared baking sheets.

5. Bake the biscotti in the center of the oven until they are golden at the edges and baked through, about 20 minutes. Remove from the oven and transfer to wire racks to cool completely.

Biscotti

*I*n the United States when we think biscotti, we think of those tasty rusklike cookies that make perfect companions to coffee in any of its steamy hot or chilled variations. To make these rusks, the dough is baked twice, first in a flattened log shape, then again after the logs have been sliced into cookies. In fact, *biscotto* literally means twice *(bis)* cooked *(cotto)*. However, on the Italian farm, many of the delicious cookies that are served—both sweet and savory—are called biscotti, whether they've been baked twice or not. These cookies show up in the morning, the afternoon, or before an evening meal with a glass of young wine or afterward, when they can be dunked in espresso or sweet wine.

Not all the cookies in this chapter are twice cooked either, but many are still called biscotti, and they offer up a tempting array of delicate aromas, crisp textures, and wonderfully intense flavors. In fact, they are a little dangerous—once you've tasted them, you may have a hard time keeping your hands from the cookie plate or tin.

Anise Cookies

**BISCOTTI
ALL'ANICE**

90
BISCOTTI

I helped make these little cookies at Agriturismo Malvarina, near Assisi (see essay, page 363). I'd spent the afternoon cooking with Maria Maurillo, who owns the *agriturismo,* a farm that offers meals and rooms, with her son, Claudio Fabrizzi. When she saw there was an hour left before dinner, she mixed up this dough.

The cookies were baked and resting on cooling racks, but Maria wouldn't let me taste one. "They aren't good yet. They need some time to age," she said. "We'll taste them tonight."

She was right to make me wait, for the flavors of anise, oil, and wine developed even in a couple of hours into a rich and subtle perfume. We had them after dinner with coffee, and their rich and heady flavor and rustic texture made an ideal end to the meal.

3⅓ cups all-purpose flour
½ teaspoon baking powder
¼ teaspoon fine sea salt
⅓ cup extra-virgin olive oil

⅔ cup sugar
2 tablespoons anise seeds
¾ cup plus 2 tablespoons dry
    white wine

Segreti

When rolling the dough into ropes, press on it firmly to compress any air pockets in the dough.

1. Sift the flour, baking powder, and salt onto a large piece of waxed paper.

2. Pour the flour mixture into a wide, shallow bowl and make a well in the center. Add the oil, sugar, and anise seeds to the well and begin to mix in some of the flour from the sides of the well. Gradually add the white wine as you continue to slowly mix the ingredients together. The dough should be soft and somewhat sticky but not too wet or difficult to handle.

3. Turn the dough out onto a lightly floured surface and knead it gently for a minute or two until it is completely mixed. Oil your hands to prevent the dough from

sticking to them and divide the dough into 90 equal pieces. Roll each piece firmly into a thin rope about 7 inches long; firmness is necessary so there are no air pockets in the ropes. Let the ropes rest for about 15 minutes to allow any gluten in the flour to relax.

4. Preheat the oven to 350°F. Line 2 baking sheets with parchment paper.

5. Form the dough ropes into circles, slightly overlapping and pressing the ends gently together. Place as many as will fit about ½ inch apart on the prepared baking sheets.

6. Bake in the center of the oven until the cookies are hard, slightly puffed, and just lightly

golden on the bottom, about 20 minutes. Remove from the oven and the parchment and let cool on wire racks. Continue baking the cookies in batches on fresh parchment. These are better the next day and even better several days later. Be sure to store them in an airtight container.

NOTE: These cookies are very pale in color, which is exactly as they should be. They improve a great deal after sitting in an airtight container for at least a week and will be even more delicious after 3 weeks.

Szdena's Amaretti

AMARETTI DI SZDENA

ABOUT 78 AMARETTI

These sweet little almond bites are a specialty of Szdena Lancellotti, who cooks at the family restaurant, Ristorante Lancellotti (see essay, page 80), outside Modena in Emilia-Romagna. Szdena does most of the baking for the restaurant, working in the large, well-lit kitchen opposite her husband, Angelo. They bicker in a friendly way as they work, teasing and talking with other members of the family who are at work elsewhere in the restaurant.

Szdena makes these cookies almost every day, for they are served after dinner with espresso. They are delicious and will keep several days in an airtight container.

3⅓ cups almonds, skins removed (see box, page 351)
1½ cups plus 3 tablespoons sugar

3 large egg whites, at room temperature

1. Grind the almonds in a food processor until they are coarsely chopped. They will be unevenly chopped, with larger bits and dusty bits, which is just fine. You can also coarsely chop

them by hand, making sure some are chopped as fine as dust.

2. In the work bowl of an electric mixer, whisk together the sugar and the egg whites until they make a thick, white foam but don't form stiff peaks. You don't want the egg whites and sugar to form a meringue but rather a white, foamy soup. This should take 3 to 4 minutes. Fold in the almonds until completely incorporated, cover the bowl loosely with a tea towel, and let sit for 2 hours.

3. Preheat the oven to 350°F. Line 2 baking sheets with parchment paper.

4. Quickly stir the batter. Using a teaspoon measure, scoop up a spoonful of batter and drop it on one of the prepared baking sheets, using another spoon to scrape out the batter. Repeat, leaving at least 2 inches between the cookies. If the batter sticks to the spoons, dip the spoons first into warm water and shake off the excess water.

5. Bake the amaretti just until they are very pale golden around the edges and crisp on top, 12 to 14 minutes. Slide the cookies, still on the paper, onto wire racks. Let cool for 10 minutes, then remove the amaretti from the parchment and let cool completely. Continue baking the cookies in batches on fresh parchment.

Hazelnut Truffles

TARTUFI DI NOCCIOLE

26 TARTUFI

Rich, pleasantly bitter, filled with flavors everyone (it seems) loves, these little chocolate and hazelnut nuggets make a lusciously satisfying mouthful, and they are very impressive to serve with after-dinner coffee. They, too, come from Szdena Lancellotti, of Ristorante Lancellotti, near Modena in Emilia-Romagna (see essay, page 80).

*10 ounces best-quality bittersweet
chocolate, preferably Lindt
Excellence
2 tablespoons extra-virgin olive oil
1⅓ cups (7 ounces) whole hazelnuts,*

*toasted and skins removed (see
box, page 351)
2 ounces (about 2 cups)
unsweetened flaked coconut*

1. Place the chocolate and oil in the top of a double boiler over simmering water and melt without stirring. When the chocolate has melted, whisk it until smooth and remove from the heat, leaving the top of the double boiler over the hot water.

2. Reserve 26 of the whole hazelnuts. Crush the remaining hazelnuts until they are in very uneven pieces—some will be powdered, others will be finely to coarsely chopped. The best way to crush the nuts is to put them on a large piece of parchment paper, fold half the paper over them, and roll over them with a rolling pin. Stir the nuts into the chocolate mixture and set aside to cool and harden.

3. When the chocolate is firm enough to hold its shape when rolled, pour the coconut out onto a work surface. Roll 1 tablespoon of the chocolate mixture into a ball, stuff a hazelnut inside it, and reshape the chocolate around it so that the nut is completely hidden. Roll it in the coconut, coating it on all sides. Repeat with the remaining chocolate mixture. Check all the truffles; if some aren't as evenly covered with coconut as you'd like, roll them in it again. You may serve these immediately.

NOTE: These are at their peak within 48 hours after they are made.

Cornmeal Cookies from the Veneto

ZALETI

ABOUT 70 COOKIES

I sampled these delicate little cookies all around the Veneto region, where they are as traditional as the ruby radicchio and green asparagus that grow there in the fertile soil. These were my favorites, and they come from the hands of pastry chef Mariagrazia Zanette, who bakes at Da Domenico, a lovely country trattoria outside Treviso. There chef Domenico Camerotto uses only local ingredients in his menu, which offers one startling delicious dish after another. The quality of the desserts matches the food, and these little cookies are no exception. Light, sweet, crunchy with polenta, and perfumed with fennel, these are as good at any time of day with coffee as they are after supper with a glass of chilled Passit, a sweet wine from the Veneto region that is made from partially dried grapes.

1 cup all-purpose flour
Generous pinch of fine sea salt
3 large eggs, at room temperature
½ cup sugar
8 tablespoons (1 stick) unsalted
   butter, melted

1½ cups finely ground polenta or
   cornmeal
1 cup sultanas or dark raisins
6 tablespoons pine nuts, untoasted
1½ teaspoons fennel seeds

1. Preheat the oven to 375°F. Line 2 baking sheets with parchment paper.

2. Sift together the flour and salt onto a sheet of waxed paper.

3. In a large bowl or the work bowl of an electric mixer, whisk together the eggs and sugar until pale yellow, light, and fluffy, about 5 minutes. Add the butter and mix well. Add the polenta and flour mixture and mix well, then add the raisins, pine nuts, and fennel seeds

and stir until evenly distributed.

4. Place even tablespoonsful of the dough at least 2 inches apart on the prepared baking sheets. Bake the cookies in the center of the oven until they are golden around the edges and set, about 12 minutes. Remove from the oven and the parchment and let cool on wire racks. Continue baking the cookies in batches on fresh parchment.

Sicilian Chocolate Spice Christmas Cookies

NUCATOLI

ABOUT 7 DOZEN 2-INCH COOKIES

Although Giuseppe Morello was married in May, his mother brought these traditional Christmas cookies to the wedding, along with every other Sicilian specialty she could fit in her voluminous baggage. The aroma of cloves wafted from the small sampler box she gave me, which I served to my family after dinner one night several days later. We were all seduced by the delicate flavor of the cookies, which resonates both of almonds and cloves.

Mama Morello frosts them with the icing suggested here. We like them better plain, though the icing makes them festive.

FOR THE COOKIES
1 pound almonds in their skins
2¼ cups sugar
2½ cups all-purpose flour, plus additional for rolling out the dough
¾ cup unsweetened cocoa
½ teaspoon baking powder
½ teaspoon freshly ground cloves
Pinch of fine sea salt

3 large eggs, at room temperature

FOR THE ICING (OPTIONAL)
2 large egg whites, at room temperature
Tiny pinch of fine sea salt
1½ cups Confectioners' Vanilla Sugar (see box, page 356)

Cacao, or the cocoa bean, introduced by the Spanish to the Italians in the 16th century, was considered a dangerous stimulant by the Catholic Church.

1. Preheat the oven to 400°F. Line several baking sheets with parchment paper.

2. Grind the almonds with ½ cup of the sugar in a food processor almost to a powder.

3. Sift together the flour, cocoa, baking powder, cloves, and salt onto a sheet of waxed paper.

4. In a large bowl or the work bowl of an electric mixer, whisk the eggs with the remaining 1¾ cups sugar until pale yellow and light; they should not become fluffy but should be thoroughly combined. Add 1 cup of the flour mixture, then the almond mixture, mixing well after each addition. Add the remaining flour mixture and mix until combined. Make sure the almonds are incorporated, for they tend to fall to the bottom of the bowl. The dough will be quite stiff and thick (see Note).

5. Knead the dough on a lightly floured work surface once or twice. Cut the dough into quarters. Roll out one-quarter of the dough at a time to ⅛ inch thick and cut out the shapes you desire. Place them on the prepared baking sheets.

6. Bake the cookies in the center of the oven until they are baked through and the tops have a matte finish, about 12 minutes. Remove from the oven and let cool completely before removing from the parchment. Continue baking the cookies in batches on fresh parchment.

7. For the icing, whisk the egg whites with the salt until foamy. Sift the sugar over the egg whites and whisk until smooth. The icing will resemble white paste. When the cookies are cool, spread them with a thin layer of icing. Let the icing harden before storing the cookies in an airtight container.

NOTE: This dough is quite stiff but easy enough to work. Have flour on hand to lightly dust the work surface as you roll out the cookies. The dough has a tendency to dry out when exposed to air, so keep covered what you aren't working with. Once you have cut shapes, gather the scraps and form into a 1-inch-thick roll. Refrigerate until thoroughly chilled, then simply cut the roll into ¼-inch-thick slices and bake as for the other cookies. The dough will keep well in the refrigerator for several days.

Fabulous Sicilian Almond Cookies

I first tasted these in the company of Giusto Occhipinti, an architect and winemaker who lives on a small farm near Caltagirone, in Sicily. We sat outside his house, a jar of these biscotti and glasses of his remarkable Cerasuolo di Vittoria at hand. I asked him if he'd made them—not such an unusual question to pose to this young and versatile man, who is architect, successful vintner, and sometime cook. He hadn't, and he gave me precise directions to the bakery where he'd purchased them. At first light the following day, I was bakery bound.

I found II Fornaio di Fatantoni & Angilletti in the small town of Pedalino, where baker Maria Grazia Leggio makes these and many other rustic country desserts (see her *ciambella,* page 342). She willingly gave me the recipe, but from tasting them at her bakery on that warm, bright sunny morning to this recipe was a long and biscotti-strewn road. I baked dozens of variations of that recipe, trying to achieve Maria Grazia's perfect balance of dry, crisp texture and sweet, nutty flavor.

Finally I achieved the results I wanted. These are addictive—satisfying and rich with toasty almond flavor. You will find it difficult to stop at one or even two. They are good for breakfast, as well as after dinner, and will keep very well in an airtight container for several weeks.

4¼ cups all-purpose flour
2 teaspoons baking powder
Pinch of fine sea salt
1½ cups almonds in their skins,
    toasted (see box, page 348) and
    coarsely chopped

1 cup plus 4 tablespoons sugar
10 tablespoons (1¼ sticks)
    unsalted butter, at room
    temperature
4 large eggs, at room temperature

Segreti

• Leave the skins on the almonds, as Maria Grazia does, for a richer flavor, and be sure to include a pinch of salt in the dough to balance the flavor.

• To test whether or not these are baked through, break one in half; if it still looks slightly wet and solid, it needs more baking. If it seems nearly dry, remove it from the oven.

1. Preheat the oven to 350°F. Line 2 baking sheets with parchment paper.

2. Sift together the flour, baking powder, and salt onto a large piece of waxed paper.

3. Grind the almonds with 2 tablespoons of the sugar in a food processor until they are of uneven texture, pulsing 7 or 8 times. There shouldn't be any large chunks, but they shouldn't be uniformly fine either.

4. In a large bowl or the work bowl of an electric mixer, beat the butter until pale yellow and light. Add the remaining 1 cup plus 2 tablespoons sugar and mix until thoroughly combined. Add 3 eggs, one at a time, mixing well after each addition. Mix in the flour mixture, 1 cup at a time, then add the ground almonds and mix just until combined. Turn the dough out onto a lightly floured work surface and gently knead it several times to completely incorporate the almonds.

5. Whisk together the remaining egg and 2 teaspoons water in a small bowl to make an egg wash.

6. Divide the dough into quarters. On a lightly floured work surface, roll each quarter into a 1-inch-thick log. Lightly press on the log to flatten it slightly and brush lightly with egg wash. With a sharp knife, cut diamond-shaped pieces that measure 1½ x 1 inch. Place them at least ¾ inch apart on a prepared baking sheet. Repeat with the remaining dough.

7. Bake the cookies in the center of the oven until they are golden and baked all the way through, 35 to 40 minutes. To test for doneness, break apart a *mandorlata;* if it appears moist in the center, continue baking for about 5 minutes. Remove from the oven and the parchment let cool on a wire rack. Continue baking the cookies in batches on fresh parchment.

Hazelnut Cookies

CANTUCCI CON NOCCIOLI

ABOUT 48 COOKIES

These crisp, sweet, hazelnut-rich cookies are typical to Tuscany, and according to Francesco Giuntini, owner of the Selvapiana winery in Rufina, Chianti, who has an encyclopedic knowledge of Italian history, Tuscan peasants traditionally baked these and gave them to nobles as a gift.

Cantucci are made with almonds in Tuscany, but I've made them here with hazelnuts. Why? Well, so many Italian sweets incorporate almonds that using halzelnuts seemed a welcome, if untraditional, change, and since Italy produces some of Europe's finest hazelnuts, it isn't so farfetched either.

If you prefer to stick with Tuscan tradition, simply substitute almonds for the hazelnuts. Whichever nut you use, serve these as Francesco Giuntini does—after a meal with a rich cup of espresso. They are also delicious dipped into a good Vin Santo, Tuscan sweet wine, or a glass of richly flavored Chianti Rufina Riserva from Selvapiana. They keep well in an airtight container for several weeks.

1¾ cups all-purpose flour
1 teaspoon baking powder
½ teaspoon fine sea salt
4 tablespoons (½ stick) unsalted
    butter, at room temperature
½ cup Vanilla Sugar (page 441)

2 large eggs, at room temperature
1 large egg yolk, at room temperature
1 cup hazelnuts, toasted and skins
    removed, coarsely chopped (see
    box, page 348, for toasting nuts)

1. Preheat the oven to 350°F. Line 2 baking sheets with parchment paper.

2. Sift together the flour, baking powder, and salt onto a piece of waxed paper.

3. In a large bowl or the work bowl of an electric mixer, beat the butter until pale yellow and light. Gradually add the

Tuscan Privation

*I*n the old days on the farm in Chianti, the heart of Tuscany, there were just two days a week allotted for dessert eating: Thursdays because half the week's work was done and Sunday because it was a day of rest and celebration.

sugar and mix until thoroughly combined. Add the eggs, one at a time, then the egg yolk, mixing well after each addition. Add the flour mixture and mix just until combined. Fold in the nuts.

4. Divide the dough into quarters and shape each quarter into a 6-inch-long log about 1½ inches thick. Place the logs about 1½ inches apart on the prepared baking sheets.

5. Bake the logs in the center of the oven until they are puffed and golden, about 25 minutes. Remove from the oven and let cool on a wire rack for 10 minutes. Leave the oven on.

6. With a sharp knife, cut the logs on the diagonal into ½-inch-thick slices. Place the slices, cut side down, on the parchment-lined baking sheets and bake until they are golden on one side, about 15 minutes. Turn the slices and bake until they are golden on the other side, 5 to 10 minutes more. Remove from the oven and let cool on a wire rack. Continue baking the cookies in batches.

Lemon Biscotti

BISCOTTI AL LIMONE

ABOUT 48 BISCOTTI

I got this recipe from a delightful woman in Abruzzo, Lucilla Curato, a noblewoman who owns about 140 acres of land outside the town of Pianella, as well as a large and beautiful villa in town.

She is somewhat unusual even in the Abruzzo, where women dominate not just the family but often the family business, for she prefers not to use her title and actually does much of the physical work on the farm herself. She was my generous guide to the area when I visited in October, which was just before olive season. Each day her first stop was to check the progress of her olive trees, then consult with the two men who help her farm the land.

Lucilla also takes tremendous interest in the traditional farm foods of her area, and this is a classic recipe. She says the biscotti are often seasoned with anise seeds and make a good dunking cookie for morning coffee or espresso.

These have a light and lovely but distinct lemon flavor. I prefer them without the anise, but you must try for yourself.

3¼ cups all-purpose flour
1 teaspoon baking powder
½ teaspoon fine sea salt
3 large eggs, at room temperature
1¼ cups sugar
¼ cup olive oil

Zest of 3 lemons, preferably organic
or at least untreated after harvest,
minced
1½ teaspoons anise seeds (optional)
½ cup whole milk

1. Preheat the oven to 350°F. Line 2 baking sheets with parchment paper.

2. Sift together the flour, baking powder, and salt onto a piece of waxed paper.

3. In a large bowl or the work bowl of an electric mixer, whisk 2 of the eggs until they are foamy. Gradually whisk in the sugar and continue whisking until the mixture is pale yellow and light, about 4 minutes. Whisk in the oil, then add the lemon zest and anise if using; mix well. Mix in the flour mixture alternately with the milk, beginning and ending with the flour mixture.

4. Turn out the dough onto a lightly floured work surface and divide it in half. Shape each half into an 8-inch-long log about 2 inches thick. Flatten the tops slightly and place the logs about 2 inches apart on one of the prepared baking sheets. Mix the remaining egg with 2 teaspoons water for an egg wash and brush it lightly on the logs.

5. Bake the logs in the

center of the oven until they are puffed and golden, 25 to 30 minutes. Remove from the oven and let cool on a wire rack for 10 minutes. Leave the oven on.

6. With a sharp knife, cut each of the logs on the diagonal into about twenty-four ½-inch-thick slices. Place the slices, cut side down, on the parchment-lined sheets and bake until they are golden on one side, about 15 minutes. Turn the slices and bake until golden on the other side, about 10 minutes more. Remove from the oven and let cool on wire racks. Continue baking the biscotti in batches.

Apricot Ice

CREMOLATA DI ALBICOCCHE

6 SERVINGS

One sees castles on the shore of the Amalfi peninsula, solid remnants of the Saracens, a nomadic tribe from northern Africa who came and conquered Italy some hundreds of years ago. The castles are forbidding, prominently placed to fend off attacks.

Some have been restored and converted into hotels, restaurants, living quarters. It is odd to see their squat towers brightened with a parasol or an edge of a curtain flying from a window cut into the thick walls. I preferred seeing the ruins sitting lonely and vacant, leaving room for imagination.

The Saracens were generous with all the countries they visited, leaving much more than well-built strongholds. It is thanks to them that Italians now have many different fruits, spices, and dishes. Among their most prominent contributions is the apricot, or *albicocca,* which has nearly become the national fruit of Italy. It is turned into everything from jam to crostata filling to this refreshing ice.

I stumbled across this recipe in the company of Grazia Caso, chef at La Taverna del Capitano, in Marina del Cantone, a small fishing village on the Amalfi coast. I spent two weeks there, which gave Grazia and me ample time to converse, sample, and try many different dishes. I owe her a great deal, not the least of which is this recipe.

My favorite way to serve *cremolata di albicocca* is with a slice of Apricot Tart (page 358) and some oozingly ripe apricots.

1 cup sugar
1½ pounds apricots, cut in half
  and pitted

2 tablespoons fresh lemon juice

1. Place the sugar and 2 cups water in a medium-size saucepan and whisk to combine. Cover and bring to a boil over medium-high heat. Remove the lid, reduce the heat so the mixture simmers merrily, and cook, stirring from time to time, just until the sugar is dissolved, which will take about 5 minutes. Let cool to room temperature.

2. Purée the apricots in a food processor. Add the lemon juice and process with one or two quick pulses to blend it into the purée. When the sugar syrup is cool, stir in the apricot purée and refrigerate it for at least 1 hour.

3. Freeze in an ice cream maker according to the manufacturer's instructions.

Lemon Ice

**SORBETTO DI
LIMONE**

4 TO 6
SERVINGS;
3 GENEROUS
CUPS

On the Amalfi peninsula lemons grow year-round, some getting as big as small footballs. More impressive than their size, however, is their round, tart, fruity flavor, which develops over months of sunshine and cool sea breezes that waft continually over the peninsula.

I visited Il Convento, a former monastery and now a farm not far from Sorrento, amidst a lush grove of lemon trees, because I wanted to see how they made their lemon grappa, a vivid alcohol served chilled after meals. I walked through a vast lemon orchard that was covered with black netting to keep it cool and to protect the trees from the winds that might knock the fruit from the branches. I also got a quick look at the grappa process and a tour of the wine cellar, which was connected to the former monastery building by a low-ceilinged tunnel once used by monks on the run from various invaders of the peninsula.

I knew I wouldn't be able to perfectly recreate the grappa from Il Convento, so instead I made this ice, which was so delicious and easy I knew it had to be included in my book. Each time I make it, which is often, it reminds me of the aroma of Il Convento's orchard.

1 cup sugar
Zest of 2 lemons, minced

1 cup lemon juice

1. Place the sugar and 2 cups water in a medium-size saucepan and whisk to combine. Cover and bring to a boil over medium-high heat. Remove the lid, reduce the heat so the mixture simmers merrily, and cook, stirring from time to time, just until the sugar is dissolved, which will take about 5 minutes. Stir in the lemon zest and let cool to room temperature.

2. When the sugar syrup is cool, strain out the lemon zest and discard. Whisk in the lemon juice and refrigerate the mixture for at least 1 hour.

3. Freeze in an ice cream maker according to the manufacturer's instructions.

NOTE: You might ask, shouldn't this be called *gelato?* No, for technically a gelato is made with a custard base, like ice cream. In some parts of Italy, this would be called a *cremolata.*

Red Fruit Sorbet

SORBETTO DI FRUTTI DI BOSCO

4 TO 6 SERVINGS

Sicily is the recognized home of the best *sorbetti,* or sorbets, and *gelati,* or ice creams, in Italy. Sicilian cooks—both professional and home—have incredibly flavored fruits at their disposal and a knack for combining them with just the right amount of sugar to make a rich-tasting blend. They also observe the seasons strictly, making ices only when it's hot outside and only when the fruit is at its peak of ripeness, a good habit to develop.

In the Sicilian farm tradition, ices would be reserved for a *festa,* or celebration, such as the Feast of the Assumption in August, when people take to the streets in a grand procession, then return home to feast on the summer bounty. Feast days are still a vital part of the Sicilian tradition, but ices are served throughout the summer season now. One no longer needs to wait for a certain saint's day to enjoy a Sicilian *sorbetto.*

Typically, Sicilian ices are made with citrus fruits or with melon, but red fruits lend themselves perfectly as well, as you will find in this clean, clear, and fresh-tasting blend. I advise against using strawberries, for their heavier flavor can mask the lightness. Although a personal addition, I highly recommend adding a handful of red currants to whatever blend you choose. Their bright, tart flavor is incomparable.

1 cup sugar
6 cups mixed red fruit, including

red currants, raspberries,
blackberries

1. Place the sugar and 2 cups water in a medium-size saucepan and whisk to combine. Cover and bring to a boil over medium-high heat. Remove the lid, reduce the heat so the mixture simmers merrily, and cook, stirring from time to time, just

until the sugar is dissolved, which will take about 5 minutes. Let cool to room temperature.

2. When the sugar syrup is completely cool, purée the berries in a food processor, then strain the purée into a medium-size bowl to remove excess seeds (particularly necessary when using raspberries).

3. Refrigerate the mixture for at least 1 hour. Freeze in an ice cream maker according to the manufacturer's instructions.

Berry and Apricot Sorbet

**SORBETTO DI
LAMPONI E
ALBICOCCHE**

**6 TO 8
SERVINGS**

This sorbet is my own invention, a creation inspired by a visit to the incredible organic farm of Livia and Alfonso Iaccarino on the tip of the Amalfi peninsula. Owners of Don Alfonso, one of Italy's few Michelin three-star restaurants, the Iaccarinos are known for the inventiveness of their cuisine, which is more international than regional.

The eight acres Alfoso and his crew tend was always a farm, and the small farmhouse on the property, built many hundreds of years ago in a distinctly Arabian style, now houses pigs and chickens. Lucky pigs and chickens, for they have an unparalleled view of the isle of Capri, surrounded by its nearly turquoise waters.

The farm slopes steeply down the hillside, stopping well above the sea, but the sea mist rises to lavish its gentle moisture on the lettuces, lemons, artichokes, beans, onions, apricots, squash, herbs, and other fruits and vegetables, all of which are cultivated organically. The fragrance of the produce I saw made me wish that all farmland could be blessed with such an abundance of natural advantages. Of course, Alfonso has installed irrigation, a costly proposition that few on the peninsula can afford, for otherwise his produce would suffer, and he counts on it for the restaurant.

Both Livia and Alfonso grew up in very comfortable circum-
stances, and they inherited not only the restaurant, with its two
luxurious apartments upstairs, but also a villa, which they sold to
buy the farm. "Our families thought we were insane," Livia told
me. "They still do, but this is what we believe in, what we want,
and where we want to live someday."

This sorbet tastes clearly of summer, and it was inspired by the
freshness of all that is produced on that farm. Nothing could be
simpler to make. Just remember to use the freshest fruit you can
find, preferably over, rather than under, ripe.

Do not freeze this rock hard, for it is best with a slightly soft texture.

1 cup sugar
1 pound ripe apricots, cut in half
  and pitted

3 cups ripe raspberries

1. Place the sugar and 2
cups water in a medium-size
saucepan and whisk to combine.
Cover and bring to a boil over
medium-high heat. Remove the
lid, reduce the heat so the mixture simmers merrily, and cook,
stirring from time to time, just
until the sugar is dissolved,
which will take about 5 minutes.
Let cool to room temperature.

2. When the sugar syrup is
completely cool, purée the apricots in a food processor. Transfer
them to a medium-size bowl and
whisk in the sugar syrup. Purée
the berries, strain them to remove excess seeds, and whisk the
purée into the apricot mixture.

3. Refrigerate the mixture
for at least 1 hour. Freeze in an
ice cream maker according to the
manufacturer's instructions.

LA DISPENSA

What a lively place is the Italian *dispensa,* or pantry, for on its shelves one finds the vibrant flavors that deliver vigor and freshness to Italian farmhouse cooking.

Often the *dispensa* is a cupboard in the kitchen where jars of everything from simple tomato sauce to peppers marinated in oil and vinegar rest in cool darkness, far from the heat of the stove. Pulled into the light, their vivid, intense colors shine when they are arranged on a platter for a simple antipasto, added to soup, or heated and poured over pasta.

Part of the *dispensa* is usually a venerable armoire in the dining room where, behind wooden doors, sit tall, narrow bottles of lemon grappa, jars of fig and grape jam with carefully handwritten labels, and small crocks of fiery peppers marinating in olive oil, which are used as a table condiment, but not by the faint of palate.

What I love about the Italian farmhouse pantry
almost as much as what it contains is the history of how the
boldly flavored seasonings, sauces, and vegetables get there. In
Gragnano, an ancient town in the Lactari mountains of the
Amalfi peninsula, which is thought to be one of the oldest
pasta-producing towns in Italy, I visited the Albertino family,
whose seven grown daughters assemble each August for a
marathon of cooking that fills all of their families'
dispense for the year to come. They make rich tomato sauce
and pickle artichoke hearts, zucchini, cauliflower, and just
about every other vegetable a neighboring garden provides.

Summer's end on the Italian farm finds most families

doing as the Albertinos do, cooking and preserv-

ing in a happy, steamy, rousing time that
results in laden shelves and the promise of
many tasty meals to come.

So wander through this chapter and
avail yourself of the abundance of flavors
in the Italian farmhouse *dispensa*. It will
make your cooking sing with the
flavors of the Italian farm.

Hot Pepper (Or Holy) Oil

OLIO SANTO

2 CUPS OIL

I found hot pepper oil throughout Italy, though I determined that it originated in the southern regions of Puglia, Basilicata, Campania, and Sicily, where food is decidedly more *piccante,* or spicy hot, than in other regions. Hot pepper oil undoubtedly moved north with the immigration of southern Italians, who brought with them not only their culinary tastes but also their hot pepper seeds.

Particularly in Sicily, hot pepper oil is called *olio santo,* or holy oil, and it anoints many a dish. This quick method for making it works well. Be aware that the longer you leave the oil on the peppers, the hotter it gets, so you will want to adjust it according to your tastes, sampling the oil each day. Once you've strained the oil, you may discard the peppers. Or put them in a jar, cover them with oil, and use that heavily infused oil by tiny drops when you want real fire on your tongue!

The Devil's Own

Hot peppers in Abruzzo are called *diavolicchio* (relating to the devil); in Sicily, they are called *pipi* or *ardenti* (ardent).

¾ *cup tiny dried hot red peppers, such as bird's-eye peppers, crushed slightly with a mortar and pestle (see Notes)*

2 *cups extra-virgin olive oil (see Notes)*

Spread the peppers in an even layer in a large shallow dish or non-reactive pan and pour the oil over them. Cover and let sit at room temperature until the oil is hot enough for your liking, about 48 hours for a nice, hot oil. Strain the oil into a bottle. It will keep several months if stored in a cool, dark place.

NOTES: Use top-quality extra-virgin olive oil, for its flavor is important.

• Don't crush the peppers to dust, but just enough to crack and allow them to give their fullest heat and flavor.

Toasted Hot Pepper Oil

This recipe comes from the Peduzzi family of Pianella, in Abruzzo, who own Rustichella, a company that produces and markets some of Italy's best artisanally made pasta. Abruzzo is known for its fiery cuisine, and I certainly experienced a great deal of it in the company of the Peduzzis, for they have more ways to heat up their food than any other Italian family I had the good fortune to spend time with. This is just one of the condiments they drizzle on food, particularly meat dishes, and it is one of my favorites, for it adds the dusky flavor of toasted peppers along with heat.

⅓ cup small dried hot red peppers, such as bird's-eye peppers, finely ground with a mortar and pestle or a spice mill (see Note)

1 cup extra-virgin olive oil

1. Place the ground peppers in a heavy skillet and toast them, frequently shaking the pan, over medium heat until they begin to turn dark brick red, 3½ to 4 minutes. Immediately pour the oil over them, shake the pan, and heat just until the oil shimmers, but not until it smokes, 1 to 2 minutes. Remove the pan from the heat and transfer the oil to a cool container so it won't continue to cook. The oil will keep for several months if stored in a cool, dark place.

2. To serve, do as the Peduzzis do and stir the oil before using so you get peppers and oil together. CAUTION: This oil is HOT.

NOTE: The seeds of the pepper won't grind into a powder but will stay whole, which is fine.

Hot Peppers Abruzzese

**PEPERONCINI
D'ABRUZZO**

**2 ½   C U P S
P E P P E R S**

This condiment, along with oil infused with toasted dried peppers (facing page), is a staple in the *dispensa,* or pantry, of Abruzzo, land of rugged mountains, fertile plains, and spicy food. Once the peppers are salted and covered with oil, they look like bright jewels and beg to be sprinkled over everything from pasta to lamb skewers to thick slabs of bread. You may simply use the oil, which has a hot tang, or do as the Abruzzese do and sprinkle the peppers themselves atop whatever you are seasoning.

*1 pound skinny fresh hot peppers,
    such as Hungarian hot wax or
    cayenne, rinsed, dried, and cut
    into ¼-inch-thick rounds with
    their seeds*

*½ teaspoon fine sea salt
2½ cups extra-virgin
    olive oil*

1. Place the peppers and salt in a medium-size bowl and toss until they are combined. Cover and let sit for 24 hours.

2. Drain the peppers, which will have given up some liquid, and spread them out on a double thickness of tea towel. Cover with another double thickness of towel and leave the peppers, patting them now and then, to dry completely, about 8 hours.

3. Place the peppers in a quart jar, pour the oil over them, and let them sit for at least 1 week before using. The peppers will keep for several weeks if stored in a cool, dark place or in the refrigerator. Be sure to remove them at least 30 minutes before using if they're stored in the refrigerator.

The Italian Pantry
La Dispensa

Your family will bless you and your friends will be astonished when you put together a fabulous meal from "nothing," if you have the following on hand in your *dispensa,* or pantry:

Pine nuts (store in airtight containers in the freezer)

Fresh walnuts (store in airtight containers in the freezer)

Fresh almonds (store in airtight containers in the freezer)

Flavorful extra-virgin olive oil

Aceto balsamico tradizionale (balsamic vinegar)

Capers, preferably salt-preserved (see box, page 66)

Cured olives

Anchovies

Sun-dried tomatoes, packed dry and/or in oil

Hot Pepper Oil (page 389)

Sage Oil (page 393)

Crushed red pepper flakes

Hot paprika

Dried oregano

Imported dried bay leaves

Lemon Rosemary Salt (page 394)

Fine and coarse sea salt

Vanilla Sugar (page 441)

Parmigiano-Reggiano

Prosciutto and/or pancetta

Legumi svariati, a variety of legumes, such as cannellini and borlotti beans, favas, chickpeas, lentils

Dried pasta, a variety of shapes both long and short

Lemons (organic, if possible)

Basil (in a pot on the windowsill or outside)

Nunzio's Tomato Sauce (page 424; stored in airtight containers in the freezer)

Light and Lively Tomato Sauce (page 423; stored in airtight containers in the freezer)

Mandarin Orange Marmalade (page 412)

Toasted Bread Crumbs (*mollica,* page 427; stored in airtight containers in the refrigerator or freezer)

Sage Oil

OLIO ALLA
SALVIA

3 CUPS OIL

On farms throughout Italy I found many different flavored oils, simple preparations in which fresh herbs or citrus zests were put into a full bottle of extra-virgin olive oil to give it additional depth and flavor. I had oils flavored with lemon, with hot peppers, with sage, rosemary, and garlic. This sage oil was one of my favorites, for the headiness of the herb is captured and softened in the oil, lending a distinct but gentle flavor to everything it touches, from pizza to roast chicken to fish.

There is some concern that flavored oils may develop bacteria; to avoid this, store them in the refrigerator. Remember to remove the oil 30 minutes before you plan to use it so that it warms enough to pour.

1½ cups fresh sage leaves (see Note)   *3 cups extra-virgin olive oil*

Place the sage in a clean, dry jar. Add the oil, close tightly, and let sit for at least 1 week before using. The oil will keep for many months in the refrigerator. When the oil gets low in the jar, remove the sage leaves, add fresh sage leaves, and top up the jar with more oil.

NOTE: You don't need to wash the sage if it is clean and fresh from the garden, and it is better if it has not come into contact with water before it is put in the oil. If you do need to rinse it, make sure it is completely dry before adding the oil to it.

Lemon Rosemary Salt

Alfredo Cavalli, chief cook for the feast of San Giovanni in the tiny farming village of the same name, in Emilia-Romagna near Bologna, motioned me into the makeshift kitchen under a large white canopy. He was preparing *spiedini*, mixed meat skewers (page 204), for two hundred people, and he wanted me to sample his secret seasoning. We he opened a jar of this salt, the aroma that emerged was citrusy and rich. He sprinkled it all over the *spiedini* and told me he always keeps some on hand at home as well.

I find myself using this salt often, for it turns a simple preparation into one that is more dressy and flavorful. It complements roast chicken, grilled fish, and oven-baked potatoes, and is also delicious sprinkled on steamed vegetables or atop fresh cheese spread over a slice of bread.

3 cloves garlic, 2 cut in half, green germ removed
1 cup coarse sea salt or kosher salt
Zest of 2 lemons, minced

1 tablespoon fresh rosemary leaves, minced
¼ to ½ teaspoon freshly ground black pepper

1. Mince 2 of the garlic cloves and reserve the remaining one.

2. Place everything but the reserved whole garlic clove in a food processor and process with 2 or 3 pulses, just until the salt has been slightly ground and the ingredients are combined. Alternatively you may crush the ingredients together in a mortar with a pestle.

3. Pour the salt mixture into a half-pint jar, push the remaining garlic clove down into the salt, and cover. Let sit for at least 3 days before using. This salt will keep at least 3 months if kept airtight.

Vinegar and Oil Pickled Bell Peppers

PEPERONI SOTT'ACETO E OLIO

ABOUT 5 CUPS PEPPERS

The tiny hamlet of Badia Montemurro in Tuscany, long ago a religious agricultural community surrounding an abbey, is now home to about twenty people whose main work is raising iris bulbs (ground for perfume and potpourri). My family spent a week in a sweet stone house there, and afternoons were taken up sitting on the small terrace outside, gazing over the Chianti hills.

Andreina and Andre Bucci were our landlords, and they lived just steps away. Friendly and eager for us to enjoy ourselves, they quickly drew us into conversation. When Andreina found out I was working on a book about Italian food, her face lit up. She loves to cook, and they both love to eat. "Andreina's mother, Linda, is the best cook in Italy," Andre said. "It's true," Andreina said. "Whenever I go into Florence to see her, I come back laden with sacks of pastas, vegetables she's pickled, sauces she's made. I put them in the freezer, and we eat well for a month!"

In our visit at Badia Montemurro, we became the lucky recipients of many of Andreina's mother's delicacies. Among them were these simple pickled peppers, which we ate as an appetizer spooned over Tuscan bread, on *panini*, and tossed with pasta.

Andreina said her mother typically uses green bell peppers for this recipe. I like to use a combination of colors, which look lovely in the jar.

1 cup best-quality white wine vinegar, 5 percent acidity
1½ pounds bell peppers, stemmed, seeds and pith removed, cut lengthwise into ¼-inch-wide strips

2 cloves garlic, green germ removed, cut lengthwise into paper-thin slices
1¾ to 2 cups extra-virgin olive oil

1. Place the vinegar and 5 cups of water in a large saucepan, cover, and bring to a boil over medium-high heat. Add the peppers, cover, return to a boil, and cook until they are to your liking (they will be perfectly crisp-tender after 5 minutes).

2. Drain the peppers, spread them out on a tea towel, pat them dry, and let cool.

3. Place the cooled peppers in a wide-mouth 1-quart jar, interspersing the slices of garlic among them and packing the peppers tightly. Pour the oil slowly over them. It should completely cover the peppers.

4. Cover the jar and let sit in the refrigerator for at least 3 days before sampling.

NOTE: Although peppers prepared this way will keep indefinitely as long as they are completely covered with oil, they are best if eaten within 3 months. Refrigerate them to be on the safe side. Just remember to remove them from the refrigerator several hours before serving so the peppers come to room temperature.

Pickled Eggplant

MELANZANE SOTT'ACETO E OLIO

ABOUT 1 QUART EGGPLANT

This recipe for pickling eggplant is another from Andreina Bucci's mother, Linda, who is originally from Emilia-Romagna but now calls Tuscany home. The eggplant has a gorgeous celadon color, tender and toothsome texture, and delicate peppery flavor. I like to serve it as a condiment for roasted meats and poultry or along with other tasty antipasti.

1½ cups best-quality white wine
vinegar, 5 percent acidity
2 medium eggplants (about 12
ounces each), peeled and cut
lengthwise into ¼-inch-thick
strips

1 clove garlic, green germ removed,
cut lengthwise into paper-thin
slices
2 small dried hot red peppers, such
as bird's-eye peppers
1 cup extra-virgin olive oil

Segreti

Peel and slice the eggplant right before you add it to the vinegar; the seeds will quickly begin to brown, as will the flesh, if it sits.

1. Place the vinegar and 7½ cups of water in a large saucepan, cover, and bring to a boil over medium-high heat. Immediately add the eggplant, stir, cover, and return to a boil. Cook the eggplant until tender and translucent, 5 to 6 minutes from the time you first add it to the pan.

2. Drain the eggplant, spread the strips out on a tea towel, pat them dry, and let cool.

3. Place the eggplant strips in a wide-mouth 1-quart jar, evenly interspersing the garlic and hot peppers among the strips. Pour in the oil, sticking a stainless-steel knife blade or a chopstick down into the jar and pulling back gently on the eggplant so the oil seeps throughout, leaving no air pockets.

4. Cover the jar and let sit in the refrigerator for at least 3 days before tasting.

NOTE: Eggplant will keep indefinitely prepared this way as long as it is completely covered with oil, but it is best if eaten within 3 months. Refrigerate it to be on the safe side. Just re-member to remove it from the refrigerator several hours before serving so the eggplant comes to room temperature.

Pickled Eggplant with Herbs

**MELANZANE
SOTT'ACETO E
OLIO CON ERBE**

ABOUT 1 QUART
EGGPLANT

This recipe, with its aromatic blend of flavors, is inspired by one for Pickled Eggplant (page 396), which I got from Andreina Bucci in Tuscany. Serve the two together as part of an antipasto platter. You may want to include the Eggplant Preserved in Oil (page 399) too, yet another—and completely different—pickled eggplant recipe. You'll be amazed at how varied eggplant can be, depending on its preparation.

Be prepared to have guests taste this and get a quizzical look on their faces as they try and figure out just what it is they are eating!

1½ cups best-quality white wine
    vinegar, 5 percent acidity
2 medium eggplants (about
    12 ounces each), peeled
    and cut lengthwise into
    ¼-inch-thick strips (see Segreti,
    page 397)

2 imported dried bay leaves
1½ teaspoons fennel seeds
3 tablespoons capers, preferably
    preserved in salt (see box, page 66)
1 clove garlic, peeled, left whole
1 cup extra-virgin olive oil

1. Place the vinegar and 7½ cups of water in a large saucepan, cover, and bring to a boil over medium-high heat. Immediately add the eggplant, stir, cover, and return to a boil. Cook the eggplant until tender and translucent, 5 to 6 minutes from the time you first add it to the pan.

2. Drain the eggplant, spread the strips out on a tea towel, pat them dry, and let cool.

3. Place the eggplant strips in a wide-mouth 1-quart jar, interspersing the bay leaves, fennel seeds, and capers among the strips. Place the garlic about halfway down into the strips. Pour in the oil, sticking a stainless-steel knife blade or a chopstick down into the jar and pulling back gently on the eggplant so the oil seeps through-

out, leaving no air pockets.

4. Cover the jar and let sit in the refrigerator for at least 3 days before tasting.

Note: Eggplant will keep indefinitely prepared this way as long as it is completely covered with oil, but it is best if eaten within 3 months. Refrigerate it to be on the safe side. Just remember to remove it from the refrigerator several hours before serving so the eggplant comes to room temperature.

Eggplant Preserved in Oil

MELANZANE SOTT'OLIO

ABOUT 2 CUPS EGGPLANT

Eggplants—and many other vegetables too—grow incredibly well during the hot summer in the Pollino hills of Basilicata, a wild and rugged region where many farmers still cultivate the land with the help of donkeys, a tradition maintained by necessity because the fields are too steep and small to accommodate tractors.

I got this recipe from Filomena Lufrano, the daughter of the successful Lufrano-Riccardi farm family (see essay, page 401), known locally for their busty red chickens and buttery sheep's milk cheese.

Filomena dreams of leaving the farm one day to go to America or another far-off country. At nineteen, however, she is content to look for accounting work locally and help out on the farm. She and her mother spend a lot of time together in the kitchen, particularly at summer's end when they produce dozens of pickled vegetables, all highly seasoned with the local chili pepper reverently called *il forte,* the strong one.

They brought this mixture out of their *dispensa,* or pantry, for me to try, and while I like eggplant pickled just about any way, this became an instant favorite and the recipe I turn to most often when I have an abundance of the vegetable on hand. Serve it with plenty of crusty fresh bread or savory biscotti as they do on the Lufrano-Riccardi farm in Basilicata.

2 tablespoons fine sea salt

2 good-size eggplants (about 12 ounces each)

2 cups best-quality white wine vinegar, 5 percent acidity

2 cloves garlic, green germ removed, cut lengthwise into paper-thin slices

¼ cup (gently packed) fresh oregano leaves, or 1 teaspoon dried

½ cup (gently packed) fresh mint leaves

1⅓ cups extra-virgin olive oil

Mint

1. Pour water into a large bowl, add 1 tablespoon of the salt, and stir to dissolve it.

2. Peel the eggplants and cut them into ½-inch-thick rounds. Immediately place the slices in the salt water to prevent them from darkening.

3. Place the vinegar, 8 cups of water, and the remaining 1 tablespoon salt in a large saucepan, cover, and bring to a boil over high heat. Drain the eggplant slices and add them to the pan. Cover, return to a boil, and cook the eggplant until soft but not mushy, 3 to 4 minutes.

4. Drain the eggplant, spread the slices out on a tea towel, cover with another towel, and press gently to remove as much liquid as possible. Replace the towels with dry ones and leave the eggplant to dry for about 12 hours.

5. Cut the eggplant into cubes and place it in a 1-pint jar. Add the garlic and herbs, then pour the olive oil over all. Cover, shake gently so all the ingredients are combined, and check to be sure that all the eggplant and herbs are completely covered with oil. If anything is exposed, either add more oil to the jar or shake it to submerge everything in oil.

6. Cover the jar and let sit in the refrigerator for at least 3 days before tasting.

NOTE: Eggplant will keep indefinitely prepared this way as long as it is completely covered with oil, but it is best if eaten within 3 months. Refrigerate it to be on the safe side. Just remember to remove it from the refrigerator several hours before serving so the eggplant comes to room temperature.

DOMINIC AND TERRANOVA

The Basilicata mountains run through south-central Italy. Remote, rigorous, and harsh, they provide a rugged and slightly intimidating landscape. Traditionally an agricultural area where farmers often just eked out an existence, it hasn't changed a great deal. Stooped figures dressed in black still work the rough and rocky soil. As I drove the winding roads, I often passed farmers coming home from their fields leading donkeys laden with huge and beautifully woven chestnut baskets piled with grapes, peppers, various vegetables from the fields. It is not a sight one easily forgets, for aside from the cars and the paved roads (some of which are surprisingly ample for such a remote area), it could be a moment in history a hundred years ago.

I was headed to the town of Terranova di Pollino to search out a farm that produced the region's noted sheep's milk cheese.

My guide was Dominic Tufaro, a warm and lively acquaintance with a compelling story. Dominic is a native of Terranova who left the area in his teens because it offered him no work or future. Farming had been a meager, sometimes miserable life for his parents' generation, even after the agricultural reforms instituted following the Second World War. At age fourteen Dominic went to Turin, where he apprenticed as a tailor.

Fully trained and in his twenties, he made his way to New York City. Despite his lack of English, he found work. It wasn't long before his boss noticed that he was skilled with more than a needle and thread and promoted him to shop manager in charge of all the non-English-speaking workers.

Dominic married, prospered, and moved to Albuquerque to start his own business. He is now a wealthy man; his three grown children have gone to the best schools and have families of their own.

"I grew up here in Terranova with nothing. I started working when I was six. I had no youth, and I was determined that my kids would have it all," he told me. It is a typical rags-to-riches story, but this one happened in the 1960s, for Dominic is still a young man, just sixty.

Dominic has maintained a fierce love for his native village, and he returns each year to live there for six months. I caught him at the end of his visit; he'd timed his departure after the grape harvest so he could be sure the wine from his vineyard would actually be bottled.

Dominic knew that I was looking for some real farmstead cheese, and he agreed to help me find a farm.

He arrived promptly at 9:30 in the morning, dressed in up-to-date rain gear, his Jeep Cherokee purring. Before we embarked on our day's journey, Dominic wanted to be sure that everyone in the village agreed with where he was taking me. We stopped at a dry goods store and he consulted with the owner, who had a constellation of fat round cheeses hanging above the cash registers. They looked delicious, and I bought one just in case we didn't ever get to a farm.

We went on to the grocery store and spoke first with the owner, then with Antonio di Masi, Dominic's best friend, who had stopped in. Before I knew it, Dominic, Antonio, and I were in the Cherokee and on our way out of town.

"There used to be thirty thousand head of sheep and goats here, but now there are just a few. These people need to figure out another way to make a living," Dominic said as he navigated the road. "I left here because there was no work. Things are changing slowly and there will be work, but it won't be in agriculture. It will be in tourism."

Dominic explained that the designation of a national park across the valley the year before was the best thing that could have happened to the area. "It is the largest park in Italy," he said. "Now all kinds of money is available for development, and Terranova is going to change."

He turned sharply up a steep and winding gravel road. "When I was a boy, I used to drive out here just to look at Maria, the woman who lives on this farm. She was the most beautiful girl in town!"

Fig trees laden with late-season fruit hung over the road. Chestnut trees were dropping their spiny-husked fruit. You could almost hear porcini mushrooms sprouting in the undergrowth. We arrived and were greeted by a group of friendly barking dogs.

Signora Maria Riccardi, holding the chicken she'd just caught by the feet in one hand, stepped out of the farmyard to greet us. Wiry, a plaid scarf framing her distinctively beautiful face, she greeted us in Terranovese, the town dialect. Her nineteen-year-old daughter, Filomena Lufrano, who spoke both the dialect and fluent Italian, brought us into the house and sat us at the dining-room table. Old on the outside, modern inside, this farmhouse was one of only a few I'd entered in Italy that didn't have a television blaring.

Soon Maria's husband, Giovanni Lufrano, a serious-looking man whose bright smile came as a complete surprise, arrived carrying a flask of rosé wine. We were joined by one of their sons, and glasses were passed all around. Maria brought out a loaf of bread—her own sourdough baked in a wood-fired oven—and began cutting thick slices. Then out came savory biscotti—ropes of boiled and baked dough flavored with anise seeds, rounds of homemade sausage red with ground hot peppers, and slabs of the family's hard yet almost buttery cheese. This was the rustic, true creamery flavor I'd been searching for.

We were a merry group sitting together at this table. Dominic looked at me and winked, and he, Antonio, and Filomena translated the short, choppy dialect so I could follow. As soon as our glasses were empty, Signore Lufrano refilled them. When the sausage was gone, more replaced it.

No cheese was being made at the moment because the sheep were about to give birth, so we talked food, and I asked Filomena for family favorites. She immediately mentioned *ciambutella* (page 178), and her mother perked up. The two disappeared, to the garden it turned out, and returned with a basket full of peppers. They motioned me into the kitchen. Filomena went to work, cutting peppers into a pan moistened with olive oil, following that with a small onion and two tomatoes, then a bit of water and some salt. All of this cooked until the peppers were tender, then Filomena stirred in eggs and hunks of farm-made sausage.

It was placed on the table with more cheese and bread. No dish, I was given to understand, is more typical of the Terranova farm table. Nothing, I thought, could be as delicious. Spooned over a slice of Maria's bread it was, quite simply, divine.

Why It Works

The Riccardi-Lufrano family has prospered on the farm in large part because they cultivate many different crops and raise animals, and as Dominic said to me in English, because Giovanni is extremely good at business. They were lucky enough to start with a sizable piece of arable land, and they have worked hard to carve out a niche for themselves with their cheese and grapes, chickens and vegetables. I was fascinated by their success because they were one of the few farmer families in the area who had achieved it. But what they were proudest of was the gravel road to their farm that they'd built themselves.

"It was too steep for machinery," Dominic

said. "And the city wouldn't give them any help, so they did it alone."

We walked outside to tour the farm, Filomena my welcome shadow. We went around the farmhouse, where chickens pecked picturesquely against the backdrop of the valley and the mountains beyond. We peeked into the barn to see the pigs and climbed a steep path to see the sheep. Behind the house we entered Giovanni's domain, the winery. He was wiping out glasses, which he then filled with new and bubbly wine from a cask.

Dominic turned to me and said, "Don't worry, this is just like grape juice. You can drink as much as you want and never feel a thing."

The light was fading as we returned to the house. I assumed we would say our good-byes and leave, but Filomena went into the kitchen and returned with a *ciambella,* a simple butter cake she had made the day before (page 342).

Many hours after we'd arrived, we prepared to leave. Before we could go, another bottle emerged, this one, however a liqueur. "Be careful of this," Dominic said. "It will make you sing."

Maria had chosen two varieties of their cheese, a *cacio* (a younger version of the aged *caciocavallo*) and a *cacio ricotta.* I bought them both, remembering that the reason for the trip had been to find an artisanal cheese production. I'd found one, though I hadn't seen anyone make any cheese. Instead, I'd had an unforgettable experience, a look into the life of a farm family tucked way up in the mountains of Basilicata.

Preserved Roasted Bell Peppers

**PEPERONI
ARROSTO
SOTT'OLIO**

A B O U T   2
Q U A R T S
P E P P E R S

I had the best preserved roasted peppers in Sardegna, made by Roberta Camboule, who lives and cooks at Zia Maria, a farm-restaurant outside Alghero. Roberta's brothers run the farm, and in a field behind the restaurant they grow dozens of pepper plants whose fruit hangs heavy all summer. Roberta roasts and preserves them in oil, then serves them along with a variety of antipasti.

For this preparation, a mix of red and green is prettiest, but using all red peppers is easiest and most flavorful. Why? Red peppers, which are simply ripened green peppers, have more flavor and sweetness, and they roast better than green peppers because their flesh is more developed.

Roberta doesn't process her peppers because she goes through them in a matter of days. If you want to keep them for any length of time, they must be canned in a water bath or they will ferment in the jar, despite their being completely covered with oil.

8 pounds red and green bell peppers
¼ cup capers, preferably preserved
*   in salt (see box, page 66)*
8 imported dried bay leaves
4 cloves garlic, green germ removed,
*   cut lengthwise into paper-thin*
*   slices*

2½ cups (gently packed)
*   fresh basil leaves*
4 to 4¾ cups
*   extra-virgin*
*   olive oil*

1. Roast the peppers over the open flame of a gas burner, on a grill, or under the broiler, charring the skins evenly all over. Transfer to heavy brown paper bags or wrap loosely in aluminum foil and let steam until they are cool enough to handle, at least 15 minutes.

2. When the peppers are

cool, remove the stems, seeds, and skin. The skin should simply slide off the pepper, but you may need to scrape off stubborn bits with a sharp knife. Do not rinse the peppers, for you will rinse away valuable flavor.

3. Cut the peppers into 1½-inch squares, lay them on a tea towel, and carefully pat them dry.

4. Divide the peppers between 2 wide-mouth 1-quart jars, interspersing the capers, bay leaves, garlic, and basil among the peppers. Cover completely with oil, leaving at least ½ inch of headroom. At this point you can serve them after several hours, or refrigerate if you aren't going to process them (see Note).

5. To process, place the jars in a kettle, cover by at least 4 inches of water, and cover the pot. Bring to a full boil and boil for 20 minutes (the temperature should reach 210°F). Turn off the heat, leave the jars in the water until the water is cool, then remove and store the jars in a cool, dark place. Leaving the jars in the water until it has cooled is vital, for removing them while they are hot may cause them to burst. Let the processed peppers sit for 1 week before eating.

NOTE: Even though these peppers are completely covered with oil, I have learned from sad experience that they will not keep out of the refrigerator without fermenting. If you do not process them in a water bath, reduce the amount of oil and eat the peppers as an antipasto the day you prepare them, or refrigerate them on the coldest shelf at the bottom of the refrigerator no longer than 1 week. There is a flavor and texture difference between the fresh and the canned peppers, but each is delicious in its own way.

ALCATRAZ

The morning was hot, sunny, dry, and the hilltop towns and open spaces of Tuscany gradually melted into the lush and humid foothills of the Umbrian Apennines. I was going to visit an organic farm called Alcatraz and its owner, Jacopo Fo. The actual name of the farm is Università Libera di Alcatraz, or Free University of Alcatraz, and I wasn't quite sure what to expect.

Situated outside the tiny village center of Santa Cristina (which is two houses big), Alcatraz is reached by a long, sloping, pitted gravel road that winds through verdant wooded hills and steep valleys. These are punctuated by fields planted in wheat, forage, and beans and partially divided by *siepi*, tangled hedges of wild tobacco and herbs, and by olive trees.

I arrived at an old stone farmhouse, which had a hodgepodge of rooms added on. In Alcatraz's busy front-room office I found Jacopo, an ascetic-looking young man with a spring in his step. We walked outside, and as he swept his hand to include several hills, the large valley before us, and the old house, he said, "This is Alcatraz. My parents and I developed it sixteen years ago. We wanted to get out into the country and create a place where people could be free. We named it after a prison because we felt that freedom is a state of mind."

"Uh-oh," I thought. This could be far-fetched.

"My family and I are from Milano, and when we first came, we were regarded with suspicion as foreigners. It was terrible. My father started a theater school here (Jacopo's father, Dario Fo, winner of the Nobel Prize for Literature in 1998, is Italy's best-known playwright and an actor), and the community wouldn't help at all, even though we were communists and this is a communist region."

After five years Jacopo's parents left to start another school elsewhere. Jacopo stayed to develop a theater, writing, and art school. Alcatraz has become an artists' retreat of sorts, as well as a productive organic farm with a restaurant that offers food made with the ingredients grown at Alcatraz or on neighboring farms. Sixteen years of persistence and Jacopo's national success with his own plays and books have meant that he and Alcatraz are not only accepted locally but also loved.

"People now know that we aren't a bunch of hippies who swim in the nude, that we aren't here to take anything away," he said, laughing. "In fact, I think we've given. When we came, Santa Cristina consisted of eighteen people. Now there are more than one hundred, young and old, who've returned because there is work."

We were interrupted for lunch, which was served in a restaurant that overlooks the valley. Pickled artichokes and zucchini strips were already on the table, followed by *polpette,* tiny meatballs flavored with lemon. On another platter came *bruschetta,* toast rubbed with garlic and topped with diced tomatoes mixed with basil and oregano. All was beautifully presented, flavorful, and fresh.

As we ate, Jacopo explained more.

"Alcatraz comprises three hundred fifty hectares [about seven hundred acres] of land, much of it in woods. Part of our woods are native, which we got the government to declare protected," he said. "Within them we find as many porcini mushrooms as we can eat and sell and other rare varieties as well. On the borders are enough wild berries to feed Bangladesh, and there are countless edible herbs and plants here. We've mapped where they are, and we use that as part of the curriculum for the children."

Conversation stopped to make way for the remaining courses of tender ravioli filled with spinach and ricotta cheese and dressed in a creamy tomato sauce, grilled local lamb, and *panna cotta,* or cooked cream, a custardy dessert topped with fresh strawberry sauce.

After coffee we climbed in a Land Rover to tour Jacopo's holdings. He stopped at the base of a gravel road, and we got out to look down to a square patch of land carved out of the woods, which was planted in strawberries and cane berries. "Our newest

project is making organic jam on an industrial level," he said. "We want to keep increasing our acreage of red fruits. They are the perfect crop here." For irrigation Jacopo tapped the river Resine, which runs through the valley.

The Land Rover was almost vertical as we drove up the hillside, and its wheels kept slipping. I was petrified, and I could tell Jacopo was nervous, but he made it to one crest, went around a corner, and crossed a field to a higher crest. Spread before us were small oak, hazelnut, olive, and willow trees that climbed the hills like a battalion of foot soldiers, irrigation hoses strung along their rows. I was amazed. This represented a huge investment, and I couldn't understand why it was hidden away.

"It's a truffle plantation," Jacopo said, and the light dawned.

"We'll harvest them next year," he said with a certainty I had a hard time crediting, for truffles are notoriously fickle, and as far as I knew, no one had ever guaranteed their presence anywhere. When I mentioned my doubt, he explained. "We planted these trees five years ago and trucked in unbelievable amounts of sheep manure, leaves, and trimmings from all the varieties of trees that foster truffles. We have analyzed the soil and found the truffle mycelium."

I shrugged, hoping he was correct. It would be fitting for truffles to thrive here, since Umbria is Italy's black truffle kingdom.

Leaving the hidden truffle field, we came upon a stone house and ancient mill above a small stream, which was almost completely restored. "This will be for the children," Jacopo said. "We want to show them how our ancestors worked the mill, ground the grain, and turned the flour into bread." He pointed to a restored wood-fired oven outside the house where they would bake the bread. "We've already roasted a lot of lamb in there," he said. "It is incredibly good."

We continued driving through fields, down paths, across valleys, and as we went, a rich aroma wafted up from under the tires as we crushed herbs and other fragrant plants. It had gotten warm, and I felt I was traveling in a cloud of rosemary and sage. Elm trees, their tiny new leaves sticky with pollen, contributed their own intense propolis aroma.

I did a double take when I smelled and saw the elms. I had thought that every single elm had vanished in the wake of the devastating Dutch elm disease that swept through Europe in the middle of the century. According to Jacopo, this is the only known patch of elms on the continent, and it is visited often by scientists seeking their secret for survival.

I was astounded at the breadth of Jacopo's holdings and his ambitious attempts not only to introduce new types of viable agriculture into this obviously fertile area but also to save woodlands and native species and to turn hundreds of acres into a thriving, singing paradise. Not a shred of my initial skepticism remained.

Jacopo acknowledged that having wealthy parents has helped, but he thinks persistence has been equally important. He now understands Italian bureaucracy and suffers through it, fighting the rules when necessary until he is victorious, then abiding by them so Alcatraz won't be closed on a technicality.

"My next project is a health farm—conference center at Alcatraz," he said. "I've been thinking about it for a long time, but it takes time to prove yourself, to win friends, to become established. I've done that now, so it's the right time."

Marinated Zucchini of Alcatraz

**ZUCCHINE
SOTT'ACETO E
OLIO**

ABOUT 3 CUPS
ZUCCHINI

I tasted these crisp pickled zucchini slices at the Università Libera di Alcatraz, in the Umbrian hills not far from Perugia (see essay, page 406). There Jacopo Fo leads a most interesting and ambitious project to cultivate the hills organically and create a school of art, theater, and writing for people of all ages, and he offers simple, rustic accommodations and wonderfully intense and clean-tasting food. I was captivated by what he is doing, and this is just one of the flavors I chose to represent the cooking of Alcatraz.

At Alcatraz it accompanied other antipasti and made a crisp foil. It seems also to be a tasty and unusual way to use up summer zucchini. You may be tempted to add herbs to this, but taste it first as it is presented here, for you'll find its simple flavor satisfying in itself.

1 pound medium zucchini, trimmed
2 cups best-quality white wine vinegar, 5 percent acidity
1 large strip (3 x ½ inch) lemon zest

1 clove garlic, green germ removed, cut lengthwise into paper-thin slices
1¼ cups extra-virgin olive oil

1. Cut the zucchini lengthwise in half and scoop the seeds out with the tip of a small spoon. Cut them crosswise into ¼-inch-thick slices. (You should have about 2⅔ cups sliced zucchini.)

2. Place the vinegar and 2 cups of water in a medium-size saucepan, cover, and bring to a boil over medium-high heat. Add the zucchini, cover, and return to a boil. Cook the zucchini just until crisp-tender, 1½ to 2 minutes. Drain, spread the slices out on a tea towel, pat dry, and let cool.

3. Place the zucchini slices in a wide-mouth 1-quart jar, interspersing the lemon zest and garlic among the slices. Pour in the oil, sticking a stainless-steel knife blade

or a chopstick down into the jar and pulling back gently on the zucchini so the oil seeps throughout, leaving no air pockets.

4. Cover the jar and let sit for at least 3 days before tasting.

NOTE: Zucchini will keep indefinitely prepared this way as long as it is completely covered with oil, but it is best if eaten within 3 months. Refrigerate it to be on the safe side. Just remember to remove it from the refrigerator several hours before serving so the zucchini comes to room temperature.

Zucchini

Frozen Basil Leaves

4 CUPS FROZEN LEAVES

Freezing basil leaves is a trick I learned from Nunzio San Filippo, who cooks for the Sapuppo family on Alcala farm, outside Catania in Sicily. While he was making his rich, thick tomato sauce, he went to the freezer and pulled forth a carefully wrapped package of frozen basil leaves. I could not believe the aroma that filled the kitchen when he unwrapped the leaves. It was as if he'd brought in an entire fresh plant.

Nunzio removed the leaves he needed, closed and returned the bag to the freezer, and proceeded with his recipe. The sauce was redolent of basil.

I do not generally use ingredients out of season, but I do now freeze basil to add to sauces when I have none fresh. The leaves keep well in the freezer for about two months.

4 cups fresh basil leaves, preferably not rinsed so they are completely dry

Wrap the basil leaves carefully in parchment paper, then aluminum foil. Place in a plastic bag with an airtight seal, press out all the air, and seal. Freeze. To use, simply open the bag and pull out as many leaves as you need, then return the remaining leaves to the freezer.

Sparkling Strawberry Jam

Segreti

Shaking the pan rather than stirring the ingredients allows the berries to stay whole.

This is from the Poce di Stries, a comfortable *agriturismo* just outside Udine, in Friuli. I stayed there on a stormy off-season evening when the electricity kept going out and the wind howled, but the whole place felt very cozy and warm. The following morning brought brilliant blue skies and a simple breakfast in which this jam, made with organic berries grown in the fields outside the farmhouse door, was the star.

Strawberry jam was never a favorite of mine until I tasted this one, which is light and tangy because of the ample lemon juice. Now I can hardly get enough of it. Spread this liberally on bread or toast—you'll be rewarded with a mouthful of vivid flavor.

2 pounds strawberries, rinsed gently and hulled

2 pounds sugar (about 5 cups)
⅔ cup fresh lemon juice

1. Place the strawberries and sugar in a large stainless-steel kettle and add the lemon juice. Bring to a boil over medium heat, shaking the pan to blend the ingredients. Reduce the heat so the mixture simmers merrily and continue cooking, shaking the pan occasionally, until the jam jells medium-firm (see Note), about 40 minutes.

2. Remove the jam from the heat and seal in jars according to the manufacturer's instructions.

NOTE: How can you tell if your jam is jelled enough? Drizzle some of it on a plate and put it in the refrigerator for a minute or two, then check its consistency. If it is runny, your jam will be runny; if it is jelled, so will be your jam. It is up to you to decide the consistency you prefer.

Mandarin Orange Marmalade

MARMELLATA DI MANDARINO

5 GENEROUS CUPS MARMALADE

Mandarin oranges, what most Americans call tangerines and what are known as clementines in many countries, grow in profusion in Sicily. When I stayed on the Sapuppo farm near Catania, in eastern Sicily, each morning I had only to walk from my door and out into the citrus groves to pick handsful of mandarin oranges for breakfast. Now when I eat a mandarin orange, its heady aroma and flavor take me right back to those fragrant groves.

This recipe comes from Nunzio San Filippo, the cook at the Sapuppo farm (see essay, page 216), who makes good use of all the citrus grown on the farm. He soaks the mandarins in water for two days to remove any bitterness in their skins, so that what remains is sweet flavor with a pleasant tang. This marmalade is delicious on toast in the morning and even better heated slightly and spooned over fresh vanilla ice cream! You must also make a tart using this flavorful marmalade. Follow the recipe for Lemon Marmalade Tart (page 357), substituting an equal quantity of Mandarin Orange Marmalade for the lemon and baking the tart for 20 to 25 minutes.

4 pounds mandarin oranges,
preferably organic, washed
and pricked all over with
a skewer
4¾ cups sugar

Segreti

• **Prick each mandarin about 10 times before soaking in water, using a metal skewer and going right through the skin into the flesh.**

• **Once the mandarins have soaked and the flesh has been scooped out, dice the skins by hand so the pieces are nice and even. If done in a food processor, the results are less appealing.**

1. Place the pricked mandarin oranges in a large nonreactive bowl or kettle, cover amply with water, and soak for 48 hours, changing the water 4 times.

2. Drain the mandarins and cut them horizontally in half. Carefully scoop out the flesh with a stainless-steel spoon into a strainer set over a bowl. (The soaking substantially loosens the skin from the fruit, making this step very easy.) Press the pulp to remove the juice and discard the pulp. Cut the skins into ¼-inch dice by hand (see *Segreti*).

3. Combine the mandarin orange juice and skins and the sugar in a large, heavy, nonreactive kettle. Stir, cover, and bring to a boil over medium heat. Uncover and boil the mixture, stirring often, until it begins to thicken, 25 to 30 minutes. Reduce the heat to medium and continue cooking, stirring often, until it begins to caramelize and darkens slightly, about 15 minutes more. Remove from the heat and seal in jars according to the manufacturer's instructions.

NOTES: Mandarin oranges are at their peak of freshness in winter, right around Christmastime. Use organic mandarin oranges or at least those whose skins have not been treated with a post-harvest fungicide.

Each time you rinse the

mandarin oranges, you will notice globules of a clear gelatinous substance at the bottom of the pan. This is pectin, which seeps out of the fruit and skin as it soaks, but don't be alarmed, for there will be plenty more to make a good, solid jam.

Ghiselda's Lemon Marmalade

**MARMELLATA DI
LIMONE ALLA
GHISELDA**

ABOUT 3
CUPS
MARMALADE

Ghiselda Bini, who lives on a richly productive farm in Tuscany, makes this marmalade with lemons that grow profusely in her own garden, after she's removed the zest to make Lemon Liqueur (page 419). It is rich and golden, with a wonderful sweet-bitter tang. Its intense flavor is delicious on a fresh, warm piece of toast or used as a filling for Lemon Marmalade Tart (page 357).

This is rustic and thick, with good-size pieces of lemon in it. It's almost closer to candied lemons than a true marmalade. Don't be concerned if there isn't enough liquid to completely cover the pieces of lemon when you are ready to seal the jars.

*10 to 12 lemons, preferably organic
(3 pounds), zest removed, pith
trimmed if necessary (see Note)*

*1 pound (2 cups plus 2 tablespoons)
sugar*

1. Cut the lemons lengthwise in half and remove the seeds. Cut the halves into ⅛-inch-thick half rounds. Place the lemons and sugar in a large stainless-steel saucepan over medium heat, stir so the sugar is evenly distributed among the lemons, and cook until the lemons give up some liquid and the sugar begins to melt and comes to a light boil. Reduce the heat to low and cook, stirring occasionally, until the mixture thickens and becomes

pale golden, about 50 minutes.

2. Remove the marmalade from the heat and seal in jars according to the manufacturer's instructions.

NOTE: Look for lemons with thin skins. If you have thick-skinned lemons with a great deal of pith that remains after you've removed the zest, simply trim and discard the extra pith. For a desirable degree of bitterness in the marmalade, the pith should be about $1/16$ inch thick.

Fig and Grape Jam

MARMELLATA DI FICHI E UVA

ABOUT 10 CUPS JAM

This is another gem from Lisa Bonacossi, doyenne of the Capezzana winery in Tuscany, outside Florence, whose lush property produces abundant vegetables and fruits, including figs. Grapes come from the vineyards, and Lisa combines them with soft ripe figs to make this luscious jam. The fruit cooks gently for a long time, allowing the figs to melt and release all of their dusky sweet flavor. Combined with the grapes and the tang of lemon, they are simply delicious.

I love this jam over fresh ricotta for a simple dessert, spread on freshly made Tuscan or potato bread (page 311 or 306), and even spooned over vanilla ice cream.

Segreti

Always make jam in small batches to keep its flavors fresh and pure. Four pounds of fruit is maximum for the best results.

4 pounds fresh figs, coarsely chopped
4 pounds flavorful table grapes (see Note), well rinsed, stemmed, and seeded

Zest of 2 (preferably organic) lemons, minced
⅓ cup water
5 cups sugar

1. Place all the ingredients in a large stainless-steel kettle and bring to a boil over medium-high heat. Reduce the heat so the mixture is boiling gently and cook, stirring occasionally to be sure it isn't sticking, until the mixture thickens to the consistency you prefer and turns an appealing dark golden color. A good, thick jam with a fabulous flavor will take about 2 hours to cook.

2. Remove the jam from the heat and seal in jars according to the manufacturer's instructions.

NOTE: Get the most fragrant grapes you can find, such as Moscato or Moscatella, for this jam.

Spirited Apricots

ALBICOCCHE SOTTO SPIRITO

8 TO 10 SERVINGS

From Maria Manera, who cultivates grapes with her husband, Luciano, in Piedmont, these juicy, soft apricots are reserved for an after-dinner treat, when they emerge from her *dispensa,* or pantry, where she has carefully stored them since the apricot harvest. She serves them in a glass so the alcohol they swim in can be sipped after the fruit is gone. The flavor is a sweet combination of apricot

and almond—which comes from the apricot pits—with a gentle warm kick from the alcohol. In short it is *famoso!*

The apricots Maria harvests from her trees are very small, about the size of a large walnut, and she serves two or three at a time. They become somewhat dark and very soft but are delicious. I like to serve them, along with some of the alcohol, over vanilla ice cream.

Scant 2½ cups unflavored vodka
*   or grappa*
1 cup sugar

1½ pounds whole apricots, rinsed
*   and thoroughly dried*
1 vanilla bean

Tips for Preserving Apricots

• **The apricots in this recipe have an annoying tendency to float to the top of the alcohol, where they stick above the surface and turn brown as they macerate. To circumvent this problem, place the ingredients in a jar with plenty of extra room, then invert a small glass jar or drinking glass on the top of the apricots and gently push down on it until you can close the larger jar. The smaller jar or glass will keep the apricots well under the surface of the alcohol and sugar so they macerate evenly!**

• **Do not seal the jar airtight, for pressure will build from the fermentation of the sugar and it may explode; simply close it loosely.**

• **The apricots will maintain their texture for about 2 months; after that, they melt into softness. Their flavor remains wonderful, but the texture will have lost some of its allure.**

1. In a large glass measure, whisk together the vodka and sugar until the sugar is almost completely dissolved. Place the apricots in a 3-quart or larger jar. Poke the vanilla bean among the apricots and pour the vodka mixture over all.

2. Place a 6- to 8-ounce glass in the jar (see *Segreti*) and cover the mouth of the jar with a piece of parchment paper, then with the lid, which shouldn't be airtight. Leave in a cool, dark place for at least 1 month before sampling.

NOTE: This is a basic recipe. You may increase the quantities as you like.

Walnut Liqueur

Segreti

To test the state of
the walnuts, which
must be soft through,
simply run a long
needle through one
still on the tree. If it
goes through easily,
the moment is right
for making this rich,
spiced liqueur.

At dawn in early summer around the feast of San Giovanni Battista on June 24, when young, tender walnuts are still damp from dew, farmwives near the Po River in Emilia-Romagna pick them to make this rich and warming liqueur.

Although the tradition of making walnut liqueur was first documented in Emilia-Romagna, it has spread to regions in the west and the south. I came across this liqueur in Liguria at a simple country trattoria called Ligagin. After a meal of traditional dishes that revolved around vegetables from the garden outside the front door, I was offered a glass of this as a finish to the meal. I enjoyed its spicy warmth, which carried me out into the night, and I find its reputation as a good digestive well deserved.

30 green walnuts (see Segreti), cut
lengthwise into quarters
3 large strips (3 x 1/2 inch)
lemon zest
2 cinnamon sticks

5 whole cloves
1 quart unflavored vodka or grappa,
plus additional if needed
1 3/4 cups sugar

1. Place the walnuts, lemon zest, cinnamon sticks, and cloves in a 2-quart jar that you can seal airtight. Pour the vodka over them; it should cover them completely. If it doesn't, add more vodka until it does. Seal the bottle and place it outside where it is in the sun for part of the day. Leave it for 30 days, shaking it once each day.

2. After 30 days, strain the alcohol through a double thickness of cheesecloth into a large measure or pitcher with a pouring lip. Discard the walnuts and spices.

3. Place the sugar and 2 cups of water in a medium-size saucepan and bring to a boil over medium-high heat. Reduce the heat to medium-low and sim-

mer, stirring frequently, until the sugar is dissolved. Remove from the heat and let cool to room temperature, then add it to the alcohol and stir to mix well.

4. Decant the mixture into bottles, seal, and let sit for 2 weeks outside in the same sunny spot, shaking the bottles once each day. Taste, store in a cool, dark place, and forget it for at least 2 months (see Note).

NOTE: This liqueur is traditionally made one year and drunk the next. Sample it 2 weeks after the walnuts and spices have been strained out, then put it away and forget about it for at least 2 months or up to 12.

Lemon Liqueur

LIQUORE DI LIMONI

ABOUT 7 CUPS LIQUEUR

Ghiselda Bini and her farmer husband, Bruno, have carved out a beautiful home and garden for themselves amid the vineyards and olive trees in the Chianti region of Tuscany. There Ghiselda has a productive garden that features, as do many Tuscan gardens, lemon trees that provide fragrant fruit most of the year.

Ghiselda has a cupboard filled with homemade liqueurs too, and she served this to me on a late summer afternoon in the cool darkness of her dining room. I found it delightfully refreshing with its caramel sweetness and immediately recreated it when I returned home. I like to serve it, lightly chilled, after dinner as the evening winds down.

Segreti

This liqueur can be sampled after about 2 weeks in the bottle, but it improves with age. I suggest making it, forgetting about it for several months, then bringing it out for a special occaision some time in the future.

3 cups minced lemon zest (18 to 20 good-size lemons; see Note)

1 quart unflavored vodka
1¾ cups sugar

1. Place the lemon zest in a 2-quart jar, then pour the vodka over it. Cover with the lid and store in a dark place for 40 days, shaking it once every day.

2. After 40 days, strain the alcohol into a large measure or pitcher with a pouring lip. Discard the zest.

3. Place the sugar and 2 cups of water in a medium-size saucepan and bring to a boil over medium-high heat. Reduce the heat to medium-low and simmer, stirring frequently, until the sugar is dissolved. Remove the heat and cool to room temperature, then add it to the alcohol and stir to mix well.

4. Decant the mixture into bottles, cover, and let sit in a cool, dark place for at least 2 weeks before serving.

NOTE: Try to find organic lemons for this recipe or at least lemons that have not been treated with a post-harvest fungicide.

RICETTE DI BASE

THE BASICS

I have developed a culinary golden rule and it is this: Keep your eyes and palate open to the best basics you can find, because with those in your repertoire, your own skill, inventiveness, and confidence will continue to grow. Italian farmhouse basics are the recipes that every Italian farm cook knows in her bones: rich tomato sauce; pasta made simply with flour and eggs or with a special blend of herbs and oil; polenta that satisfies; sugared almonds that heighten desserts; dough that makes farm pizzas tender and delicious. Each farm cook has her own particular version of the basics, and learning them has been one of the most rewarding parts of my culinary education, for it is in the basics where the secrets lie.

Each basic recipe in this chapter is a flavorful element on its own. Combined with fresh, carefully chosen ingredients and used in the recipes collected in this book, they make dishes act Italian—lively, spirited, forthright, and easy to love.

Beef Broth

BRODO DI CARNE

ABOUT 8 CUPS
BROTH

This richly flavored broth prepared from a combination of veal and chicken bones is key to many different recipes. If you'd like to jazz it up, do as they do around Naples and add a stick of cinnamon and two or three cloves as it simmers.

3 pounds uncooked veal or
 beef bones
1 pound chicken bones, preferably
 uncooked
2 small carrots, cut into
 ½-inch-thick slices
1 medium onion, diced

2 medium ribs celery, cut into
 ½-inch-thick slices
1 handful fresh flat-leaf parsley
 leaves
10 black peppercorns
1 cinnamon stick (optional)
2 or 3 cloves (optional)

1. Place all the ingredients in a large heavy stockpot and add water to cover by about 4 inches. Cover and bring to a boil over high heat. Reduce the heat so the liquid is simmering and cook, partially covered, until the liquid is golden and all of the flavor has cooked out of the bones and vegetables, at least 3 hours. Check from time to time, skimming off any impurities that rise to the surface as the broth simmers. Strain the broth, discarding the bones and vegetables. Use immediately or cool, transfer to a covered container, and refrigerate for up to 3 days or freeze for up to 1 month.

Light and Lively Tomato Sauce

Segreti

Be sure to salt the fresh tomatoes, as the salt draws water from them, resulting in a livelier, more intense, and freshly flavored sauce.

This is a basic tomato sauce that, of all the dozens of different tomato sauces I have tried, has become my favorite. From Massimo Gangeni, who raises organic tomatoes just outside Genoa, it does what I think a tomato sauce should do—it preserves the integrity of the tomato's red ripeness without interference. It is light and basil scented, just like the air in Liguria where it originated, and it adds life to every dish it touches. Make this sauce in summer with vine-ripened tomatoes and freeze it for a year-round supply of fresh tomato flavor.

12 pounds ripe, flavorful tomatoes, cored and peeled
Fine sea salt
9 tablespoons extra-virgin olive oil
3 large onions, diced

6 cloves garlic, green germ removed, minced
1½ cups (gently packed) fresh basil leaves

1. Cut the tomatoes horizontally in half. Sprinkle the cut sides with 1 tablespoon of salt, place the halves upside down in a colander or on a metal rack, and let drain for 30 minutes so they can give up excess juice, which will help to concentrate their flavor. Coarsely chop the tomatoes without rinsing them and reserve any juice that collects while cutting them.

2. Place the oil, onions, and garlic in a large heavy saucepan and cook, stirring occasionally, over medium heat until the onions turn translucent but not brown, about 8 minutes. Add the tomatoes, cover, and bring to a boil. Reduce the heat so that the tomatoes are simmering, uncover, and cook until the tomatoes are softened but haven't really lost their shape, about 15 minutes.

3. Coarsely chop the basil, stir it into the sauce, and continue to cook until the tomatoes are very soft but still bright and not mushy, about 15 minutes

more. Remove from the heat and let cool. The sauce can be frozen up to 3 months or sealed in canning jars and processed in a water bath according to the jar manufacturer's instructions. The sauce will need seasoning depending on what dish it is being added to.

Nunzio's Tomato Sauce

SUGO DI NUNZIO

3 CUPS
SAUCE

Segreti

If you don't think you'll use up the sauce within a week, I suggest freezing it in ¼-cup portions. Then when you've got a dish that needs a dash of flavor, simply take out as many portions as you think it requires. The sauce will keep well for 2 months in the freezer.

Nunzio San Filippo, the cook at Alcala farm in the citrus country outside Catania, on Sicily, always has this sauce on hand. The children of the family like to dress pasta with it and Nunzio, his brow furrowed with concentration, his dark-lashed eyes clearly focused, adds it to innumerable dishes he prepares for the family and guests at Alcala, a farm that offers beds and meals (see essay, page 216). It adds intense tomato-rich flavor and color to sauces, soups, pastas, pizzas, and stews alike. Nunzio always uses canned tomatoes for this sauce, which he makes year-round. I do the same. It will keep well for a week if refrigerated and tightly covered.

2 cans (each 28 ounces) best-quality
   peeled plum tomatoes with
   juice
4 cloves garlic, crushed with the flat
   of a knife and peeled
1 tablespoon coarse sea salt
2 tablespoons sugar
6 tablespoons extra-virgin olive oil
½ cup (gently packed) fresh basil
   leaves

Place all the ingredients in a medium-size saucepan, cover, and bring to a boil over medium-high heat. Reduce the heat to medium so the sauce is boiling gently, uncover, and cook, stirring occasionally and crushing the tomatoes, until all of the liquid is evaporated, about 1¼ hours. Stir it often as it thickens to be sure that it doesn't stick to the bottom of the pan.

Herb and Lemon Sauce

SALMORIGLIO

**ABOUT
¾ CUP SAUCE**

Nunzio San Filippo uses this sauce for roasted rabbit or chicken. It is bright and tart with the flavors of Sicily—oregano that has been dried to accent its intensity, fresh lemon juice from just-picked ripe lemons, and rich extra-virgin olive oil.

I follow Nunzio's example but also prepare it for fish, using the sauce as a marinade before the fish is cooked or as a seasoning after it's done. It also makes a sprightly dressing for braised or steamed vegetables, as well as a dip for crusty bread.

¼ cup fresh lemon juice
½ cup extra-virgin olive oil
1 tablespoon dried oregano
*1 cup (gently packed) fresh flat-leaf
  parsley leaves*

*1 cloves garlic, green germ
  removed, minced*
Fine sea salt

1. Pour the lemon juice into a medium-size bowl and whisk in the oil gradually to emulsify the two.
2. Crush the oregano with your fingers and whisk it into the sauce.
3. Mince the parsley with the garlic and whisk into the olive oil mixture. Season to taste with salt.

NOTE: This amount of sauce is enough to marinate 1 average-size (3½- to 4-pound) rabbit, chicken, or fish and should be used on the day it is prepared.

Béchamel Sauce

Béchamel is as basic to northern Italian cooking as is pasta, and northern Italian cooks are masters of the sauce, making it rich, creamy, yet light. You may use béchamel in many ways, including as the foundation of a sumptuous vegetarian lasagne, in a meat lasagna, or simply as a garnish for freshly steamed vegetables . . . the possibilities are nearly endless!

Segreti

• When making béchamel, first rinse out the pan for the scalded milk with water, leaving it wet so the milk won't stick to the pan.

• Cook the flour in the butter for 2 minutes so the flour taste cooks out.

• Rub the top of the finished béchamel with a piece of butter, leaving a thin layer of melted butter, which prevents a skin from forming.

3½ cups whole milk
7 tablespoons unsalted butter

7 tablespoons all-purpose flour
Fine sea salt

1. Pour the milk into a medium-size saucepan and scald it (look for small bubbles forming around the edge) over low heat. Remove from the heat but keep warm.

2. Melt the butter in another medium-size saucepan over medium heat until completely melted. Whisk in the flour and let the mixture foam and cook, whisking occasionally, for 2 minutes. Whisk in the hot milk and cook, whisking regularly, until the sauce thickens, about 5 minutes. If the sauce isn't thickening, increase the heat slightly and whisk constantly so as not to burn the sauce.

3. Season the béchamel with salt to taste and remove from the heat. The sauce is ready to use immediately on steamed vegetables or pasta; if you are using it in lasagne, let it cool first.

Toasted Bread Crumbs

MOLLICA

¾ CUP
CRUMBS

Segreti

I let bread dry on the counter for about 3 days before grinding it as fine as possible in the food processor. I sift the crumbs, then grind the larger crumbs that remain until I have a batch of very fine crumbs to toast.

Mollica is an essential ingredient in all of Sicilian cooking. Simple as it sounds, there are many different "rules" for making it, and they vary according to the different regions of Sicily. In some parts of this island, it is thought that a good *mollica* demands bread that has dried outdoors, hung from a rafter, for at least two days. In other parts of the island, the bread must also dry for at least two days, but indoors.

Once the bread is ground, some farm cooks toast it with a bit of oil, and others leave it dry. I prefer it the way I had it most often in Sicily—without oil. That way it adds a neutral crunch, which can be flavored according to the needs of the individual dish.

Once toasted, use *mollica* on everything from pasta to steamed vegetables; you'll find it adds an intriguing dimension. Keep *mollica* on hand, refrigerated in an airtight container.

6 slices very dry unsweetened white bread

1. Break the bread into chunks and grind them into fine crumbs in the food processor. If you want uniformly fine crumbs (which is preferable), sift the crumbs, then grind the larger crumbs that remain in the sifter. Repeat until all the crumbs are consistently fine.

2. Place the crumbs in a cast-iron skillet over medium-low heat and toast, stirring frequently, until they are an even and toasty golden brown, about 4 minutes. Remove from the heat and immediately transfer the *mollica* to a bowl so it doesn't continue to cook. Let cool completely, then store in an airtight container in the refrigerator for up to 1 month.

Polenta

8 TO 10 SERVINGS

In northern Italy, polenta is the nutty, golden staple. In the Val d'Aosta it is made with richly flavored stone-ground corn, and it has a thread of smokiness from the wood fire it is cooked over. In Friuli, polenta is made with bright yellow or white cornmeal and has a more delicate flavor. In northern Lombardy cornmeal is blended with ground buckwheat and cooked to make hearty *polenta taragna,* which is dressed in garlic butter and fontina cheese (page 176). In the Veneto polenta is often made with white cornmeal and achieves yet a different flavor note.

If I learned one thing in all my Italian travels, it is that polenta must be made with care and attention. I also learned that when one is served

Grilled Polenta

If you want to grill or fry polenta rather than eat it straight from the pan, turn the cooked polenta onto a lightly oiled work surface and spread it out to form a rectangle that's about 20 x 14½ inches and about ½ inch thick. When it has firmed up (it doesn't need to be cool), cut it into shapes of your choice. (If using refrigerated leftover polenta, let it come to room temperature, then spread it out into a rectangle.)

To grill, preheat a barbecue grill or broiler. Brush the top and bottom of each polenta piece with olive oil and grill until the polenta is golden crisp on the outside and hot throughout, 4 to 5 minutes per side.

To fry, heat olive oil to a depth of ¼ inch in a heavy skillet over medium-high heat until it is hot but not smoking. Add enough polenta pieces to fill the pan without crowding and fry until they are golden crisp on the outside and hot on the inside, 4 to 5 minutes per side.

Once prepared, eat the polenta as is with a salad, or sprinkle it with Parmesan or pecorino cheese, or use it as a base for chopped tomatoes and basil.

polenta in a northern Italian home it is an honor akin to being asked to join the family, for polenta is home cooking and not for "company."

I make polenta at home more often than I thought I would, considering the amount of stirring involved. I never skimp on time. I've tried polenta at many different stages, and one hour of stirring is necessary to make it truly smooth and rich tasting. I serve it plain with just olive oil or butter and a dusting of salt and pepper, or with *fonduta* (page 153), or cooled and cut in slabs that are then either fried or roasted. It makes a terrific after-school snack for a hungry child and a delicious foundation for a warming supper. It is also good doused in butter and maple syrup for breakfast!

5 teaspoons fine sea salt

4½ cups coarse cornmeal, preferably stone ground

1. Bring 3 quarts of water and the salt to a rolling boil in a large (at least 6-quart) heavy saucepan or Dutch oven. When the water is at a rolling boil, sprinkle in the cornmeal in a fine rain, whisking it vigorously to avoid lumps, until it is all in the pan.

2. Retire the whisk, reduce the heat so the polenta is gently simmering (bubbles pop occasionally to the surface), and using a wooden spoon, stir constantly until the polenta is very thick and smooth, at least 1 hour.

3. Remove from the heat and let sit for about 10 minutes so it releases itself from the pan. Turn the polenta out of the pan onto a cutting board or a warmed platter. Serve immediately, scooping or slicing it, depending on how thick it is, onto individual plates.

PECORINO, AS IT ONCE WAS

Before going to Tuscany I assumed that all its landmark percorino, a creamy-hard sheep's milk cheese, was made the old way, with raw milk. But once I got there, I found out differently. Out of the tons of pecorino produced in Tuscany, most is made with pasteurized milk.

Why? The reasons have to do with international marketing and ease. As borders in Europe blend, one country's rules and food standards naturally affect another's. Cheeses made with raw milk are less stable than those made with pasteurized milk, because harmless bacteria in the raw milk are constantly "working" to develop flavor and texture in the cheese. Raw-milk cheeses are more perishable and more demanding of special shipping and storage conditions.

Thus, for large pecorino producers in Tuscany, who naturally want to sell their cheese to neighboring countries, pasteurization has become a necessity. My quest for a producer who made ultra-flavorful raw-milk cheese began to seem impossible. Pecorino in Tuscany has become a standardized product.

I bemoaned the state of affairs to my friend Rolando Beremendi, and he pulled out his address book. "Call this number. You'll find what you want." I did, and I did.

I drove north of Florence and out into the heart of the Mugello, a little-visited rural area of Tuscany. My destination was the farm of Giovanna Baciotti who, with her son, Roberto, raises sheep and all the feed. Roberto still milks about 150 sheep by hand. Once the milk is in, he and his mother make their cheese in the small workroom on the ground floor of their home.

They make cheese as it's always been done—first gently heating the milk, then adding a natural substance to promote fermentation, and later rennet to coagulate the curd. After forty minutes, Roberto mixes the cheese with a stringed instrument called a *mestole,* which breaks up the curd. This he drains, presses, and fits into a mold.

To make ricotta he scalds the whey and adds a bit of milk for richness, vinegar to help the milk solids separate from the liquids, then a bit of salt for seasoning. The resulting ricotta is immediately ready to consume. It is sumptuous, warm, rich, and creamy. Although the Baciottis sell every cheese they make and are sometimes tempted to expand, they know it would be folly to do so, for it's just the two of them and the methods they use are too labor-intensive for expansion. So they provide for the customers they have—one of whom runs a mail-order business for local specialty foods. The rest they sell to local shops and to customers who drive from as far away as Florence, about an hour and a half away.

Pizza Dough

PASTA PER PIZZA

**2 POUNDS DOUGH;
ENOUGH FOR
1 THICK OR 2 THIN
PIZZA CRUSTS**

This pizza dough, which I use for most of the pizzas I make, gets its flavor from the technique for Tuscan Bread (page 311). It employs a *madre*, or mother, that is made the night before and delivers a lively yeasty presence, subtle sweetness, and superior flavor to the baked dough. Salt and oil are added to soften and elevate the flavor.

If you want to make pizza and haven't thought about it in advance, turn to Maria's Pizza Dough (page 432), or, even faster, Simple Dough (page 432).

FOR THE MADRE
1 teaspoon active dry yeast
1 cup lukewarm water
2 cups all-purpose flour

FOR THE DOUGH
⅓ cup lukewarm water
¼ cup extra-virgin olive oil
1 teaspoon fine sea salt
About 2⅓ cups all-purpose flour

1. To make the *madre*, whisk together the yeast and water in a large bowl or the work bowl of an electric mixer, then slowly whisk in the flour to make a smooth batter. Cover and let sit at room temperature (68° to 70°F) 9 to 12 hours.

2. When the *madre* has risen and is filled with air holes (like a sponge), make the dough. Whisk the water, oil, and salt into the *madre*. Gradually add enough of the flour, working with a wooden spoon, your hands, or the paddle on an electric mixer, to make a soft dough. Knead until the dough is soft and satiny. If it is very sticky, continue adding flour until you have a soft dough that does not stick to a clean finger.

3. Transfer the dough to a clean bowl, cover it with aluminum foil, and let it rest in the refrigerator for 30 minutes. It should be rise slightly, but it will not double its size.

4. Proceed with the pizza recipe of your choice.

Maria's Pizza Dough

**PASTA PER PIZZA
DI MARIA**

**ABOUT
2 POUNDS DOUGH;
ENOUGH FOR
1 THICK OR 2 THIN
PIZZA OR FOCACCIA
CRUSTS;
6 TO 8 SERVINGS**

This is from Maria Maurillo, one of the best cooks I met in Italy, who prepares meals nightly for guests at her farm, Agriturismo Malvarina, just outside Assisi (see essay, page 363). The secret to its charm is a generous amount of extra-virgin olive oil, which makes it easy to work, even easier to eat!

Maria prepared most of the dough for pizza. The rest she cut in small pieces, rolled out, and fried in hot olive oil. These would later be spread with a savory blend of tomato sauce and tuna and served as a delectable appetizer. "It's an all-purpose dough," she declared as she finished up. "You can do just about anything with it." In fact, I like to bake it as a loaf or as rolls, as well as use it as a basis for pizza.

1⅓ cups lukewarm water
2 teaspoons active dry yeast
½ cup extra-virgin olive oil

4 to 4½ cups all-purpose flour
1 tablespoon fine sea salt

1. In a large bowl or the work bowl of an electric mixer, whisk together the water and yeast. Add the oil and mix well. Add 1 cup of the flour and mix until smooth. Stir in the salt and enough of the remaining flour to make a soft dough. Because of the oil, the dough will feel somewhat slippery, and it may not be a homogeneous lump at first. Knead, adding as little flour as necessary, until it comes together and is satiny and elastic, about 5 minutes. The dough should be moist because of the oil but not wet, and it shouldn't stick to your clean finger.

2. Place the dough in a clean (unoiled) large bowl, cover with a tea towel, and let rise at room temperature (68° to 70°F) until it is doubled in bulk, about 1½ hours. Punch down the dough and use in recipes as called for.

Simple Dough

PASTA

**ABOUT 2½
POUNDS
DOUGH**

Savory pastries in Sicily are legion, ranging from round, fat little rolls filled with ricotta and pork or studded with olives to double-crusted pizza stuffed with vegetables (see recipes, pages 322 to 329). They all use the same dough, and this is my version of what is made daily in just about every Sicilian farm kitchen.

Dough made outside Sicily can only be a replica, for the flour there is unique (see essay, page 319) and the tradition calls for making a rather brittle and hard dough. I developed this version after trying dozens of different farm recipes, and I'm very satisfied with the result. It is easy to work with, versatile, and delectable.

1 cup lukewarm water
½ teaspoon active dry yeast
* (see Note)*
5 to 6½ cups all-purpose flour

2 teaspoons fine sea salt
3 large eggs, at room temperature
2 tablespoons extra-virgin olive oil

1. In a large bowl or the work bowl of an electric mixer, whisk together the water and yeast. Let the yeast dissolve if necessary. Whisk in enough flour to make a soft dough. Add the salt, eggs, and oil and whisk until thoroughly blended. Gradually add enough of the remaining flour to make a firm but pliable dough. Knead the dough until it is satiny, about 8 minutes by hand, 5 minutes by mixer.

2. Transfer the dough to a clean (unoiled) large bowl. Cover with a tea towel and let rise at room temperature (68° to 70°F) until it has doubled in bulk, about 1 hour.

3. Turn out the dough onto a lightly floured surface, punch it down, and proceed with the recipe as directed.

NOTE: If you want to use instant-rise yeast, try Saf brand, which is commonly used throughout Europe, as well as in better bakeries in the United States.

Fresh Pasta Dough

PASTA FRESCA

ABOUT 1¾ POUNDS PASTA; 4 TO 6 SERVINGS

This recipe for pasta dough comes from Maria Manera, a lovely, energetic farmer and cook from Piedmont. She and her husband, Luciano, cultivate grapes that are turned into lush Piedmont wines like Barbera and Dolcetto. Even though Maria works full-time with Luciano in the vineyards, she also manages to assemble delicious meals for her family and the farmworkers. After staying with the Maneras for several days, I finally asked Maria for the secret to her productivity. "I don't need much sleep," she said. "So early in the morning before anyone else is up, I do as much of the cooking for the day as I can."

From observing Maria in the kitchen, I also know that she works very quickly and efficiently, producing dishes she grew up learning to make. She makes this dough often, and once it is ready she rolls, fills, or simply cuts it and leaves it to dry, loosely covered with a tea towel, until she is ready to cook it later in the day.

You'll find this dough very easy to assemble. The amount of flour will vary depending on the humidity in the atmosphere, but don't add too much—just enough to keep the dough from sticking and tearing as you roll it out.

pasta wheel

1¾ cups bleached all-purpose flour
1¾ to 2 cups unbleached all-

purpose flour
5 large eggs, at room temperature
1 tablespoon extra-virgin olive oil

Segreti

• **Olive oil gives character and substance to homemade pasta without affecting its tenderness.**

• **Letting the pasta dough rest on a wooden surface allows it to dry out, as the wood absorbs any moisture given off by the dough. If it rests on a nonporous surface, such as tile or marble, the liquid cannot evaporate, and more flour must be added to the dough, making it tough, but this problem can be circumvented by covering the surface with tea towels.**

• **Using two types of flour is another trick of Maria's to add substance and texture to her pasta.**

1. Combine 1¾ cups of each of the flours in a mound on a work surface and make a well in the center. Break the eggs into the well and add the oil. Using a knife, break up the eggs without breaking through the flour "walls" of the well, mixing them just until they are combined; they do not need to be completely homogeneous.

2. Gradually work the flour into the eggs with your fingers by bringing it from the top of the edges without breaking the well, so the eggs don't run all over the counter. When the eggs have absorbed enough flour to keep them from running, you can be more physical about mixing the eggs and flour, using your hands and a dough scraper if necessary to work them together. At first the dough will be messy, but it will gradually come together as you work it. Once you've got a relatively homogeneous ball, knead it until it becomes satiny (the surface will not be entirely smooth), about 4 minutes. Cover the dough with an inverted bowl and let it rest on the work surface for 30 minutes so the gluten in the flour has

a chance to relax.

3. Cut the dough into 8 equal pieces. Lightly flour a work surface. Using a pasta machine and working with one piece of dough at a time (leave the remaining dough under the bowl so it doesn't dry out), run the dough through the widest notch of the machine. Fold the dough in thirds, like a business letter, so it is slightly narrower than the width of the rollers and run it over the work surface so it gets a light overlay of flour. Place it, edges first, between the rollers set at the widest thickness and roll it through again. Repeat the process 6 more times, for a total of 8 times through the widest setting. This is the kneading stage, when the pasta develops most of its texture. Try not to add too much flour, but just enough so the dough rolls smoothly through the machine. Run each piece of dough through the machine 8 times.

4. Now the dough is ready to turn into strips that are thin enough for pasta. Move the width regulator on the pasta rollers a notch so the rollers are closer together, and run each strip of pasta through them. If

Mama Lancellotti's Pasta Variation

To make Ida Lancellotti's pasta is easy. Simply prepare the recipe for Fresh Pasta Dough (page 434) without the 1 tablespoon of olive oil. All other directions remain the same. However, to actually watch Ida in action is pure pleasure. First her son, Emilio, transforms the dining room of the family's restaurant (Ristorante Lancellotti in Soliera, near Modena in Emilia-Romagna; see essay, page 80) into a small pasta production room. He moves all but one table from the center of the room, and on that he places a large board, making sure it is well balanced. Then he clears out of the room. Ida pours a mountain of flour on the board and makes a well. She breaks eggs into it and blends them with a knife, then slowly and surely incorporates the flour into the eggs, which at first looks like it will be impossible. In her capable hands, however, which work while she talks as though they were completely autonomous, a soft, golden dough comes quickly together. She kneads it for about four minutes

with vigor, then lets the dough sit for a good fifteen minutes, before she kneads it again, searching for just the right elasticity.

Emilio appears and hands her a four-foot rolling pin. She flattens the dough, then slips an end between her stomach and the edge of the table to hold it as she rolls, rolls, and rolls, never hurrying but never letting up. Within half an hour she gracefully transforms the lump of dough into a beautiful veil of nearly transparent pasta. She lets it sit for just a minute or two, then cuts it in wide bands, which she loosely rolls and slices into thin strips. These she gathers up with her hand, shaking them loose and carefully letting them drop into little golden piles.

"Two of these bunches will feed one person," she told me.

Later in the kitchen, I watched her husband, Camillo, size up the golden piles of pasta and set aside two per hungry diner. She hadn't told him to do it; he knew from years of experience.

the dough is sticky, run it over the lightly floured work surface, then run it through the machine. Repeat through all the notches of the rollers, until you have long, thin strips of dough. If the strips become too long to handle, simply cut them crosswise in half and roll the 2 pieces separately.

5. Hang the dough strips on broom handles placed between 2 chairs or lay them out on a

Italians consume more than sixty pounds of pasta per person per year.

lightly floured wooden or tea-towel-covered work surface to dry just slightly so that they can be cut easily. Depending on the ambient temperature and humidity in the air, this will take from 8 to 15 minutes. They shouldn't be brittle, but they shouldn't be too damp either.

6. When the pasta has dried enough to be cut, run the strips through the cutter on the pasta machine to make tagliatelle, or roll each strip up loosely and cut it

by hand into ¼-inch-thick strips. Take each bunch of cut pasta loosely in your hands and drop it on a lightly floured surface from at least 18 inches above the surface so it lands in a nice loose pile and can continue to dry slightly before it is cooked. You may cook the pasta immediately (for about 30 seconds), but it tends to have a bit more presence and texture if left to dry for about 2 hours, at which point it will still cook very quickly, in 1 to 3 minutes.

Chestnut Pasta

PASTA DI CASTAGNE

ABOUT 1¾ POUNDS; 4 TO 6 SERVINGS

Walter Tripodi, the chef at the Frateria di Padre Eligio (see essay, page 146) in Cetona, near Siena, served chestnut pasta to me when I spent the day there. I was immediately enamored of its sweet, toothsome richness, for the chestnut flour gives it a surprising amount of flavor and body.

I always have some in my freezer, which is the best place to keep it if you're not going to use it immediately, for it can spoil. Chestnut pasta is sumptuous as a foil for Walter's flavorful artichoke sauce, but if I want something simpler, I dress it with flavorful extra-virgin olive oil and some fresh herbs.

Segreti

Salt balances the
sweetness of the
chestnut flour and is
necessary in this
recipe.

*2¼ to 3¼ cups bleached
    all-purpose flour
2 cups chestnut flour*

*1 teaspoon fine sea salt
5 large eggs, at room temperature
1 tablespoon extra-virgin olive oil*

1. Mix 2¼ cups of the all-purpose flour, the chestnut flour, and salt on a work surface, shape into a mound, and make a well in the center. Break the eggs into the well, add the oil, and mix them with a fork or your fingers. Gradually incorporate the flour into the eggs until you have a fairly firm but easy-to-work dough. Knead it just until the ingredients are blended and the dough is homogeneous, then cover the dough with an inverted bowl and let it rest on the work surface for 15 minutes.

2. To roll out the pasta and cut it into tagliatelle, proceed as directed in Fresh Pasta Dough (page 434), steps 3 through 6.

Perfect Chestnut Pasta

This pasta dough is very easy to mix together and knead because the chestnut flour has no gluten, which keeps the dough soft. It does require more flour while rolling than other pasta, so have 1 cup of all-purpose flour on hand for lightly flouring the dough on both sides each time you roll it through the pasta machine. The operative word when using flour is "lightly"; you have to judge the amount of flour carefully, for you don't want the pasta to get too firm. If the dough goes easily through the machine with no tears or wrinkles or sticking, you're doing just fine. If it does stick or act reluctant, lightly dust it—even once it's in the machine—with flour. If the pasta emerges from the machine with very jagged edges, you've used too much flour. This situation is not disastrous—just hold off on the flour a bit and keep rolling. If you've misjudged and the dough is too moist and comes out of the machine looking like lace, simply fold it back together and roll it back through with a light, even dusting of flour.

Franca's Sweet-Tart Pastry

**PASTAFROLLA DI
FRANCA**

**PASTRY FOR
A 9 ½ - INCH
TART WITH
LATTICE
TOP**

Segreti

**Make sure the butter
and the room you are
working in are nei-
ther too cold nor too
hot, for it has an ef-
fect on the pastry. A
temperature of 65° to
68°F for both the but-
ter and the room is
ideal for making and
rolling out the pastry.
Any warmer and the
pastry becomes too
soft to handle; any
colder and it tends to
break and fall apart.**

Franca Franzoni is a perfectionist, one of the few I've met in whom I could truly appreciate the mania. Her livelihood is honey mak-ing, which she does in a beautiful old building near her home in the hills outside Florence. She is also an avid baker; so while with her I asked for her tips on making *pasta frolla,* one of the cornerstones of Italian baking. I had many recipes for it but none that I absolutely loved. This one I love. It has the right balance of ingredients and a hint of lemon zest, and it elevates every tart to star status.

This makes the perfect amount of pastry for a *crostata,* using two-thirds of it to line the pan and the other third for lattice strips on top. It is also ideal for a simple one-crust tart. For a double-crust *torta,* double the amount.

1½ cups plus 1 tablespoon
   all-purpose flour
7 tablespoons unsalted butter,
   at room temperature

2 large egg yolks, at room temperature
½ cup sugar
Pinch of fine sea salt
Zest of 1 lemon, minced

Place the flour in a mound in a wide, shallow bowl and make a well in the center. Place the butter, egg yolks, sugar, salt, and lemon zest in the well and mix them to-gether with your fingertips. Grad-ually work the flour into the butter mixture by scooping it in with your fingers from the sides of the well. When the mixture is al-most uniformly crumbly, transfer it to a work surface. Use the heel of your hand to push gently down and away on the dough, as though you were smearing it across the work surface. This effectively blends all the ingredients together. When the dough holds together, pat it into a small, flat disk, cover it with an inverted bowl, and let it sit at room temperature for 30 minutes.

Baked Almonds and Sugar

**MANDORLE CON
ZUCCHERO AL
FORNO**

**ABOUT
2 CUPS
ALMONDS**

Maria Maurillo, who owns Agriturismo Malvarina, outside Assisi (see essay, page 363), always has a batch of these almonds on hand to put on biscotti, in tarts, and atop cakes. To make them, she simply dusts almonds with sugar and bakes them in the oven until they are toasty and the sugar has caramelized around them. It's very simple, and the results make a satisfying little sweet all on their own.

*1 large egg white, at room
   temperature*

*⅓ cup Vanilla Sugar
   (page 441)
2 cups almonds in their skins*

1. Preheat the oven to 400°F. Line a baking sheet with parchment paper.

2. Whisk the egg white and sugar together in a mixing bowl until blended and slightly foamy. Add the almonds and stir until they are thoroughly coated. Spread them out on the prepared baking sheet and drizzle with the excess egg white mixture if there is any.

3. Bake the almonds in the center of the oven until they are deep golden and the egg white mixture is pale golden, about twelve minutes.

4. Remove from the oven and let cool on the baking sheet to room temperature. Break the almonds apart, discarding any excess egg white, and store them in an airtight container in a cool place. They will keep well for at least 2 weeks.

Vanilla Sugar

**ZUCCHERO ALLA
VANIGLIA**

**4 CUPS
SUGAR**

In Italy vanilla extract isn't as common as it is in the States, the substitute being little packets of granulated vanilla sugar that are not very tasty. I've gotten around this by flavoring my sugar with vanilla beans and using the resulting vanilla-flavored sugar in pastries that call for vanilla. I always keep several vanilla beans in my sugar, changing them regularly (they offer good flavor for at least two months) so the flavor stays strong and pure.

Spoon some vanilla sugar into your next cup of coffee, or sprinkle it on buttered toast or atop a freshly baked tart. You'll find vanilla sugar has dozens of uses.

4 cups sugar

*1 never-used or 2 used-once-before
vanilla beans*

Pour the sugar into an airtight container and push the vanilla bean down into it. Cover and let ripen for at least 1 week. Replenish the sugar as you use it, pouring out what is already flavored, adding new sugar to the container, and topping it with the flavored sugar. Replace the vanilla bean every 2 months or so.

Conversion Table

LIQUID CONVERSIONS

US	IMPERIAL	METRIC
2 tbs	2 fl oz	30 ml
3 tbs	1½ fl oz	45 ml
¼ cup	2 fl oz	60 ml
⅓ cup	2½ fl oz	75 ml
⅓ cup + 1 tbs	3 fl oz	90 ml
⅓ cup + 2 tbs	3½ fl oz	100 ml
½ cup	4 fl oz	125 ml
⅔ cup	5 fl oz	150 ml
¾ cup	6 fl oz	175 ml
¾ cup + 2 tbs	7 fl oz	200 ml
1 cup	8 fl oz	250 ml
1 cup + 2 tbs	9 fl oz	275 ml
1¼ cups	10 fl oz	300 ml
1⅓ cups	11 fl oz	325 ml
1½ cups	12 fl oz	350 ml
1⅔ cups	13 fl oz	375 ml
1¾ cups	14 fl oz	400 ml
1¾ cups + 2 tbs	15 fl oz	450 ml
1 pint (2 cups)	16 fl oz	500 ml
2½ cups	1 pint	600 ml
3¾ cups	1½ pints	900 ml
4 cups	1¾ pints	1 liter

APPROXIMATE EQUIVALENTS

1 stick butter = 8 tbs = 4 oz = ½ cup

1 cup all-purpose presifted flour/
    dried bread crumbs = 5 oz

1 cup granulated sugar = 8 oz

1 cup (packed) brown sugar = 6 oz

1 cup confectioners' sugar = 4½ oz

1 cup honey/syrup = 11 oz

1 cup grated cheese = 4 oz

1 cup dried beans = 6 oz

1 large egg = 2 oz = about ½ cup

1 egg yolk = about 1 tbs

1 egg white = about 2 tbs

WEIGHT CONVERSIONS

US/UK	METRIC	US/UK	METRIC
½ oz	15 g	7 oz	200 g
1 oz	30 g	8 oz	250 g
1½ oz	45 g	9 oz	275 g
2 oz	60 g	10 oz	300 g
2½ oz	75 g	11 oz	325 g
3 oz	90 g	12 oz	350 g
3½ oz	100 g	13 oz	375 g
4 oz	125 g	14 oz	400 g
5 oz	150 g	15 oz	450 g
6 oz	175 g	1 lb	500 g

OVEN TEMPERATURES

FAHRENHEIT	GAS MARK	CELSIUS
250	½	120
275	1	140
300	2	150
325	3	160
350	4	180
375	5	190
400	6	200
425	7	220
450	8	230
475	9	240
500	10	260

Note: Reduce the temperature by 20°C (68°F) for fan-assisted ovens

Please note that all the above conversions are approximate, but close enough to be useful when converting from one system to another.

Index